SEX AND THE SINGLE SAVIOR

SEX AND THE SINGLE SAVIOR

Gender and Sexuality in Biblical Interpretation

Dale B. Martin

Westminster John Knox Press
LOUISVILLE • LONDON

Book design by Sharon Adams
Cover design by Lisa Buckley

First edition
Published by Westminster John Knox Press
Louisville, Kentucky

This book is printed on acid-free paper that meets the American National Standards Institute Z39.48 standard. ♾

PRINTED IN THE UNITED STATES OF AMERICA

06 07 08 09 10 11 12 13 14 15—10 9 8 7 6 5 4 3 2 1

Library of Congress Cataloging-in-Publication Data is on file at the Library of Congress, Washington, D.C.

ISBN-13: 978-0-664-23046-3
ISBN-10: 0-664-23046-6

To Bart D. Ehrman

Contents

Preface

The essays published in this book were written over several years, the first published in 1995 and the most recent having just been written. Six have been previously published. All address issues of sexuality, gender, and biblical interpretation. Several speak explicitly about homosexuality. Another recurring theme is family, including marriage and divorce. Some chapters are more explicit than others in their discussion of interpretation theory and its relation to how we do and how we should interpret the Bible. Though these different chapters are somewhat diverse in both subject matter and style—some more exegetical, others more historical, some more "scholarly," and others more popular—they still cohere well together. They all were written to demonstrate the inadequacies of much modern use of the Bible in debates about gender and sexuality, and they all attempt in some way to advocate a different approach to scriptural interpretation.

Since this book is a collection of essays, readers may wish to pick and choose which chapters to concentrate on and the order in which each will be read. Chapters 3 and 4, for instance, were written more for a scholarly audience and are thus a bit more "technical" and dense. Chapter 10, unlike most of the others, has few footnotes, since it was initially designed as a public talk and not published subsequently. Chapters 1, 2, and 11 were written particularly for this collection and are geared for a general audience; thus they assume no specialized knowledge on the part of the reader. I resisted the temptation to revise all the essays in order to render them more uniform in style and presentation. Differences among the chapters reflect the different situations for which they were originally composed, and I hope readers will experience that as a pleasant variety rather than a distraction.

The introduction in chapter 1 presents a general account of my own views about interpretation theory, recent debates about scriptural interpretation, and the failure of what I call "textual foundationalism." The conclusion in chapter 11 continues those themes but goes further to advocate different ways of thinking about what Scripture is and how contemporary Christians should read it. Much of the introduction and the conclusion, along with much of what now makes up chapter 2, "The Rhetoric of Biblical Scholarship," were originally presented as the Gustafson Lectures in Biblical Studies at United Theological Seminary of the Twin Cities, Minnesota, in 2004. I am grateful to the faculty and students of United Theological Seminary for the invitation to deliver the lectures and for discussion and feedback on my ideas.

Chapter 3, "*Arsenokoitês* and *Malakos*," was originally published in *Biblical Ethics and Homosexuality: Listening to Scripture* (ed. Robert L. Brawley [Louisville, KY: Westminster John Knox, 1996], 117–36). I thank Professor Brawley for the invitation to write the paper in the first place and for accepting it for publication. I also thank Elizabeth A. Clark and Anthony Neil Whitley for assistance in the research for the essay. It is published by permission of Westminster John Knox Press.

Chapter 4, "Heterosexism and the Interpretation of Romans 1:18–32," was originally published in *Biblical Interpretation* (vol. 3 [1995]: 332–55). It was republished in *The Boswell Thesis: Essays for the Twenty-Fifth Anniversary of John Boswell's Christianity, Social Tolerance, and Homosexuality* (ed. Mathew Kuefler [Chicago: University of Chicago Press, 2006]). I thank Koninklijke Brill N.V. and the University of Chicago Press for permission to republish the article.

Chapter 5, "Paul without Passion," was originally written for a conference on the family in early Christianity at the University of Oslo, Norway, in 1995. It was published in *Constructing Early Christian Families: Family as Social Reality and Metaphor* (ed. Halvor Moxnes [London: Routledge, 1997], 201–15). I am grateful to Professor Moxnes for the original invitation and for including the article in his collection. More importantly, I am grateful for his generosity and friendship over many years. The writing of the essay as well as travel to and from the conference where it was originally presented were funded by the Alexander von Humboldt Foundation, Germany. I am grateful to the foundation as well as to my host in Tübingen, Professor Hubert Cancik, for their kind hospitality and gracious support.

Chapter 6, "The Queer History of Galatians 3:28," was originally read at a conference on "Identity, (Homo)Sexuality and Gender in Christian Antiquity" at the University of Oslo in 1998. It was also read at Yale University Divinity School in 1998, and a shorter version was read at the Society of Biblical Literature Annual Meeting, Orlando, Florida, on November 23, 1998. It has never been published in English, but a Norwegian translation was published as "'Ikke mannlig og kvinnelig': Likestilling, androgyni og kjønnsoverskridelse hos Paulus" ["No Male and Female": Equality, Androgyny, and Gender Transgression in Paul], in *Naturlig sex? Seksualitet og kjønn i den kristne antikken* [Natural Sex? Sexuality and Gender in Ancient Christianity] (ed. Halvor Moxnes, Jostein Børtnes, and Dag Øistein Endsjø [Oslo: Gyldendal, 2002], 99–125). Again, I am grateful especially to Halvor Moxnes for invitations and support. I thank Hugo Lundhaug for translating the essay into Norwegian. And I thank Elizabeth

A. Clark and Halvor Moxnes for their reading of and suggestions toward the improvement of the article. It is published by permission of Gyldendal Akademisk of Norway, for which I am grateful.

Chapter 7, "Sex and the Single Savior," was originally an invited paper for the Studiorum Novi Testamenti Societas Annual Meeting in Montreal, Quebec, August 2, 2001. It was also read at the University of Uppsala, the University of Helsinki, the University of Copenhagen, and the University of Aarhus in 2001. I am grateful to members of all those audiences for comments and suggestions. The essay was first published in a shorter form in the *Svensk Exegetisk Årsbok* (vol. 67 [2002]: 47–60). It was republished, with revisions, in Martti Nissinen and Risto Uro, eds., *Sacred Marriages in the Ancient World* (Winona Lake, IN: Eisenbrauns, 2006). I am grateful to Eisenbrauns and particularly to James Eisenbraun for permission to republish the article here.

Chapter 8, "Familiar Idolatry and the Christian Case against Marriage," was prepared for the Alexander Robertson Lectureship at the University of Glasgow in 2003. It was also read at a conference on "Sex, Marriage, and the Family and the Religions of the Book" at the Center for the Interdisciplinary Study of Religion, Emory University, in 2003. I am grateful especially to John Barclay for the invitation to Glasgow and to Mark Jordan for inviting me to participate in the conference at Emory. The article is published in *Authorizing Marriage? Canon, Tradition, and Critique in the Blessing of Same-Sex Unions*, ed. Mark Jordan (Princeton, NJ: Princeton University Press, 2006). I thank Princeton University Press for permission to republish the essay.

The beginnings of what became chapter 9, "The Hermeneutics of Divorce," and chapter 10, "Community-shaped Scripture," were presentations to a seminar of faculty and graduate students at the University of Copenhagen in 2001. The latter paper was also presented at the University of Oslo, also in 2001. I am grateful for the discussion, debate, and suggestions provided by both audiences.

As is already apparent, much of the initial work on several of these chapters was accomplished and presented at the University of Copenhagen in 2001, when I was fortunate to work there as a Fulbright Fellow. I am grateful to my hosts in Denmark, especially Professor Troels Engberg-Pedersen, and to the Fulbright Commission for the support. I also benefited greatly from friendly discussions with other members of the faculty there, especially Lone Fatum, Henrik Tronier, and Geert Hallbäck. It was a wonderful time, and I cherish the long-lasting friendships nourished during that time and since in Denmark, Norway, Sweden, and Finland. Would that all of us could live in such gentle and civilized nations.

Yale University is generous with allowing research leaves for faculty. Much of the work for these essays was accomplished during a leave in 2001, and the project was completed during a leave in 2005–2006. I am grateful to Yale for these leaves that have facilitated its composition.

I give heartfelt thanks to Denise Thorpe for detailed comments and suggestions that vastly improved key essays of this collection. I also wish to thank my sister, Ferryn Martin, for reading several chapters and discussing them with me, and for her encouragement. These essays went through many forms over the past eleven years, and I am sure I owe thanks to far more people than I can list here. I apologize to those I have inadvertently left unnamed.

Finally, I thank Bart D. Ehrman and dedicate the book to him. His incisive mind and scholarship have been an inspiration and a model. But more importantly, his friendship for more than twenty-five years has been one of the most valued treasures of my life.

Chapter 1

Introduction

The Myth of Textual Agency

One of the central goals of much of my writing over the past several years has been to undermine a common assumption, common among lay Christians as well as scholars: that the Bible "speaks" and our job is just to "listen." Repeatedly we encounter biblical scholars talking as if the text of the Bible contains certain, identifiable "meaning" that it "communicates" to us, and our task is to be as passive as possible and "receive" that message without distorting it too much. My scholarship, on the other hand, has attempted to highlight the *activities of interpretation* by which people "make meaning" of the biblical texts. I have insisted that the texts don't "speak"—except in the most tenuous of metaphorical senses of that term—and that we humans have to do lots of hard work to interpret the texts before they have any meaning for us at all. I have tried to expose the complications of biblical interpretation in order to shine light on the agency of human interpreters and to insist that the "text itself" does not exercise its own "agency" in its own interpretation. Texts do not interpret themselves; they must be interpreted by human beings. To repeat a slogan I have often used in speaking to various audiences: "Texts don't mean. People mean with texts." Thus much of my work has been an attempt to disabuse people of the myth of textual agency.

I hasten to point out that I still believe we may read texts to derive legitimate meanings. The notion that Christians read Scripture in order to find answers to their questions and meaning for their lives is entirely appropriate. My point is that when we do so, we have to recognize that it is not the *text itself* that is simply "giving" us that meaning. The "finding" of meaning in Scripture necessitates interpretation and cannot be done outside interpretation. Human beings are necessary for meaning to take place, and we can experience no interpretation without human agency. Therefore, the responsibility for interpretation—the responsibility for the "meaning" we "find"—lies with us human readers of the text, not with the text itself understood apart from interpretation.

For me, this is not only a point about literary theory. It is also an ethical issue. I believe that one of the most serious impediments to the ethical use of Scripture, especially with regard to issues of gender and sexuality, has been the myth of textual agency. One regularly comes across a certain tone in debates about Christian ethics, a tone by which one or both parties in the debate seem to say, "Don't blame me! *I'm* not opposed to gay people (or the ordination of women, or name your issue). The *Bible* is. The Bible tells us. . . ." Such people never admit that the Bible doesn't actually talk. They do not acknowledge their own interpretive practices by which they have arrived at what they think the Bible "says." People throughout history, therefore, have committed grave ethical offenses—supporting slavery, oppressing women, fighting unjust wars, killing, torturing, and harming their fellow human beings—under cover of "the Bible says." As long as the text itself is thought to provide its own interpretation or to constrain or direct its own meaning, the ethical and political responsibility of interpreters can be masked, denied, or slighted. Immoral interpretations can be—and have been—blamed on the text rather than the interpreter. Today, one of the places this kind of deceptive rhetoric occurs most often is in debates about sexuality.

I call this the sin of Christian textual foundationalism.[1] The text of the Bible is taken to be a relatively firm basis from which we can derive all sorts of knowledge, about doctrine or ethics, by simply reading the text and passively "hearing" its message. The idea is that the text of the Bible is a stable, reliable source for certain kinds of knowledge (doctrine and ethics, mainly) similar to the way "nature" is thought to function as a source for scientific knowledge.[2] As scientists just "look at nature" for correct knowledge about how the world works (or so the assumption goes) so Christians can just "look to the text" of the Bible for correct knowledge about doctrine and ethics.

Foundationalism is not the same as fundamentalism. Fundamentalism grew up in the United States in the nineteenth and twentieth centuries as a response to modernism and intellectual shifts resulting from the modern Enlightenment. Fundamentalism typically held that the Bible is completely inerrant not only with regard to necessary issues of doctrine and ethics, but also with regard to matters of history, nature, and science. The literal inerrancy of Scripture is still the most commonly cited marker of modern fundamentalism, at least when it comes to Christianity.

Foundationalism is different. Foundationalism does not necessarily hold to the complete inerrancy of Scripture, at least not in matters of history and nature. Foundationalism, however, holds that the Bible provides, or should provide, a secure basis for doctrine and ethics, at least if we interpret it by the appropriate methods. Whereas *fundamentalists* might believe that one must accept the fact that "Job" was a historical figure, *foundationalists* may have no problem doubting that there was a "historical Job" or that our biblical book "correctly" relates his "history," but they would nonetheless insist that the book of Job should provide a basis for knowledge about God and human relations with God. *Fundamentalists* may believe that Christians must accept the Pauline authorship of all those letters that bear his name. *Foundationalists* may accept that some of those letters were not actually written by Paul, but they would nonetheless teach that *if they are read according to the proper methods* the texts furnish Christians with firm foundations on which to build contemporary ethical guidelines. Whereas *fundamentalists* might insist that the creation accounts in Genesis are historically accurate, that there was a historical Adam and Eve, and that "the fall" was an actual historical event, *foundationalists* might identify the stories as originary myths with no historical referent, but they nonetheless appeal to the stories as a basis for ethical guidelines on male-female relations. Even if the stories are not *historically* true, therefore, they still "speak a message" about God's will for human existence. They provide some foundationalists even with *negative* rules for human behavior: by creating "Adam and Eve" and not "Adam and Steve," they claim, God made it abundantly clear that human wholeness is fulfilled only in the complementariness of male and female, and that therefore the only moral sexual relationship is heterosexual.

Textual foundationalism is not the only kind of foundationalism. As I have already implied, it is merely a literary version of modern science's notions that we can obtain secure and true knowledge about nature by carefully observing nature. Studied correctly, nature itself will yield its own "meaning," and nature therefore may function as a foundation for the formation of other types of knowledge.[3] In a previous generation of Christian thinkers, "human experience" was evoked as another epistemological foundation. Human beings, it was thought, could observe "human experience," perhaps even "universal human experience," and derive from those observations secure guidelines for ethical norms.[4] In all these foundationalisms, the driving desire is to find something outside the vagaries of interpretation by which to test the validity of interpretation: if we wonder whether our ethical notions are correct, we should test them against some source of knowledge outside that process of interpretation itself, whether in "nature," or "science," or "experience," or the "text." Those I call biblical foundationalists are just as much invested in foundationalism as other modernists; they just insist that the text of Scripture is the most important foundation that ultimately trumps any other source of knowledge.

LITERARY THEORY AND TEXTUAL MEANING

The most significant challenge to textual foundationalism has come from post-structuralist literary theories that emphasize the instability of textual "meaning." What does a text "mean"? When we have disagreements about the meaning of a text, how do we settle those disagreements? Textual foundationalists insist that we must read the texts more carefully, put aside our prejudices as much as possible, use more reliable methods, and "listen" to the text better. Nonfoundationalists such as myself insist that those ideas are misleading, ultimately unworkable, and even morally questionable. We believe, rather, that texts don't have *any meaning* apart from particular interpretations that must be performed by human beings.[5] Since meaning does not reside "in the text itself" but is provided by the reading activity, simply insisting on "what the text says" won't get us anywhere, nor will we be able to devise a method of interpretation that will insure a predictably "true" or "correct" or "ethical" interpretation of the text.[6] We insist that human agency in interpretation be firmly reintroduced into debates about the meanings of texts.

Let me illustrate with an example. In the second century, the church father Irenaeus wrote against all sorts of groups he considered heretical. Some Christians noted that in the gospel account of the baptism of Jesus a dove is said to come down upon Jesus, and a voice proclaims, "This is my beloved son." Some manuscripts even had the additional phrase "Today I have begotten you."[7] At least some interpreters noted that the word in the text for "dove" is *peristera*. As is well known, Greek numbers in the ancient world were designated by letters of the alphabet: A is 1, B is 2, and so forth. The numerical value of the addition of the letters in *peristera* is 801, which providentially equals alpha plus omega (A = 1, Ω = 800), which we learn from Revelation denotes the identity of divinity (Rev. 21:6; 22:13). The text could thus be cited as proof that divinity descended upon Jesus at his baptism, rather than that Jesus had always been divine. This sort of reading apparently was used to support a Christology we call "adoptionism" because it taught that Jesus was "adopted" as the son of God at some point in his life, variously taken to be at his birth, or baptism, or resurrection.[8] The truth of this Christology could be argued by appeal to the Scriptures. It was right there in the text: *peristera* = 801 = A + Ω.

This is a reading of the text that few of us would be willing to accept today, but how could we convince them that the interpretation is not "correct"? We might point out that there are no other indications in Mark of adoptionist Christology, but they could say that does not matter because this indication is sufficient. We might say that the author surely didn't *intend* such a reading, but they could answer that he certainly must have done so since he wrote the clue into his text; or they might respond that even if the *human* author Mark didn't "intend" this meaning, the *real* author of the text is God or the Spirit, and we all know that God the Father and the Spirit have sprinkled the Scriptures with many meanings not immediately accessible to just anyone. We might say that an adoptionist Christology contradicts other indications in the New Testament, but they could simply point out that we are not reading the other texts correctly, or that other texts that imply an adoptionist Christology should be given more weight.[9] I am not saying that we could never convince them that their interpretation is wrong—*if* we and they share some assumptions about "proper" interpretation. But I am insisting that just pointing to the text itself won't solve the problem. The text *cannot* interpret itself.

I sometimes illustrate my point when asked to speak about "what the Bible says about homosexuality." I put the Bible in the middle of the room or on the speaker's podium, step back, and say, "Okay, let's see what it says. Listen!" After a few seconds of uncomfortable silence and some snickers, I say, "Apparently, the Bible can't talk." This is not the frivolous gimmick it may initially seem. Our language about "what texts say" tends to make us forget that the expression is a metaphor. Texts don't "say" anything: they must be read. And even in the reading process, interpretation has already begun. And if we want to move on from reading the text out loud, say, to paraphrasing it or commenting upon what it "means," we have simply moved further into human interpretation.

Now, textual foundationalists may object that I am taking the language of "texts speaking" or "meaning" too literally, and that of course they realize that texts must be read and interpreted. They will still insist, however, that the meaning of the text is not completely indeterminate: read responsibly, texts can and do constrain our interpretations of their meaning. But that way of thinking about making meaning is still too metaphorical. Texts *in themselves* do not and cannot constrain one's interpretation of them. What influences interpretation are the social constraints surrounding and constituting the interpreter, especially other human interpreters. We read certain ways because we are socialized to do so; we change our readings in interaction with other human beings; we read differently on a second reading because we ourselves have been (socially!) changed in the meantime. There are constraints on reading, but they are social and psychological constraints, not constraints exercised directly by the "text itself." We may "feel" that the text is indicating its meaning, but I insist that there is no meaning "there" in the text. It is created by readers using the text.[10]

AUTHORIAL INTENTION

Some scholars agree that the text itself cannot settle disagreements about its meaning, but they insist that all texts do have authors, and authors can make meaning, and that the meaning of a text resides in the author's intention. Appeals to authorial intention to settle disagreements of textual meaning appear commonsensical to many of us because our speech acts often do seem to be the communication of an idea or request or command from one person to another. "Meaning" therefore resembles a "thing" passed from one person to another, so if misunderstanding occurs, the "receiver" should go to the "source" and check for the "correct meaning."[11] Reader response theory, which I am here advocating, does not insist that authors have no intentions, or that when we read a text we may not legitimately imagine what an author may have intended. Reader response theory simply insists that the *meaning of the text* is not *identical* to an author's intention, nor can an author's intention actually constrain the meaning of the text or control its interpretation.

Notice what actually happens when someone appeals to authorial intention. We can never actually *go to* the author's intention; we cannot point to it in nature; we cannot "see" or "hear" it. Even in those cases where we ask an actual human being what she or he "meant" by a statement, what we will get is at most a memory of what the author may have been thinking at the time, or a guess on the part of the author based on the statement itself, or a memory of the writing activity. In other words, we are still getting an *interpretation* of the text, even from the author of the text. Authorial intention is not the answer to the vagaries of interpretation because it is part of interpretation itself.

The most compelling argument against authorial intention as establishing the meaning of an utterance, though, is to point out that we actually do not, in much of our interpreting of speech or writing, take "the meaning" to be equivalent to the intentions of the author. Examples from common experience could be multiplied infinitely, but I will offer a few. When my brother was young, he was briefly hospitalized due to a collapsed lung. The doctor told my parents that he couldn't say precisely what caused the lung to collapse, that the condition was congenital, and that it could happen again with little or no warning. My sister, a teenager at the time, overheard this conversation and for days went around telling family friends that my brother was in the hospital because of a "genital disease." How do we decide about "the meaning" of my sister's statement? Certainly not by simply attempting to ascertain "what she meant." For one thing, at this distance (many years later) she probably cannot remember accurately what she was thinking at the time. Even if we could settle what her intentions were, that in itself wouldn't provide the meaning of the statement. If she now told us that she *meant* the sense of "congenital" rather than "genital," even that wouldn't change the meaning of what she actually *said*, as if we could just alternate the two words back and forth without the meaning changing because now we knew her "intention." The statement's meaning (both the fact that it is meaningful for us at all and the meaning we take it to signify about my brother, my sister, and the situation) is a complicated conjunction of several different factors: our knowledge of the normal meanings of the terms "genital" and "congenital," which are social facts, not "intentions"; our knowledge that such misunderstandings are not unlikely for a young girl; our knowledge that there is a certain "joking" quality to the whole story; our knowledge that part of the humor comes from the sexual innuendo, even if none was "intended." The meaning of the statement, that is, comes from our knowledge of complicated social conventions: of similar-sounding words, of doctors' explanations, of adolescent misunderstandings, and of social scandal. Even if we do attempt to figure out "what she meant" (and we *need* not do so to understand the statement), that bit of information would do nothing more than add to the process of interpretation; it wouldn't "fix" the meaning of the statement.

The problem with theories of interpretation that insist on authorial intention is that they are incapable of accounting for *all* the ways we regularly interpret texts, even if we may imagine that they do correctly portray the way we interpret in certain circumstances (say, when thinking about commands issued or letters between two people). For instance, "the meaning" of poetry, most poets would insist, is not limited to what the poet "intended" to communicate. Poetry, in the minds of many people, poets included, is *supposed* to be patient of many different interpretations and kinds of interpretation. Or take the example of racist or profane language. Let us imagine that a young man for whom English is still a new language repeats a phrase from a music video that contains profanity or a racist statement, perhaps without even understanding its normal meaning. If he insists that he didn't *mean* the words in an offensive sense, would that mean that the words were in fact not profane or racist? No. We may legitimately explain to him that the language is offensive *in spite of his intentions*. I am not saying that the offensive nature of the language exists *inherently* in the words. I am saying that the meaning of the language derives from its function, and that the meaning is usually a function of the way the language would be "normally" understood by "competent" speakers of the language. We might excuse the person for the offense because he didn't really understand the meaning of the words. But his *intention* is not the same thing as the *meaning* of the words.

It simply misrepresents how we actually do interpret language to insist that the meaning of the statement is the author's intention. The meaning of the statement is a result of a complex interpretive process that takes place in specific social and historical contexts. It is a matter of what the statement is *taken to mean*, not what it *may have meant* to the original author. Theories about authorial intentions providing the meaning of texts must show that to be the case not only in *ideal* or even *most* cases; they must show that authorial intention is the meaning of a text in *all* cases. Otherwise, authorial intention becomes just one more act of the imagination we employ when we interpret texts.

HISTORICAL "RECOVERY"

Some scholars admit that we can never have access to the author's intention itself, especially when reading the texts of authors long since dead, but they then insist that such intentions, though never actually producible, are relatively "recoverable" by historical methods. Here again, the metaphorical language needs breaking down. The word "recover" invokes the image of, say, digging up an artifact from the ground and displaying it again as a real object, not just one of our imagination. It may be excusable to speak of "reconstructing" something like an archeological object: we may "recover" the pieces of the Titanic, for instance, haul them to land, and "reconstruct" the ship using "recovered pieces" of the original. But that is not really what scholars do when they say they are "recovering" or "reconstructing" an author's intentions. For one thing, there is nothing physical there to "recover." The "reconstruction" is actually a "construction." The scholars are again just reading texts and, using their imaginations informed by *other* interpretations of *other* texts, imagining what an author *may* have meant to communicate when writing the text. No scholar has ever *recovered* an ancient author's intention. They have constructed it out of the very processes of interpretation that they are attempting to regulate by appealing to "authorial intention."

My argument thus far about authorial intention as providing "the meaning" of a text may be summarized like this:

1. Authorial intentions do not really exist anywhere in nature so that we could hold up our interpretations against them for testing purposes.
2. Authorial intentions, when used as a factor in interpreting texts, are themselves products of people interpreting texts.
3. In our everyday practices we actually do *not* always use notions of authorial intention to settle the meanings of texts.
4. Even if authorial intention is something we may legitimately imagine for purposes of interpreting a text, there is no reason to limit interpretations of all texts to attempts to ascertain intentions.[12]

SCRIPTURE, THEOLOGY, INTENTION, AND THE USE OF HISTORY

Thus far I've offered simply arguments from everyday observation to disprove the commonsensical assumption that the meaning of a text lies either in the text itself or in the intentions of the author. But there are also very good theological issues to address here as well. After all, the Bible has never been considered just a "text" by Christians. It is the Word of God. What does it mean to call this text "Word of God"? How should we think about interpreting a text once we believe it is "Scripture," the "Word of God"? These questions also have something to contribute to the debate about both authorial intention and the use of historical criticism in biblical interpretation.

There are good theological reasons to reject making authorial intention the goal of the interpretation of Scripture. First, we must recognize that what has traditionally been considered authoritative for the church is Scripture, not the intentions, real or imagined, of the original authors. Yes, Christian interpreters throughout history have talked about what Paul or some other biblical writer may have *meant* to say, but that has traditionally not been taken to *limit* the meaning of the text to that intention.[13] Thus, even if the psalmist intended to speak of David or some other king of ancient Israel, the church has always considered it legitimate to interpret the psalm as referring also—or even only or supremely—to Christ. Even if the human authors of the New Testament did not *intend* to affirm the Trinity in the first century, the church may legitimately interpret Scripture in Trinitarian terms.[14] The church has traditionally not located the site of inspiration to be in the mind of the human author but in the text of Scripture itself.[15] The shift to concentrating on the intentions of the human author is something that happened only in the modern era, with the rise of historical criticism.[16]

Second, how useful is authorial intention for many of the kinds of texts we find in the Bible? Which "author" do we consider, for instance, when reading Genesis: the "Yahwist" or the "Elohist"?[17] Or do we consider the scribe or scribes who redacted the earlier sources to produce the final version of Genesis? And what precisely *is* "the final version": some particular Hebrew recension; the form of the "Masoretic" text reproduced in modern editions; a critical edition produced by modern scholars comparing different ancient Hebrew and Greek manuscripts? Who is the "author" of composite texts? Appealing to "the author" is simply a technique we use to shape our imaginations in certain directions, but it is not a secure method or resource for ascertaining meaning—much less *limiting* meaning.

Third, according to Christian understanding "the author" of Scripture is the Holy Spirit or God. Even if we could "recover" the authorial intention of Paul, for instance, that should not be allowed, *from a theological point of view*, to limit our interpretation about the meaning of the text. Since the author of Scripture is God, and since God is not immediately accessible to us present human beings as an arbiter for disagreements about interpretation, appeal to authorial intention to settle disagreements about meanings of scriptural texts will not get us very far.

Before the Reformation, the assumption was that the church itself, through its hierarchy and leadership, had the authority to settle disputes about the meaning of Scripture. Since the author of Scripture is the Holy Spirit, and since the mind of the Spirit is not readily and easily accessible to all people, the church hierarchy reserved for itself the right to interpret Scripture. The "teaching office" of the Roman Catholic Church that is supposed to decide such matters is called the magisterium.

The early Protestants, of course, rejected the right of the Roman Catholic hierarchy, the magisterium, to decide "the meaning" of Scripture. The reformers insisted that "only Scripture," *sola scriptura*, should serve as the source for doctrine and moral teaching, and they increasingly insisted that the fundamental meaning of Scripture resided in its "plain" or "literal" sense.[18] But they discovered that settling on the "literal sense" was itself not easy to do. In fact, it increasingly seemed to offer no more reliable guidance to "the meaning" of the text than had methods such as allegory or typology. People couldn't agree about what "the literal sense" was.

Eventually, in the modern world historical criticism was offered as a control over meaning: the *ancient* meaning of the language. In this book, when I speak of the "historical-critical meaning" of the text, I refer to this notion that the primary or most fundamental meaning of the text is that suggested by historical research about what the original human author intended or the original readers understood. In the modern period, the primary meaning of the text has had to be anchored in its ancient meaning.[19]

But there are also very good reasons to reject the notion that Christians should insist on the *necessity* of historical criticism for the interpretation of Scripture or that the historical-critical meaning of the text should be the primary or controlling meaning of the text. In the first place, any survey of actual historical-critical studies demonstrates that different scholars come to widely different interpretations about even the historical meaning of the text.[20] Even using the same methods of historical research, biblical scholars are able to offer widely divergent, even mutually contradictory, readings of the same text. Much of the work of the essays in this book demonstrates this fact: historical criticism simply has not been able to deliver what it promised: a workable consensus on the meaning of the text. Moreover, even when scholars agree about the ancient meaning of the text, they often disagree about the ethical or doctrinal consequences or application. Historical criticism simply cannot provide the security or controls for reliable interpretation that it originally hoped to deliver.

But the most important problem with insisting on the necessity of historical criticism of the Bible is a theological one. Since the historical method of interpretation was invented and developed only in the modern period, no premodern Christian used that method. To say that the historical method is *necessary* for Christian interpretation is to say that all premodern interpreters were not Christians or were completely incapable of interpreting Scripture Christianly. This would cut the modern church off from eighteen centuries of Christian tradition and life, which would in turn offend the Christian doctrine of "the communion of the saints." The doctrine of the communion of the saints teaches that all Christians are members of the body of Christ that exists in every place today and has always existed. If we modern Christians insist that Christian interpretation of Scripture *must* proceed by using the methods of historical criticism, we cut ourselves off from premodern Christian interpreters and declare their practices of interpretation non-Christian.[21] We disrupt the body of Christ, the communion of the saints. From a theological perspective, there can be no particular method of interpreting Scripture deemed *necessary* that has not been available to Christians throughout the history of the church. I should make it clear that I am not arguing that Christians should *avoid* historical criticism. As one method for reading Scripture among others, it is not only appropriate but often quite valuable. What I am arguing is that any insistence that historical criticism is *necessary* or provides the *ruling or controlling* meaning of the text offends the theological notion of the communion of the saints and is therefore not theologically defensible.

ATTEMPTS AT THEOLOGICAL RATIONALES FOR HISTORICAL CRITICISM

Most modern scholars, even Christians, have made no attempt to defend the use of historical criticism in their interpretations of Scripture. They simply assume it. But as the dominance of historical criticism in biblical scholarship has come under attack in recent years, some scholars have attempted to offer theological reasons for their advocacy of history as providing the foundational meaning of the text.

Some scholars, for example, have noted (rightly) that throughout history Christian theologians have insisted that the "plain sense" or the "literal sense" (*sensus literalis*) of the text must be primary. They then claim (wrongly) that the "historical sense" *is* what Christian theologians have always considered the "literal sense." N. T. Wright, for instance, says, "Genuine historical scholarship is still the appropriate tool with which to work at discovering more fully what precisely the biblical authors intended to say."[22] He defends this assertion by insisting that this is what even premodern Christian theologians meant by the "literal sense," the *sensus literalis* of Scripture: "discovering what the authors meant," "the sense originally intended," "the original sense" (67, 132–33), which is just what modern historical critics are also seeking. But this characterization of what premodern theologians meant by the "literal sense" is simply wrong.

First, we should note that in the long sweep of Christian theological thinking about Scripture, it is not true that the "literal sense" was considered the most important sense of the text. At different times and by many Christians, the "literal sense" was actually considered *inferior* to the "spiritual" or figurative sense of Scripture. To imply that focusing on the primacy of the literal sense is "the traditional Christian view" ignores much theology and actual Christian practice, especially from the first thousand years of Christian theology.[23] But even more crucial than that observation is the fact that for most of Christian history and theology, the "literal sense" did not mean "the original historical sense" or "the human author's intention." Rather, here in the words of Charles Wood, "literal sense" in premodern theology is "the 'natural,' 'plain,' 'obvious' meaning which the community of faith has normally acknowledged as basic, regardless of whatever other constructions might also properly be put upon the text." It is "the sense whose discernment has become second nature to the members of the community."[24]

Augustine (354–430), for example, certainly took the *sensus literalis* to be important, and he also advocated that the reader attempt to discern the human author's meaning. But the two were not necessarily identical. One reason was because Augustine, like almost all Christian writers, took the *main* author of Scripture to be God or the Holy Spirit. The human author may not have discerned the meaning intended by the divine author. Thus, Augustine believes that the "literal sense" of one author may be clarified even by using texts of Scripture written by different authors at different times:

> Sometimes not just one meaning but two or more meanings are perceived in the same words of scripture. Even if the writer's meaning is obscure, there is no danger here, provided that it can be shown from other passages of the holy scriptures that each of these interpretations is consistent with the truth. The person examining the divine utterances must of course do his best to arrive at the intention of the writer through whom the Holy Spirit produced that part of scripture; he may reach that meaning or carve out from the words another meaning which does not run counter to the faith, using the evidence of any other passage of divine utterances.[25]

What Augustine is advocating as the literal sense is not the modern notion of the historical-critical sense. If the author's meaning is obscure, the interpreter may explain it by recourse to any other part of Scripture deemed relevant, even those of other authors separated by centuries. This is a practice rejected by historical criticism. Moreover, for Augustine the literal sense could be a meaning that the human author did not at all perceive himself.[26]

Whereas for many modern scholars, the literal sense is that intended by the author, Augustine's test for whether a biblical text is literal or figurative is whether it accords with true doctrine or ethics: "We must first explain the way to discover whether an expression is literal or figurative. Generally speaking, it is this: anything in the divine discourse that cannot be related either to good morals or to the true faith should be taken as figurative. Good morals have to do with our love of God and our neighbour, the true faith with our understanding of God and our neighbour"(*De doctrina christiana* 3.33–34 [10.14]). Texts that accord with Christian doctrine and an ethic of love are literal; those that do not are figurative: "If scripture seems to advocate love, it is literal; if it seems to advocate malice, it is figurative" (3.55 [16.24]). So Augustine interprets the first part of Romans 12:20 ("If your enemy is hungry, feed him; if he is thirsty, give him a drink") as literal, but the following phrase ("For by doing this you will pile coals of fire on his head") as figurative. For Augustine, the interpreter may indeed take the human author's intention into account, but that is certainly *not* what establishes the literal sense of the text. The literal sense is established by ethical and doctrinal criteria. This is *not* what modern scholars mean by the "historical sense" or the "author's intention."

Thomas Aquinas (1225–1274) drew on the theories of Augustine and modified them. Thomas wanted to argue that the different meanings of Scripture, including the anagogical or allegorical, were actually *not separate* meanings of Scripture but were really *contained in* the literal meaning. Moreover, he believed that the "literal sense" was the sense "intended by the author," but he did not mean the *human* author: "Now because the literal sense is that which the author intends, and the author of holy Scripture is God who comprehends everything all at once in his understanding, it comes not amiss, as St. Augustine observes, if many meanings are present even in the literal sense of one passage of Scripture."[27] Nicholas of Lyra (d. 1340) built on Thomas's ideas. He agreed that the literal sense was the sense intended by the author, who was God. For Nicholas, there could be two literal senses of the same text. Thus, in 1 Chronicles 17, God is speaking to Solomon when he says, "I will be a father to him," and this is the literal sense of the text. But the text also refers to Christ, and this is also its literal meaning. "Furthermore," as James Preus explains, "in harmony with Thomas' theory, Lyra makes no appeal to the intention of the Old Testament author to support the New Testament meaning."[28] Preus goes further to trace the notion of literal sense into the Reformation and the early writings of Martin Luther. As he demonstrates, these premodern Christian theologians worked with a notion of the original intention of the human author. So it is not just that they didn't *explicitly consider* identifying the literal sense of the text with the intention of the human author. Rather, they both considered *and rejected* the idea that the *sensus literalis* could be identified with the intentions of the human author or the understandings of the original audience.[29]

Theologians and historians of theology, therefore, have increasingly come to recognize that *sensus literalis* in premodern theology did not generally mean what modern historical critics mean by the "original historical meaning" or the "author's intention." As Hans Frei noted years ago, "established or 'plain' readings are warranted by their agreement with a religious community's rules for reading its sacred text."[30] George Lindbeck agrees that the literal sense is "that which a community of readers takes to be the plain, primary, and controlling signification of a text (a less problematic move than appealing to authorial intention or to some property ingredient in the text)."[31] And Kathryn Tanner argues that the "plain" or "literal sense" of the text is not a property of the text itself, nor the human author's intention, nor the original historical meaning, but

> a function of communal use: it is the obvious or direct sense of the text according to the *usus loquendi* established by the community in question. . . . [T]he plain sense of a text is not considered here as if it were anything "in itself," apart from an interpretive practice of using texts. . . . The plain sense is itself a product of an interpretive tradition; the distinction between what is and is not the plain sense of a text becomes, therefore, a relative distinction between different sorts of communal uses of a text.[32]

The attempt, therefore, by historical critics such as N. T. Wright to invoke the premodern notion of *sensus literalis* to support the necessity of historical criticism ignores the vast historical evidence about the actual use of *sensus literalis* in Christian history as well as the arguments of contemporary theologians. The Christian tradition of valuing the "literal sense" of Scripture does not support the claim that historical criticism is *necessary* for Christian readings of Scripture.

Another common way modern scholars have argued for the necessity of history is by declaring that Christianity is, by its very nature, a "historical" religion. For example, scholars will sometimes point to the centrality of the incarnation for Christianity.[33] They then note that the incarnation happened in time, in history, so historical criticism is necessary for Christian theology. This argument is wrongheaded because scholars are here using the term "history" in two very different senses.[34] When modern historians say an event is "historical," they are not simply saying it may have "happened" or that it is "in the past." They are saying that it can be verified as an event by the normal means of modern historiography.[35] No good historian, playing by the professional disciplinary rules of modern historiography, can demonstrate that the incarnation is an "historical fact." This is *not* the same as saying that it is "false" or "didn't happen." It is just saying that it cannot be treated as an historical fact when judged by the normal disciplinary rules of modern historiography. The doctrine of the incarnation teaches that God became human in the person of Jesus. Now, of course Jesus of Nazareth was a historical person, and we may apply historical methods to establish what we may say about his life as a human being. But we could never demonstrate *anything* about whether or not God was "in" him or that he could be identified with God. God is not one of those things that can be tested or proved by the practices of modern historiography. Thus, although we can affirm that Jesus was a historical person (meaning simply that historians, doing historiographical research, can point to evidence that he existed), we cannot affirm (or deny), *historically speaking*, the truth of the incarnation.[36]

Richard Hays also attempts to argue for the necessity of historical criticism when he claims that the Gospels are "history-like narratives," and therefore modern historical criticism is the appropriate place to start in reading the Bible.[37] But Hays never explains why "history-like narratives" need modern historiography to confirm their "truth" or supply their "meaning." One could admit that the Gospels are history-like narratives (which I do not) in the same way that Hamlet is a history-like character in the history-like narrative of Shakespeare's play, but that *need not* mean that we must use modern historiography to ascertain anything about the "historical Hamlet" at all, nor that we would need modern historical criticism to ascertain "Shakespeare's intentions," before we could read and interpret *Hamlet*.[38] *Hamlet* was interpreted quite well long before the rise of modern historical criticism, so that method is not *necessary* for an interpretation of *Hamlet*. Likewise, even *if* the Gospels are "history-like narratives" one does not *need* historical criticism in order to interpret them Christianly.[39]

In sum, when apologists for historical criticism say that history is necessary because Christianity is an historical religion, they are using the term "history" in two very different ways: one to refer to something as having happened in the past, and the other to a set of disciplinary practices and rules. History, in the latter sense, as a *discipline*, *cannot* serve as the epistemological foundation for theology, nor should Christians insist that the "historical-critical meaning" of the biblical text serve as a *necessary foundation* for theological use of Scripture.

THE ANXIETY OF UNCERTAINTY

Instead of admitting or trying to defend their assumptions that texts "have" their meaning in themselves simply waiting to be unlocked by readers, or that historical criticism can and should provide sufficiently defensible controls on interpretation, most scholars seek merely to alarm their readers by saying that if texts can't constrain their own interpretation or if historical criticism cannot deliver reliable consensus, we will be left in absolute interpretive anarchy and all meaning will disappear. People will be able to make a text mean whatever they want it to mean.[40] Churches will simply read texts to reinforce their own prejudices and beliefs. Individual readers will see in the text what they already believe. If texts cannot resist readings or constrain interpretation, we will all look into texts and see only our own reflections. Unethical readings of Scripture will abound.

This sort of argument is not theologically thoughtful or reasonable. It is persuasion by fear. It is also false. It pretends that if texts themselves cannot control their own interpretation then there are no controls at all on interpretation. But that is false. None of us can interpret a text in just any way—not because we are constrained by the text, but because we are constrained by many other things. We are all socialized to read in certain ways. As modern people, for instance, we tend to read ancient texts with a modern historical consciousness. We *want* to know what the ancient author may have intended to communicate, what the text may have meant in its ancient context. Therefore, most modern people will resist a reading of a text that they realize is highly anachronistic. But this is not a constraint exercised on the reader by the text; it is rather a constraint exercised by modern consciousness and the socialization of the reader.

To cite another possible control: human beings are not hermetically sealed individuals; we are influenced by people and other social forces all around us. Therefore, our readings of texts may be challenged by other human beings, and that experience may in turn change our own reading. The fear expressed by many scholars that "anything goes" if we do not assume that texts control their own interpretation simply ignores that there are many other factors that control and constrain human interpretations of texts. [41] Those are things such as the contingency and socialization of readers themselves, the cultural formation of the self, and other people and institutions. These controls on interpretation never completely disappear, as much as we may try to step away from them. Therefore it is *not* true that people interpret texts in just "any old way." They interpret texts according to assumptions and rules of interpretation they have internalized and that are reinforced by human society and culture.

Equally ironic is the insistence of some Christian scholars that without the control of historical criticism or the "foundation" of the text people will interpret the Bible to support unethical actions. The irony is that some of the pioneers of modern historical criticism actually *did* use the Bible, even interpreted by the methods of historical criticism, to support the most heinous beliefs and policies. Famous historians who supported the Nazis in Germany were respected historical critics of the Bible, who used their own historical scholarship to support anti-Semitic readings of Scripture and public policy.[42] Supporters of slavery in the American South used the Bible to back up their racism, and from a historical point of view their readings were more defensible than those of abolitionists.[43] My point is not that we should blame the method of historical criticism for the Holocaust, or slavery, or racism. My point is that historical criticism is powerless to prevent such readings. Historical criticism cannot be depended on to provide reliably ethical readings of Scripture, as history itself easily proves.

It is also ironic when Christian scholars insist that without a foundationalist use of the Bible for ethics we will be plunged into conflict and even violence. Some people evoke images of neotribalism taking up arms as the last resort to "establish the truth" if we give up common-sense ideas that things like "texts" themselves can provide secure foundations for knowledge and ethics. The lie is given to this argument by the universally observable fact that it is now foundationalists—even fundamentalists—who are key players in the current epidemic of violence, especially religious violence. Islamic fundamentalists, Jewish fundamentalists, Hindu fundamentalists, *and* Christian fundamentalists (and the conservative government of the United States at this time is for all practical purposes a Christian fundamentalist political force) are all much more central to the engines of current international and interreligious violence than is anyone under the influence of postmodernism, deconstruction, or antifoundationalist theories. The people who are nowadays the most violent are also those most secure in their theological-epistemological foundations. For biblical scholars to cry that without a foundationalist understanding of textual meaning we may have no recourse against using the Bible for unethical and violent ends is glaringly ironic if not simply disingenuous.

SCRIPTURE WITHOUT FOUNDATIONS

These arguments for the necessity of textual foundationalism or historical criticism are wrong-headed. We must admit that we are without secure foundations for knowledge. In the end, there are no guarantees that we or anyone else will not use the text unethically. There are no reliable foundations. The answer to that problem is not just to keep insisting that there are but to learn to live faithful and ethical lives without secure foundations.

Though written separately and for different purposes, each of the essays collected in this book attempts to demonstrate that textual foundationalism will not work. But that is not all. In these essays I outline my belief that foundationalism is ethically *dangerous*. Foundationalism often leads to unethical practices because it masks the very real interpretive agency of the human interpreter and thus allows the interpreter to avoid responsibility for the truth, goodness, morality, and social effect of her or his interpretation. Moreover, the modern method of historical criticism, though certainly a useful tool, cannot be depended on to deliver secure, ethical interpretations of Scripture. I do believe there is a way forward, beyond textual foundationalism and the hegemony of the historical-critical method. The conclusion of this book constitutes an attempt to point in that direction. But before we can seriously entertain alternatives, we must demonstrate the inadequacies of much contemporary thinking about Scripture and its interpretation. The essays of this book, in a variety of ways, offer that demonstration.

Chapter 2

The Rhetoric of Biblical Scholarship

A Primer for Critical Reading of Historical Criticism

As noted in the previous chapter, Christians of many different stripes in the modern world have turned to historical criticism in an attempt to find a method for interpreting Scripture that will create consensus about the meaning of biblical texts. With the Protestant rejection of the Roman Catholic claim that the Church's hierarchy itself should decide the meaning of the text, and Protestantism's substitution of *sola scriptura* for the Roman Catholic magisterium, it gradually became apparent that some method was needed for ascertaining the correct reading of the text. And also gradually, the traditional notion of *sensus literalis*, the text's "literal sense," came to be associated in the minds of moderns with the "original" meaning of the text. That original meaning was supposed to be established either by guessing what the original human author intended or by suggesting how original, native speakers would have understood the text. The historical meaning of the text—or at least a limited range of meanings that could be defended by the methods of modern historiography supplementing traditional grammatical analysis—came to be proposed as the meaning that could eventually command consensus among all reasonable Christians of good will.

It hasn't worked. A simple empirical survey of the ways different scholars use historical criticism to arrive at very different, sometimes diametrically opposed, readings of texts demonstrates that historical criticism simply *cannot* provide the security or controls for reliable interpretation it has promised. Moreover, it can't provide "*the* meaning" even in the sense of what the text meant in its ancient context, much less its meaning for modern ethical applications. To demonstrate this point, I offer in this essay a brief survey of the different kinds of arguments and interpretations—a rhetorical analysis—of recent New Testament scholarship on homosexuality, concentrating especially on disagreements over interpretations of Romans 1. For the sake of simplifying a confusing array of differences, I have organized these different "rhetorics of history and ethics" into a few main categories. We may think of these as categories of arguments or types of "historical proofs."[1]

This chapter also urges that people be educated in rhetorical analysis of scholarship and that theological education of students include education not only in *what* scholars say but also in *how* they say it. "Rhetoric" refers to the use of language to persuade. Any linguistic statement, no matter what its original speaker intended, can be analyzed as an "attempt to persuade." When people have disagreements about what the Bible "says" or means on a topic, they often use different ways of arguing to persuade others of their interpretation. But too often even students in seminaries and divinity schools, not to mention average Christians "in the pews," are never really taught how to recognize, use, or question common ways of arguing. When we analyze how someone marshals arguments in order to persuade, we are analyzing those statements *as rhetoric*.

This is not to say that rhetoric is bad. Nor is it to dismiss arguments as "mere rhetoric." Rhetoric is, in fact, unavoidable if we want to communicate with one another and sway others to our way of seeing or thinking. But people should be educated in rhetorical analysis, certainly students and would-be scholars but also laypersons. If we are incapable of recognizing and "naming" different rhetorical moves, we are usually incapable of resisting those arguments even when they are wrong or inadequate. Learning to recognize rhetoric—typical ways of arguing or persuading—becomes a powerful tool people may then use either to construct arguments themselves or to resist problematic arguments put forward by others. What I offer in this chapter is a rhetorical analysis of biblical scholarship on sexuality, something like a "road map" for negotiating the diverse arguments presented by people about biblical interpretation. I concentrate initially on scholarship on Romans 1 and homosexuality.[2] First, I provide a list of "typical arguments" scholars make when interpreting the text. Then I analyze the writings of four individual scholars, demonstrating how their arguments sometimes mislead and how they each invoke the false notion that their ethics are based on the "foundation" of the text of Scripture.

A PRIMER ON SOME BASIC ARGUMENTS

For the convenience of my readers, I provide here a quotation of Romans 1:18–27, the text addressed by the scholarship below. Though I usually provide my own translation of New Testament texts, I here provide that of the New Revised Standard Version. If I were to provide my own translation, I would then need to explain or defend it, and my purpose here is not to argue for my own reading of the passage but to highlight aspects of the arguments of other scholars. This very admission, though, demonstrates one important point about all interpretation of the Bible: it usually begins with translation, which is itself a highly interpretive and creative activity.

> For the wrath of God is revealed from heaven against all ungodliness and wickedness of those who by their wickedness suppress the truth. For what can be known about God is plain to them, because God has shown it to them. Ever since the creation of the world his eternal power and divine nature, invisible though they are, have been understood and seen through the things he has made. So they are without excuse; for though they knew God, they did not honor him as God or give thanks to him, but they became futile in their thinking, and their senseless minds were darkened. Claiming to be wise, they became fools; and they exchanged the glory of the immortal God for images resembling a mortal human being or birds or four-footed animals or reptiles.
>
> Therefore God gave them up in the lusts of their hearts to impurity, to the degrading of their bodies among themselves, because they exchanged the truth about God for a lie and worshiped and served the creature rather than the Creator, who is blessed forever! Amen.
>
> For this reason God gave them up to degrading passions. Their women exchanged natural intercourse for unnatural, and in the same way also the men, giving up natural intercourse with women, were consumed with passion for one another. Men committed shameless acts with men and received in their own persons the due penalty for their error. (Rom. 1:18–27, NRSV)

"Difference in times," or "The times they have a-changed"

This kind of argument emphasizes the differences in culture separating modern Christians from the ancient situation. It is sometimes admitted that Paul in Romans 1 does condemn same-sex intercourse, but that these condemnations are so wrapped up in other ancient cultural assumptions, which we either do not or should not share, that they should not be used to condemn homosexuality today. For example, Paul's condemnations of homosexuality are completely implicated in his assumptions of hierarchy, especially gender hierarchy. Since Paul assumed something we should not assume—that male is always superior to female and that the penetrator in intercourse is always superior to the penetrated—to transfer his condemnations to our day would implicate us in those hierarchical assumptions.[3]

In a different version of this kind of argument, William Countryman has argued that Paul is worried about "purity" issues in Romans 1, and that we ourselves do not and should not share those purity concerns; indeed, Paul himself, in his better moments, transcended the structures of purity and honor-shame that his language in Romans 1 invokes.[4] Ancient purity notions were understandable in the ancient Near East, and even in Paul's time, but they must be seen today as oppressive and foreign to most current notions of Christian ethics.

Still others have argued that the only homosexual relationships that could have been imagined by Paul would have been pederastic, or between a slave and the slave owner. Paul could not imagine, because it was not a part of his culture, the kinds of mutual, loving, egalitarian homosexual relations we see all the time.[5] In addition, many people have argued that there was no ancient knowledge of "homosexual orientation," which we in the modern world take for granted; had Paul had access to our knowledge, he may not have condemned homosexuality as he did.[6]

Such arguments can be turned around to serve the other side of the debate as well. More conservative scholars simply play the "culture" card differently.[7] They argue that the category of "sexual orientation" is a modern construction that may or may not truly reflect reality. Had Paul known about sexual orientation, he would simply have ascribed it to the fall, and it would have made no difference to his ethics.[8] This does in some ways miss the point attempted by the more liberal interpreters: they needn't have meant that Paul would approve of homosexuality if we could just resurrect him and give him information about orientation; they just mean that since he did not share our views of the psychology of sexuality, his condemnations should not simply be taken over by us for a very different cultural environment. But this shows how the cultural argument (that "times were different then," that Paul's ideas were implicated in his culture) can be turned either way.[9]

A related argument says that Paul's prejudices against homosexuality reflect the "Jewish" views of his time and that Jews regularly took homosexuality to be an especially heinous example of Gentile sin and godlessness. But again, this kind of appeal to a specific culture and a different time has been used on both sides of the debate, with some scholars using that connection to argue against Christian acceptance of homosexuality.[10] Some scholars tend to identify "Judaism" with "truth" or "revelation" as opposed to "the world" or "paganism," and since we as Christians must fall on "the Jewish" side of that equation, the fact that the Jews were against the pagans by opposing homosexuality means that we Christians must also oppose homosexuality. On the other side, David Bartlett used this identification to argue that Paul's condemnation of homosexuality, being part of his Jewishness, is as dispensable for us Christians as has been circumcision, or concerns about idol meat, or kosher, or keeping the Sabbath.[11] The Jewishness of Paul's condemnations can be used either way.

All of the arguments that I've discussed up to this point under the category of "a difference in times" tend to make problematic assumptions about "culture" and "Christianity." Embedded in them is the idea, usually implied but not explicit, that things that are "just culture" can be dispensed with, that the "husk" of culture can be thrown out in order to retain the "kernel" of whatever ethical truth may lie within.

Other arguments turn this into a "Christ against culture" kind of rhetoric: those advocating a change in ethics for sexuality are abandoning Christian values and giving in to dominant secular forces, or Enlightenment prejudices, or just "popular" ideas. Culture is set up as something negative or dispensable, and opposed to "nature" or to "Christ" or to "Christian values." This is completely misleading, obfuscating, even hypocritical rhetoric. Everything we human beings think or say is "cultural."[12]

"Culture" nowadays refers to the entire complex of symbol systems, language, behaviors, beliefs, artifacts, and actions that distinguish one "people" from another. All human communities, in this reckoning, have culture. Culture is the very way human beings make meaning of our existence. It is only through the complex symbolic systems of culture that the human beings of a community can make any "meaning" at all.[13] Thus there is no human observation of "nature" that is not already absolutely implicated in culture. "Nature" is mediated to us humans *only* through culture of some sort. Furthermore, every expression of Christianity we can say anything about is completely implicated in culture. Christians do believe that there is "Christ" that transcends every particular human culture, but for any of us to imply that *we limited human beings* have unmediated access to that Christ is false and arrogant—even idolatrous. As human beings, we are all cultural in our language and thoughts. It can be no other way. So since neither nature nor Christ is immediate to us apart from the mediation of language, *all* our notions of nature and Christ are cultural. There is nothing more "natural" than culture (it exists everywhere there are human beings), and there is nothing more "cultural" than nature (the precise human understandings of "nature" are everywhere and always cultural). Furthermore, as the incarnation should have taught us long ago, Christ is never present to us *except* by mediation, and that mediation, at least as soon as it is *talked* about, as soon as it is *debated*, is cultural. The "Christ against Culture" and "Culture versus Nature" rhetorics are misleading and should be recognized and unmasked whenever they make an appearance in an argument over ethics.

"Scripture against Scripture"

Throughout history Christians have often quoted one passage of Scripture as a counterpoint to another passage. Some scholars, following suit, argue that Paul may have been condemning homosexual acts, but his condemnation should be set aside in deference to other scriptural texts that offer a more ethical notion of love and sexuality, such as the Song of Songs, or the "high" commandment to love one another.[14] Or the offensive aspects of ancient anxieties about impurity or the honor-shame culture are rejected in light of prophetic calls for justice.[15] This is an ancient practice with a respectable pedigree. As Elizabeth Clark has shown, the church fathers repeatedly set one biblical text against another in their case to make Scripture speak more ascetically—that is, to make Scripture teach the avoidance of sex or its severe control.[16] Jesus himself quoted Genesis 1 and 2 to forbid divorce, even though his opponents had already demonstrated that there existed a much clearer Scripture that explicitly permitted divorce.[17] So it is not at all surprising that in our age Christians would find some Scripture passages more relevant for speaking about sexuality than others. This too is a rhetorical strategy.

"The passage is about something else"

A common way of arguing over interpretation of texts is to dispute the very assumption that the text is "about" the issue under debate. In relation to Romans 1, a popular interpretive move, made usually by those who take a more liberal stance on the issue, is to insist that though the passage may *seem* to condemn homosexuality, it is a mistake to interpret it that way since the passage is actually about something else. Paul clearly links the sexual activity to idolatry, so what Paul is really talking about here is idolatry, which should make the passage less relevant for Christians today.[18] Or the passage is about "lust" but not "love."[19] Or the passage is really presenting *theological* reflections by Paul, and to take those as offering fundamental ethical *rules* actually changes the subject.[20] Other scholars argue that Paul's phrase *para physin*, though regularly meaning "contrary to nature," should here be interpreted "contrary to convention" as it seems to mean in other contexts, Pauline and otherwise. So the passage is actually not about "natural sex" but social conventions.[21]

John Boswell offered one of the most interesting, and to many people least convincing, arguments along this line. He argued that Paul was condemning those who had sex contrary to *their* natures, but since homosexual sex is *not* contrary to the natures of homosexual persons, Paul was condemning only heterosexual people who were "exchanging" their "natural" sex for same-sex intercourse, which would admittedly be "unnatural" for them. Thus, the passage is not about homosexuals at all, but about adventurous heterosexuals.[22]

More conservative scholars may not use this kind of argument when discussing Romans 1 because they usually *want* to see the text as condemning homosexuality in general and completely. But they do use the same strategy when discussing other issues and texts. They may interpret 1 Corinthians 11:14–15, where Paul insists that "nature" teaches that men must have short hair and women long hair, by insisting that Paul is not after all referring to "nature" but actually to "cultural convention."[23] Again, the rhetorical strategy may be used to different ends—even opposite ends.

"Not the text, but the author's intention"

In this kind of argument, an interpreter changes the focus of attention away from "what the text says" and focuses instead on "the author's intention." This is a rather tricky rhetorical move because those who use it seldom draw attention to the fact that they are using it, and therefore diverting attention from "what the text says" to "what the author may have intended." For example, the conservative Robert Gagnon and the liberal Bernadette Brooten both use this strategy. They both believe that Paul is condemning female-female sexual intercourse in

Romans 1, though they both admit that the passage itself does not *explicitly* condemn female same-sex activity.[24] They then move the attention from what the text *says* to what Paul *must have* meant. Since Paul was a Jew and an ancient man, and since just about every ancient Jewish male we know about, and ancient *men* for that matter, disapproved of female homoeroticism, that must be the meaning of the text here. In my view, this is highly misleading rhetoric, shifting the "location" of the meaning of the text away from an interpretation of the words of the text and onto an imagined intention of the author, or even of some abstract construction of an author we may imagine on the basis of general ancient ideas ("the ancient Jewish man," for instance).[25] This rhetorical technique is nonetheless quite common in New Testament scholarship.

"Rules from narratives"

Scripture contains much more than doctrinal statements or ethical rules. Much of it is narrative. One interpretive device that needs more critical examination, because it is usually done in an unreflective manner, is the derivation of rules or abstract principles from narratives. On the conservative side, this rhetorical move is most often expressed by claiming that in Romans 1 Paul is assuming or invoking the Genesis account of creation. The scholars then read the creation stories of Genesis and insist that those narratives somehow clearly and obviously teach not only the "complementariness" of male and female, but that this principle of gender complementariness must be both exclusive and reflected in the individual sexual lives of all people who have sex. In other words, the narrative of Genesis does not *merely* teach the complementariness of male and female—so that we could imagine masculinity and femininity existing in all of us, even as individuals (as the ancients so thought).[26] It must rather express itself sexually in the joining of particular men and women—and any other joining is forbidden by that principle.[27] What is remarkable is that conservative interpreters can get such specific sexual rules from a narrative.

It is even more surprising that they can get one from a narrative that could just as easily be read to emphasize sameness rather than difference. After all, when Adam sees Eve he doesn't say, "Look what I've got that she needs!" He rather says, "Bone of my bone, and flesh of my flesh" (Gen. 2:23). The main point, I would think, would be the sameness of the two halves of the human couple, not the difference. This demonstrates that when people derive rules or principles from a narrative, the text itself has no ability to control *what* rules or principles they derive from it.

Some scholars advocating the inclusion of gay men and lesbians in Christian churches have turned attention to a different narrative for guidance. They point to the narrative about the radical change in what was taken to be God's will depicted in Acts 15, when the Gentiles are suddenly included in "Israel" against all tradition and against the ways Jewish Scripture had theretofore been read. Jeffrey Siker, for instance, points to the narrative from Acts as a model for how the church may and should radically rethink its traditional exclusion of gay and lesbian people. Homosexuals are the "Gentiles" of the twenty-first-century church.[28] Again, deriving principles from narratives is a long and respected practice in Christian interpretation, but we should recognize when we or others are doing it.

"Texts as quotations"

I could go on and on, but I will close this survey by noting just one more common rhetorical move in historical-critical debates about sexuality and gender: the rhetorical argument that a statement in the text does not represent the "true view" of the text or the author but is being quoted as the view of someone else. Some scholars, for instance, have argued that Paul's condemnations about homosexuality represent views, perhaps typical "Jewish" views about Gentiles, that Paul here is merely quoting. Perhaps Paul quotes someone else's position, so the argument goes, only to supply an example that he doesn't necessarily buy into himself, or perhaps so that he may refute the view in what follows.[29] "Conservative" or "evangelical" interpreters use this technique when they claim that Paul's statement in 1 Corinthians 7:1 ("It is better not to touch a woman") is a more radically ascetic position held by other members of the church at Corinth with whom Paul is disagreeing. Paul is merely quoting the slogan in order to refute it. This interpretation of the situation helps modern conservative Christians, for they want to base their condemnations of gays and lesbians on "Paul's view" but don't want their own heterosexual relations and ideologies to be challenged by any possible Pauline asceticism. More moderate conservatives follow this tactic when they argue that 1 Corinthians 14:34–35, which seems to present Paul as forbidding any speech by women in church, is actually a scribal statement later interpolated into Paul's text. They ascribe a condemnation of homosexuality to Paul's "true view," but still find some Pauline foundation for the gender egalitarianism of their own churches.

This survey could go further, both more broadly and more deeply. For example, I could discuss the common use of "shaming" rhetoric by which some scholars simply imply that if others don't "see" in the text what they themselves "see" it is because their opponents are somehow blind, deaf, insensitive, or even perverted.[30] (I do provide some examples of this kind of rhetoric in my analysis of the individual scholars below.) But I believe the categories of rhetoric I have provided are enough to illustrate my main points. First, scholars must give up on the fiction that historical criticism can create consensus on meaning, especially on the ethical use of Scripture. The scholars I have cited are not marginal. They are good, usually well-trained historical critics. And I have pointed out these rhetorical commonplaces not in order to suggest that we should get rid of rhetoric and just get to "the real thing." We *have* to use rhetoric, and there is nothing wrong with most of these rhetorical practices. But once we are cognizant of them, that in itself should convince us that the methods of historical criticism *cannot* deliver dependably objective or final or "true" interpretations, either "true" historically or "good" ethically. Historical criticism may legitimately be used (when judged by the criteria of history itself) and yet still arrive at diametrically opposed interpretations of texts.[31]

We ought to be aware of rhetoric and the categories people employ. One of the reasons for my rhetorical survey is to draw attention to *agency* and *power* in rhetoric and interpretation. This is not to say that I am arguing that Scripture is irrelevant for ethical reflection. It simply cannot be used in the modern foundationalist way with the expectation that reliable, secure ethical guidance will result. This exercise has also demonstrated that *how we read* is what produces "meaning," not the text itself—nor even particularly the historical-critical method of reading.

With this sort of rhetorical analysis in mind, let us spend more time looking at some individual scholars who have recently published on sexuality and biblical interpretation.

ROBERT A. J. GAGNON

Robert Gagnon's book *The Bible and Homosexual Practice*, already cited, has generated much discussion since it appeared in 2001. It is a long and involved study that comes down firmly on the conservative side of the debate, and it provides an excellent opportunity for rhetorical analysis of modern scholarship on the question. I draw attention to it first because it presents a position that is theoretically the most traditional—that is, it is firmly committed to the necessity of historical criticism. There is no influence here of contemporary literary or hermeneutical theories, and Gagnon flatly rejects any notion that textual interpretation is an uncertain endeavor.

Gagnon constantly, and with no hint that he is using a metaphor, portrays the Bible as "speaking," or "condemning," or performing some kind of action. In fact, the texts speak "clearly" and "obviously." But Gagnon's own rhetoric undermines such claims. For one thing, if these texts really did speak so clearly and obviously, Gagnon wouldn't need to insist so often and vociferously that they do. But even beyond that fact, Gagnon repeatedly slips up and reveals by his very wording and interpretations that the texts do not speak. At one point, Gagnon says that Romans 1 "makes an explicit statement not only about same-sex intercourse among men but also about lesbianism" (229). But later he admits that there is no such "explicit statement" (298), although he believes that the passage does clearly and obviously condemn female same-sex intercourse anyway. In the second passage, though, he ends up using words such as "infer" and "imply." He doesn't seem to realize that he has contradicted himself, but that regularly happens when people believe so firmly that what *they* see in the text is *really there* objectively.

In another context, Gagnon admits that Jesus seems never to have addressed the issue of homosexuality, but that does not keep Gagnon from enlisting the historical Jesus as an opponent of homosexuality. He says that "the inferential data speaks loud and clear about Jesus' perspective" (187). Note the oxymoronic language: "data" is a "scientific" sounding word; it is supposed to conjure up ideas of hard, concrete evidence. One would think, therefore, that the adjective "inferential" wouldn't work well with the noun "data." For Gagnon, though, the "data" not only "speak" but speak "loud and clear," even though the message of the "data" is only "inferred" by Gagnon from guesses about what Jesus *would have* thought.

Gagnon's own exegetical practices belie the simplicity of listening to the text that his rhetoric invokes. He does not seem to recognize how many gaps in the text he must regularly fill to get to his preferred meaning. Let us walk though just one example. Gagnon takes the story about the cursing of Ham, Noah's son, as being really about homosexuality (Gen. 9:20–27; Gagnon, 63–71). First, Gagnon supplies a translation, which as anyone who translates knows, requires countless decisions, not always conscious, about interpretation among different possibilities. Next, he argues that the "outercoat" used to cover the naked Noah should be taken to be Noah's own coat—something not specified in the text. Next, Gagnon argues that since we know of no other ancient restrictions against simply seeing one's father naked, something more must be involved here, and that must be "incestuous, homosexual rape" of Noah by Ham (64). Although the story does not tell us that Ham went into the tent, he must have, because he is said to have "told it to his brothers outside" (65). Since Gagnon has assumed that the outercoat was Noah's, and that Shem and Japheth take it from outside the tent inside in order to cover Noah up, this must mean that Ham had taken the garment outside the tent after raping Noah. Why would Ham have taken the garment outside? Gagnon suggests that Ham uses it as proof of what he had done and "to establish his bragging rights" (66). The passive statement that noted that Noah "was uncovered" suggests that someone else had "uncovered" him, and that must have been Ham (66–67). Gagnon then argues that since men in other ancient Near Eastern texts are depicted as raping other men to establish social superiority, that must be what is going on here (68). The special care on the part of the other brothers *not* to "see their father's nakedness" demonstrates that Ham's action was rape and not something else (69). Why the severity of the "curse" on Ham? It must be due to the fact that the action was incestuous rape (70).

I emphasize that I have highlighted only some of the textual gaps filled by Gagnon's reading. And I point out that I don't fault him for filling in gaps; I believe that is the only way we can and do read texts.[32] But it is amazing to me that Gagnon can conduct himself through all this elaborate interpretation, with all the decisions and speculations it necessitates, and then convince himself that any reasonable, responsible, unbiased reader would see in the text precisely what he sees. After such a parade of assumptions, to believe that the text itself is dispensing its meaning is astounding.

What is also surprising for me is that Gagnon uses the modern, historical-critical method without ever realizing that he should supply some kind of theoretical or theological defense of that practice. Furthermore, he does not use the modern method as one among others. He insists that the *only* possible way to read Scripture is by ascertaining the original author's intention, which he also insists is "recoverable" (439–40), though he never actually demonstrates that it is.

Gagnon's uncritical acceptance of such assumptions, though, does get him into trouble. One of Gagnon's favorite and most curious interpretive devices is to move from considering what the text says, and even what the intentions of the author were, to imagining what a presumed author *would have* thought about a hypothetical question, a strategy I mentioned in the first part of this essay. For example, even if other biblical texts that mention Sodom do not condemn homosexuality, surely their authors would not have accepted homosexuality, which is then taken by Gagnon as evidence that the Sodom story in Genesis *does* condemn homosexuality (90). Despite the fact that there is very little (if anything) in the New Testament about consensual, loving homosexual relationships, as Gagnon admits, he still insists that "there is very little likelihood that any writer of Scripture, or Jesus, would have supported homosexual behavior of any sort" (485). Note the slippage in the location of scriptural authority: it is now not the text, nor even the actual authorial intentions of the historical writer, but what Gagnon imagines Jesus or Paul would say if they could be transported to the twenty-first century and asked a question.

Gagnon misses the point of why scholars sometimes insist on placing ancient texts in ancient contexts (see, e.g., 182). It is not to claim that Jesus or Paul "would have" had different views if they could be transported into our world (it should not need pointing out, although I'm afraid it does, that if they could be so transported, they would not be the same people they were). The point is rather that their reconstructed views should not be simply taken *apart from* the worldview and assumptions that provided meaningfulness to what they may have believed. The problem is in Gagnon's assumption that we can "distill" principles and rules from the complex ancient contexts without substantially changing the *meaning* of those rules. Thus Gagnon is confused on two issues here: (1) the nature of contextual historiography along with the complexity of meaning, and (2) what actually counts as "Scripture" in Christianity: Scripture is the text as read in faith and led by the Spirit, not the imagined psyches or views of an imaginatively fabricated ancient author.[33]

Gagnon is also a modern foundationalist when it comes to other sources for knowledge, especially "nature." According to Gagnon, the Bible, by "clearly" teaching the "complementariness" of male and female, "unequivocally defines same-sex intercourse as sin" and "presents the anatomical, sexual, and procreative complementarity of male and female as clear and convincing proof of God's will for sexual unions" (37; again, note the rhetoric of agency: the *Bible* is teaching and presenting, not Gagnon the interpreter). But this knowledge is just as clearly presented, according to Gagnon, in "nature" itself. "Procreation is God's clue," he writes, "given in nature, that the male penis and the female vagina/womb are complementary organs. No other sexual activity results in new life. Therefore the only acceptable form of sexual intercourse is between a man and a woman" (164).[34]

Besides the obvious problems with this way of reasoning (if these indications of God's will in nature are so obvious and clear, such "convincing proof," why is it that so many other people can't see it? Can't "nature" be taken to "mean" just about anything?), Gagnon's own arguments use faulty syllogisms. Gagnon's stated syllogism is as follows:

> (A) Procreation provides the meaning of sex in God's will;
> (B) only penis-vaginal penetration can result in procreation;
> (C) *therefore* only heterosexual sex accords with God's will.
> (see 164, 168–69)

But logically, "C" should read, "therefore only penis-vaginal penetration accords with God's will and God disapproves of *all* sexual contact other than such penetration that may result in conception." Gagnon, however, believes that other forms of *heterosexual* behavior are permissible. The syllogism is taken to mean only that all forms of *homosexual* eroticism are forbidden by God.[35] Gagnon is so enamored of what he thinks he sees "in nature" that he cannot see the logical flaws in his syllogism. Nature, like the text, does not interpret itself and is not "clear and convincing" in what it "says"; otherwise we wouldn't have so many disagreements about "the meaning" of nature or what is "natural."

Gagnon's foundationalism extends also to modern science and human experience. He appeals to scientific studies of homosexuality, though selectively and tendentiously. And he appeals to the experiences of human beings, but only to those who have found their homosexuality oppressive and have experienced heterosexual "conversion," ignoring the vast majority of gay and lesbian Christians who testify to the goodness of their sexual experiences and identities. One of the problems with foundationalism, besides the fact that those foundations tend to crumble on critical inspection, is that the *choice* of foundational data is up to the interpreter and therefore provides no *external* control on the interpretation itself.

In the end, Gagnon seems to sense that all his intricate, complex biblical interpretations—his appeals to nature, science, or experience—may not be as "convincing" as he says they are. Thus he often resorts finally to shaming rhetoric. He repeatedly insults gay men (though much less lesbians): "The willingly penetrated male takes up a complaint with nature for failing to supply him with a vagina" (169). He depicts all of gay subculture with the most negative stereotypes (see, e.g., 178). He questions the motives and rationality of other interpreters. Those who read Paul differently than does Gagnon are offering "clever and self-serving sophistry," mostly as an excuse to satisfy their lust (296). They are "desperate" (154). Their interpretations are "sophistic folly" in contrast to Gagnon's own "mature socio-scientific wisdom" (182). Recourse to shaming rhetoric is often the final recourse of one who truly believes that "nature" or "the text itself" provides a clear, self-interpreting foundation for ethics. If other people cannot see it, there must be something wrong with *them*.[36]

RICHARD B. HAYS

A bit more sophisticated theoretically, though in the end just as foundationalist, is Richard Hays's *Moral Vision of the New Testament.* Hays does offer a few comments that admit that others may read the texts differently and that all readings are interpretations. His own proposal, he says, "is not an exact method that can yield foolproof scientific results . . . the conclusions reached here are offered as one *performance* of the imaginative task of New Testament ethics" (462, his emphasis). Yet Hays repeatedly slips back into foundationalist rhetoric when speaking of the New Testament itself: he calls the church to a "renewed encounter with the witness of the New Testament itself," to "a disciplined reading of the New Testament witness" (463). Indeed, Hays repeatedly speaks of his approach in at least two stages (sometimes broken down into more than two, but still containing these two): the first is "hearing" the witness of the New Testament; the second is "appropriating" that "witness" in the life of the church (462). We may have to use our "imagination" to figure out how to "use" the New Testament to arrive at ethical norms, but that is secondary to accepting "the world articulated by the texts," to "listen[ing] patiently to the Word of God in Scripture" (298–99). The first task is regularly presented as a passive one in which the real action is done by the New Testament itself: it "speaks"; we "listen."[37]

Throughout, Hays is worried about the possible lack of security in ethical use of the New Testament. Some methods of interpretation "leave the door open for selfish and sinful human beings to justify their own wills while cloaking their action in religious language" (237). Theologians who attempt to derive basic "principles" from the text of Scripture can hardly thus avoid "unfaithful capriciousness" (249). For example, because Stanley Hauerwas believes that the meaning of Scripture must always be mediated through the community of the church, Hauerwas, according to Hays, "finds himself with no theoretical grounds for an appeal to Scripture against the church's practices" (266).[38]

Unlike Gagnon, Hays strongly senses the *lack* of "obvious" meanings of the text. He is therefore in search of a method and guidelines that will constrain our readings in some way: "The goal of the inquiry will be to clarify how the church can read Scripture in a faithful and disciplined manner so that Scripture might come to shape the life of the church" (3); "we need a cluster of focal images to govern our construal of New Testament ethics" (5). Hays attempts to offer "practicable guidelines for New Testament ethics as a normative theological discipline," and to those who object to his own method, he challenges them "to articulate alternative guidelines that will promote equal methodological clarity" (310). As we have seen, though, what Hays is really after is not simply "methodological clarity" but some assurance that the method is "true" to the "witness" or "vision" or "speech" of the New Testament itself. But if the meaning of the text is not already simply "there" in the text waiting to be "seen" or "heard," *no method of reading* will insure that readers "really see" what is "really there."

No method of reading, no matter how "clear" or well thought-out, will deliver predictably ethical interpretations of Scripture.[39] Thus, Hays's account should be critiqued partly because of his repeated rhetoric that makes the text itself into an agent (it "speaks," it "witnesses," it "shapes the church"), but also because it gives false hope that a method of reading will render innocuous our own interpretive agencies. Neither the text itself nor any method will provide the firm foundation for good interpretations or the bulwark against false readings that Hays desires.

Thus, like Gagnon, Hays is in the end very much a modernist, though he seeks his foundations in a method as well as a text. Hays's modernism is revealed also in the centrality he ascribes to historical criticism in his method. He appeals to original authorial intention (found via historical criticism) as containing and constraining meaning.[40] Hays criticizes Stanley Hauerwas because Hauerwas does not use historical criticism, and Hays praises John Howard Yoder because he does (259–60). Karl Barth's readings are faulted on historical-critical grounds.[41] Indeed, *all* of Hays's approach fully assumes not only the validity but even the necessity of historical-critical methods. For example, the meaning of the text is dependent on ancient authorial intention; allegory is not permitted; anachronism is to be avoided; different New Testament authors must be treated as independent "witnesses"; ancient context governs meaning (see esp. 3–4, 14–15). The tropes are everywhere, and these are all common interpretive principles of modern historical criticism.[42]

What is remarkable is that this reliance on the historical-critical method is completely at odds with another aspect of method on which Hays also insists: Hays repeatedly says that *the way* we interpret the text must proceed from the texts themselves (see 294–95). The "unifying images" we use to read Scripture "must be derived from the texts themselves rather than superimposed artificially" (5, 194). "New Testament texts must be granted authority (or not) in the mode in which they speak (i.e., rule, principle, paradigm, symbolic world)" (310). But if that is true, by what rights does Hays not only use but insist on historical criticism, a method foreign to the New Testament's own "methods" of interpretation and its "modes of speaking"? Hays wants to derive our ethics from a rather passive "listening" to the text, and he wants even the method itself to be derived in some way from the text itself. But this runs counter to his demand for historical criticism, a totally modern invention.

Interestingly, it also contradicts Hays's earlier writings on biblical hermeneutics. At the end of his 1989 book *Echoes of Scripture in the Letters of Paul,* Hays admitted that Paul's interpretive methods often seem far-fetched to us. They are not at all constrained, or even informed, by the sort of historical sensitivity modernist interpretation demands, nor are they focused on "the original meaning of the text."[43] Yet there Hays argues not only that Paul's interpretations are valid, but that even we modern Christians should feel free to imitate Paul's freedoms of interpretation. Hays ends up with a remarkably postmodern, nonfoundationalist statement: "No longer can we think of meaning as something contained by a text; texts have meaning only as they are read and used by communities of readers . . . [T]he attempt to separate Paul's hermeneutical freedom from ours cuts off the word at its roots" (189).[44] This is an astounding statement given the severe restrictions Hays attempts to place on interpretation in *The Moral Vision*, in which he regularly refutes *other people's* readings precisely on historical-critical grounds. I know of no place where Hays admits that he changed his mind between the publications of these two books. In any case, *Moral Vision* is suffused by anxieties about interpretive freedom and textual indeterminacy, and it tries again and again to restrain the kind of interpretive freedom raised as a model in *Echoes*. Perhaps the terror of issues such as divorce, abortion, and homosexuality finally drove Hays away from the insecurity of reader response realizations and into the more "secure" arms of textual and methodological foundationalism.

FRANCIS WATSON

Another scholar whose rhetoric about interpretation has changed significantly is Francis Watson. Watson began his career as a New Testament scholar with a well-respected book on Paul, the Jews, and Gentiles that used mainly social-scientific or social-historical methods in a historical-critical project.[45] He later, though, moved away from a strictly historical-critical approach and began urging the discipline to take theological hermeneutics more seriously. He edited a book of essays, published in 1993, called *The Open Text: New Directions for Biblical Studies?*[46] In the introduction, Watson questioned the role of historical criticism, not to throw it out, but to place it in a more "pluralistic" context of different approaches, including but not limited to theological.[47] In the exegetical essay he contributed to the volume, significantly titled "Liberating the Reader," Watson went so far as to argue, "The hermeneutical principle of the absence of the author from the text is a useful way of countering the reductionist tendency to confine textual meaning to the reconstructed circumstances of origin."[48] He urged readers to establish their independence from the text in order to avoid succumbing to its own possibly unethical ideological tendencies. Speaking of androcentrism, for instance, he writes, "Awareness of such limitations will exclude all idealizing of the biblical text, all claims that one must submit one's critical faculties beneath the imperious demands of a semi-divinized book" (68).

Watson made similar comments in his 1994 book *Text, Church and World*.[49] There Watson practically mocks the sense of "progress" in interpretation one regularly discerns in modernist historical-critical writing on the Bible. The multiplicity of different, even contradictory, "meanings" of the text advanced, even by purely historical-critical readings, *should* shake modernist confidence in the "progress" of the discipline. Thus far, one gets the sense that Watson has little faith in either the necessity of historical criticism or in its promises to supply even consensus about meaning, much less "the" meaning.

The tone in Watson's more recent work, however, is crucially different. Increasingly, Watson seems to fear textual indeterminacy and even to fall back on historical criticism to stave off readings of Scripture he finds offensive or dangerous—especially *sexually*. Whereas multiplicity of different interpretations served in the 1994 book as an argument *against* the reliability of historical criticism, in a 1997 book, now titled, I think tellingly, *Text and Truth*, the very same multiplicity is invoked, but this time as evidence that there is some kind of "stable meaning" over which scholars can disagree but which can be "approximated" by the "progress" of interpretation![50] Though Watson continues to admit that "truth is textually mediated" (which one would think means that we have no access to "reality" apart from textuality, and that there is no access to "the real" that is not part of the process of interpretation), by 1997 he seems concerned more about textual indeterminacy and variable interpretation than broadening the discipline methodologically and theoretically.[51] In the 1997 book, he seems to have become much more conservative, insisting now on "literal sense," "authorial intention," and "a set of 'objective,' non-context-dependent interpretative procedures" (11).[52] Texts "say" what they want to say, and we are supposed to listen.[53] What happened to "liberating the reader"?

It is therefore perhaps not surprising that Watson sounds almost hysterical in a review of Stephen Moore's book *God's Beauty Parlor*, a sequel to his brilliant *God's Gym*.[54] Moore used queer theory and other poststructuralist approaches to analyze "heteronormativity" of biblical texts and their traditional interpreters. What is surprising about Watson's reaction is not that he doesn't like Moore's project (he doesn't, but that is hardly surprising given his own more conservative views of sexuality), but that he seems to think it is enough just to insist that "the text" does not "say" what Moore takes it to mean. Watson just points to the text and proclaims that the text "says" something else. According to Watson, the role of the interpreter is completely passive: "The interpreter's role is to *help* the text to say what it has to say—playing the part of the Socratic midwife" (110; emphasis in original). Contrary to the interpretations of many scholars, myself included, Watson insists that gender hierarchy is simply not an issue in Romans 1, and Moore is rather perverted for reading it into the text (116). Indeed, Watson seems to believe that the text has such strong agency that it can *reject* readings of itself it doesn't like: "Paul's texts steadfastly refuse to co-operate in this projected rewriting of Pauline theology" (116–117).[55] Of course, "Paul's texts" do not "refuse" to do *anything* (a fact that is empirically verifiable if any is), which is precisely why Moore and others *can* and *do* read them differently than Watson would like. What is most interesting to me, though, is again the curious shift in Watson's own position over the years. He is no longer concerned with advocating new interpretive options and freedom. Perhaps again anxiety about sex is coupled with anxiety about texts.

L. WILLIAM COUNTRYMAN

Contrary to what we might suppose, foundationalism is not a mistake made only by conservatives. Scholars arguing on the liberal side of the homosexuality debate often also fall into problems with foundationalism. William Countryman provides a good example for me because his work is recent and progressive, and because I actually agree with him on issues of ethics, gender, and sexuality. Yet I believe his ideas of texts and interpretation are fundamentally flawed.

In his 2003 book *Interpreting the Truth*, Countryman initially seems to realize that interpretation is a very creative act.[56] He notes that even translation is interpretation, and *creative* interpretation at that (11). Yet he quickly makes many unsupported, and unsupportable, claims about meaning and the text. He dismisses reader-response theory and insists that the text "has a voice and is *capable* of entering into the broad human conversation" (28, his emphasis), yet he never *shows* "the voice" of a text actually speaking (playing a recording would convince me, as long as there wasn't a human being or something else between us and "the text" doing the actual speaking). He insists that "constructionism" is false and disproved by the "fact" that "the reality behind and beyond social construction keeps intruding on reality as socially constructed and disrupting it" (31), yet he cannot demonstrate this happening without reintroducing *some* kind of "social construction" (language, symbol systems) that will "represent" that "reality" to and for us.[57] In other words, "reality" itself never does actually *by itself* alter our perception of "reality." It is always mediated through some interpretation, or else it can have no meaning for us at all in any discursive sense (that is, in a sense in which we could *say* anything about it at all).

Countryman becomes entrapped in self-contradiction. On the one hand, arguing against poststructuralist notions of the variability of textual meaning, Countryman insists that "whether we recognize this in theory or only in practice," a text "raises questions" and "offers us perspectives that are scarcely available" to us otherwise.[58] But Countryman does this immediately after criticizing another interpretation for *not* reading the text correctly. In other words, with one hand he says that texts *themselves* provide their meaning—they "speak" to us—and with the other hand he faults another scholar's understanding of "what the text says." One would think that the very existence of another sincere and scholarly interpretation would count as empirical proof that "the text" actually *does not* do what Countryman claims it does.[59] Elsewhere, after insisting that texts possess their own meaning and are themselves partners in "human conversation," Countryman slips up and says, "Whether it [i.e., the text] succeeds in doing so is largely a result of how interpreters and readers engage with it" (28). But if this interpretation is necessary before the text can "speak," and if even the *method* of interpretation has to be specified (modern historical criticism), doesn't that demonstrate that meaning is *not* in the text itself but rather the interpretation of the text?[60]

Countryman's only "evidence" brought forward to convince us that texts "speak" and have their own meanings in themselves are appeals to commonsensical *feelings* we often experience that reality really does communicate with us and the common experience that consensus on the meaning of texts is often possible. "Without acknowledging that some readings are better than others, there is no way to explain the common experience of 'coming to understand' a text, especially insofar as it includes the recognition that one had previously understood it only in part or even out-and-out misunderstood it" (57). The fallacies of this way of thinking have been repeatedly pointed out. The first fallacy is the assumption that since many people read a text the same way, therefore the text itself is somehow dispensing its meaning. But readers read the same way insofar, and only insofar, as they have been socialized to read the same way or similarly. The people in a "reading community" (to use Stanley Fish's terminology) *learn* to read in certain ways, so it is not at all a mystery that they often "see" the same meaning in a text.[61] The second fallacy is assuming that since we change our minds about the meanings of texts, it must be the texts themselves that are stable, and only that *our minds are changed by the texts*. But this presupposes that human selves are completely stable and do not themselves change. On the contrary, the reason we repeatedly read a text in different ways is because *we* change constantly. I see the text differently at different readings because it is literally not the same "I" doing the reading. As I change, so my readings change. None of these rather commonsensical objections to reader-response theories overturns the theories. On the contrary, the best evidence that texts *do not* contain or control their own meanings is that no one can ever *show* a text doing so. Simple empirical evidence (just looking at how people get meaning from texts) demonstrates that "texts don't mean; people mean with texts."

In spite of the fact that I very much agree with Countryman's goals and much of his ethics, and I often find his interpretations of Scripture compelling, I believe his textual foundationalism is theoretically and theologically problematic.[62] Even with the best methods in place, simply paying more attention to "what the text says" will never in itself protect us from the capricious or self-serving "impositions" onto the text Countryman fears. The textual and methodological foundationalism of Countryman cannot provide the protection against the vagaries of interpretation Countryman desires.

CONCLUSIONS

I do not offer this rhetorical survey and critique of modernist, foundationalist interpretation of Scripture in order to convince readers that the Bible is irrelevant for contemporary Christian understandings of sexuality and ethics. I believe Christians *must* read Scripture when dealing with the difficult issues confronted in our lives. My goal has been, rather, to demonstrate that appeals to the agency of "the text itself" or to "authorial intention" or to any other entity taken to be stable and able to constrain and control interpretation are theoretically and theologically indefensible. Appeals to "what the text says" actually serve to mask the very real interpretive agency of the human interpreter. Texts mean nothing until human beings interpret them. Therefore the true focus of ethical debate must be not on some mythical meaning of "the text itself," but on the very real activities of the interpreter. Interpretation is never a passive event. It is the exercise of power and is always implicated in rhetoric and ideology. In order to teach Christians and theological students how to read the Bible and biblical scholarship, we should begin with teaching them to recognize rhetoric for what it is: the powerful attempt to persuade.

Chapter 3

Arsenokoitês and *Malakos*

Meanings and Consequences

The New Testament provides little ammunition to those wishing to condemn modern homosexuality. Compared to the much more certain condemnations of anger, wealth (sometimes anything but poverty), adultery, or disobedience of wives and children, the few passages that might be taken as condemning homosexuality are meager. It is not surprising, therefore, that the interpretation of two mere words has commanded a disproportionate amount of attention. Both words, *arsenokoitês* and *malakos*, occur in a vice list in 1 Corinthians 6:9, and *arsenokoitês* recurs in 1 Timothy 1:10. Although the translation of these two words has varied through the years, in the twentieth century they have often been taken to refer to people who engage in homosexual, or at least male homosexual, sex, and the conclusion sometimes then follows that the New Testament or Paul condemns homosexual "activity."

Usually the statement is accompanied by a shrugged-shoulder expression, as if to say, I'm not condemning homosexuality! I'm just reading the Bible. It's there in the text. Such protestations of objectivity, however, become untenable when examined closely. By analyzing ancient meanings of the terms, on the one hand, and historical changes in the translation of the terms, on the other, we discover that interpretations of *arsenokoitês* and *malakos* as condemning modern homosexuality have been driven more by ideological interests in marginalizing gay and lesbian people than by the general strictures of historical criticism.

In the end, the goal of this chapter is not mere historical or philological accuracy. By emphasizing the ideological contexts in which interpretation has taken place and will always take place, I intend to challenge the objectivist notion that the Bible or historical criticism can provide contemporary Christians with a reliable foundation for ethical reflection. Neither a simple reading of "what the Bible says" nor a professional historical-critical reconstruction of the ancient meaning of the texts will provide a prescription for contemporary Christian ethics. Indeed, the naive attempts by conservative Christians, well-meaning though they may be, to derive their ethics from a "simple" reading of the Bible have meant merely that they impute to the Bible their own destructive ideologies.[1] The destruction is today nowhere more evident than in the church's mistreatment of lesbian and gay Christians.

ARSENOKOITÊS

From the earliest English translations of the Bible, *arsenokoitês* has suffered confusing treatment. Wyclif (in 1380) translated it as "thei that don leccherie with men" and until the twentieth century similar translations prevailed, primarily "abusars of them selves with the mankynde" (Tyndale 1534; see also Coverdale 1535, Cranmer 1539, Geneva Bible 1557, KJV 1611, and ASV 1901; the Douai-Rheims version of 1582 was a bit clearer: "the liers vvith mankinde"). A curious shift in translation occurred in the mid-twentieth century. Suddenly, the language of psychology and "normalcy" creeps into English versions. Although some still use archaic terms, like "sodomite" (OB 1966; NAB 1970; NRSV 1989), several influential versions substitute more modern concepts, such as "sexual perverts" (RSV 1946; REB 1992) or terms that reflect the nineteenth century's invention of the category of the "homosexual," such as the NIV's (1973) "homosexual offenders." Some translations even go so far as to collapse *arsenokoitês* and *malakos* together into one term: "homosexual perverts" or "homosexual perversion" (TEV 1966; NEB 1970). Modern commentators also offer a variety of interpretations. Some explain that *malakos* refers to the "passive" partner in male-male anal intercourse and *arsenokoitês* the "active" partner; thus the two disputable terms are taken care of mutually.[2] Some simply import wholesale the modern category and translate *arsenokoitês* as "male homosexual."[3] Others, in an attempt, I suppose, to separate the "sin" from the "sinner," have suggested "practicing homosexuals."[4]

Between the end of the nineteenth and the middle of the twentieth century, therefore, the translation of *arsenokoitês* shifted from being the reference to an action that any man might well perform, regardless of orientation or disorientation, to refer to a "perversion," either an action or a propensity taken to be self-evidently abnormal and diseased. The shift in translation, that is, reflected the invention of the category of "homosexuality" as an abnormal orientation, an invention that occurred in the nineteenth century but gained popular currency only gradually in the twentieth.[5] Furthermore, whereas earlier translations had all taken the term (correctly) to refer to men, the newer translations broadened the reference to include people of either sex who could be diagnosed as suffering from the new, modern neurosis of homosexuality. Thorough historical or philological evidence was never adduced to support this shift in translation. The interpretations were prompted not by criteria of historical criticism but by shifts in modern sexual ideology.

As the debate over homosexuality and the Bible has become more explicit, various attempts have been made to defend the interpretation of *arsenokoitês* as a reference to male-male or homosexual sex in general. A common error made in such attempts is to point to its two parts, *arsên* and *koitês*, and say that "obviously" the word refers to men who have sex with men.[6] Scholars sometimes support this reading by pointing out that the two words occur together, though not joined, in Greek translations of the Hebrew Bible and in Philo in a context in which he condemns male homosexual sex.[7] Either Paul, it is suggested, or someone before him simply combined the two words together to form a new term for men who have sex with men.

This approach is linguistically invalid. It is highly precarious to try to ascertain the meaning of a word by taking it apart, getting the meanings of its component parts, and then assuming, with no supporting evidence, that the meaning of the longer word is a simple combination of its component parts. To "understand" does not mean to "stand under." In fact, nothing about the basic meanings of either "stand" or "under" has any direct bearing on the meaning of "understand." This phenomenon of language is sometimes even more obvious with terms that designate social roles, since the nature of the roles themselves often changes over time and becomes separated from any original reference. None of us, for example, takes the word "chairman" to have any necessary reference to a chair, even if it originally did. Thus, all definitions of *arsenokoitês* that derive its meaning from its components are naive and indefensible. Furthermore, the claim that *arsenokoitês* came from a combination of these two words and *therefore* means "men who have sex with men" makes the additional error of defining a word by its (assumed) etymology. The etymology of a word is its history, not its meaning.[8]

The only reliable way to define a word is to analyze its use in as many different contexts as possible. The word "means" according to its function, according to how particular people use the word in different situations. Unfortunately, we have very few uses of *arsenokoitês*, and most of those occur in simple lists of sins, mostly in quotations of the biblical lists, thus providing no explanation of the term, no independent usage, and few clues from the context about the term's meaning. But having analyzed these different occurrences of *arsenokoitês*, especially cases where it occurs in vice lists that do not merely quote 1 Corinthians 6:9 or 1 Timothy 1:10, I am convinced that we can make some guarded statements.

As others have noted, vice lists are sometimes organized into groups of "sins," with sins put together that have something to do with one another.[9] First are listed, say, vices of sex, then those of violence, then others related to economics or injustice. Analyzing the occurrence of *arsenokoitês* in different vice lists, I noticed that it often occurs not where we would expect to find reference to homosexual intercourse—that is, along with adultery (*moicheia*) and prostitution or illicit sex (*porneia*)—but among vices related to economic injustice or exploitation. Though this provides little to go on, I suggest that a careful analysis of the actual context of the use of *arsenokoitês*, free from linguistically specious arguments from etymology or the word's separate parts, indicates that *arsenokoitês* had a more specific meaning in Greco-Roman culture than homosexual penetration in general, a meaning that is now lost to us. It seems to have referred to some kind of economic exploitation by means of sex, perhaps but not necessarily homosexual sex.

One of the earliest appearances of the word (here the verb) occurs in *Sibylline Oracle* 2.70–77.[10] Although the date of this section of the oracle—indeed, of the finished oracle itself—is uncertain, there is no reason to take the text as dependent on Paul or the New Testament. The oracle probably provides an independent use of the word. It occurs in a section listing acts of economic injustice and exploitation; in fact, the editors of the English translation here quoted (J. J. Collins) label the section "On Justice":

> (Never accept in your hand a gift which derives from unjust deeds.)
>
> Do not steal seeds. Whoever takes for himself is accursed (to generations of generations, to the scattering of life.
>
> Do not *arsenokoitein*, do not betray information, do not murder.)
>
> Give one who has labored his wage. Do not oppress a poor man.
>
> Take heed of your speech. Keep a secret matter in your heart.
>
> (Make provision for orphans and widows and those in need.)
>
> Do not be willing to act unjustly, and therefore do not give leave to one who is acting unjustly.

The term occurs in a list of what we might call "economic sins," actions related to economic injustice or exploitation: accepting gifts from unjust sources, extortion, withholding wages, oppressing the poor. "Stealing seeds" probably refers to the hoarding of grain; in the ancient world, the poor often accused the rich of withholding grain from the market as a price-fixing strategy.[11] I would argue that other sins here mentioned that have no necessary economic connotation probably do here. Thus the references to speech and keeping secrets may connote the use of information for unjust gain, like fraud, extortion, or blackmail; and "murder" here may hint at motivations of economic gain, recalling, for example, the murder of Naboth by Jezebel (1 Kgs. 21). In any case, no other term in the section refers to sex. Indeed, nothing in the context (including what precedes and follows this quotation) suggests that a sexual action in general is being referred to at all. If we take the context as indicating the meaning, we should assume that *arsenokoitein* here refers to some kind of economic exploitation, probably by sexual means: rape or sex by economic coercion, prostitution, pimping, or something of the sort.

This suggestion is supported by the fact that a list of sexual sins does occur elsewhere in the same oracle, which is where we might expect to find a reference to male-male sex (2.279–82). The author condemns "defiling the flesh by licentiousness," "undoing the girdle of virginity by secret intercourse," abortion, and exposure of infants (the last two often taken to be means of birth control used by people enslaved to sex; such people proved by these deeds that they had sex purely out of lust rather than from the "nobler" motive of procreation). If the prohibition against *arsenokoitein* was taken to condemn homosexual intercourse in general, one would expect the term to occur here, rather than among the terms condemning unjust exploitation.[12]

A similar case exists in the second-century *Acts of John*. "John" is condemning the rich men of Ephesus:

> You who delight in gold and ivory and jewels, do you see your loved (possessions) when night comes on? And you who give way to soft clothing, and then depart from life, will these things be useful in the place where you are going? And let the murderer know that the punishment he has earned awaits him in double measure after he leaves this (world). So also the poisoner, sorcerer, robber, swindler, and *arsenokoitês*, the thief and all of this band. . . . So, men of Ephesus, change your ways; for you know this also, that kings, rulers, tyrants, boasters, and warmongers shall go naked from this world and come to eternal misery and torment.[13]

Here also, *arsenokoitês* occurs in a list of sins related to economics and injustice: delighting in wealth, robbery, swindling, thievery. Note also the list of those who prosper by their power over others: kings, rulers, tyrants, boasters, warmongers. The emphasis throughout the section is on power, money, and unjust exploitation, not sex.

As was the case in the *Sibylline Oracle*, "John" *does* denounce sexual sins elsewhere in the text, and the word *arsenokoitês* is absent (section 35). If this author took *arsenokoitês* to refer generally to homosexual sex or penetration, we would expect him to mention it among the other sexual sins, rather than in the section condemning the rich for economic exploitation. Thus, here also *arsenokoitês* probably refers to some kind of economic exploitation, again perhaps by sexual means.

Another second-century Christian document offers corroborative, though a bit less obvious, evidence. Theophilus of Antioch, in his treatise addressed *To Autolychus*, provides a vice list.[14] First come the two sexual sins of adultery and fornication or prostitution.[15] Next come three economic sinners: thief, plunderer, and defrauder (or robber). Sixth is *arsenokoitês*. The next group includes savagery, abusive behavior, wrath, and jealousy or envy, all of which the ancients would recognize as sins of "passion": that is, uncontrolled emotion. Next come instances of pride: boastfulness and conceit or haughtiness. I take the next term, *plêktês* ("striker"), to denote someone who thinks he can go around hitting people as if they were his slaves. Then occurs the term "avaricious," or "greedy." Finally are two phrases related to the family: disobedience to parents and selling one's children. These last three may all have been taken as belonging to the category of greed, surely in the case of selling one's children and also perhaps in the reference to parents, if the particular action is understood as a refusal to support one's parents in their old age.

Arsenokoitês is separated from the sexual sins by three terms that refer to economic injustice. Would this be the case if it were understood as a condemnation of simple male homosexual intercourse? Furthermore, as Robert Grant notes, Theophilus takes these terms, with the exceptions of *phthoneros* and *hyperoptês*, from vice lists in the Pauline corpus. Therefore, it is notable that Theophilus places *arsenokoitês* in a different position. Grouping it with economic sins, I suggest, reflects his understanding of the social role to which it referred and his rhetorical goal of grouping the vices by category.

Later in the same work, *arsenokoitia* occurs in another list: again adultery and *porneia* come first, then *arsenokoitia*, followed by greed (*pleonexia*) and *athemitoi eidôlolatreia*, referring to idolatry. This list is not very helpful, since the term could here be taken as a sexual vice, grouped with the two preceding terms, or as an economic vice, grouped with the following. One possible explanation is that it is both: it is economic exploitation by some sexual means.[16]

There are two texts in which one might reasonably take *arsenokoitia* as referring to homosexual sex. In each case, however, I believe a careful reading encourages more cautious conclusions. The first occurs in Hippolytus's *Refutation of All Heresies* 5.26.22–23. Hippolytus claims to be passing along a Gnostic myth about the seduction of Eve and Adam by the evil being Naas. Naas came to Eve, deceived her, and committed adultery with her. He then came to Adam and "possessed him like a boy (slave)." This is how, according to the myth, *moicheia* (adultery) and *arsenokoitia* came into the world. Since *arsenokoitia* is in parallel construction with *moicheia*, it would be reasonable for the reader to take its reference as simply homosexual penetration. We should note, nonetheless, the element of deception and fraud here. The language about Naas's treatment of Adam, indeed, which could be read "taking or possessing him like a slave," could connote exploitation and even rape. Certainly the context allows a reading of *arsenokoitia* to imply the unjust and coercive use of another person sexually.

The second debatable use of the term occurs in a quotation of the second- to third-century writer Bardesanes found in Eusebius's *Preparation for the Gospel*.[17] Bardesanes is remarking that the peoples who live east of the Euphrates River take the charge of *arsenokoitia* very seriously: "From the Euphrates River all the way to the ocean in the East, a man who is derided as a murderer or thief will not be the least bit angry; but if he is derided as an *arsenokoitês*, he will defend himself to the point of murder. [Among the Greeks, wise men who have lovers (*erômenous echontes*, males whom they love; "favorites") are not condemned]" (my trans.).

On the surface, this passage appears to equate being an *arsenokoitês* and having a favorite. But there are complicating factors. In the first place, the text seems to have gone through some corruption in transmission. The sentence I have given in brackets does not occur in the Syriac fragments of Bardesanes' text or in the other ancient authors who seem to know Bardesanes' account, leading Jacoby, the editor of the Greek fragments, to suggest that Eusebius himself supplied the comment.[18] Thus Eusebius's text would provide evidence only that he or other late-Christian scribes wanted to equate *arsenokoitês* with "having a favorite." This fourth-century usage would therefore be less important for ascertaining an earlier, perhaps more specific, meaning of the term. Furthermore, we should note that the phrases occur in Eusebius in a parallel construction, but this does not necessarily mean that the second phrase is a defining gloss on the first. The point could be that "wise men" among the Greeks are not condemned for an action that is similar to one found offensive to Easterners. The equation of the terms is not absolutely clear. I offer these thoughts only as speculations meant to urge caution, but caution is justified. Especially since this text from Eusebius is the only one that might reasonably be taken to equate *arsenokoitia* with simple homosexual penetration, we should be wary of saying that it always does.[19]

I should be clear about my claims here. I am not claiming to know what *arsenokoitês* meant. I am claiming that no one knows what it meant. I freely admit that it *could* have been taken as a reference to homosexual sex.[20] But given the scarcity of evidence and the several contexts just analyzed, in which *arsenokoitês* appears to refer to some particular kind of economic exploitation, no one should be allowed to get away with claiming that "of course" the term refers to "men who have sex with other men." It is certainly possible, I think probable, that *arsenokoitês* referred to a particular role of exploiting others by means of sex, perhaps but not necessarily by homosexual sex. The more important question, I think, is why some scholars are certain it refers to simple male-male sex in the face of evidence to the contrary. Perhaps ideology has been more important than philology.

MALAKOS

The translations and interpretations of *malakos* provide an even clearer case of ideological scholarship. For one thing, in contrast to the case with *arsenokoitês*, in which we have too few occurrences of the term to make confident claims, we possess many occurrences of *malakos* and can be fairly confident about its meaning. Moreover, the changes in translation of *malakos* provide an even clearer record of how interpretive decisions have changed due to historical shifts in the ideology of sexuality.

Early English translations render *malakos* by terms that denote a general weakness of character or degeneracy, usually "weaklinges" (Tyndale 1534; Coverdale 1535; Cranmer 1539; see also Wyclif 1380, "lechouris ayens kynde," and Geneva

Bible 1557, "wantons"). From the end of the sixteenth century to the twentieth, the preferred translation was "effeminate" (Douai-Rheims 1582; KJV 1611; ASV 1901). As was the case with *arsenokoitês*, however, a curious shift takes place in the mid-twentieth century. The translation of *malakos* as "effeminate" is universally rejected, and some term that denotes a particular sexual action or orientation is substituted. The JB (1966) chooses "catamite"; the NAB (1970) renders *arsenokoitês* and *malakos* together as "sodomite"; others translate *malakos* as "male prostitute" (NIV 1973; NRSV 1989); and again some combine both terms and offer the modern medicalized categories of sexual, or particularly homosexual, "perversion" (RSV 1946; TEV 1966; NEB 1970; REB 1992). As was the case with *arsenokoitês*, no real historical or philological evidence has been marshaled to support these shifts in translation, especially not that from the "effeminacy" of earlier versions to the "homosexual perversion" of the last fifty years. In fact, all the historical and philological evidence is on the side of the earlier versions. The shift in translation resulted not from the findings of historical scholarship but from shifts in sexual ideology.

This hypothesis is easy to support because *malakos* is easy to define. Evidence from the ancient sources is abundant and easily accessible. *Malakos* can refer to many things: the softness of expensive clothes, the richness and delicacy of gourmet food, the gentleness of light winds and breezes. When used as a term of moral condemnation, the word still refers to something perceived as "soft": laziness, degeneracy, decadence, lack of courage, or, to sum up all these vices in one ancient category, the feminine. For the ancients, or at least for the men who produced almost all our ancient literature, the connection was commonsensical and natural. Women are weak, fearful, vulnerable, tender. They stay indoors and protect their soft skin and nature: their flesh is moister, more flaccid, and more porous than male flesh, which is why their bodies retain all that excess fluid that must be expelled every month. The female is quintessentially penetrable; their pores are looser than men's. One might even say that in the ancient male ideology women exist to be penetrated. It is their purpose (*telos*). And their "softness" or "porousness" is nature's way of inscribing on and within their bodies this reason for their existence.[21]

And so it was that a man who allowed himself to be penetrated—by either a man or a woman—could be labeled a *malakos*. But to say that *malakos* meant a man who was penetrated is simply wrong. In fact, a perfectly good word existed that seems to have had that narrower meaning: *kinaedos*. *Malakos*, rather, referred to this entire complex of femininity.[22] This can be recognized by looking at the range of ways men condemned other men by calling them *malakoi*.

As I mentioned, a man could, by submitting to penetration, leave himself open to charges of *malakia*.[23] But in those cases, the term refers to the effeminacy of which the penetration is only a sign or proof; it does not refer to the sexual act itself. The category of effeminate men was much broader than that. In philosophical texts, for example, *malakoi* are those people who cannot put up with hard work. Xenophon uses the term for lazy men.[24] For Epictetus and the Cynic Epistles, the term refers to men who take life easy rather than enduring the hardships of philosophy.[25] In Dio Cassius, Plutarch, and Josephus, cowards are *malakoi*.[26] Throughout ancient literature, *malakoi* are men who live lives of decadence and luxury.[27] They drink too much wine, have too much sex, love gourmet food, and hire professional cooks. According to Josephus, a man may be accused of *malakia* if he is weak in battle, enjoys luxury, or is reluctant to commit suicide (*War* 7.338; *Antiquities* 5.246; 10.194). Dio Chrysostom says that the common crowd might stupidly call a man *malakos* just because he studies a lot—that is, a bookworm might be called a sissy (66.25).

The term *malakos* occurs repeatedly in the Pseudo-Aristotelian *Physiognomy*, a book that tells how to recognize someone's character by body type and body language, including whether a man is really effeminate even if he outwardly appears virile. The word never refers specifically to penetration in homosexual sex (although men who endure it are discussed in the book). Rather, it denotes the feminine, whether the reference is to feet, ankles, thighs, bones, flesh, or whatever (see esp. chap. 6 passim). It always represents the negative female characteristic to which the positive masculine characteristic is contrasted. For example, if a man has weak eyes, it means one of two things: either he is *malakos* and *thêlu*, or he is a depressive and lacks spirit (808a10). Each option contains a pair of synonyms: just as "depressive" and "lacking spirit" (*katêphês*, *athymos*) are synonyms, so are *malakos* and *thêlu*, both referring to effeminacy. *Malakia*, therefore, was a rather broad social category. It included, of course, penetrated men, but many others besides. To put it simply, all penetrated men were *malakoi*, but not all *malakoi* were penetrated men.[28]

In fact, *malakos* more often referred to men who prettied themselves up to further their heterosexual exploits. In Greco-Roman culture, it seems generally to have been assumed that both men and women would be attracted to a pretty boy. And boys who worked to make themselves more attractive, whether they were trying to attract men or women, were called effeminate. An old hag in a play by Aristophanes drags off a young man, saying, "Come along, my little softie" (*malakion*), although she has perfectly heterosexual things in mind (*Ecclesiazusae* 1058). The Roman playwright Plautus uses the Latin transliteration *malacus* to indicate effeminate men. But whereas in one comedy the term is *cinaedus malacus*, referring to a penetrated man, in another it is *moechus malacus*, referring to a man who seduces other men's wives (*Miles Gloriosus* 3.1 [1.668]; *Truculentus* 2.7.49 [1.610]).

In the ancient world, effeminacy was implicated in heterosexual sex as much as homosexual—or more so.[29] When Diogenes the Cynic sees a young man prettied up, he cannot tell whether the boy is trying to attract a man or a woman; in either case the boy is equally effeminate (Diogenes Laertius, *Lives* 6.54; the term *malakos* does not occur here, but effeminacy is the subject).[30] Chariton, in his novel *Chaereas and Callirhoe*, provides a typical portrait of an effeminate man (1.4.9): he has a fresh hairdo, scented with perfume; he wears eye makeup, a soft (*malakon*) mantle, and light, swishy slippers; his fingers glisten with rings. Only a modern audience would find it strange that he is off to seduce not a man but a maiden.[31] When the author of the Pseudo-Aristotelian *Physiognomy* wants to portray the

"Charitable Type" of man, he makes him typically effeminate—and very heterosexual. Such men, he says, are delicate, pale, with shining eyes and wrinkled noses; they cry a lot, are "reminiscent," warmhearted, and have nice dispositions. They are particularly fond of women, with whom they have lots of sex, and they tend to produce female children (808a34).

Ancient sexist ideology was quite different from modern sexist—and heterosexist—ideology. The ancients operated with an axis that represented masculinity at one end and femininity at the other. All people theoretically could be assigned a particular place on the axis. The ancients could also assume, rather less often or obviously, an axis on which men-who-love-boys occupied one end and men-who-love-women the other, with most men assumed to fall somewhere in the middle as naturally omnisexual. To some extent, therefore, we can recognize analogies to the modern axes of masculine-feminine and heterosexual-homosexual. But whereas in modern ideology the two axes are usually collapsed together, with queer men of all sexual positions considered feminine and straight guys masculine (and even more masculine the lustier they are), the two axes had no relation to one another in the ancient ideology. A man could be branded as effeminate whether he had sex with men or with women. Effeminacy had no relation to the sex of one's partner but to a complex system of signals with a much wider reference code. Thus it would never have occurred to an ancient person to think that *malakos* or any other word indicating the feminine in itself referred to homosexual sex at all. It could just as easily refer to heterosexual sex.[32]

This can be demonstrated by analyzing those famous texts in which men argue about whether the love of women is inferior or superior to the love of boys. Each side accuses the other of effeminacy and can claim some logical grounds for doing so. In Plato's *Symposium*, where Aristophanes is made to relate his fanciful myth about the origins of the different kinds of loves, man for man, man for woman, and woman for woman, it is taken as natural that male-male love is the most "manly" (*andreiotatoi*) of all three (192A). In the *Symposium* no one attempts to argue the opposite, more difficult case. In Plutarch's *Dialogue on Love* (*Moralia* 748E–771E), the man defending the love of women does accuse the penetrated man of *malakia* and *thêlytês*, but the speaker advocating the love of boys is given the stronger case. He says that the love of females is, of course, more effeminate (750F); the love of women is "moist" (*hygron*), "housebound," "unmanly" (*anandrois*), and implicated in *ta malaka*, "softness" (751A–B). Men who fall in love with women demonstrate their effeminacy (*malakia*) and weakness (*astheneia*, 753F; 760D) by the fact that they are controlled by women.

Similar mutual insults are exchanged in the Pseudo-Lucianic *Affairs of the Heart*. The man advocating the love of women is portrayed by the author as the more effeminate. He is said to be skilled in the use of makeup, presumably, the narrator comments, in order to attract women, who like that kind of thing (9). True, in his own turn, the "woman lover" complains that the penetrated man in homosexual sex is feminized; it is masculine to ejaculate seed and feminine to receive it (28, 19; note *malakizesthai*). But the man advocating the love of boys counters that *heterosexual* sex taints a man with femininity, which is why men are so eager to take a bath after copulating with women (43). Male love, on the other hand, is manly, he says, associated with athletics, learning, books, and sports equipment, rather than with cosmetics and combs (9, 44).[33]

I cite these texts not to celebrate homosexual love. What strikes me about them is rather their rank misogyny.[34] But that is just the point. The real problem with being penetrated was that it implicated the man in the feminine, and *malakos* referred not to the penetration per se but to the perceived aspects of femaleness associated with it. The word *malakos* refers to the entire ancient complex of the devaluation of the feminine. Thus people could use *malakos* as an insult directed against men who love women too much.[35]

At issue here is the ancient horror of the feminine, which can be gruesomely illustrated by an example from Epictetus. In one of his especially "manly" moments, Epictetus praises an athlete who died rather than submit to an operation that would have saved his life by amputating his diseased genitals (1.2.25–26). Whereas we might think the paramount issue would be the man's wish to avoid an excruciatingly painful operation, the issue for Epictetus is the man's manly refusal to go on living if he must do so without his masculine equipment—the things that set him apart from despised femininity. It is better to die than be less than a man. Or, perhaps more to the point, any sensible person would rather be dead than be a woman.

There is no question, then, about what *malakos* referred to in the ancient world. In moral contexts it always referred either obviously or obliquely to the feminine. There is no historical reason to take *malakos* as a specific reference to the penetrated man in homosexual intercourse.[36] It is even less defensible to narrow that reference down further to mean "male prostitute."[37] The meaning of the word is clear, even if too broad to be taken to refer to a single act or role. *Malakos* means "effeminate."

Why has this obvious translation been universally rejected in recent English versions? Doubtless because contemporary scholars have been loath to consider effeminacy a moral category but have been less hesitant in condemning gay and lesbian people. Today, effeminacy may be perceived as a quaint or distasteful personal mannerism, but the prissy church musician or stereotyped interior designer is not, merely on the basis of a limp wrist, to be considered fuel for hell. For most English-speaking Christians in the twentieth century, effeminacy may be unattractive, but it is not a sin. Their Bibles could not be allowed to condemn so vociferously something that was a mere embarrassment. So the obvious translation of *malakos* as "effeminate" was jettisoned.

CONSEQUENCES

Being faced with a Pauline condemnation of effeminacy hardly solves the more important hermeneutical issues. Suppose that we wanted to be historically and philologically rigorous and restore the translation "effeminate" to our Bibles. What do we then tell our congregations "effeminacy" means? As I have already illustrated in part, in the ancient world a man could be condemned as effeminate for, among many other things, eating or drinking too much, enjoying gourmet cooking, wearing nice underwear or shoes, wearing much of anything on his head, having long hair, shaving, caring for his skin, wearing cologne or aftershave, dancing too much, laughing too much, or gesticulating too much. Keeping one's knees together is effeminate, as well as swaying when walking, or bowing the head. And of course there were the sexual acts and positions: being penetrated (by a man or a woman), enjoying sex with women too much, or masturbating.[38] The list could go on—and that contributed to the usefulness of the word as a weapon. It was a malleable condemnation.

Naturally, many of these things do not make a man effeminate today. If in trying to be "biblical," then, we attempt to "take seriously" Paul's condemnation, do we condemn what Paul and his readers are likely to have considered effeminate—that is, take the historical route? Or do we condemn only those things that our culture considers effeminate? And what might that be? Taking piano lessons? ballet dancing? singing falsetto in the men and boys' choir? shaving one's body hair for anything but a swim meet or a bicycle race? being a drag queen? having a transsexual operation? camping it up? or wearing any article of "women's clothes" (unless you are a TV talk show host trying to make a point)? refusing to own a gun? driving an automatic transmission instead of a stick shift? drinking tea? actually requesting sherry? Or do we just narrow the category to include only those people most heterosexist Christians would really like to condemn: "gays" and "manly men" who are careless enough to get caught? Condemning penetrated men for being effeminate would also implicate us in a more elusive and pervasive problem: the misogyny of degrading the penetrated. The ancient condemnation of the penetrated man was possible only because sexist ideology had already inscribed the inferiority of women into heterosexual sex. To be penetrated was to be inferior because women were inferior.

Let us also be clear that our modern culture has in no way liberated itself from this sexism. This should be obvious every time a frat boy says, "This sucks!" or "Fuck you!"—thus implicating both his girlfriend and possibly his roommate in the despised role of the penetrated. The particular form taken by modern heterosexism is derived largely from sexism. People who retain Paul's condemnation of effeminacy as ethical grounding for a condemnation of contemporary gay sex must face the fact that they thereby participate in the hatred of women inherent in the ancient use of the term. In the face of such confusion and uncertainty, no wonder modern heterosexist scholars and Christians have shrunk from translating *malakos* as "effeminate." I myself would not advocate reading a condemnation of effeminacy out loud in church as the "word of the Lord." But to mask such problems and tell our fellow Christians that the word "really" refers just to boy prostitutes or, worse, "passive homosexuals" is by this time just willful ignorance or dishonesty.

Some scholars and Christians have wanted to make *arsenokoitês* and *malakos* mean both more and less than the words actually mean, according to the heterosexist goals of the moment. Rather than noting that *arsenokoitês* may refer to a specific role of exploitation, they say it refers to all "active homosexuals" or "sodomites" or some such catchall term, often broadening its reference even more to include all homosexual eroticism. And rather than admitting the obvious, that *malakos* is a blanket condemnation of all effeminacy, they explain that it refers quite particularly to the penetrated man in homosexual sex. Modern scholars have conveniently narrowed down the wide range of meanings of *malakia* so that it now condemns one group: gay men—in particular, "bottoms." In order to use 1 Corinthians 6:9 to condemn contemporary homosexual relationships, they must insist that the two words mean no more but also no less than what they say they mean. It should be clear that this exercise is driven more by heterosexist ideology than historical criticism.

My goal is not to deny that Paul condemned homosexual acts but to highlight the ideological contexts in which such discussions have taken place. My goal is to dispute appeals to "what the Bible says" as a foundation for Christian ethical arguments. It really is time to cut the Gordian knot of fundamentalism. And do not be fooled: any argument that tries to defend its ethical position by an appeal to "what the Bible says" without explicitly acknowledging the agency and contingency of the interpreter is fundamentalism, whether it comes from a right-wing Southern Baptist or a moderate Presbyterian. We must simply stop giving that kind of argument any credibility. Furthermore, we will not find the answers merely by becoming better historians or exegetes. The test for whether an interpretation is Christian or not does not hang on whether it is historically accurate or exegetically nuanced. The touchstone is not the historically reconstructed meaning in the past, nor is it the fancifully imagined, modernly constructed intentions of the biblical writers.[39] Nor can any responsible Christian—after the revolutionary changes in Christian thought in the past twenty years, much less in the past three hundred—maintain that Christian interpretations are those conforming to Christian tradition. The traditions, all of them, have changed too much and are far too open to cynical manipulation to be taken as foundations for gauging the ethical value of a reading of Scripture.

The only recourse in our radical contingency is to accept our contingency and look for guidance within the discourse that we occupy and that forms our very selves. The best place to find criteria for talking about ethics and interpretation will be in Christian discourse itself, which includes Scripture and tradition but not in a "foundational" sense. Nor do I mean that Christian discourse can itself furnish a stable base on which to secure ethical positions; it is merely the context in which those positions are formed and discussed. Conscious of this precarious contingency, and looking for guiding lights within the discourse, I take my stand with a quotation from an impeccably traditional witness, Augustine, who wrote, "Whoever, therefore, thinks that he understands the divine Scriptures or any part of them so that it does not build the double love of God and of our neighbor does not understand it at all" (*Christian Doctrine* 1.35.40).

By this light, any interpretation of Scripture that hurts people, oppresses people, or destroys people cannot be the right interpretation, no matter how traditional, historical, or exegetically respectable. There can be no debate about the fact that the church's stand on homosexuality has caused oppression, loneliness, self-hatred, violence, sickness, and suicide for millions of people. If the church wishes to continue with its traditional interpretation it must *demonstrate*, not just claim, that it is more loving to condemn homosexuality than to affirm homosexuals. Can the church *show* that same-sex loving relationships damage those involved in them? Can the church give compelling reasons to believe that it really would be better for all lesbian and gay Christians to live alone, without the joy of intimate touch, without hearing a lover's voice when they go to sleep or awake? Is it really better for lesbian and gay teenagers to despise themselves and endlessly pray that their very personalities be reconstructed so that they may experience romance like their straight friends? Is it really more loving for the church to continue its worship of "heterosexual fulfillment" (a "nonbiblical" concept, by the way) while consigning thousands of its members to a life of either celibacy or endless psychological manipulations that masquerade as "healing"?

The burden of proof in the last twenty years has shifted. There are too many of us who are not sick, or inverted, or perverted, or even "effeminate," but who just have a knack for falling in love with people of our own sex. When we have been damaged, it has not been due to our homosexuality but to others' and our own denial of it. The burden of proof now is not on us, to show that we are not sick, but rather on those who insist that we would be better off going back into the closet. What will "build the double love of God and of our neighbor"?

I have tried to illustrate how all appeals to "what the Bible says" are ideological and problematic. But in the end, all appeals, whether to the Bible or anything else, must submit to the test of love. To people who say this is simplistic, I say, far from it. There are no easy answers. "Love" will not work as a foundation for ethics in a prescriptive or predictable fashion either—as can be seen by all the injustices, imperialisms, and violence committed in the name of love. But rather than expecting the answer to come from a particular method of reading the Bible, we at least push the discussion to where it ought to be: into the realm of debates about Christian love, rather than into either fundamentalism or modernist historicism.

We ask the question that must be asked: "What is the loving thing to do?"

Chapter 4

Heterosexism and the Interpretation of Romans 1:18–32

In the religious debate surrounding homosexuality, Romans 1 has commanded, perhaps unduly, a great deal of attention. It is not my purpose in this chapter to offer yet another interpretation of the passage, although I will in passing pose some exegetical arguments. Rather, I am interested in how modern heterosexism has ruled interpretations of Paul's rhetoric. This chapter is thus less an exegesis of Paul's text than an ideological analysis of modern scholarship on Romans 1:18–32.

According to Patricia Beattie Jung and Ralph F. Smith, *heterosexism* is "a reasoned system of bias regarding sexual orientation. It denotes prejudice in favor of heterosexual people and connotes prejudice against bisexual and, especially, homosexual people. . . . It is rooted in a largely cognitive constellation of beliefs about human sexuality." Heterosexism maintains that "heterosexuality is *the* normative form of human sexuality. It is the measure by which all other sexual orientations are judged."[1] In this chapter, I analyze the logic of modern heterosexism as it has read Paul's remarks on homosexual acts in Romans 1. My purpose is not to argue that Paul approves of homosexual sex or would consider it acceptable behavior for Christians.[2] I will demonstrate, however, that modern scholars are being disingenuous or self-deluding when they claim that their position—the heterosexist position—is simply an appropriation of "the biblical view." Their reading of Paul is prompted not by the constraints of historical criticism or their passive perception of the "clear meaning" of the text, as they claim, but by their inclination (not necessarily intentional) to reinforce modern heterosexist constructions of human sexuality.

Although I refer in passing to several exegetes, I concentrate on two articles by my colleague Richard Hays, not because he represents a particularly egregious example of prejudice (his conclusions are less offensive than those of many others) but because the particular constellation of issues I wish to highlight can all be found in his work. Those issues are as follows: (1) the claim that the etiology of homosexuality, according to Paul, lies in the corruption of universal human nature that occurred in the fall; (2) the assumption that Paul is differentiating homosexual desire from heterosexual desire in Romans 1, ascribing the former to the fall and the latter to pristine creation; and (3) the importation of a modern concept of acts "contrary to nature" when explaining Paul's term *para physin.*

THE ORIGINS OF HOMOSEXUALITY

Hays attempts the laudable task of convincing conservative Christians that Paul does not single out homosexuality as a particularly heinous sin. Believing he advocates a more compassionate position, Hays argues that Romans 1 refers to "the unrighteousness of fallen humanity," to "the human race in general."[3] Quoting Robin Scroggs, Hays agrees that "the whole passage is 'Paul's real story of the universal fall.'"[4] It is "an illustration of human depravity," an "apocalyptic 'long-view' which indicts fallen humanity as a whole."[5] Homosexuality is no more (but no less) than a symptom of the depravity of all of human nature due to humanity's rebellion against God.

Hays is not alone in taking Paul's comments to refer to the beginning chapters of Genesis. Years ago, Helmut Thielicke similarly argued that homosexuality, according to Paul, is "a kind of symptomatic participation in the fate of the fallen world." Thus, in what is assumed to be a liberal stance, Thielicke insists that those with a homosexual orientation are no more sinful than other people: "We are all under the same condemnation."[6]

This inscription of homosexuality into "fallen human nature" is remarkable in light of the fact that Paul does not here mention Adam, Eve, Eden, the fall, or the universal bondage of humanity to sin. Elsewhere, to be sure, Paul does cite Adam as the point at which sin entered cosmic and mythological history (Rom. 5:12), but, as many other scholars have noted, the scenario Paul sketches in Romans 1 has to do with the invention of idolatry and its consequences, not the fall of Adam.[7] In Romans 1 Paul refers not to Adam or "he"—a single person—but to "they." Furthermore, we have no evidence that Paul considered Adam an idolater. I suggest that Paul's assumed narrative is as follows: Once upon a time, even after the sin of Adam, all humanity was safely and securely monotheistic. At some point in ancient history most of humanity rebelled against God, rejected the knowledge of the true God that they certainly possessed, willfully turned their collective back on God, made idols for themselves, and proceeded to worship those things that by nature are not gods. As punishment for their invention of idolatry and polytheism, God "handed them over" to depravity, allowing them to follow their "passions," which led them into sexual immorality, particularly same-sex coupling. Homosexual activity was the punishment meted out by God for the sin of idolatry and polytheism.

Paul apparently presupposes a Jewish mythological narrative about the origins of idolatry. Since the first chapters of Genesis do not explicitly recount the beginnings of idolatry and polytheism, Jews in Paul's day had filled in the missing data in different ways. Although accounts differ from one another, all of them place the beginnings of idolatry and polytheism at some point after the time of Adam: rabbinic sources variously ascribe the invention of idolatry to Kenan, Enosh (son of Seth), or the people of Enosh's generation.[8]

These Jewish accounts about polytheism's origins were part of a literary tradition that blamed many evils of contemporary Gentile civilization on some ancient turn in human history. A famous example is the story of the fall of the Watchers in *1 Enoch:* heavenly beings, the "sons of God" from Genesis 6, descend to earth, lust after women, mate with them, produce giants or monsters, and introduce the evils of civilization into the world: magic, astrology, warfare, cosmetics, and so forth. In these narratives, one result of the evil angelic influence is sexual immorality. None of the accounts I have examined explicitly names homosexuality as one of the "sins" introduced by the fallen angels, but sexual immorality in general, linked with impurity and corruption, is almost always mentioned, and Paul, along with other Jews, probably assumed that this "immorality" included same-sex intercourse. Stories such as these, which Stanley Stowers calls "decline of civilization narratives," were common in Greek, Roman, and Jewish circles; in the Jewish traditions, they usually function to set Israel off from the impurities and gross sins of the Gentiles.[9] For Jews, the stories served to highlight the fallenness not of Jewish culture or even of humanity in general, but of the Gentiles due to the corruption brought about by civilization. *Porneia,* as the sin of the Gentiles par excellence, is a polluted and polluting consequence of Gentile rebellion.

For example, the book of *Jubilees* offers a series of stories that depict the increasingly profound corruption of the world. In *Jubilees,* the introduction of idolatry occurs several chapters after the account of the sin of the Watchers. According to this text, Ur built the city named after him, the citizens of which then began to make images and worship them. Heavenly beings encouraged them: "And cruel spirits assisted them and led them astray so that they might commit sin and pollution" (11:4). Here we have the usual constellation of motifs: civilization advances due at least in part to inspiration by evil heavenly beings; different aspects of urban culture (and empire) are introduced (in this case idolatry); impurity (often described as sexual) results; and strife (often including the invention of war itself) among human beings is intensified.

Accounts such as these provide the context for Paul's comments about the origins of homosexuality. The narrative flow of Paul's rhetoric mimics the linear structure of these "decline narratives." For Paul, knowledge of God has been available to human beings since the creation of the world (Rom. 1:20). The different peoples, however, willfully plunged themselves into foolishness and darkness of mind (vv. 21–22). They exchanged the glory of the immortal God for images of mortal humans, birds, beasts, and reptiles (v. 23).[10] Therefore (*dio*), that is, as a direct punishment for idolatry and polytheism, God handed over the nations to the "desires of their hearts," leading to uncleanness, pollution, and dishonoring of their bodies (v. 24). In verses 25–32, Paul repeats the sequence: people exchanged monotheism for idolatry and polytheism (v. 25); for that reason (*dia touto*) God gave them over to passions of dishonor, leading to sexual actions "beyond nature" (*para physin,* v. 26).[11] The result of the corruption was further and deeper bondage to sin, strife, social conflict, and chaos (vv. 28–32).

That Paul is referring not to the "universal human condition" but to Gentile culture in particular is confirmed by a rhetorical analysis of the first few chapters of Romans. As Hays realizes, in Romans 1 Paul sets up a "sting" operation, first against the self-righteousness of Gentile moralists (2:1–16), and then against that of the Jewish moralist who puts himself forward as a teacher of the Gentiles (2:17–3:31).[12] He condemns first the Gentiles, and then turns his attention to the Jews. If Romans 1:18–32 is taken as a depiction of the fallenness of human nature in general, the structure and power of Paul's argument collapse. As it is, Paul entices his "Jewish" hearer to nod in agreement with this traditional Jewish indictment of Gentile corruption, of which sexual impurity, as usual, is offered as a prime example.

My reading of Romans 1 as a reference to the origin of idolatry rather than to the fall is not original or unusual. Even those scholars who read into the text the "fallen nature of humanity" often acknowledge that homosexual acts result as a punishment for idol worship.[13] Hays, for example, recognizes that Paul's contemporary readers would have heard the passage "as a condemnation of the pagan Gentiles."[14] This makes it especially notable when Hays shifts the rhetoric from Paul's condemnation of Gentile polytheism to a general condemnation of perverse human nature.[15] Such inconsistencies betoken the ideological bias at work in the interpretations—a bias I identify as "heterosexist."

I will comment further below on possible reasons for reading Romans 1 as referring to the fall, but some observations can here be offered. In the first place, modern scholars tend to read Paul through Augustinian lenses, seeking references to general theological anthropology in the most unlikely places.[16] Paul here makes a characteristic statement about Jewish ethnic purity—or rather, Gentile ethnic *impurity*—which is transformed by modern scholars, in good Augustinian fashion, into a statement about universal concupiscence.[17] Moreover, most modern scholars do not have the texts of *Jubilees* or the Rabbis foremost in their minds when they read Paul, but rather tend to see him as constantly alluding to or echoing the (Protestant!) Old Testament. More importantly, modern scholars read the fall into Romans 1 because it renders the text more serviceable for heterosexist purposes.

Paul's own logic assumes a mythological structure unknown to most modern persons, Christians included. Most of us do not believe that all of humanity was once upon a time neatly monotheistic, only later, at a particular historical point, to turn to polytheism and idolatry; nor are we likely to believe that homosexuality did not exist until a sudden invention of polytheism. According to his etiology of homosexuality, Paul must not have believed that it ever existed among the Jews, at least those who abstained from idolatry. Importantly, when Paul finally indicts the Jews in Romans, he does not accuse them of idolatry or homosexual immorality; Jewish immorality is revealed, at most, in adultery and dishonesty regarding the property of temples (2:22). This is perfectly consistent with Paul's assumption that homosexuality is punishment for idolatry and polytheism: the Jews have not been so punished because they have not, in general, been guilty of that particular sin. If we were to follow Paul's logic, we would have to assume that once idolatry and polytheism were forsaken, homosexuality would cease to exist, which is probably what Paul believed; after all, he never even hints that any Jew or Christian engages in homosexuality.

Even if we take the problematic terms *malakos* and *arsenokoitês* in 1 Corinthians 6:9 to refer to simple homosexual coupling (which is doubtful), Paul's point is "such *were* some of you"—in the past. The vice list functions again to characterize the Gentile world that these newly made "people of Israel" have left behind. Most of us, on the other hand, probably do not believe that the abolition of idolatrous cults and polytheism would spell the end of homosexuality. In sum, modern people, even Christians, do not believe the mythological structure that provides the logic for Paul's statements about homosexuality in Romans 1. Heterosexist scholars alter Paul's reference to a myth that most modern Christians do not even know, much less believe (that is, a myth about the beginnings of idolatry), and pretend that Paul refers to a myth that many modern Christians do believe, at least on some level (the myth about the fall). Heterosexism can retain Paul's condemnation of same-sex coupling only by eliding the supporting logic of that condemnation.

NATURAL DESIRE AND UNNATURAL ACTS

Another telling inconsistency in heterosexist scholarship on Romans 1 lies in its assumption that Paul is not only addressing the question of homosexual *activity* but also providing an explanation for the existence of homosexual *desire.* On the one hand, most of these scholars, in an attempt to be more "compassionate" and "liberal," point out that Paul condemns not homosexual orientation or desire but only homosexual acts. Thus gay and lesbian people should take comfort that, although their emotions are shameful, they are not exactly culpable. On the other hand, these scholars continue to read Romans 1 as offering an explanation for the existence of homosexual desire (that such an explanation is felt to be necessary is itself, of course, the result of heterosexism). Helmut Thielicke, for example, arguing against Karl Barth and others for a more "liberal" view of homosexuality, speaks of "the predisposition itself, the homosexual potentiality as such," and claims that it is "a kind of symptomatic participation in the fate of the fallen world." The "constitutional homosexual," therefore, should not be condemned any more than any other fallen human being.[18] According to a Church of England document, the "invert" is "an anomaly whose sexual disorientation bears its own tragic witness to the disordering of humanity by sin."[19] And Richard Hays, in spite of his insistence that Paul is condemning not homosexual desire or orientation but only homosexual activity, cannot in the end help but slip into reading Romans 1 as providing an etiology of homosexual orientation: "Paul, if confronted by a study demonstrating that (say) 10 percent of the population favor sexual partners of the same gender, would no doubt regard it as corroborative evidence for his proclamation that the wrath of God is being made manifest in rampant human unrighteousness."[20] Thus, though Hays insists (I think rightly) that Paul had no conception of homosexual orientation and thus no conception of homosexual people in the modern sense,[21] Hays nevertheless also insists that the presence of such people in the world is a sign of the wrath of God. All of these scholars, indeed, believe that Paul is referring to homosexual desire, even if he is not actually condemning it.[22]

To some extent, it is understandable that modern scholars read Paul's comments as a reference to homosexual desire; Paul does, after all, mention desire and passion in the passage. In verse 24 Paul says that God "gave them up in the desires [*epithymiai*] of their hearts to uncleanness with the result that they dishonor their bodies in themselves." Paul uses the term "passions of dishonor" (*pathê atimias,* v. 26), and he writes that males "burned in their yearning [*orexis*] for one another" (v. 27). But it is a mistake to read into these comments the kind of modernist dichotomy between homosexual and heterosexual desire, in which a difference in *kind*—between an unnatural, abnormal desire and a natural, normal desire—is assumed. The question is, Does Paul here assume a category of homosexual desire that is a different kind of desire from heterosexual desire?

First, it should be noted that Paul uses the term "contrary to nature" or "unnatural" only when referring to actions, not desires. In verse 26, Paul says that females exchanged the "natural use" (*physikê chrêsis*) for that which is "contrary to" or "beyond nature" (*para physin*). Paul also mentions males forsaking the "natural use of females" (v. 27). Paul does not, however, link the language of "nature" to "desire." The absence in Paul's language of any reference to "unnatural desire" is understandable when we place him in the context of ancient, rather than modern, notions of homosexual sex.

As has been often noted, ancient Greco-Roman moralists (and we should include most Jewish moralists of Paul's day) generally believed homosexual behavior sprang from the same desire that motivated heterosexual sex.[23] According to these moralists, some people, due to unrestrained sexual desire, grew bored with "basic" sexual activity and went cruising for new and untried pleasures. Women, no longer satisfied by sex with their husbands, would be led in their lasciviousness to experiment with bestiality.[24] Men were so enslaved to their lusts that they were eager to try activities out of the ordinary, such as sex with one another. The problem had to do not with a *disoriented* desire, but with *inordinate* desire. Degree of passion, rather than object choice, was the defining factor of desire.

This ancient logic surfaces in discussions about "unnatural" sex in the ancient texts. In a speech by Dio Chrysostom, for example, a rustic moralist bemoans the excesses of civilization and criticizes men who have gotten their fill of seducing women:

> The man whose appetite is insatiate in such things, when he finds there is no scarcity, no resistance, in this field, will have contempt for the easy conquest and scorn for a woman's love, as a thing too readily given—in fact, too utterly feminine—and will turn his assault against the male quarters, eager to befoul the youth who will very soon be magistrates and judges and generals, believing that in them he will find a kind of pleasure difficult and hard to procure.[25]

As Victor Paul Furnish notes, the ancient moralists, and here we must include Paul, considered homosexual behavior to be "the most extreme expression of heterosexual lust."[26] Or as John Chrysostom put it, "You will see that all such desire stems from a greed which will not remain within its usual bounds."[27] In other words, a basically "natural" desire is taken to an "unnatural extreme."

It may be helpful here to note the analogy with eating. Ancient moralists often couple condemnations about sexual misdeeds with similar remarks about eating. Gluttony is "unnatural" because the glutton is insatiable: whereas "nature" intends human beings to be satisfied with a decent meal, gluttons stuff themselves until they become sick, even making themselves vomit so they can continue eating. Human beings should be content with basic nourishment— bread, vegetables, and water, according to some of the more ascetic Greco-Roman traditions; but gormandizers are never satisfied until they have searched out exotic and expensive delicacies. The glutton and gourmand act "contrary to nature" not because they have perverted desires (for example, to eat things not found "in nature" or that will kill them) but because they have indulged their desires to excess, thus losing control of them. In this regard, it is significant that the Greek phrase *para physin,* usually translated "contrary to nature" or "unnatural," more exactly means "beyond nature" or "in excess of what is natural." For the ancient writers, certain behaviors were "contrary to nature" because they went beyond the proper limits prescribed by nature. Gluttony was "too much eating"; homosexuality was "too much sex." We should compare this ancient logic of "unnatural acts" to modern heterosexist rhetoric about homosexuality as "unnatural." In modern discourse homosexuality is unnatural in that it results from disoriented desire, wrong "object choice": some people have perverted passions and desire things that are, in themselves, disgusting and harmful.[28] In this logic, homosexual desire is like a craving to eat excrement. This is, however, *not* what the ancients meant when they spoke of certain acts as "unnatural": for them, the actions could be "unnatural" but still sprang from basically natural desire. This is why the ancients had no notion of "homosexual orientation" or "homosexuals"; it was not a question of "disoriented desires" but of legitimate desires that were allowed illegitimate freedoms.[29]

It is true that Greco-Roman texts in rare cases speak of "unnatural desires," and an analysis of such cases reveals why some moralists considered same-sex intercourse "unnatural acts." What is at issue in these cases, however, is unlike anything modern discourse means when it sometimes labels same-sex eroticism "unnatural." For example, an Aristotelian discussion (the topic occurs in Aristotle's own texts and pseudo-Aristotelian accounts) ponders why some men, contrary to their nature as males, desire to *be* sexually penetrated. Males, by definition, are those "on top," those who penetrate. It is "unnatural," therefore, for a man to be willing—and even eager!—to allow himself to be penetrated.[30] The "unnaturalness" of the desire has nothing to do with one man's erotic interest in another, but with the "unnaturalness" of a man desiring to demean himself by enthusiastically assuming the despised, lower position appropriate for women. Sex in Greco-Roman society, as is well known, was hierarchical, and sex acts (whether the couple was male-male, male-female, female-female, or any combination of human and animal) were almost always inscribed by the assumed superiority of the penetrator to the penetrated. A man's desire to be penetrated was considered unnatural because he thereby renounced his natural position of male superiority and honor: his desire frustrated the gender hierarchy of "nature."[31]

This is precisely the argument mounted against homosexual sex by Plato: a man's *desire* for another male is assumed to be "natural"; but homosexual penetration affronts nature due to its disruption of the male-female cosmic hierarchy.[32] As Plutarch later puts it, homosexual sex is "contrary to nature," because of "the weakness and effeminacy on the part of those who, contrary to nature, allow themselves in Plato's words 'to be covered and mounted like cattle.'"[33] What is unspoken but clearly presupposed is that it is perfectly "natural" for *women* to be "covered and mounted like cattle."

Philo's writings demonstrate that Jews shared these Greco-Roman common senses about hierarchized sex roles, nature, and the implicit devaluation of the feminine. With the Greek and Roman authors, Philo also assumes an etiology of homosexual desire that is no different from heterosexual desire. Sexual desires exceed their bounds precisely like desires for food. In fact, an excess of indulgence in food may lead to an excess of sexual desire. Thus Philo writes,

> These persons begin with making themselves experts in dainty feeding, wine-bibbing, and the other pleasures of the belly and parts below it. Then sated with these they reach such a pitch of wantonness, the natural offspring of satiety, that losing their senses they conceive a frantic passion, no longer for human beings male or female, but even for brute beasts.[34]

Once led to act out their excessive sexual desire, people grow more and more brazen, and eventually "throw off nature" in their excess.[35] The aspects of same-sex intercourse Philo considers unnatural are the feminization of the penetrated man and the unfruitful expenditure of seed by the penetrator. The complex of desire and nature assumed by Philo is like that of other intellectuals of Greco-Roman culture: (1) male *attraction* to beautiful males is considered "natural" ("the natural offspring of satiety"), thus homosexual *desire* is not itself "contrary to nature"; (2) same-sex intercourse, however, may spring from an *excess* of desire, and allowing desire to exceed its bounds leads to actions "beyond nature"; (3) the aspects of same-sex intercourse assumed to be "unnatural" are (a) disruption of the male-female hierarchy and (b) sexual intercourse that does not have procreation as its goal.[36]

Paul, as a product of his culture, certainly shared many of these assumptions—with the exception that Paul shows no concerns for procreation whatsoever (see 1 Corinthians 7). Thus he describes homosexual activity in Romans 1 as inordinate passion.[37] As a possible objection to my argument one might note that Paul does speak of "dishonorable passions" (v. 26) as the motivation for homosexual activity. Does this not imply that Paul believed that homosexual acts sprang from a different kind of desire than heterosexual acts? This would be the case only if we could demonstrate that there was such a thing for Paul as "honorable passion," that is, heterosexual desire that was the positive counterpart of perverted homosexual desire. Such is not the case. Paul never has a positive word to say about sexual passion or desire.[38] The only other place in Paul's undisputed letters where the word *pathos* occurs is 1 Thessalonians 4:5, again linked with *epithymia* to denote sexual desire. Here also, passion is characteristic of Gentiles and must be avoided completely by Christians. Christian men are to have sex with their own wives *and thus avoid passion and desire.*[39] To be sure, Paul sometimes uses the term *epithymia* in a neutral or positive sense (Phil. 1:23; 1 Thess. 2:17), but never when referring to sexual desire. And when giving instructions to Christians in 1 Corinthians 7, Paul counsels people to get married—if they are too weak to control themselves otherwise—not so that they may have an arena for the proper expression of sexual desire but in order to *preclude* the possibility of it.[40] "It is better to marry than to burn" means, in spite of its incomprehensibility for modern persons, that Paul encouraged sex within marriage only as a prophylaxis against desire. Sex is not so much the problem for Paul as desire: marital sex acts thus assist in the precluding of passion. It is a mistake, therefore, for us to interpret Paul's phrase "passion of dishonor" as implying the possibility for him of "honorable passion," since for him *all* passion is dishonorable. For Paul, homosexuality was simply a further extreme of the corruption inherent in sexual passion itself. It did not spring from a different kind of desire, but simply from desire itself.

Doubtless, Paul also objects to same-sex intercourse due in part to his assumption about the cosmic hierarchy of male over female. While this is not made explicit in Romans 1, it is probably assumed.[41] Indeed, in only one other instance do we have an ethical argument from Paul based on "nature." In 1 Corinthians 11:2–16 Paul argues that women should be veiled when they pray and prophesy. While there are several exegetical problems of this passage I cannot address here, certain points must be highlighted for what they tell us about Paul's concept of "nature."[42] In the first place, Paul is here concerned to maintain the male-female gender hierarchy assumed to exist in the cosmos. God is to Christ as Christ is to man as man is to woman (11:3). Man is the reflection of God, and woman is the reflection of man (v. 7).[43] To support his point, Paul offers an argument from "nature" to convince his readers that women "naturally" should be covered: "nature" teaches, according to Paul, that women are to have long hair and men short. Any disruption of that natural order results in "shame," either for the man with long hair or the woman with short. Paul assumes a cosmic hierarchy of male and female that is expressed in the "natural" facts of hair length. For men to wear long hair is "contrary to nature." And what makes such a situation "unnatural" is its disruption of gender hierarchy.[44]

It is not clear whether the modern apologists for heterosexism intend also to appropriate Paul's views about "nature" when it comes to the maintenance of patriarchal gender hierarchy. It is certain, however, that heterosexism has led them to introject their own modern conceptions of sexual desire and its relation to "nature" into the biblical text. Romans 1 offers no etiology of homosexual desire or orientation; its etiology of homosexual sex is one no modern scholar has advocated as factual; and its assumptions about "nature" and sex are not those generally held by the modern apologists for heterosexism.

THE POWER OF HETEROSEXISM

By now it should be clear that I am not arguing that Paul was pro-gay or even neutral on the topic of homosexual sex. My purpose, rather, has been to expose the radical difference between the logics of sexuality that underwrite Romans 1, on the one hand, and the modern logic, on the other, that rules virtually every current discussion, including those by people priding themselves on being "true to the Bible." Whether we are talking about the origins of homosexuality, the mythological presuppositions of Paul's text, the nature of desire, or the logic of the "unnatural," I have highlighted the disjunctions between Paul's presuppositions and those of modern Christian heterosexism. In each case, contemporary scholars read Paul through the lenses of modern categories and assumptions, either ignoring, masking, or dismissing the logic of Paul's own account.

I am attempting, of course, to unmask what parades as "objectivity." Heterosexist scholars regularly impugn the motives of their foes, accusing them of seeing in the text only what they want to see (due, doubtless, to their disoriented nature). Richard Hays, for example, claims that others import anachronisms into the Pauline text; those who argue that the Bible does not condemn homosexuality (in the modern sense of the term) have simply "imposed a wishful interpretation on the biblical passages."[45] Hays criticizes John Boswell for "scrutiniz[ing] the text through the hermeneutical lenses of modern categories alien to the first-century historical setting."[46] Would Hays have us assume, then, that *he* is simply letting the texts "speak for themselves," that he is passively submitting to their penetrating word about homosexuality? Hays's rhetoric, of course, comes as no surprise; oppressive ideologies have always in the modern world masqueraded as objective descriptions of "the way things are."

I believe I have demonstrated, by using the same historical methods as these scholars who claim objectivity, that they are no more "objective" than the rest of us. Indeed, they construe Paul's argument the way they do because of the modern heterosexist assumptions they themselves bring to the text. As they see it, Paul inscribes disturbing desires and orientations into fallen human nature, and they see their own conceptions of "natural" and "unnatural" reflected back at them in the text—none of which would be possible apart from particularly modern forms of heterosexism. Ultimately, my purpose is to insist that modern scholars cannot blame their heterosexism on Paul precisely because the form their heterosexism takes—its assumptions, logics, ways of framing the question—is completely different from the form of Paul's heterosexism, as can be seen through my sketch of the different (indeed, conflicting) grammars of the ancient and modern ideologies.

Why have modern scholars read Romans 1 as a reference to universal fallen human nature? Why read the fall into this text? Furthermore, why read Romans 1 as offering an etiology not just of homosexual activity but of homosexual desire? One possible explanation, though I recognize that it will be a controversial one, is that the modern accounts represent a classic case of homophobia.

Charges of homophobia should not be cast breezily or indiscriminately, so I will explain why I suggest it here. Homophobia is the loathing of homosexuality that arises from a deep-seated (and I think, irrational) fear of homosexuality, often including an unconscious or unacknowledged fear of one's own homoerotic tendencies.[47] Homophobia results when people (regardless of their orientation, for there are homophobic homosexuals) fear the homosexual within. Not all heterosexism springs from homophobia, any more than all sexism necessarily springs from misogyny, but some does.

Much scholarship on Romans 1 and religious writing on homosexuality in general could be read as a classic case of such internalized fear and loathing. I should be clear in making this point that I am unconcerned about the individual psychologies of particular biblical scholars. I am not claiming that these particular men are themselves homophobic. Rather, I would argue that their writings about homosexuality participate in a cultural homophobia, an irrational fear and loathing of homosexuality—and by extension (in spite of protestations to the contrary) lesbian, gay, and bisexual people—that pervades much of modern Western culture and expresses itself in discourses about sexuality, institutionalized marginalization of gay and lesbian people, and social structures that discriminate against them.

The homophobia of Hays's writing occurs in his stereotypical depiction of the "gay subculture" and "homosexual lifestyle" as depressing and loathsome. Hays introduces, as the spokesperson for gay experience, a self-loathing, conservative homosexual Christian who is dying of AIDS—and who had died by the time of the writing of the article, significantly rendering him unavailable for further discussion. His "condition"—referring to his identity as a homosexual man or to his medical diagnosis?—is "tragic." He experiences his homosexuality as "a compulsion and an affliction." (At this point, any distinction between his sexuality and his sickness has become blurred—or was perhaps never really possible at all.) He is "wracked" by his sexual orientation. (The language of torture is not accidental.) "Gary," the gay spokesman in the article, testifies that homosexual people tend (more than straights?) to "draw their identity from their sexuality." (It is a common heterosexist stereotype that gay men and lesbians are quintessentially defined by their sexual desires and activities, whereas the identities of "normal" heterosexuals are complex and constructed by many different aspects of personhood, such as relations, geographical origin, career, interests, hobbies, age, gender, talents, etc.) In the end, it seems, the only hope for gay Christians is the kind of miraculous healing of their homosexuality experienced by "Gary" at the end of his life; they must pray that the "great weight" of their sexuality be lifted off them. Through this amazing rhetorical sleight of hand and ventriloquism, Hays himself avoids explicitly accusing "gay subculture" of any of these faults and diseases; he simply lets the gay spokesman tell his own story about "the depressing reality of the gay subculture."[48]

This exclusively negative portrait of "gay subculture" and the tortured homosexual is surprising given the fact that Hays himself has for years known lesbian and gay Christians who have quite different, *positive* experiences of their sexuality and who have borne witness to the supportive alternative communities they have built outside heterosexist culture, including that of the church. The simultaneous presence of such persons in Hays's experience with the absolute absence of such voices in Hays's articles betrays the irrationality of ideological stereotypes. Like racism and sexism, homophobia must construct and advance stereotypes of the "other" that are belied by the experiences of its very proponents.

Whereas Hays's article represents the *loathing* aspect of homophobia, irrational *fear* is the salient factor in an article published by a group of Jewish and Christian conservative scholars who call themselves the "Ramsey Colloquium." Although the article "The Homosexual Movement" does not attempt an exegesis of Romans 1, it also, like Hays, inscribes homosexual orientation into "humanity's fallen condition," thereby invoking fears of the "homosexual within" corporate humanity.[49]

The authors of the article question the famous claim that 10 percent of men experience predominantly or exclusively homosexual desires, insisting that such data "have now been convincingly discredited." Neglecting to cite the research to which they refer or to analyze it critically, they nevertheless continue: "Current research suggests that the percentage of males whose sexual desires and behavior are exclusively homosexual is as low as 1 percent or 2 percent in developed societies."[50] In spite of their claims that homosexuals are relatively insignificant demographically, however, the authors proceed with their argument by invoking fears that homosexuality, unless kept firmly in the closet, will destroy the existence of heterosexuality and the fabric of the heterosexually oriented nuclear family. They single out "the homosexual subculture" as particularly responsible for "sexual promiscuity, depression, and suicide and the ominous presence of AIDS." Even more broadly, they decry "the harm done to the social order when policies are advanced that would increase incidence of the gay lifestyle and undermine the normative character of marriage and family life." The mere presence of lesbians and gay men constitutes an "attack" upon "the heterosexual norm."[51] Invoking even the dangerous stereotype of the lecherous homosexual preying on and recruiting children, the authors advocate job "discrimination" (their word) "in education and programs involving young people." They argue, "Public anxiety about homosexuality is preeminently a concern about the vulnerabilities of the young. This, we are persuaded, is a legitimate and urgent public concern."[52]

One might reasonably expect that members of the Ramsey Colloquium would have settled on a coherent logic before going into print: Is the incidence of homosexuality really as rare as they claim (in which case it is hard to imagine how dangerous an attack upon heterosexuality it could effectively mount), *or* is heterosexuality truly threatened (in which case we must imagine a far higher percentage of the population choosing exclusively homosexual relations)? Even if 20 or 30 percent of the population—a figure far higher than suggested by Kinsey's data—were in same-sex alternative families, it is difficult to imagine how that would disable the rest of the population from pursuing opposite-sex ones. Are the authors afraid that our society is on the brink of population extinction? How does the love of two men or two women for one another pose a significant threat to the existence of heterosexual relations or structures? The Ramsey Colloquium nowhere offers any reasoned arguments to demonstrate how even a large majority of gay men and lesbians could conceivably bring about the demise of heterosexuality; and the irrationality of their anxiety becomes even more glaring since they argue that only 1 or at most 2 percent of the population is homosexual. The homophobia of the article "The Homosexual Movement" is revealed, as is often the case with marginalizing ideologies, by its internal contradictions.

I have gone to such lengths to illustrate why I call certain positions homophobic (rather than simply heterosexist) for an important reason. Having denied that heterosexist scholars interpret Paul the way they do because they are simply "reading the text," I wished to propose other reasons to explain why they have misconstrued Paul's writings in the particular way they have. I suggest that a specifically modern form of homophobia—an irrational and exaggerated loathing and fear of homosexuality—has motivated many such interpretations.[53] By implanting homosexual desire into the body of universal, fallen human nature—which Paul does not do—conservative scholars closet homosexual desire in the deep recesses of humanity itself, manifesting the classic tendency of homophobia to portray the danger of homosexuality as that which threatens from within. Instead of representing homosexuality as something "they" do (for example, Paul's

Gentiles), such modern readings curiously make it something "we" do—or that we (and our children!) may very well do if we are not careful to police our inmost urges and those of our fellow citizens. What for Paul functioned as a sign of the boundary separating idolatrous civilization from monotheistic faith has become a symptom par excellence of what is wrong with "all of us." Homosexual desire now lurks somewhere within us all. The fear of its outbreak motivates the current interpretive politics of heterosexism.

Chapter 5

Paul without Passion

On Paul's Rejection of Desire in Sex and Marriage

Paul was apparently not a very romantic fellow. While most modern Christians consider marriage the proper sphere for the expression of desire (perhaps we should specify *heterosexual* desire), Paul considered marriage a mechanism by which desire could be extinguished. In Paul's view, unlike that of some other ascetic-oriented writers of his day, sex was not so much the problem as desire. And sexual intercourse within the bounds of marriage functioned to keep desire from happening. Sex within marriage was not the expression of desire, proper or improper; rather it was the prophylaxis against desire.[1]

Paul's particular brand of asceticism, the control of desire, is not exactly like other ancient attempts to control it. But a comparison with some of those other attempts shows, in the first place, that Paul was not absolutely peculiar in the ancient world in his belief that sexual desire could and should be completely extirpated, even by means of sexual intercourse if necessary. As other scholars have pointed out, Stoics also advocated sex without desire. In the second place, such a comparison shows that the precise structure of Paul's asceticism—his assumptions about its meanings, his reasons for it, and the ways he believes desire can and ought to be controlled—is different from that of others. This essay will compare Paul's rationality of desire and its avoidance with those of ancient medical writers, on the one hand, and Stoics, on the other. The control of desire was a common concern in the early Roman Empire, at least among many intellectuals, but the logics or rationalities underwriting such control differed among different social groups.

THE EXTIRPATION OF DESIRE IN PAUL'S WRITINGS

The key passage that brings out Paul's position is 1 Corinthians 7, which is devoted to the argument that people who are too weak for celibacy should get married, and that people who are strong enough for celibacy should remain unmarried and chaste. A central point in Paul's argument is an enigmatic statement in which he urges marriage for those who are "out of control." They should get married, he says, because "it is better to marry than to burn" (1 Cor. 7:9). Taking the "burning" here as a reference to eschatological judgment is possible but not, in the end, compelling. Throughout the chapter Paul is concerned about the here and now of people who are having trouble controlling their sexual desires (7:2, 5, 9, 36). The theme of judgment, though playing a role elsewhere in 1 Corinthians, has not been mentioned in this section and plays little part in chapter 7. Furthermore, as I have argued elsewhere, conceiving sexual desire as a "burning" within the body, metaphorically and physically, was so common in Paul's day, as seen in medical, magical, physiological, philosophical, and "artistic" texts, that it is unimaginable that Greco-Roman readers would have missed such a reference here.[2] In fact, Paul elsewhere (as I will analyze further below) quite clearly speaks of sexual desire as a burning (Rom. 1:27). Even if we decide that Paul's "burning" of 1 Corinthians 7 includes a reference to eschatological judgment, we cannot exclude a reference here to sexual passion and desire.

This means, of course, that Paul believed that it was not only possible but preferable—in fact, *necessary*—that Christians experience sexual intercourse only within the context of marriage and only in the absence of sexual passion and desire. As remarkable as this may be for modern people, it seems to be the case. Paul can, indeed, use the term "desire" (*epithymia*) in a morally neutral sense, as when he says that he "desires" to see someone or do something (Phil. 1:23; 1 Thess. 2:17). But whenever Paul broaches the subject of sex and the desire associated with it, he has nothing good to say about it. In 1 Corinthians 7, for example, Paul nowhere mentions a positive kind of desire as opposed to the "burning" that he hopes marriage will quench. He says that sex within marriage functions to guard weak Christians from the pollution of *porneia* (7:2); it is a duty Christian spouses owe to one another (7:3); and it protects Christians from satanic testing (7:5). The romanticism of modern Christian (especially Protestant) attitudes about marriage—that it functions as the "fulfillment" of divinely created and "healthy" human sexuality, or at least heterosexuality; that it is the "normal" outcome of love between a man and a woman; that human beings were practically created *for it*—is strikingly, though not surprisingly, absent. Paul's either/or of 7:9, therefore, should be taken seriously: marriage is the option for weak Christians who cannot otherwise avoid desire.

This complete exclusion of sexual desire is reflected in other Pauline passages. In 1 Thessalonians 4, Paul says that the will of God is the "holiness" or "sanctification" of the Thessalonians (*ho hagiasmos*), and the first issue threatening that holiness Paul mentions is *porneia*. Christian men should "possess" their wives not in the passion of desire (*en pathei epithymias*) like the Gentiles who do not know God. As in 1 Corinthians, Paul is concerned about *porneia*, which is taken to be the characteristic sin of the Gentile world "outside" the closed boundary of the body of Christ. The passion of sexual desire is part of the polluting complex of the cosmos that threatens the church. The problem of *porneia* is that it is unclean (*akatharsia*; 4:7), as opposed to the holy *pneuma* of God that inhabits the church. The passion of desire, therefore, is part of the dirty, polluted cosmos in opposition to God. The way to avoid the pollution is for men to possess and control their "vessels" (their wives) as safe receptacles for their sexual overflow. But the idea that passion could be a part of that process is not entertained; in fact, it is excluded.

This connection of sexual desire with the Gentile world "out there" is also important for Paul's interpretation of Numbers 11 in 1 Corinthians 10. The people of Israel, according to Paul's reading, pursued a catastrophic path from "desire" (*epithymia*) to idolatry (v. 7) to *porneia* (v. 8) to "testing Christ" and subsequent destruction (v. 9). Paul here stands in a long tradition of both Greek and Jewish placements of *epithymia* at the center of the destructions wrought by the passions. For Paul, as for most Jewish writers on the subject, *epithymia* is linked particularly to idolatry. But for all sorts of writers—Greek, Roman, and Jewish—it was a problem. Moreover, as G. D. Collier has argued, in 1 Corinthians 10 *epithymia* "is not merely one of the listed sins, but *the source* of sin to be explicated." What follows in Paul's argument, his warning about idolatry, *porneia*, and rebellion, is simply a "spelling out" of the passion of desire.[3]

This "downhill slide" from desire to destruction occurs also in Romans 1, which is again a place where the uncleanness of *porneia*, idolatry, Gentiles, and sexual passion are connected in Paul's argument. Many readers have taken Paul's comments in Romans 1 to refer only to homosexual desire. But this is a tendentious reading prompted by a modern urge to condemn homosexual desire while sparing heterosexual desire. Paul's argument actually does not differentiate between the two kinds of desire, which is understandable when we recognize that desire itself is the problem for Paul, not just what moderns call "homosexual" desire.[4]

Whereas the sequence in 1 Corinthians 10 was from desire to idolatry to *porneia* to destruction, in Romans 1 the rebellion of idolatry comes first, which merely demonstrates that Paul is less concerned about the *order* of events than the general complex of idolatry, *porneia*, and passion, and their connection to the Gentile world that must be rejected by Christians. Due to their willful rejection of the true God and preference for idolatry and polytheism, God "gave up" the Gentiles "in the desires [*epithymiai*] of their hearts into uncleanness" (1:24). That this reference to *epithymia* includes sexual passion is confirmed by the parallel statement in verse 26, where "passions of dishonor" express themselves sexually. In verse 27 we have the reference to the "burning" of the Gentiles' urge for one another. Here as elsewhere, *epithymia* and *pathos*, when referring to sexual desires, are in a complex of idolatry, *porneia*, pollution, and the Gentile world from which Christians need protection.

Modern Christian interpreters of Paul, often wishing to find some Pauline support for modern notions of romance and marriage, read all these texts as condemning not sexual desire in general but illicit, unnatural, or excessive passions. Paul *must* have had, so the thinking goes, a notion of good, healthy, heterosexual desire; otherwise, why get married at all? Why have sex at all? But I argue that such appeals to what "must" have been the case just beg the question. The worst historians and cultural anthropologists often appeal to "common sense" or what "must" be the case; even good scholars appeal to such arguments when they have no evidence.[5] But all such appeals are problematic. Rather than insisting on what "must" have been the case based on modern common sense, we would do better to look for structures of plausibility in the ancient world by which the absence of sexual desire would be not only possible but preferable.

MEDICAL AND ARISTOTELIAN CONTROL OF DESIRE

The medical writers of Paul's day would have found his extreme position puzzling. They also viewed sexual desire as dangerous. They speak of it as a disease—in particular, a disease of burning—and they offer therapies and regimens to control the burning of desire. But they would have considered any absolute avoidance of desire to be impossible. For the medical doctors, the disease of desire sprang from the natural heat of the body, and any body, to be alive at all, had to have some heat. Health was the appropriate balance (dry and moist, hot and cold) of the constituents and dispositions of the body, usually including the body's elements, like the humors. What needed to be kept in balance was debated by doctors and scientists, but they pretty much all agreed that balance was health.[6] A complete quenching of heat would mean death. Furthermore, the doctors were in service to those male heads-of-households who paid the bills, and those men were almost all interested, at least to some degree, in producing babies. According to the dominant theories of sex, the heat of desire was necessary for the concoction of sperm or semen. Some doctors understood semen as the foam from concocted blood and *pneuma*, the most powerful material of the body, that resulted from the natural coming together of these different corporeal elements. Others explained that semen came from the concoction of humors. Still others held that the friction of sex itself caused the foam. In all cases, however, the heat of desire, as either the compulsion towards friction or the friction that led to compulsion, was essential for ejaculation (and for most of the doctors, it seems, both men and women had to produce semen for pregnancy to result). No more heat would mean no more semen and no more progeny. And for a Greco-Roman householder, that was usually unacceptable.

So doctors taught their patients how to control the heat of desire in themselves, and especially in their wives and daughters. Rufus, who lived perhaps slightly later than Paul, wrote an entire "Regimen for Virgins" guaranteed to ensure that young girls would not get too hot before they reached marriageable age (twelve, for Rufus).[7] Soranus, another physician roughly contemporaneous with Paul, believed that the healthiest route for both men and women was the complete avoidance of sex. (He seems to have been in the minority on this.) This did not mean, however, that they could completely avoid the burning of desire. So Soranus gives advice and prescriptions intended to contain and control the disease of desire, the heat of passion.[8]

Physicians weren't the only ones with these beliefs. Plutarch, for example, follows the Aristotelian tradition that says that desires and appetites are placed in the body by nature to assure that the body will get what it needs. There are different kinds of desires, of course. Those that arise from the body and relate to simple urges like that for food or sex are natural and need only be controlled, not extirpated. Only the fantastic and unnatural desires that arise from the mind when undisciplined must be avoided entirely.[9] Control and moderation are urged. To be most healthy, one should eat moderately, avoid working to exhaustion, and preserve one's "spermatic substance."[10] Plutarch even criticizes those therapists, including perhaps the more strenuous Stoics, who are too rigorous, urging cold baths or periodic fasting on a fixed schedule. Little wonder, then, that Plutarch never advocates either the complete avoidance of sex or the extirpation of desire. As Plutarch says, people ought "to preserve that natural constitution of our bodies, recognizing that every life has room for both disease and health" (135D; trans. F. C. Babbitt).[11]

THE STOIC CONTROL OF DESIRE

In her book *The Therapy of Desire*, Martha Nussbaum calls the view I have just outlined the Aristotelian or Peripatetic position.[12] In quite self-conscious opposition to it, according to Nussbaum, were the Stoics. Rather than taking passion or emotion as a natural compulsion that arises out of necessity, the Stoics, in this case Zeno (according to Diogenes Laertius, *Lives of Philosophers* 7.110), took it as irrational and unnatural. Seneca admits that the wise man will experience "shadows of passion" (*umbras affectuum*), but from passion itself he will be completely free (*De ira* 1.16.7). The Stoics also think of desire as disease, and so they mock the Peripatetics, who would then seem to suggest that one might be content to be just a *little* ill. No, a man with even a slight fever is still sick. If health is what we are after, we will seek complete freedom from the disease of desire, the complete extirpation of the passions (*Epistles* 85.3–4; 116).

Sexual love, Seneca explains, is particularly a state of disorder, as anyone who has experienced it can attest; it is a lack of control, like slavery.[13] Thus one must learn to have sex without love, without passion, without desire. And one *can* learn this. In fact, the real disagreement, according to Seneca, is about the *ability* of a human being to attain such a free, stable existence without the passions. Critics of the Stoics claim that such a state is against human nature. Seneca claims just the opposite: yes, we can! The real reason, according to Seneca, that Stoic ideas are rejected by other philosophers is because they are too enamored of their vices. The nature of a human being is to be rational and free. Only with the extirpation of the passions, including sexual desire, can we be free and self-sufficient (see for example *Epistles* 116.7).

The Stoics, like Paul, do not think this means an end to marriage or sex. The goal, and they seem to believe it is attainable at least by the wise man, is to have sex without desire. A favorite slogan among later ascetic Christians such as Jerome had its origin among the Stoics: "The man who loves his wife too much is also an adulterer."[14] The good Stoic will be a good citizen, a member of the community of humanity, and therefore he will marry, have children, participate in society. But he must do all of these things without suffering from *pathos* or *epithymia*. He must completely extirpate desires.

For the question "How could or why would a person have sex at all without any compulsion to do so?" the Stoics had an answer, following a lead from Aristotle. They taught that the natural compulsion for intercourse, like that for food, did spring from nature and that human beings shared these impulses with animals (who were not rational beings and therefore could not experience passions or emotions, which are "misjudgments," and not possible for nonrational beings; see Diogenes Laertius, *Lives* 7.85, 7.110). But the natural impulse is not *pathos* or *epithymia*; it is *hormê*, which occurs in plants and animals as well as humans.[15] All living beings have an impulse to self-preservation placed there by nature. This includes hunger and an impulse towards self-preservation through sex. Giving in to such an impulse is no more immoral than scratching an itch. But this impulse must not be confused with that harmful and dangerous emotion that people experience when they fall in love or feel as if they can't live without that special someone. The line between "impulse" and "desire" is a fine but important one. The wise man may follow the natural, unemotional impulse to propagate, like, say, an impulse to defecate. But to get too involved in it is disgusting and harmful. In fact, it is "sick."

The Stoics offered a system of therapy, based on discussion, reasoning, self-questioning, analysis, and critique of conventional beliefs, by which anyone with a strong-enough will could learn to control and finally extirpate the passions: grief, pleasure, anger, and desires of all kinds. They claimed to be able to teach people how to live lives of self-control and self-sufficiency. They offered *eudaimonia*, a word difficult to translate but meaning something like well-being, contentedness, happiness, the "blessed" life. Furthermore, according to Nussbaum, the philosophers (the Stoics and other schools as well) offered their therapy as an alternative to other, perhaps more popular methods of attaining "the good life," that is, therapies of desire practiced by doctors, popular healers, astrologers, priests, and other religious leaders, to mention a few.

DESIRE AND RATIONALITY(-IES)

As I hinted at the beginning of this chapter, Nussbaum's account of the Stoics' therapy of desire is important for me because it presents another system of thought in the Greco-Roman world that advocated, and believed possible, the complete extirpation of sexual desire even within the sexual activities of marriage. What may appear highly improbable and perhaps impossible to modern readers, and to ancient doctors, was quite possible at least to some segment of ancient society. Nussbaum's account is also important because it helps us place Paul's position in relation to other therapies of desire in ancient culture. We have here, to simplify somewhat, three different understandings of desire and its treatment: the physicians', the Stoics', and Paul's.

All three treat desire like a disease and agree that it is dangerous. With the Stoics, Paul shares the belief that the complete extirpation of desire is both possible and preferable, even within sexual relations in marriage. But along with the doctors, Paul would doubtless reject the Stoics' doctrine that complete self-sufficiency is possible, since both Paul and the physicians take the self to be a part of its environment and too constituted by that environment to be able to achieve radical self-sufficiency. The Stoics and the medical writers, however, would share a belief that self-sufficiency is an ideal towards which people may strive. Only Paul's position, of these three, takes marriage to be a tool for guarding against desire. And Paul, against both other positions, would certainly reject self-sufficiency as an ideal towards which Christians should strive. This is such an important point that I will return to it later.

What are the more fundamental differences among these three therapies? How or why did these people arrive at these particular differences in understandings and treatments of desire? Nussbaum's answer to such questions is that the philosophical position (and I will concentrate on the Stoics as more important for Paul's position as well as the one given most attention by Nussbaum) differs from all other ancient therapies of desire because it is, well, philosophical. By that she means it is "rational"; it cures the patient by means of discourse rather than drugs, and critical reasoning rather than miracles or salvation. For Nussbaum, philosophy is basically "the pursuit of logical validity, intellectual coherence, and truth," and it will deliver "freedom from the tyranny of custom and convention." Religious and other therapies depend on dogma, conventional beliefs, or external agents, whether they be divinities, demons, doctors, or drugs. Only philosophy offers a therapy that depends on the rationality of the self; therefore it is the rational therapy.[16]

This argument about rationality is difficult to evaluate because, for one thing, Nussbaum actually uses "rationality" in two different ways in the book. When attempting to define or describe philosophy or rationality, she concentrates on issues of procedure, not the actual content of beliefs. Thus, rationality or reason is the process of seeking truth by questioning; it is dialogical, open-ended with regard to results, free from custom and convention, nondogmatic. It scrutinizes assumptions and the self and is open to self-revision at every point. It avoids prejudice by employing critical thinking and examining every issue from every relevant perspective (see, for example, 148). This kind of definition, however, is unusable for comparative purposes, as can be seen when one notes the "question-begging" terms that inevitably occur in such definitions. For example, how open to any possible end must one be before being accepted as rational? How critical must one be of how many assumptions? In any actual situation, I would argue, no one can be truly open to any possible end nor completely critical of all assumptions, given our own contingency and finitude. The parameters of possibility are simply set to some extent. To cite another example, who gets to decide what is or is not a "relevant" perspective? We would certainly have to admit that no one could consider all possible perspectives on an ethical issue, since perspective, as the very mathematical metaphor reveals, is as infinite as the number of possible fractions. These are only examples, but similar question-begging conditions occur in each section where Nussbaum tries to describe "rationality" by concentrating purely on method in the abstract.

The other way Nussbaum speaks of rationality or reason is more revealing but just as problematic. Throughout the book Nussbaum uses these terms to refer not to a method for arriving at truths but to particular truths themselves.[17] There simply *are* beliefs that are rational, and most of the time Nussbaum makes no attempt to argue for the rationality of such beliefs from the ground up (see, for example, 353–54). A list of such cases is revealing. Rational positions are those that assume the existence of a stable individual self. Even though human beings live within society and should be part of it, they are individually free beings with free will and capable of free moral agency (326). Rationality will convince these free agents that they possess universal citizenship and have available to them universal rationality (318). That is, every human being of all places and times has the ability (at least) to reason alike, and if they would just do so they would arrive at the same truth (96, 325). Also rational is a belief in the equality of the sexes (324). Rationality is critical of cultural assumptions, society, and convention. It is naturalistic, which is to say that all things in the universe must be understood to operate by similar mechanisms, the mechanics of "nature." Thus rationality may admit a notion of religion or the divine, but only one that would not threaten the freedom of the individual. In fact, a rational belief in divinity (if any is needed) recognizes the divine within the human person (160–61). The one exception permitted by Nussbaum to this free, stable self, open and visible to itself and subject to its own rule, is the presence of the unconscious. But even the unconscious can be accessed and controlled to a great extent by procedures that sound remarkably like modern psychotherapy (133–34, 490). The existence of the unconscious therefore offers no real threat to the possibility of a stable, free self.

So whereas rationality sometimes refers to a method for arriving at truth, at other times it refers to actual truths with little or no attention given to the method by which these beliefs came to be accepted as true. There is, though, no contradiction here, because Nussbaum really believes that if human beings—any, anywhere, any time—pursued these methods they would arrive at these truths.[18] In my opinion, this is a "faith statement" that, although it may be true, can be supported neither by empirical comparative evidence (experience) nor by some abstract argument that uses universal criteria of reasonableness ("rationality"). Indeed, Nussbaum seems to recognize that her position is more akin to faith than knowledge when she admits that someone like Michel Foucault would find her confidence that rationality can make us free to be an illusion—but, she insists, she still believes it.[19]

As my comments reveal, I find this appeal to rationality insufficient for explaining the differences among Paul, the doctors, and the Stoics. I want to argue, rather, that each position is rational in a sense, and that we can see its rationality when we analyze the therapy in light of its different assumptions about the world and the self. Paul's position, for example, would be rejected by both the doctors and the Stoics as hopelessly uneducated and superstitious. As I have shown elsewhere, educated people in the Greco-Roman world rejected fears of pollution from outside agents as superstition.[20] Rather than following a "logic of invasion" when thinking about disease, they thought of disease along the lines of a "logic of imbalance"; disease was the result of an imbalance of the body's normal states and elements. Thus all Paul's concerns in 1 Corinthians that the church, the body of Christ, might be polluted by idol meat, *porneia*, or desire itself would have appeared ignorant and naive to them. Although the doctors would also have rejected the radical self-sufficiency advocated by the Stoics, they would have assumed that moderate self-sufficiency was a natural ideal. But to accept notions about polluting demons and invading diseases would have posed an unacceptable challenge to the secure, stable, sufficient self that was at least an ideal for upper-class intellectuals in general. Thus their therapies of desire are understandable within the context of their views of the body and the world. And within their system, Paul's fears are irrational.

We can only imagine how Paul would critique their view, especially the more radical Stoic view of self-sufficiency. For rhetorical purposes, Paul can claim self-sufficiency. He tells the Philippians, for instance, that he appreciates their gift but didn't exactly *need* it, since he is *autarkês* and lacks nothing (Phil. 4:11). But this rhetoric carries none of the freight for Paul that it would for the philosophers.[21] Paul readily admits his absolute dependence on God and explicitly rejects the notion that human beings can be self-sufficient: "Not that we are sufficient of ourselves so that we could consider anything as really ours; rather our sufficiency comes from God" (2 Cor. 3:5–6; note the emphatic placement of "not" [*ouch*] at the beginning of the sentence). There is no attempt by Paul to establish or protect a stable, secure self. While Christians are "at home in the body" they are "away from their home that is the Lord" (2 Cor. 5:6). Even Christ is not thought of as independent and self-sufficient. Note, for example, the thick interconnections of being in Paul's statement that Christ "died for all, so that those who live live no longer for themselves but with regard to the one who died and was raised for them" (2 Cor. 5:15). Christ's existence is "for" others; because of what he did "for" them, the others no longer live "for" themselves. Such frank admissions of mutual dependence would be scorned by the Stoics.

DESIRE, SELF-SUFFICIENCY, AND IDEOLOGY

The Stoics' rejection of the passions is based on their ideal of self-sufficiency and their belief that true well-being could be had only by exercising self-control. The passions threatened the perfect control over their bodies, and indeed, their world, for which they yearned. I would argue, moreover, that, of the passions, desire was in some ways a special threat because it was a constant signal of need—insufficiency. According to both Aristotelian and early Stoic theory, the "urge" for food and sex was placed by nature in the body to meet its "needs."[22] Desire arose from unnatural confusions surrounding those needs and urges. Desire, therefore, signifies "lack," and this was a painful confession for Greco-Roman philosophers. True nobility was self-sufficient, just like the ancient aristocratic ideal of the self-sufficient household that was capable of growing all its own food, making all its own clothes and utensils, and running its own day-to-day affairs with no interference of any kind. Like the southern American plantation owner of later times, the Greco-Roman *paterfamilias* nourished an ideal of his own private community. And his body was a microcosm of that self-sufficient community. To recognize that he needed a woman to further his line was something of a shameful surprise, but it was, after all, part of "nature." The goal was to fill this lack in such a way as to demonstrate as little lack as possible within himself. Men had many ideological stratagems for getting over what appeared to be an insurmountable lack in nature and their bodies. One example is the Aristotelian theory, eventually rejected by perhaps most doctors, that all the requisite seed for the embryo came from the man, with the woman being only the fertile field in which the important substance was planted.[23] All such theories, in any case, were attempts to minimize the experience of lack, the sign that constantly pointed to the illusion of self-sufficiency.[24]

The entire ideological complex of the self-sufficient man and the stable self is absent in Paul's writings. The reality of "lack" is recognized all through his letters: Epaphroditus supplies what the Philippians lack (Phil. 2:30); the abundance of the Corinthians supplies what other Christians lack (2 Cor. 8:15); Paul wants to visit the Thessalonians to supply what they are lacking (1 Thess. 3:10). Furthermore, Paul doubtless would have none of that "moderation" so important to the philosophers. He constantly uses language celebrating both lack and abundance, even "over-abundance."[25] The philosophical idea, for example, that too much love is a bad thing would have struck Paul, as it doubtless struck most people in that society, as ridiculous.

But not only would Paul have rejected the *ideal* of self-sufficiency; he also would have believed it absolutely impossible. For Paul, every human being receives its identity by virtue of its place, either in "this cosmos" or Christ. Christians live by the *pneuma* of Christ; non-Christians have only the *pneuma* of "this world." Furthermore, every self, even Christian ones, can be threatened by disintegration due to a variety of cosmic forces: the death-dealing of *sarx* (flesh), the pollution of *porneia*, even the poison that Christ's body becomes when eaten unworthily.[26] Moreover, however we settle the tricky question of Paul's views on predestination or free will, no one can persuasively argue that Paul would have believed possible the radical kind of free choice so necessary for Stoic doctrine and therapy.[27] Paul can speak of human beings, even Christians, as predestined by God (Rom. 9–11), as hopelessly deluded apart from God's grace and revelation (1 Cor. 2:6–16; 3:18–23), or as hindered by Satan from carrying out their wills (1 Thess. 2:18). Any part of this Pauline complex renders impossible the free will and free moral agency necessary for Stoicism. Thus both the ideal and the possibility of a stable self would be rejected by Paul as illusions.

What started out in this chapter as a comparison of beliefs about desire, sex, and marriage has become an analysis of complex ideological systems. But that is what I believe is necessary for an adequate interpretation of the ancient therapies of desire. Paul's position would doubtless have been rejected by the ancient philosophers and doctors as irrational. But for a modern scholar to be satisfied with that verdict is inadequate. Paul had very good reasons, given his own assumptions about the world and the human self, to fear sexual desire as a polluting force that threatened the health of the Christian's body and Christ's body. His insistence that desire must be excluded entirely, even within sex in marriage, was reasonable—just as reasonable, in fact, as the Stoics' radical position was within their own system, based as it was on a belief in the possibility of a stable self-sufficiency. Both systems, from different rationalities, taught that sexual desire, even within sex, must be extirpated.

One of Martha Nussbaum's goals in writing *The Therapy of Desire* was to convince modern readers, especially postreligious, liberal Americans, that ancient moral philosophy can provide a method and concepts useful for modern ethics. She finds the Stoics especially appealing, with the proviso that their insistence on complete self-sufficiency and the extirpation of desires is too radical.[28] She would take up, to some extent, the Stoic cause, and she believes that cause to be a good one as long as one adds in a bit of compassion.

I don't believe that's such a good idea, mainly because it either ignores the ancient ideological context and function of their system, or it insists, wrongly I believe, that their therapeutic system can be divorced from the negative aspects of its ideological assumptions. Although Nussbaum begins by noting that ancient philosophy must be studied with a view to society and culture, there is actually very little attention to culture in this book and none to ideology.[29] And that is its problem. In my view, the ancient aristocratic ideal of self-sufficiency was possible only within a context of slavery and exploitation. Indeed, it is hard to imagine the conditions for the rise of that ideal except in a society where a small portion of the population could mask its own great dependence on other human beings by rendering them less human. The extent to which a *paterfamilias*, the owner and head of a familial estate, could convince himself that he was or could be self-sufficient was the extent to which he could close his eyes to the thick matrices of economic and social systems on which he unavoidably depended. Self-sufficiency as an ideal requires just such ideological ignorance. The ancient philosophical therapies of desire depend on notions of self-sufficiency and fear of lack; the therapies don't make sense without such presupposed values. And these values are anything but democratic and egalitarian. Of course, from a Christian point of view, and I think this is not just Paul's view, self-sufficiency is neither possible nor desirable. I also find it hard to imagine how a philosopher these days can so confidently *assume* the existence of a stable, integrated self capable of exercising unproblematic free moral agency given current biomedical and biochemical research, genetic engineering, poststructuralist psychological theories, philosophies of the mind based on artificial intelligence, and studies showing the disintegration of the self through pain and torture.[30]

In the end, I believe the myth of self-sufficiency is especially dangerous for Americans, with our tendency to splendid isolation and self-centeredness and our uncanny ability to fail to notice our domination of and dependence on other countries and our own lower class. Americans, "liberal" and "conservative" alike, are already far too enamored of the myth that social problems can be solved by individualism and volunteerism. I understand why a liberal democratic American philosopher like Nussbaum would find "self-sufficiency" an appealing goal. But I also believe that it plays into the worst aspects of modernist individualism, capitalist ideology, and American lies about the self-saving self.

Is Paul's account of desire, sex, and marriage any better? Not for me, thanks. Given our own probably unshakeable modern assumptions about love, sex, romance, and desire, we perhaps could never wholeheartedly accept the possibility, much less the desirability, of sex without desire. It is significant that no modern Christian church has attempted even to recognize, let alone appropriate, Paul's ethics of sexuality here. And I would not advocate that it do so. Both Nussbaum's advocacy of ancient philosophy and some Christians' belief that our sexual ethics should come rather simplistically "from the Bible" are just different forms of Classicism, which in my view is nostalgic and self-deluding.[31] I do not understand why modern persons would want to ground their own therapies of desire on either the ancient philosophers or Paul. I suppose I'm too much a postmodernist to find real Classicism alluring, whether in art, architecture, or morality.

Chapter 6

The Queer History of Galatians 3:28

"No Male and Female"

Biblical scholarship has too often clothed itself in a rhetoric of transparency and innocence. It portrays its method as one of natural disinterestedness; it covers its contingency. Biblical scholars freely use words like "clearly," "obviously," "naturally." They love to appeal to "common sense," that most unhistorical of concepts.[1] One of the most valuable tools for demythologizing historical criticism is the historical analysis of it. Ironically, historicizing the supposedly transparent interpretations of historical critics enables us to see through the mystification of the method and recognize its conceits. Also ironically, it may make us better historical critics—or at least help us better understand what the role of history should be in our readings of texts, including Christian readings of Scripture.

A good test case for the value of historicizing biblical interpretation is the treatment of Galatians 3:28. The interpretation of the verse has shifted through the ages, reflecting changing social situations and norms and the shifting interests of interpreters from the ancient period to the modern and postmodern. And though the interpretation of the Jew/Gentile and slave/free dualisms are today rather noncontroversial, the interpretation of the clause "no male and female" is very much a bone of contention, both in churches and the academy. For the purposes of this essay I concentrate on the phrase "no male and female" and its interpretation with regard to gender and sex.

THE "MAINSTREAM" CONSENSUS

Perhaps the majority of Christians in the world, even today, believe that women *should* occupy inferior positions in church and society. And it may be the case that the majority of Christians even in North America and Europe believe that Galatians does not mandate the complete equality of power and function between women and men in society, church, and home. But certainly the most common position in the dominant intellectual subculture within Christianity, whether of the "mainline" Protestant churches or the more prestigious educational institutions, holds that women and men should have completely equal access to power and leadership roles throughout society, and Galatians 3:28 is taken as a foundational text for advocating such equality. In fact, the verse is read as addressing the issue of gender by recognizing the reality of a dimorphic, dualistic, male-female gender construction and advocating equality between the two sides of the dualism.

One of the most influential interpretations of Galatians 3:28 along these lines was Krister Stendahl's study *The Bible and the Role of Women*, published in English in 1966 but springing from the debate about the ordination of women in Sweden in the 1950s. Stendahl argued that the "in Christ" of Galatians 3:28 should "manifest itself in the social dimensions of the church."[2] The New Testament contains "elements, glimpses which point beyond and even 'against' the prevailing view and practice of the New Testament church," and Galatians 3:28 constitutes a "breakthrough" in early Christianity's treatment of women (32–35). *The Bible and the Role of Women* had a great impact and has been cited repeatedly in scholarship on Galatians 3:28 throughout the 1970s, 1980s, and 1990s. It had much to do with placing Paul's term "no male and female" at the center of the debate, even to the extent that scholars such as Mary Hayter or Stanley Porter in the late 1980s could note that the verse had become the *locus classicus* of the debate about gender equality.[3]

The widely influential scholarship of Elisabeth Schüssler Fiorenza probably also had something to do with the popularity of the egalitarian reading. The Scripture index of her book *In Memory of Her* lists thirteen references to Galatians 3:28, far more than for any other scriptural reference, and one of those references includes all of chapter 6 (205–36). In this book, Schüssler Fiorenza builds on previous work of her own as well as the egalitarian arguments advanced by Stendahl, Robin Scroggs, Robert Jewett, and others, but her treatment is so thorough and powerfully argued that it has been cited by many subsequent treatments as most persuasively making the egalitarian-liberationist case for pre-Pauline Christianity and Galatians. Indeed, for Schüssler Fiorenza, "equality" is the basic issue addressed by Paul's "no male and female," and that equality must be taken as pertaining not just to justification or salvation but to social and ecclesial roles.[4]

Scholars who wished to champion an egalitarian reading of Galatians 3:28 recognized that their reading posed problems, since other statements by Paul intimated that he was not such a gender egalitarian after all. Even if one dismissed 1 Corinthians 14:34–35 as an interpolation (verses in which "Paul" insists that women must keep silence in the Christian assembly and even says explicitly that they are to be "subordinate": *hypotassesthôsan*), there still remains 1 Corinthians 11, where Paul insists that women cover their heads when praying and prophesying in the assembly because the man is the head of the woman as Christ is the head of man and God is the head of Christ. Even taking the problematic term "head" out of the picture, it was very hard to avoid a hierarchical reading of this passage once it was admitted that, for Paul, there is a hierarchical relationship between Christ and man and between God and Christ. Hierarchy could hardly be denied, then, in the third pair: man and woman.

Scholars have tried all sorts of hermeneutical maneuvers to circumvent the problem. Sometimes they admit that Paul might not be consistent, that although he cherished an "ideal" of gender equality, his views were also constrained by his time and place, and that he simply did not consistently carry through the implications of his egalitarian vision expressed in Galatians 3:28. Or sometimes 1 Corinthians 11 and other seemingly hierarchical Pauline texts are reinterpreted so that they don't seem so hierarchical after all. What is consistent in all these interpretations, however, is their acceptance of the notion that Paul's "no male and female" does constitute a statement about equality between men and women, certainly "in Christ" and at least potentially in society as well.[5]

THE TRADITIONAL HIERARCHICAL READING

The liberal-egalitarian interpretation was a reaction to an older reading of the verse that held sway especially throughout the late nineteenth century. Up until the 1970s, the majority of scholars insisted that the passage taught the equality of men and women "in Christ" (*coram Deo*, "in the presence of God"). But they then usually denied that this mandated or even allowed complete equality for women in society, the church, and the home.

First, we should note that an emphasis on *equality* creeps into the discussions only gradually. Earlier treatments of the issue use language less about equality than *difference* or *distinction* between the sexes. (As I will point out in a moment, this has more in common with ancient readings of the verse than those of the late twentieth century.) G. G. Findlay in 1893, for example, says that the verse teaches that in baptism "distinctions of race, or rank, even that of sex" are forgotten. He then warns, "Paul, to be sure, does not mean that these differences have ceased to exist. He fully recognizes them; and indeed insists strongly on the proprieties of sex, and on the duties of civil station."[6] Another commentary on Galatians, whose fourth edition was published the same year, 1893, takes much the same line but extends the sexual distinction even further, suggesting that sexual difference will be part of human identity even into eternity. Its author, Joseph Agar Beet, writes, "Only to sex as affecting our relation to Christ does this apply. It therefore does not absolutely deny the distinction of sex in man's future glory. And, that it belongs to man's original constitution, suggests strongly that even sex will share that glory. . . . Paul's prohibition . . . to women to speak in the church proves that in this relation also, in his view, the distinction of sex continues."[7]

Two things should be noted about these, quite typical, readings. In the first place, they make the salient issue not so explicitly *equality* as *distinction*, although one can hear concerns about equal rights in the background. In the second place, the authors insist on emphasizing Paul's words "in Christ" to argue that Paul had no intention of redefining male and female roles in society. The verse teaches the indifference of sexual distinction for justification or salvation. Other interpreters saw it as providing an ideal vision of a universal humanity that transcended sexual difference. They did *not* see it, though, as advocating or allowing the disruption or redefinition of sexual difference in society.

In the twentieth century, language about *equality* becomes more explicit and more common—in fact, ubiquitous—in interpretations of the verse. In the 1930s, for example, George Duncan raises the theme of "equality" but emphasizes the phrase "in Christ." There is no attempt here to read the verse as favoring women's social equality, though equality is recognized as an issue.[8] In 1969, Donald Guthrie's commentary on Galatians addressed the problem directly. He did take the references in Galatians 3:28 to Jews, Greeks, slave, and free to apply to mid-twentieth-century race relations. According to Guthrie, the verse teaches the abolition of all racial distinctions and social inequities. But when Guthrie considered the male-female pair, he equivocated: "There is no doubt that few outside the Christian Church in Paul's day would have maintained any form of equality of the sexes. The apostle himself drew some distinctions between the sexes as far as their functions within the Church were concerned, but no distinctions over their position in Christ."[9] Here the full complement of distinction and equality is present, along with the traditional conservative insistence that any equality or absence of distinction holds true only "in Christ," not in society.[10]

Of course, there were voices to the contrary. In fact, I would argue that these scholarly interpretations—which represent the "mainstream" of their time—were themselves a reaction to the feminist movements of the nineteenth century. *The Woman's Bible*, for example, certainly took Galatians 3:28 as a "declaration of the equality of the sexes."[11] Even established male scholars could take up the egalitarian torch. William Ramsay, for example, in 1899, comes across as quite progressive. He notes that most commentators are more willing to entertain the idea of the abolition of race and status differences than that between the sexes. And he admits that elsewhere (notably 1 Corinthians 11) Paul backs off giving women complete equality in the church. But he argues that 1 Corinthians 11 represents a special situation, and he credits Paul with a sort of misty "prevision" of an ultimate rise in women's status that would place them on completely equal footing with men throughout society.[12] Compared to most of his male contemporaries, therefore, Ramsay looks like a feminist and no doubt was influenced by the nineteenth-century women's movement. But the majority interpretation of Galatians 3:28 insisted that Paul had never intended to abolish gender distinction entirely or to promote full equality for women in society, church, or home.

In fact, this older, antiliberationist reading has continued to find advocates to this day. One of the locations where the liveliest debate over Galatians 3:28 is currently taking place is among self-described "evangelical" Christian scholars. A taxonomy of positions has been proposed by some: (1) the nonevangelical egalitarian position, which I have labeled as the liberal-egalitarianism of the "mainstream," (2) the evangelical egalitarian position, and (3) the hierarchical position.[13] Many people who call themselves "evangelical" now support full equality of status and function for women in leadership roles, even in the church and home, and they often base their arguments on Galatians 3:28.

Judith Gundry-Volf, for example, accepts the thesis of feminists such as Elisabeth Schüssler Fiorenza that the baptismal formula "no male and female" "fueled social and gender emancipation in early Christianity."[14] According to Gundry-Volf, 1 Corinthians 7 teaches equality between husband and wife. And Galatians 3:28 "negates sexual differentiation *as a basis for a hierarchical and oppressive role differentiation*" (emphasis mine, 116). Note the qualifier: the verse is taken *not* as "negating sexual differentiation" entirely, only negating it "as a basis for a hierarchical and oppressive role differentiation." Indeed, as we will see, it is important for the egalitarian interpretation to retain sexual difference while promoting sexual equality. And that is what Gundry-Volf takes Paul to do.[15]

Evangelical theologian Miroslav Volf bases an entire theological-ethical argument on this conjunction of equality and gender distinction as read from Galatians 3:28 and "natural" sexual dimorphism. According to Volf, "men and women continue to exist in a duality as male and female through all the changes of their gender identity precisely because of the stability of their sexed bodies." Galatians 3:28, Volf writes, "entails no eschatological denial of gender dimorphism. What has been erased in Christ is not the sexed body [understood, it should be noted, as a dichotomy], but some important culturally coded norms attached to sexed bodies (such as the obligation to marry and procreate and the prohibition of women from performing certain functions in the church)."[16]

These evangelical egalitarian readings have been vigorously countered by other evangelical scholars. Several have pointed out (quite rightly) that the egalitarian interpretation is recent and overturns centuries of Christian interpretation. They attribute the revisionist interpretation to twentieth-century ideology and "political correctness."[17] Robert Yarbrough, an evangelical of the more conservative variety, insists that the egalitarian reading of Galatians 3:28 was "virtually unheard of in technical exegesis prior to the latter half of the twentieth century," though he laments that it is "now widespread even in evangelical circles." He harkens back to the more traditional reading, insisting that the verse teaches "freedom, emancipation, liberty, whatever it be called, only in Christ." Notably, he also insists that the verse does *not* mean the abolition of sexual difference: "each of us is essentially human *qua* male or human *qua* female."[18] John Jefferson Davis also chides his fellow evangelicals for being swept up in the tide of "the ideals of the Enlightenment of the eighteenth century" in their reading of Galatians 3:28. The subordination of women, he insists, is inscribed in nature and supported by several New Testament passages.[19]

Of course, even the more conservative evangelicals want to affirm *some* sort of equality for women, which leads them into exegetical and philosophical nuances and complications that may appear inscrutable to many of us. Grant R. Osborne, for instance, offers this explanation: "In the body of Christ there is ontological equality and functional hierarchy. As persons, husband and wife as well as Jew and Greek or slave and free are equal—a partnership. Neither side is superior, nor is one more important than the other. At the same time there is a functional difference in the partnership, and this role is built into the hierarchical framework. The wife is equal to the husband in the marriage *relationship*, but must subject herself to him in her marital *role*" (my emphasis).[20] Perhaps this is a sort of "equality" that many of us could not recognize as such, but my point here is that even within evangelical circles, Galatians 3:28 is taken to refer to equality; the debate is over what spheres of life are to embody this equality and how. Moreover, I would point out that the more conservative exegetes have a historically accurate point: the current egalitarian reading is recent and reflects the politics and ideology of modern democraticism and feminism. I imagine that the voices here are so shrill, in part, because, in spite of being on the side of history and tradition, such evangelicals sense that they are fighting a losing battle.

We should step back a bit and note explicitly what the issues are in this debate. Throughout the discussion certain themes recur: equality, reciprocity, the mutual interdependence of the sexes. And does Galatians 3:28 refer to Christian reality "in Christ" only (whatever that would mean), or should it be used to advocate equality and mutuality also in church and home, and throughout society? What is assumed by all sides of the debate, as I have thus far presented it, is the reality of the sexual and gender distinction itself. A dichotomy of male/female—as a dichotomy and not just as a polarity—is maintained.[21] Sometimes this dichotomy is assumed; at other times it is explicitly advocated; but it is everywhere maintained. The phrase "no male and female" is read as recognizing, not negating, the male-female dichotomy in nature or creation or human experience. The verse is taken to mean that the dichotomy doesn't matter with regard to salvation or justification, or that the relation of male and female should be one of equality and reciprocity. The dichotomy itself, however, is not disrupted or dispensed with, at least not in our current human experiences and social interactions.

THE "THIRD WAVE" CHALLENGE

In opposition to this conservative *and* mainstream consensus about the verse's meaning has arisen a growing body of scholarship that argues that Galatians 3:28

is not about equality at all. These arguments usually take their lead from Wayne Meeks's seminal article "The Image of the Androgyne," in which Meeks argued, in 1974, that Galatians 3:28 alluded to a baptismal formula in which certain conflictual dichotomies of human existence were said to be overcome in an eschatological unity. The aboriginal human being had been a unified being, only later experiencing the fissures of ethnicity, status, and sex. The original Adam had been an androgyne, and the splitting of that androgynous being into male and female halves would be overcome in the salvation of the end time. In the resurrection, people would be like the angels, neither marrying nor given in marriage (Matt. 22:30; Mark 12:25; Luke 20:35). This recovery of the unity of androgyny is prefigured in Christian baptism, so that Paul can say that "in Christ" there is no male and female, but rather the restoration of the original, androgynous human being.

At the time, Meeks noted that ancient androgyny does not always imply male-female equality. Usually, in order to be "saved" the woman actually is said to become male, implying the continued inferiority of femaleness in relation to maleness. But Meeks did believe that these ideas of androgyny ended up promoting equality between women and men in Paul's churches. As he wrote then, "Paul accepts and even insists upon the equality of role of man and woman in this community which is formed already by the Spirit that belongs to the end of days."[22]

Meeks's article has been enormously influential, but also challenged, and his research on androgyny has been significantly extended. Building on and responding to his insights, scholars such as Ingvild Saelid Gilhus and Dennis MacDonald showed that there is no evidence that androgyny in the ancient world implied equality between male and female.[23] When women experience salvific gender change, they are not said to add male characteristics to their female nature, retaining male and female aspects; rather, they are usually said to "become male." In the *Gospel of Thomas* (logion 114), as Meeks himself had noted, Jesus does not say that Mary will be saved as a male-female or a female-male, but that he will "make her male." In the second-century *Acts of Paul and Thecla*, Thecla is not precisely identified as a man, but when she, at the end of the story, commissions herself to be, practically, an apostle, she is said to "sew her mantle into a cloak after the fashion of men."

In fact, the word "androgyny" can be misleading when applied to ancient ideas. We moderns usually take androgyny to mean the combination of masculine and feminine in relatively equal parts, in one being. An "androgynous" person is one whose gender identity is ambiguous because s/he possesses both male and female traits or characteristics, or not enough of one or the other to allow confident categorization.[24] Usually, androgyny in modern discourse means both feminine and masculine, or it refers to someone who looks like neither a man nor a woman, but because s/he is to some extent both.

Recent gender studies show that this was not generally the case in the ancient world. Thomas Laqueur, in his book *Making Sex*, suggests that the differences between modern and ancient understandings are due to radically different models of the human body and sexual dimorphism.[25] According to Laqueur, the modern body is a two-sexed body: male and female are taken to be different, and relatively equal, sides of a dichotomy. The ancient body, on the other hand, was a "one-sex" body: a hierarchical spectrum or continuum along which all human bodies could be placed. All humans had both male and female aspects to them, and their bodies could, and did, shift upward and downward on the continuum, depending on how much maleness (strength, heat, dryness, compactness) or femaleness (weakness, cold, moisture, or porosity) their bodies contained at any particular time. In this system, any change that would be construed as salvific must be understood as a movement higher on the spectral hierarchy. Thus, women may experience salvation as a movement upward into masculinity, but men who experience a movement downward into femininity (and both kinds of movement are noted in ancient texts) are not understood by that to experience an improvement in state or status. What we see as soteriological androgyny in ancient texts is only misleadingly called "androgyny," that is, male combined with female. It is actually the subsuming of the weaker female into the stronger male, the masculinization of the female body, the supplying of male "presence" (heat, for instance) for the former experience of female "absence" (cold, understood as a lack of fire). In this system, which is the overwhelmingly predominant kind of "androgyny" in the ancient world, it would be a mistake to portray androgyny as implying any equality at all between male and female.[26] Ancient "androgyny"—if we may still use that problematic term with something like scare quotes around it—*embodies* the unequal hierarchy of male over female; it does not dispense with it or overcome it.[27]

Building on insights such as these, more recent—and perhaps more radical—feminist scholars have argued that there is simply no compelling reason to take Paul's phrase "no male and female" as suggesting equality at all. Kari Vogt, for example, warns against reading ancient texts as advocating what we would take as egalitarian androgyny. She insists that we are dealing instead with a "sex change metaphor." The "becoming male" of early Christian texts is precisely that: sex change, "transgendering," not "androgyny."[28] Lone Fatum challenges all sorts of liberal, feminist, and egalitarian readings of Galatians 3:28. She insists that "no male and female," understood in its ancient context, does not promote equality between retained sexual differences; it rather gets rid of sexual difference entirely and substitutes for a hierarchical spread of male-female an asexual unity of completed male. As she says, "Male and Female gender are both annulled as a sexual duality in favor of male/man as an entity of asexuality. . . . Neither text nor context allow[s] us to jump to conclusions from v. 28c and speak of the equal rights of Christian women in freedom and solidarity with Christian men in the fellowship of the congregation."[29] For Paul, "sexual liberation is in fact liberation from sexuality" (76). Fatum concludes that Galatians 3:28 "does not allow Christian women any opportunity of being affirmed as women, but fixes them in a state of asexuality dependent on the androcentric concept of human normality" (79). Ironically, Fatum and more radical feminist scholars like herself read Galatians 3:28 much like the most conservative evangelical scholars, at least as far as the implications of the verse for social equality go. Paul's "no male and female," read historically, does not promote social equality or the disruption of hierarchy. Fatum differs from them, importantly, in her insistence that the verse implies a radical annulment of sexuality itself and that Paul's view was that the female would actually have to become male. She reads the verse as destroying sexual difference and saying nothing about equality. The conservative evangelicals read it as retaining sexual difference and limiting equality to the sphere of justification "in Christ."

ANCIENT CHRISTIAN READINGS

A telling piece of evidence that Fatum is on target is the fact that most of the ancient Christian authors (themselves embedded in ancient notions of gender) read Galatians 3:28 the same way.[30] The *Acts of Thomas*, for instance, contains what is probably an allusion to the verse when it has its heroine meditate on the glories of being in the presence of Jesus. Where Jesus is, "there is neither day and night, nor light and darkness, nor good and evil, nor poor and rich, male and female, no free and slave, no proud that subdues the humble" (129). Although a few of these pairs could be construed as hierarchical dualities whose hierarchy is being challenged (rich/poor, free/slave, proud/humble) others cannot. The author is certainly not, for example, equating good and evil. The vision of the beatific state, in other words, is not one that retains good and evil, now in a relationship of equality. The emphasis is on dispensing with the divisions themselves, not equating the two sides. This reflects a pervasive ancient ideology that took unity to mean peace, wholeness, and perfection, and that understood conflict, pain, and imperfection as the necessary result of division and difference. Thus, an early Hippocratic writer, in a passage admittedly several centuries prior to our text but that, I would argue, partakes of the same ideological common sense, argues that the body must be composed of different entities, in this case, different humors that comprise different combinations of the different elements of the universe. Otherwise disease would not be possible. If the body were of completely unified substance, it would not experience the conflict and change that constitute disease.[31] Correspondingly, the quotation from the *Acts of Thomas* envisions a beatific state in which societal and corporeal divisions will be overcome in perfect unity.

John Chrysostom, in his several comments on Galatians 3:28, reflects the same ideological assumptions. He is able at times to allude to Paul's "no male and female" to argue that all people are judged on the basis of their deeds before God, not on the basis of social distinction; men and women are both learners in the "philosophy" of Christianity (*Homily 5 on Acts*). And Paul's mention of noble women as his coworkers in Romans 16 proves that their sex was no hindrance to the attainment of virtue, which Chrysostom backs up by quoting Galatians 3:28 (*Homily 30 on Romans*). But Chrysostom is careful to point out that Paul does uphold the traditional hierarchy of husband over wife, man over woman (*Homily*

19 on 1 Corinthians). Most often, Galatians 3:28 is not taken as speaking to the status of women; it rather refers to the abolition of sexual distinction entirely. Commenting on the passage in Acts 1:16, which relates that men and women together awaited the Spirit in the upper room, Chrysostom writes that the sexes could then be together without fear of anything untoward occurring because they were experiencing "the angelic condition," "no male and female." He continues in a tone intended to shame his congregation: "I wish the churches were that way now! No one there had his mind full of worldly concerns. No one was worried about his household!" (*Homily 3 on Acts*). In a sermon on Matthew, Chrysostom uses the same shaming device: in the "good old days" of the church's beginnings there was "no male and female," so there was no need to separate men from women in the assembly. But those innocent days of asexuality are, lamentably for Chrysostom, long gone (*Homily 73.3 on Matthew*). Galatians 3:28 is taken as historical proof that the earliest Christians had lacked sexual desire entirely, not that men and women had been equal.

Most remarkable from our modern point of view are Chrysostom's comments on the baptismal language of Colossians 2, in which he again quotes Galatians 3:28. He says that the state immediately after baptism foreshadows the perfected heavenly state. "Immediately you take into yourself the Lord himself, you are mingled with his body, you are intermixed with that Body that lies above, where the devil cannot approach. No woman is there for him to approach and deceive as the weaker; for it is said, 'There is no female, no male'" (*Homily 6 on Colossians*). A few lines later, he alludes to the division of the sexes portrayed in Genesis, but by denying its ultimate reality: "No more shall woman be formed from your side, but we all are one from the side of Christ." For Chrysostom, Galatians 3:28 teaches the obsolescence of the female, not its elevation. The message is unity in masculinity, not equality between the sexes.[32]

The dominance of this ascetic, asexual reading of Galatians among ancient authors can be discerned even when it is being rejected. Clement of Alexandria, for example, must oppose this sort of reading in his condemnation of the asceticism of Julius Cassianus, a second-century Christian writer. Cassianus had argued that the corporeal differences between men and women should not be used to defend the goodness of sex, supporting his argument with a quotation from a noncanonical Gospel: "When Salome asked when she would know the answer to her question, the Lord replied, 'When you trample underfoot the covering of shame, and when the two become one and the male is one with the female, and there is no more male and female.'"[33]

Clement rejects Cassianus's interpretation, first by pointing out that the quotation is not from "our four traditional Gospels," but from the unacceptable *Gospel According to the Egyptians*. He then offers a Platonizing interpretation of Paul's slogan in which Paul's "male" is taken as referring to that part of the human soul from which impulse or temper arises and "female" to that part of the soul where "desire" resides. When these lower parts of the Platonic soul are submitted to the rational part, then soul and spirit are united in submission to the Word.

"The soul stands aside from the mere appearance of shape whereby male is distinguished from female and is transformed into unity, being neither male nor female." Note that Julius Cassianus was advocating what had probably become the dominant interpretation of Galatians 3:28: that it taught the abolition of sexual distinction and therefore advocated ascetic asexuality. In order to oppose that powerful reading and retain *some* respectability for sex, Clement submits Galatians 3:28 to Platonic allegorizing. Nonetheless, Clement's reading *also* assumes the abolition of sexual difference and can in no way be read as raising the status of the female. Indeed, for Clement the female represents the lowest part of the soul, desire, which must be swallowed up in the final triumph of the rational logos.

HISTORICAL SHIFTS AND IDEOLOGICAL CONTEXTS

I have wandered through several centuries, so let me summarize my argument. I believe that the recent, more radical feminist reading of Galatians 3:28 is the better historical interpretation (that is, the best reading on the basis of common historical-critical categories and criteria). We have little evidence that in Paul's day it would have occurred to anyone to take his slogan "no male and female" as implying equality between male and female or men and women. Equality was not the issue; division was. The baptismal formula reflected, I believe, a quite pervasive notion that the aboriginal human being was not divided into male and female; and it reflected a common Christian belief that the human being of the resurrection would also overcome the male-female division of current human experience. But this would *not* be a state in which male and female remained distinct but equal; rather the lower female aspects of all human beings would be subsumed into the superior, perfected, and therefore (as it seems to us) male body. This means, though, that "no male and female" promises the abolition of dimorphic sexuality, not sexual equality.

This also makes more sense of Paul's thought than do both the traditional, conservative readings and the currently dominant liberationist-egalitarian reading. Paul does not contradict himself; there is no "tension" in his writings about gender. Everything he says about men and women can be understood as reasonably consistent. He does believe that women may hold leadership roles in churches. He does believe, I think, that they may pray, prophesy, and speak in the assemblies. (I do take 1 Cor. 14:34–35 as a non-Pauline interpolation, but even if it is authentic there are other ways to interpret it so that it does not contradict indications elsewhere that women were allowed to speak in Pauline churches.)[34] Paul believes that there is a mutuality of need between men and women (1 Corinthians 11), but this does not necessitate equality.[35] After all, ancient political theory held that masters needed slaves and slaves needed masters, that the rich needed the poor and the poor needed the rich. But ancient theorists did not think this made all these people equal to one another.[36] And Paul can teach that wives may demand the same sexual accessibility of their husbands as their husbands demand of them (1 Corinthians 7); but this Pauline ethic can still easily be understood within an assumption of gender hierarchy and not as necessarily disrupting it. All interpretations that have taken Paul as advocating gender equality have used Galatians 3:28 as their main support. But it is misleading, from a historical point of view, to read Galatians 3:28 as addressing equality.

The shifts in the interpretation of this verse are significant. It was taken throughout the ancient church as referring not to sexual equality, but to the abolition of the sexes, to ascetic asexuality. It was read not as teaching equality between men and women but the overcoming of division in unity. In the nineteenth and early twentieth centuries—largely, I suggest, in response to "first wave" feminism—the verse was taken as having something to do with women's roles in society. The majority interpretation saw it as teaching equality, perhaps, but only "in Christ," not in society, the church, or the home. In the 1970s, corresponding to "second wave" feminism, the tide began turning, and Paul's "no male and female" was increasingly read as a foundation for gender equality, this time both "in Christ" and throughout society. But sexual difference was retained.[37]

Recently, the liberal-egalitarian reading has been strongly challenged by a more radical view. It is more radical in the first place because it challenges the very "reality" of the modern dimorphic, dualistic, and I would say heterosexist, construction of sexuality: the very idea that "sexuality" *means* a dichotomy of and reciprocity between male and female. It is more radical, in the second place, because it sees no need to base our evaluations of our own sexualities, our political programs, our theology, or our ethics on a historically constructed Pauline theology. I do not think it accidental that the invention of this more recent reading strategy coincides with what some people have labeled "third wave" feminism.[38] This reading of Paul's language has arisen in no more of a social or ideological vacuum than any of the others, just in a *different* social and ideological context.

It should be clear, therefore, that I am not suggesting that we will end up with the "true," "only," or "best" reading of the text by constructing the most "historical" reading of the text. There is no necessary reason why the Christian interpretation of Galatians 3:28 should be ruled by the norms of historical criticism.[39] I have used my own historical readings to disrupt what I perceive as a current "common sense" of the text, and indeed one that portrays itself as the correct historical exegesis. But actually, I see no compelling *theological* reason to allow Christian readings to be constrained or controlled by historical criticism, even if people wish, for whatever purpose, to be informed by it or to use it for their own ends.

POSTMODERN QUEER READINGS

Once we have freed ourselves from the hegemony of historical criticism, what might we do with this text? First, I will point out that the normal translation is rather sneaky. Usually, Paul's "no male and female" is translated as "*neither* male *nor* female." But if we translate the Greek more literally, we open the door for more possibilities. I have argued, for instance, that the historically constructed meaning would be that there is "no male and *female*" because, in ancient understandings, there was in Christ only male. The inferior female has been swallowed up into the eschatologically perfected male form. But we might just reverse that tendency and say that the text teaches that there is no *male* and female in Christ because the male is now *female*. In this case, we depart from the prejudice of the ancients and argue that the masculine side is what needs to be taken up into the feminine: there is no "*male* and female" because we've all become queens—or divas.

Or we could get rid of the "male and female" by saying that it is the "and" that is the problem. There is "no male and female" because in Christ everyone is both: masculifeminine or feminimascupersons. In the historical sense, this would have been true because the imperfect female was subsumed into the perfect male. But, as I've already hinted, we might imagine a sense that would retain both sides and force each to share in the essence of the other. The male would be the yin of the female yang, in a symbiosis in which neither side had any reality or meaning apart from the equal, complementary play of the other. No person could be masculine without becoming fully feminine, and no person could be feminine without also at the same time becoming fully masculine. In ethical-prescriptive terms, this would be interpreted as meaning that all femmes must become as butch as possible, and all butches must work their hardest to become flaming queens. Everyone must take the macho, made-up, cross-dressing basketball star or actor as the Christian role model—or the hyperfeminine drag queen fashion model, or the gentlemanly butch lesbian country singer. All sports stars, entertainers, and Christian saints must get their credentials by performing very good and convincing drag. In this case, the dualism is retained, but the dichotomy is destroyed.

Better yet, we could dispense with the dichotomy, the dualism, the dimorphism entirely. We admit the queer observation that gender is multiplex, not duplex. In the words of the editors of the feminist book *Third Wave Agenda*, "girls who want to be boys, boys who want to be girls, boys and girls who insist they are both, whites who want to be black, blacks who want to or refuse to be white, people who *are* white *and* black, gay *and* straight, masculine *and* feminine, or who are finding ways to be and name none of the above."[40] Once we destabilize the duality, all sorts of new ways of being human, not just two and not just combinations of two, may be invented. The gender made possible by the new creation in Christ opens as yet unknowable ways of gendering human experience, combinations of which we cannot foresee as long as we retain the dualistic male-female limitation. In this case, Christians could be gendered in many different ways. I am not saying that this is the "historical-critical" meaning of the text. I am saying that it is no *more* "unhistorical" or "anachronistic" than the overwhelmingly dominant interpretations current today. And I am also saying that it is just as supportable by appeals to "the text itself."

In any case, we should finally admit how ironic it is that the verse has been read as advocating equality between the sexes while at the same time maintaining the "naturalness" of the reality, distinction, and reciprocity of the two sexes.

It would seem that the phrase would either have to get rid of the two sexes themselves, or collapse one into the other. The force of the phrase should be to challenge heterosexuality itself and entire. That the phrase has been used to maintain that heterosexual dichotomy and mutuality and then to support "equality" between them is certainly notable. In most modern assumptions, one must be *either* male *or* female. A Christian cannot be both. A Christian cannot be neither. Indeed, if a human body is born in a confused state, it must be surgically corrected to fit the male/female dichotomy.[41] And any teenage Christian who is confused about which side of the dichotomy to fall on must be coerced onto one or the other side, by means of surgery or shock treatment if necessary. No Christian is allowed to refuse to align him/her/self on either both or neither of the two mutually exclusive sides of the dichotomy. Is this not a bizarre interpretation of a verse that *rejects* the "male and female" dichotomy? I suggest that we'd be better off recognizing just how queer a text Galatians 3:28 is. And that we should use its queerness to help us get along with the task of queering our Christian selves.

Chapter 7

Sex and the Single Savior

Jesus has been a figure of ambiguous sexuality. The vast majority of books about him have simply not raised the question of his sexuality. Was he married? Was he either accidentally or intentionally celibate? If he wasn't married, does that mean that he never experienced sexual intercourse? Did he experience sexual desires? If not, why not? If so, of what sort? Perhaps our traditions about Jesus include no reference to a wife or girlfriend because he simply was not attracted to women. Perhaps he found men sexually attractive. And of course I can't stop raising such questions without raising the question, Should we raise such questions?

Actually, I am less interested in Jesus' sexuality than in questions about whether or not that is a legitimate question and in how answers to such questions should be attempted. Is it illegitimate to raise questions about Jesus' sexual desires and activities? Some might argue that even to raise the question of Jesus' sexuality is to introduce anachronism. But who says anachronism is wrong? Why? Only if one is "playing by the rules" of modern historical criticism can anachronism even be raised as a delegitimating factor. Why should a modern person, a modern Christian or non-Christian, be worried about anachronism?

Once we have decided we are content that questions about Jesus' sexuality or singleness are admissible questions, though, we then must confront the problem of how to go about answering the questions. Most people have come to believe modern scholars, who mostly assume (they don't argue for it) that any possible right answers to questions about Jesus' sexuality will have to be settled by careful historical research. One of the purposes of this chapter is to challenge that assumption. I will pay attention to historical criticism, but only to situate it among several different interpretive methods. I will also attempt to highlight the weaknesses of historical criticism even when it is allowed to play by its own rules. I will show for one thing that history can give us no secure answer to the question of Jesus' singleness and sexuality. But I will also show that even the answers it can give are only the products of its imagination and have no right to delegitimate the answers supplied by other interpretive methods.

Though the number of possible interpretive methods that could theoretically be applied to my question is infinite, I will concentrate on just four: the popular imagination, the historical imagination, the patristic imagination, and the gay imagination. I want to make it quite clear that I privilege *none* of these imaginations. In fact, one of my most important points is that all of them *are* "imaginations" that contemplate the singleness of Jesus in different ways, applying different criteria as to what will constitute a suitable answer within their own interpretive contexts. What I want to argue is that the day of the hegemony of historical criticism should be over. I am assuming for the most part a Christian interest in Jesus. And I am urging scholars to entertain the possibility—quite seriously—that several different ways of reading the Bible should be learned, taught, and practiced in the contemporary church and academy.

THE POPULAR IMAGINATION

First, the "popular imagination." The lack of clarity in Christian sources about Jesus' sexuality has left all sorts of avenues open for speculation in popular imagination. The Jesus of the novel and film *The Last Temptation of Christ*, to take just one example, is famously conflicted about sex and desire.[1] Not that he experiences much conflict about sexual orientation. He's fairly certain that he wants Mary and not Judas or the boys. *The Last Temptation* refers to Jesus' desire to live a completely "normal" life of heterosexual fulfillment and family, if not with Mary alone, perhaps with more than one woman and several children. The struggle of Jesus here is against the very oddness or singularity to which he feels himself called. The premise of both the book and the film is that any departure from heterosexual coupling is abnormal. Jesus is queer only in that he feels that he must resist those very normal desires, and in the fact that he does indeed in the end resist them, as he must in order to become our Savior.

The huge popularity of the more recent novel by Dan Brown, *The Da Vinci Code*, adequately testifies to the hunger of the popular imagination for a rigorously heterosexual Jesus. As is thoroughly well known by now, the novel portrays a conspiracy to keep secret the "historical fact" that Jesus and Mary Magdalene were sexually involved and produced offspring. Many people may have been offended by the notion, though it seems that many more have been intrigued and titillated. I'm sure many other New Testament scholars, as I have, have been inundated by questioners eager to have the novel's "historical facts" confirmed. *The Da Vinci Code* is so captured by heterosexual normativity that it even turns the male "Beloved Disciple" of the Fourth Gospel into a female Mary. The Jesus who would be acceptable to most modern Americans, of course, may indeed have been intimate with a disciple who *appeared* to be male, as long as he/she is "truly" a woman.[2]

For alternatives to the heterosexual normativity of *The Last Temptation*, *The Da Vinci Code*, or any of a number of other popular imaginations about Jesus, we may point to a few recent depictions, mainly in theatrical plays, in which Jesus is shockingly gay—shocking, that is, if we are to believe the tone of newspaper reports and protesters that often accompany the openings of such plays.[3]

But even in the popular imagination Jesus' sexuality is seldom unambiguous. Take *Jesus Christ Superstar*.[4] Here we have a Jesus, especially in the film version, who is a bit too mousey and vacillating to fit a decent American or British stereotype of muscular heterosexuality. He sings in a high, squeaky voice, swishes a bit too much in his gauzy, white gown, and seems as ambivalent in his erotic expressions toward Mary as he does toward Judas. Though Jesus in the film is caressed mostly by female camp-followers, both women and men writhe and moan as they wallow in the problem of not knowing "how to love him." Mary and Judas compete with one another in a duet of affective confusion. *Jesus Christ Superstar* is perhaps a bit more obvious than most in its portrayal of Jesus' ambiguous sexuality, but it is just one instance of the pervasive uncertainty in the popular imagination over what to do about Jesus' desires and possible sex lives.

Let's step back and note some underlying assumptions in the popular imagination about Jesus. We could even call these "rules" of interpretation since they are like tacitly honored social agreements about what will count as a good as opposed to a bad understanding of Jesus' sexuality and singleness. First there is the assumption that Jesus *had* sexuality.[5] If the Gospels are relatively silent about Jesus' sexual desires, that need not preclude the popular imagination from wondering about it and supplying any missing information. But this is perfectly understandable: in our modern world, sexuality is everywhere, so why not in Jesus? To many modern persons, a man who experienced no sexual desire at all would not be a man. We *may* be able to imagine people who deny or control their desires and remain celibate. But not to experience desire at all renders someone, in our world, so abnormal as to be practically nonhuman. Thus, the popular imagination takes Jesus' humanity seriously.[6] In fact, it has been a regularity of popular treatments of Jesus to focus on his humanity, so they must imagine what his sexuality must have been. Second, we see that *most* of the time Jesus' sexuality is rigidly heterosexual, at least when it is made explicit in the portrait. If Jesus is agonized about sexuality, as he is in *The Last Temptation of Christ*, he must certainly be agonized about his desire *for women*. But we should also not be surprised when the portraits of Jesus show cracks in his heterosexual façade with the result that he comes across—even in those contexts in which he is ostensibly heterosexual—as sexually ambiguous. He is sometimes a bit effeminate; he seems to enjoy the company of his male disciples a bit more than some would think "normal." Thus, at least in three ways, the popular imagination reveals its own rules of interpretation: it must admit the constant reality of sexual orientation and desire; it must be dominated by assumptions about heterosexual normativity; and it must not be able completely to control the excess of sexuality within heterosexual normativity or to exclude homoeroticism.

THE HISTORICAL IMAGINATION

The previous examples represent, though, popular imagination. In the modern world, historical criticism has usually presented itself as the method that can overcome random diversity of interpretation and capriciousness of meaning. History, so the assumption has gone since the beginning of the modern period, can bring security of meaning—even perhaps singularity of meaning. With that modern goal of consensus of interpretation in mind, it is striking that there is so little consensus among biblical scholars about Jesus' sexuality and what to do with it. In the first place, the vast majority of scholars writing about the historical Jesus say absolutely nothing about his sex life or desires. In fact, one gets the feeling that the topic is for most of them rather embarrassing. When John Meier, as one of a very few, decides to address the question, he almost sheepishly admits that "the mere act of asking whether Jesus was ever married will strike some readers as imprudent, others as vulgar, and still others as blasphemous."[7] Apparently in our culture it is considered a bit radical, or perhaps only impolite, to raise questions about Jesus' sex life.

One scholar has in fact targeted that very embarrassment in his critique of traditional Christian notions about sexuality and his own argument that Jesus was probably married and experienced a "normal" sex life. William E. Phipps has argued that within Judaism of Jesus' day, celibacy was rarely tolerated. Judaism required that Jewish men be married and engage in heterosexual intercourse. In Phipps's reconstruction, Judaism had a "healthy" view toward sex in contrast both to surrounding Greco-Roman tendencies and to the later church.[8] Thus it is almost certain that Jesus would have been married and sexually active.

In spite of Phipps's pretensions to objectivity freed from "the distortion of sexuality in the Christian tradition," his own historical imagination is quite limited. For one thing, as we will see, his view of ancient Judaism is simply inaccurate. But a more glaring error is Phipps's assumption of heterosexual exclusivity. At the beginning of his treatment of the sexuality of Jesus, for instance, he says that he will deal with "the entire gamut of male-female relations."[9] What about male-male relations? Or female-female relations—not to mention the variety of permutations and combinations we could otherwise imagine? Phipps therefore presents himself as advocating unbiased scholarship, untainted by traditional Christian neuroses about sexuality. But in the end he seems able to imagine only a Jesus who is "normal," that is, "heterosexual."[10]

Other scholars have pointed out the errors in Phipps's claims about ancient Judaism and have argued that in all likelihood Jesus was celibate. John Meier surveys Jewish texts from the Second Temple period and notes different Jewish groups and individuals who apparently practiced sexual asceticism for a variety of reasons. The Qumran community, he says, probably included at least some Jews who were celibate, though discerning precisely their reasons for avoiding marriage is difficult. Perhaps they held to a "Sinai-covenant theology that demanded sexual abstinence in preparation for encounter with God (cf. Exodus 19:15)." Or they intended their actions as extending the rules for priestly purity to the entire community, "which was a living temple worshipping God in the company of the angels." Or perhaps they avoided sex as preparation for a holy war they expected to participate in along with heavenly powers arrayed against cosmic powers of evil. And it is possible, he admits, that basic misogyny, as is reflected in descriptions by Josephus and Philo, may have motivated the Qumran Jews, at least in part. In any case, Meier concludes that celibacy was practiced "among certain marginal Jewish groups."[11]

After rejecting some possible motivations for Jesus' choice of celibacy (priestly purity, holy-war ideology, misogyny) Meier guesses that Jesus may have intended his celibacy to be a puzzle to his contemporaries: "Mirroring his parabolic speech, and like his easy fellowship with the socially and spiritually marginalized in Palestine, his celibacy was a parable in action, an embodiment of a riddle-like message meant to disturb people and provoke them to thought—both about Jesus and about themselves."[12]

Dale Allison comes to similar conclusions.[13] After surveying different forms of ancient Jewish sexual renunciation, Allison suggests five different reasons for Jesus' celibacy. First, his dedication to his eschatological mission and the demands it would have made on its preachers discouraged marriage. Second, Allison notes that asceticism in millenarian groups sometimes is seen to separate the participant from "the present world order," often itself conceived as corrupt and corrupting.[14] Third, Jesus and his disciples offered their renunciation of the normal societal supports as rhetorical persuasion intended to convince others of the reality of their message that God himself would completely take care of their needs.[15] Fourth, Jesus and his disciples intended their own renunciation as a prophetic, symbolic act of judgment on those who preferred to live lives of luxury and comfort.[16] And finally, their avoidance of sexual intercourse and family was a reflection of their belief that the coming eschatological society was already beginning to break into the current world through their own actions.[17] In opposition, therefore, to those who insist that Jesus must have been a "normal" man who expressed his sexual desires and tendencies by the "normal" means, Allison and Meier argue that in all probability Jesus was celibate, and that since the "normal" in his society was defined at least in part by marriage and family, he was in this case not only single, but also singular.[18] He wasn't really "normal" after all.

Neither Meier nor Allison (nor the vast majority of scholars) even entertains the possibility that Jesus may not after all have been sexually attracted to women. Meier, for example, believes that Jesus was not married and that this was a "radical sacrifice" on his part. Is this so obvious? Meier's reconstruction is dependent on his assumption in the first place that Jesus did experience strong desires for sex, marriage, and family, and in the second place that those desires were heterosexual. Allison offers five different explanations for Jesus' celibacy (which raises the question of how satisfying a historical explanation can be that offers *five different* hypotheses)—and Allison never raises questions about Jesus' *desires*. Meier and Allison have made Jesus into an abnormal man with regard to his celibacy but a normal heterosexual with regard to his desires. In fact, if Phipps gives us a Jesus who is a normal heterosexual, Meier and Allison give us a Jesus who is an *abnormal* heterosexual: Jesus is heterosexual in his desires, yet he doesn't *act* on those desires. Jesus is singularly sexual: a queer heterosexual.[19]

Of course, there have been scholarly reconstructions of a very different sort, the most famous perhaps being Morton Smith's suggestions, based on the fragments of the so-called *Secret Gospel of Mark*. In one of the fragments Jesus raises a young man from the dead, causing the young man to "love" Jesus deeply. In the other quotation, the young man is said to come to Jesus by night, naked except for a linen robe. Jesus spends the night with the young man, apparently initiating him into mysteries of esoteric knowledge.[20] Smith suggested that the fragment constituted evidence of ancient accounts of naked initiatory rites performed by Jesus himself with select male disciples, and Smith did not demur from opining that some homosexual activity may have constituted part of those initiations.[21] Whatever one may think of Smith's hypothesis, one must admit that it would solve some conundrums. The significance of the naked young man in the canonical Gospel of Mark is just one such problem. Perplexing parallels between the Gospels of Mark and John constitute another. And the Jesus of Smith's reconstruction would go a long way toward explaining why Jesus may have never married.

I have no interest in arguing for any of these different proposals for Jesus' sexuality. I find certain assumptions undergirding each of them difficult to accept. What is more interesting for my purposes is how they illustrate what has been imaginable at different times with regard to the sexuality of Jesus—and what has been apparently unimaginable.

Nor do I believe that just practicing historical criticism more rigorously will clear up the ambiguity of Jesus' sexuality. Let us attempt, for the sake of illustration, a couple of thought experiments. First, let's argue the case for Jesus as a sexual ascetic. Christian tradition, including the evidence of the earliest Gospels, almost unanimously portrays Jesus without a wife or children. Furthermore, several sayings in the tradition imply that Jesus may have been nonmarried and maybe even a sexual ascetic, the main ones being the saying about eunuchs from Matthew (19:10–12) and the saying about the angels in heaven not being married (Mark 12:18–27 and parallels). From these and a few other hints, we *could* fairly postulate that Jesus was not married and that he was probably a sexual ascetic.

But in that case, Jesus must have been a very queer one. As I've mentioned, we now know of several different forms of Jewish asceticism current in Jesus' day. But Jesus fits none of them. The asceticism of the Dead Sea Scrolls, for example, is heavily implicated in their concerns about purity and the Temple, fastings, strict Sabbath observance, and obedience to a strictly interpreted Torah. Essenes also rejected the use of oil for anointing; bathed with cold water before meals and after relieving themselves; wore white clothing; enforced extreme physical modesty and dietary moderation; rejected animal sacrifice; and avoided the contemporary Temple cult. We find none of these concerns in the early Jesus movement.

To cite another example of Jewish asceticism, the sexual renunciation of Jewish Nazirites was pursued so that the ascetic might attain a "priestly level of holiness" by avoiding, in the words of Steven Fraade, "wine, grape products, contact with the dead, even of one's immediate family, and cutting of one's hair."[22] Jesus seems to have been well-known for *not* avoiding wine or grape products; he had no compunction about physical contact with the dead; and though he seems at times to have avoided his family, he avoided them when they were alive and showed no concerns about their deaths at all; we have no hint that Jesus avoided cutting his hair, Hollywood and the history of western art notwithstanding.

We could mention other examples, such as the "Therapeutai" as described by Philo (*De vita contemplativa*), or, closer to home as far as Jesus was concerned, the asceticism of John the Baptist. But the impression in any case is that *if* Jesus was a Jewish ascetic, he can be fitted into *none* of the forms of Jewish asceticism known to us from his day. In almost every case, sexual asceticism is accompanied by dietary asceticism and the avoidance of wine or feasting. Usually, ascetics fast. Often, they withdraw to establish an uncontaminated life apart from normal culture. Asceticism often occurs as an intensified version of normal Torah observance. Most importantly, Jewish asceticism is almost always linked to heightened concerns for purity, often with the Temple playing a central role. In contrast, Jesus shows few concerns about purity or the Temple cult;[23] if Jesus taught anything about Torah, it was apparently a rather more liberal than strict interpretation; Jesus was apparently not an ascetic with regard to food or drink; he did not regularly fast or teach his disciples to fast; though he withdrew into the wilderness on occasion, Jesus did not in principle withdraw from society. Thus, though we can now admit that sexual asceticism was indeed practiced by Jews of Jesus' day, what we know about Jesus does not fit any of the forms of ascetic Judaism we know about. If Jesus was a sexual ascetic, he was a queer one.

Perhaps, though, we have here a clue that we are looking in the wrong direction. Since it is so difficult to place Jesus' assumed asceticism in an ancient Jewish context, and the evidence *that* he was a sexual ascetic is so slim (mainly an argument from silence), maybe it is safer to assume that Jesus was *not* an ascetic after all. Perhaps Jesus had nothing against sex and desire—even if he did have much against the ancient household, for which we have much more evidence.

Perhaps Jesus never taught that sex itself was to be avoided. After all, a historical Jesus that so badly fits his environment may be too *queer* for good historiography. In other words, even when we play by the rules of modern historiography, we don't end up with satisfactory answers about Jesus' singleness—even by the standards of modern historiography: one of the central rules of modern historiography is that things must fit their historical context, that "absolutely unique" entities in history must be viewed as suspect in their historical reconstruction. A celibate Jesus, if constructed according to our available evidence, does *not* fit his historical context well, yet we have no evidence that Jesus was anything *but* single, again by normal historiographical criteria of what counts as "evidence."

THE PATRISTIC IMAGINATION

We've again ended up with a Jesus of ambiguous sexuality. Though we've searched through the popular imagination and the historical imagination, we've come up with nothing but a Jesus of uncertain sexuality. What if we turn our attentions to the writings of the early church fathers? May we find more secure answers in the Jesus of what we may call "the patristic imagination"? After all, I would think that the people who should be most concerned about the sexuality of Jesus would be Christians. And I would think that Christians would have little reason to allow modern historiography the right to settle the meaning of Jesus' desires. Invoking the Christian commitment to the "communion of the saints" should imply, I think, that the voices of earlier Christians should be given at least as much attention as the relatively recent methods and opinions of modernism. So what can we discern about the sexuality of Jesus by reading the Fathers?

In spite of a very few early Christian voices to the contrary (Carpocratians, Manicheans?),[24] all the Fathers who come to be accepted as "orthodox" are agreed that Jesus was celibate. But that doesn't mean that the *meaning* of Jesus' celibacy was unambiguous or without problems.

First, it is remarkable that there is a noticeable reluctance among the Fathers to use Jesus as a *model* for celibate life.[25] Cyril of Jerusalem, for instance, as do many others, points to the *suffering* of Jesus as a model for Christian imitation, but when he wants a model for celibacy and virginity, he points to other Christians.[26] Basil the Great speaks of the imitation of Christ that is necessary for "perfection of life" but does not mention celibacy; rather, he is thinking of Christ's gentleness, lowliness, long-suffering endurance, and death.[27] And Tertullian points to Christ as an example for Christian fasting—even though there is little portrayal in the Gospels of Jesus as fasting.[28] When the fathers want an example of virginity, they much more often point to Mary as the model.[29]

In fact, Christ plays the role more often of the bridegroom than as a model for the celibate.[30] Tertullian rather confusingly uses Christ as a model both for virgins and for married persons, in the latter case to enforce one-time marriage. Christ, just like Adam "before his exile," was "entirely unwedded," "entirely pure," and can therefore serve as a model for virgins. But "in spirit" Christ is a monogamist, "having one Church as his bride, according to the figure of Adam and Eve."[31] Thus, as a virgin Christ is a model for virgins; as a monogamist he is a model for married persons. We end up with a rather queer Christ who is both a celibate virgin and a loyal husband.

Modern Christians may find many reasons to be less than enthusiastic, therefore, about the sexuality of Jesus as interpreted in the patristic imagination. And they may be even more uncomfortable when they pay attention to the *meaning* of Jesus' asceticism as interpreted by the Fathers. According to Gregory of Nyssa, the central issue in Christian conformity to Christ lies in his *apatheia*, his lack of passion, the absence of (the vice of) passion and desire.[32] Furthermore, Christ must have been perfect and thus our model for perfecting ourselves. In the sexual ideology assumed by Gregory, sex represents lack or passion (that is, susceptibility to change), and thus Christ must not have been able to experience sex, any more than he could have experienced lack, change, and imperfection. Is this the meaning of sexuality that the church today wishes to promote?

Again, I must pass over other important patristic views about sex, such as the almost universal idea that even if marriage is not to be condemned, it is not equal to the "higher calling" of virginity, or sentiments such as Origen's when he insists that Christians not pray in bed because that is where "defiling sex" takes place.[33] The patristic imagination, in any case, much like both the popular imagination and the historical imagination, leaves modern Christians with more uncertainties and problems regarding the sexuality of Jesus than answers. Is there really anything here modern Christians should want to imitate? Is freedom from desire a Christian goal? Should we accept a hierarchy in which virginity is considered superior to sexual connection? Should sex be interpreted as signifying "lack" and "imperfection"? Do we want to promote detachment from the world and immutability as the highest virtues? And should we go along with the Fathers in viewing sex as defiling?

THE GAY IMAGINATION

With all this ambiguity surrounding Jesus' sexuality—whether in the popular imagination, the historical imagination, or the patristic imagination—is it any wonder that the gay imagination can so easily find a Jesus for itself? What happens if we read the Gospels through the eyes of the male homoerotic gaze? We may note, for starters, that there is practically no place in the Gospels where Jesus is said to "love" a woman in particular. The closest is when the Fourth Gospel tells us that Jesus loved Martha, her sister, and Lazarus (John 11:5), perhaps a *ménage à quatre*? Jesus' attraction to specific men, on the other hand, is explicit. Though he at first treated the "rich young ruler" a bit abruptly, Jesus then "looked on him and loved him" (according to Mark 10:21).[34] Even the people standing around surmised from Jesus' weeping that he must have loved Lazarus a great deal

(John 11:36). And of course there is "the disciple whom Jesus loved," who is regularly close to Jesus, who lies practically on top of him at his last dinner, whom Jesus loves so much that he seems unwilling to allow him even to die (13:23–25; 21:20–22). For those unable to imagine anything erotic going on here, just consider what people would think if we took the "beloved disciple" to be a woman (as has in fact been imagined, presumably by heterosexuals); in that case, most people wouldn't be able to resist the consequent erotic imaginings.[35] Finally, we have Jesus' last discussion with Peter in the Fourth Gospel, in which Jesus teases and flirts with Peter like a schoolgirl: "Do you *really* love me? Really? Really? Then prove it!" (21:15–19).

There are other sites of the sensual in the Gospels, but always with regard to men (is it significant that these occur almost entirely in John, the most homoerotic of the Gospels?). Thomas is invited to penetrate the holes in Jesus' body (John 20:24ff). Jesus dips his "little piece" (*psômion*) in the gravy and places it in the hand of Judas (John 13:26). And though Jesus allows a woman to wash his feet (and we biblical scholars—who know our Hebrew—recognize the hint), when it is his turn, he takes his clothes off, wraps a towel around his waist, and washes the feet of his *male* disciples, again taking time out for a special seduction of Peter (John 13:1–11).[36] In contrast, when Mary later wants a hug, Jesus won't let her even touch him (John 20:17). (Jesus' *noli me tangere* is the Gospel version of Paul's homosocial slogan "It is better for a man not to touch a woman"; 1 Cor. 7:1).

As these references imply, we needn't think of Jesus as actually "having sex" (whatever *that* means these days) in order to see him as erotic and sexual. Any sexually experienced person knows that the most intense eroticism may be had by denying oneself consummation. Flirtation, titillation, intimacy, love taken to the edge of orgasm, are often sexually more intense than mere intercourse. May that explain the intensity of Jesus' passion? *If* we take him to be an ascetic after all (though, as we've seen, that is not at all certain), do we nonetheless see in him the erotic passion and desire of the sexually charged ascetic? But in that case *again*, Jesus is certainly not a normal man—not even a "normal" *gay* man. He ends up again looking very singular—very queer.

THE NONFOUNDATIONALIST PREDICAMENT—OR POSSIBILITY

We have no direct and certain epistemological access to the "real" Jesus. The popular imagination, the historical imagination, the patristic imagination, the gay imagination—all find both possibilities and limitations in what they are able to imagine concerning the sexuality of Jesus. That is perhaps not a matter of debate. What may be a matter of debate, though, are the two points I want to stress the most.

First, all of these different methods of interpretation are indeed "imaginings." We scholars and seminarians have all been taught by our training as modern exegetes that historical criticism, if not the only way to read texts, is the one method to which all other readings must bow. We may be willing to allow a preacher in a pulpit a few flights of allegory, narrative inventiveness, or modernizations, but in the end those fanciful interpretations must submit themselves to the more serious, secure, scholarly findings of historiography. This historiography need not be totally predictable or monolithic. Many exegetes, for example, have increasingly realized how difficult, if not impossible, it is to ascertain the "author's intention" of 2,000 years ago—not to mention the fact that for biblical texts we often do not know who the author is (other than saying that the author is "God," which introduces fresh problems for discerning authorial intention). Even historical critics therefore have opened their minds enough to allow that perhaps attention to the author should be supplemented or even replaced by attentions to the ancient readers, or at least what we may imagine to have been the plausible understandings of ancient readers of the text. In other words, the reader's interpretations may have supplanted the author's intention in some contemporary interpretation, but in that case it is the *ancient* reader who is the criterion for better or worse interpretations. Most modern historical reconstructions still claim the right to judge between better and worse readings. I am insisting that that claim is theoretically naïve and theologically suspect. Moreover, historical critics should stop pretending that their own constructions of the text's meaning are any less "imaginative" than any other. They just use a different kind of imagination.

My second crucial point is that *none* of these different imaginations can offer compelling reasons to claim the position of hermeneutical hegemony over the others. In other words, I am not advocating that the patristic imagination be allowed to displace the modern hegemony of historical criticism with a new hegemony of patristic criticism. Nor do I want to substitute the gay imagination for historical criticism or patristic interpretations. I see the nonfoundationalist (postmodern?) world of biblical criticism as one in which many different interpretive methods will vie with one another for our attentions, and in which students will not be considered well trained until they have been trained in several exegetical imaginations and until they demonstrate an ability to negotiate the labyrinth of the text (or the hypertext of the text) using several different reading strategies and different hermeneutical theories. In other words, I'm not in favor of letting "narrative" criticism or "canonical" criticism or any other one approach command center stage. In the nonfoundational hermeneutical world, there is no center stage.[37]

People who have not listened to me carefully when I have talked about this topic have sometimes thought that I was basically arguing for a "gay" Jesus as the "real" Jesus. Nothing could be a more egregious misunderstanding of what I am about. I am rather interested in shining a spotlight on several aspects of biblical interpretation. For one thing, I am making the uncontroversial point (at least it should now be uncontroversial) that all interpretation is subjective and interested, that people's interpretations of texts, even those about Jesus, are a product of who they are and where they live. Thus people come up with all sorts of ways to imagine the sexuality of Jesus. And of course that has a great deal to do with what they find imaginable about sex. As is the case with so many instances in all interpretation, how people interpret the sexuality of Jesus tells us more about the meaning of sex *for them* than for some "real" Jesus freed from interpretation.

My other point, though, may be a bit more controversial. I refer to my insistence that there is nothing necessarily wrong with the fact that people interpret the Bible in many different ways and come up with widely varying Jesuses. It is part of the history of Christian interpretation—part of the way Christians have always made sense of their own sex and their very singular Savior. What makes my nonfoundationalist stance different from the foundationalism of modernism is my insistence that we can be no other way. We should learn from the facts of our contingency. If we need a hermeneutical theory (and perhaps we don't need one at all), we must come up with one that gives up on the search for security in interpretation in foundations outside the interpretive process itself. There is nothing "out there" to referee our varying and even conflicting interpretations. There is nothing "in the text" that can play the role of judge among us.

We have a right to think about the sex of Jesus, the sexuality of Jesus, the desires of Jesus, the singularity of Jesus. What none of us has a right to do, I am arguing, is to insist that he or she will supply *the* method of interpretation that will bring imagination to an end and silence the imaginations of others. For me, the sexuality and singularity of Jesus are significant issues. But the much more important issue is the question of interpretation itself in a nonfoundationalist world.

Chapter 8

Familiar Idolatry and the Christian Case against Marriage

Contemporary Christianity in the United States—whether Protestant or Catholic, liberal or conservative—has so closely aligned the basic message of Christianity with the family and "traditional family values" that it is currently in a state of idolatry.[1] Increasingly, whether they are religious or not, people in America tend to equate Christianity with the family and "family values." It is not just that gay and lesbian people have largely left their churches; single people in general often feel out of place in churches. And other people in non-"traditional" family structures—whether divorced, cohabiting, or in partial nuclear families—tend to be much less active in churches. The reason is that American churches have so identified themselves with the modern, heterosexual, nuclear family that people without such families feel less at home in most churches.[2] The religious term for the identification of anything but God at the center of Christian faith is idolatry. And the idolatry of contemporary American Christianity is the familiar idolatry of the church's current focus on the family.

Not only is contemporary Christianity idolatrous in its focus on the family and marriage; it is also hypocritical. It either explicitly states or assumes that its current values are the obvious expression of Christian Scripture and tradition. Though most Christians *assume* that the current centrality of marriage and family represents a long tradition in Christianity, it is actually only about 150 years old. One could even make the argument that the current focus on the heterosexual *nuclear* family dates back only to the 1950s.[3] In this chapter, I pass over the long tradition of Christianity, though it also provides little support for the modern family. Rather, I here concentrate mainly on the New Testament and the writings of the early church. Contrary to most contemporary opinion—Christian as well as non-Christian—there are many more resources in Christian Scripture and tradition to *criticize* the modern family than to promote it.

THE HISTORICAL JESUS

Jesus of Nazareth was not a family man. Though we could debate the construction of the historical Jesus—and all "historical Jesuses" are in fact hypothetical constructions based on the flimsiest of evidence—according to all our available evidence, Jesus never married. This *could* have been an accident of history. It wasn't unusual for men in the ancient world to put off marriage, if they married at all, until their thirties. If Jesus was about thirty years old when he began his ministry, as suggested by some traditions (deriving from Luke 3:23), he could have been unmarried just because he hadn't gotten around to it. But there are other indications that he rejected marriage and family ties and taught his disciples to do likewise. Whatever the historical Jesus taught about sex, about which we have no real evidence, his message apparently included a severe critique of the traditional family, including marriage.

One of the sayings of the Gospels that must be historical is Jesus' response when told that his mother and brothers (and sisters according to one source [a textual variant at Mark 3:32]) wanted to see him. Jesus answers, "Who is my mother and who are my brothers? . . . Whoever does the will of God, that one is my brother and sister and mother" (Mark 3:33–35; cf. Matt. 12:46–50; Luke 8:19–21). Jesus refused to identify with his traditional family and instead substituted for it the eschatological community that shared his vision of a new, divinely constituted family.

Indeed, all our Gospels present Jesus as creating and living within an alternative to the household: an itinerant group of men and women unrelated to one another by blood or marriage, most of whom had also apparently separated from their families. Jesus called his disciples away from their households. Although perhaps teaching that the commandment to honor one's parents should still be obeyed (the evidence is either nonexistent or inconclusive), he told one man not even to bury his father—a teaching that would have been perceived as an incredible and offensive affront to family values in ancient Palestine (Luke 9:59–60; Matt. 8:21–22).[4] In another saying, as passed on by Luke, Jesus says, "If anyone comes to me and does not despise [or hate: *miseô*] his own father and mother and wife and children and brothers and sisters, and yes his own life, he is not able to be my disciple" (Luke 14:26). Most modern Christians prefer to remember the saying in its Matthean version, where in place of "despise" or "hate," the author has Jesus say merely that one must not "love more" one's family than Jesus (Matt. 10:37). But the Lukan use of "hate" has support from the *Gospel of Thomas* 55, which may well be an independent witness to an early tradition. And it is more likely, many scholars believe, that the Lukan form better reflects an earlier, Aramaic source.[5] Moreover, Matthew would more likely have altered a "Q" saying to the less offensive "love more" in order to make Jesus' teaching fit his own high regard for the law of Moses.[6] Thus, the more radical version passed on by Luke and *Thomas* has the stronger claim to authenticity. A clearer indication that the historical Jesus taught the rejection of the traditional family can scarcely be demanded.

But doesn't Jesus' teaching about divorce, as contained mainly in Mark 10:6–12 and Matthew 19:4–9, imply the support of marriage? Here Jesus forbids divorce even though the law of Moses had allowed it. Wouldn't this imply that Jesus, if the saying is historical, supported marriage and the traditional family at least to the extent that the law did? Not really. After all, Matthew includes Jesus' forbidding of divorce but then follows it up with his saying about those who have "made themselves eunuchs for the sake of the kingdom of God" (Matt. 19:12). The saying is admittedly difficult to interpret and may not be historical—it is found only in Matthew, after all—but its most likely meaning is that the avoidance of procreation and marriage is preferable. The combination of the sayings is evidence that a writer could be opposed to divorce without advocating marriage and family. That possibility is upheld by almost all the church fathers, who almost without exception coupled a severe critique of marriage, in some cases all but forbidding it for truly pious Christians, with an even stronger prohibition of divorce.[7] Even if Jesus did forbid divorce, therefore, that cannot be taken as evidence that he advocated marriage.

What was the meaning, though, of Jesus' rejection of marriage and the family for himself and his disciples? One clue comes from his saying about the resurrection and marriage. Jesus says, "In the resurrection of the dead, people neither marry nor are married, but they are as angels in heaven" (Mark 12:25; Matt. 22:30). Or at least that is how the saying appears in Mark and Matthew. Luke, perhaps realizing that the saying was too cryptic, expands it, having Jesus explain it this way: "For they [that is, the resurrected dead] are no longer able to die, for they are equal to the angels and are sons of God, being sons of the resurrection" (Luke 20:36). Luke's version may be epexegetical, but it probably does correctly portray the basic meaning of the saying about angels. A common understanding among ancient Jews and Christians was that angels are androgynous, or perhaps completely male. They needn't, in any case, reproduce themselves the way human beings do because they are not subject to death. The understanding throughout much of the ancient world was that marriage was for the purposes of legitimate and controlled procreation, which was necessary only because of the fact of death. Marriage, therefore, was completely implicated in the dreaded cycle of sex, birth, death, and decay, followed by more sex, birth, death, and decay. As John Chrysostom put it many years later, "where there is death, there is marriage" (*On Virginity* 14.6). In the resurrection, Jesus taught, that cycle will have been broken. Marriage will be obsolete and even offensive in the kingdom of God. Jesus' rejection of the traditional family and his creation of an alternative community signaled the imminent, or perhaps incipient, in-breaking of the kingdom of God.

All our evidence pointing to the historical Jesus, therefore, indicates that he not only avoided marriage and family himself but also taught people to forsake those institutions and enter into an alternative, eschatological society. The household was part of the world order he was challenging. It, along with other institutions of power, would be destroyed with the coming kingdom. The household, moreover, represented traditional authority, which he was challenging at every turn. The household was implicated in the cycle of death. Indeed, the household, as the site of procreation, birth, and burial, was the very technology of life *and death* in the ancient world. For the historical Jesus, the rejection of marriage and the family was as necessary as the proclamation of the resurrection and the eternal kingdom of God.

THE GOSPEL OF LUKE AND THE ACTS OF THE APOSTLES

Different Christians in the early church took these early Jesus traditions in different directions. We've already seen that Matthew toned down Jesus' antifamilial teachings somewhat, apparently uncomfortable with having Jesus speak of "hating" one's family. As we will see, later Christians actually turned the gospel around so that it supported rather than challenged the traditional household. Still other Christians carried on the antifamilial tendencies of the historical Jesus. The author of the Gospel of Luke and the Acts of the Apostles laces his entire narrative with the theme.

First, we should note how he himself may have edited the saying I've already quoted about "hating" one's family. Only Luke includes "wives and children" in the list of those a disciple is supposed to "despise." Although Thomas also uses the word "hate" or "despise," Thomas's account agrees with Matthew in *not* including wives in the list. It is possible, therefore, that Luke added "wives and children" to a list of family members he found in Q. This suggestion is supported by an analysis of the rest of the Gospel.

There occur a few small details special to Luke's Gospel that tip his hand about his stance on the traditional family. Only Luke contains Jesus' teaching that people should not invite their friends and family to a dinner they host, but that they should instead invite the poor, outcasts, those who cannot return the favor (14:12–14). A few sentences later, in the parable of the Great Banquet, only Luke has a character decline the invitation because he has just been married (14:20), an excuse not found in Matthew's version.[8]

Other details in the early portions of Luke's Gospel, details usually overlooked, can also suddenly appear significant when seen in a larger context of Luke's critical stance toward the traditional family. Luke portrays the birth of Jesus, for example, as a very "public" event, not at all a "family affair." And toward the close of that narrative, Luke ominously adds that Mary "pondered in her heart" all that had happened (2:19). The next ominous foreshadowing concerning Mary occurs just a few verses later, when Simeon prophesies that a sword will pierce Mary's soul (2:35). And then again only a few verses later things become more explicit. At the age of twelve, Jesus in the Temple, though "obedient" to his parents (2:51), clearly expresses his ultimate independence from his fleshly family. He names God as his "father" and his "business" as God's "business" (2:41–51). The Greek here—*en tois tou patros mou*—could refer to the "matters" or "business" of the father (so the KJV?), the "household" of the father (and thus the RSV?), or even the "people" of the father (if taken to be masculine).[9] In any case, the contrast between Jesus' traditional family and the household of God is here early highlighted. Mary's soul is already being pierced.

The author of Luke-Acts then constructs his narrative to emphasize this contrast between the community of Jesus and the traditional family. In Luke 8:1–3, we are informed about Jesus' entourage, which includes the twelve male disciples, Mary Magdalene, Joanna, Susanna, and "many other" women. Jesus' "household" now consists of twelve men and several women, none of whom is mentioned as traveling with a spouse or family. It is no surprise, therefore, when a few verses later Jesus gets explicit about his substitution of this new community for his traditional family (8:19–21). Those who travel with him, not the nuclear family of his birth, are his family. In the next chapter Jesus tells the young man to forget burying his father and to follow Jesus instead (9:59–62), which is followed a few verses later by a description of the intimacy of Jesus with his true father: "Everything has been given to me by my father. No one knows who the son is except the father, and who the father is except the son and whomever the son chooses to reveal it to" (10:22). The contrast is thus made between the disruption Jesus brings to "normal" father-son relations and the intimacy of Jesus' own relation to his heavenly father.

Even clearer contrasts occur in the narrative of Acts. At the beginning of the book, for instance, the communal life of the disciples in Jerusalem is described (Acts 2:42–47). They meet in the Temple and in different houses all together. They share belongings and common meals. They hold all things in common (*eichon apanta koina*, 2:44). To make sure we get the point, the author rehearses the account two chapters later. He says that the disciples were all happily united; no one claimed any private property, but they rather held all things in common; whoever owned land or houses (think "households") sold them and delivered the proceeds to the whole group, to be administered by the apostles, who gave to each according to need. Joseph, an apparently single man called "Barnabas" by the apostles, is cited as a particular example: he sold a field and gave the entire proceeds to the community (4:32–37).[10]

Immediately and in direct contrast to this description of communal life, the author introduces the negative countertype: the married couple Ananias and

Sapphira, to this point the only married couple mentioned in Acts.[11] In fact, they are the only married couple explicitly mentioned in Acts apart from Prisca and Aquila, who are themselves anything but the "normal," traditional married couple.[12] Note how the actions of Ananias and Sapphira are described (5:1–11). They are Christians with their own private possessions. But instead of doing as the others have done, they sell their possessions and bring only a portion of the proceeds to the church. Twice in the text, the author emphasizes that the two *conspire together* to deceive the church and avoid the communalism of the others (5:2, 9). As usual, the author of Acts presents Satan as the instigator of actions opposite those demanded in the kingdom of God, and also as usual, the actor on the side of the church is the Holy Spirit, to whom, Peter says, the couple has actually lied (5:3).[13] When Ananias and Sapphira die, we are told that they are carried out and buried by "young men," a detail repeated twice that is hard to explain but may represent the "new" thing happening in this eschatological community of the future (the Greek word for "young men" builds on the Greek word that may also be translated "new"; 5:6, 10; cf. 2:17). Finally, the text emphasizes that the couple is buried together, the wife "right by her husband" (*pros ton andra autês*; 5:10), together now in death as they were together in their conspiratorial marriage that sought its own interests before the communal interests of the spirit-led church.[14] Then, at the end of the story about the married couple, the narrative returns our vision once again to the (nonhousehold) community, telling us that "great fear fell on the whole church and on all those who heard about these events" (5:11).

I think it cannot be an accident that a married couple, one of only two named in the book of Acts, serves as the negative countertype to the nonhousehold, eschatological community of the first part of the book, a community clearly foreshadowing and representing the coming community of God that will replace the traditional family for good. The solidarity of the married couple represents the old, self-serving order of the traditional family and familial solidarity, with its concerns for economic stability, inheritance, and continuity, in contrast to the new, young, growing, communal, eschatological household, whose procreation is a miraculous gift of the spirit and whose survival is assured by common solidarity and the gifts of God, a household of brothers and sisters rather than husbands and wives, fathers and mothers. Or to use another early and fundamental social metaphor for the church, the traditional couple is opposed to the *ekklêsia*, the "town gathering," the new polity of the gathered people of God that outgrows, transcends, and ultimately rejects the traditional family.

More such examples of the Christian critique of marriage and the family from Luke and Acts could be given, but I will mention only one. It has not often been noted that there is no explicit condemnation of divorce in Luke, though there is in both Matthew and Mark. Luke, unlike Matthew, does not appropriate the material from Mark 10:2–12, in which Jesus explicitly prohibits divorce. The only place where the subject comes up explicitly in Luke is in his quotation of a Q saying, but its precise wording should be analyzed carefully. According to

Luke's wording, Jesus said, "Everyone who divorces his wife and marries another commits adultery, and any woman who has been divorced from her husband and marries another commits adultery" (Luke 16:18; compare Matt. 5:32; 19:9). According to most interpretations, this is read as a prohibition of *both* divorce *and* remarriage. But that, I argue, is to read the Lukan passage under the influence of the explicit prohibitions of divorce in Mark and Matthew. Luke's statement could easily be read as a prohibition only of the *combination of divorce with remarriage*. And that is the way I think it must be read. After all, we have already seen that Jesus in Luke, in contrast to the accounts in Matthew and Mark, *urges* his disciples to "hate" their wives. In Luke, Jesus demands that his disciples give up wives and children as well as their other family members in order to follow him. If Luke had Jesus forbid divorce or separation (and we must remember that for most people in the ancient world there was no real difference between divorce and separation)[15] while at the same time implying that his disciples must leave behind their wives, he would be caught in an obvious contradiction. But there is no contradiction if we assume that what Luke believed Jesus was prohibiting here was not divorce, but remarriage after divorce. This would also explain why he would *not* want to reproduce Mark 10:2–12 in his Gospel. Thus, Luke leaves out of his Gospel any prohibition of divorce; he has Jesus allow divorce but forbid remarriage. This fits perfectly with the other indications in Luke and Acts that the author took marriage and the traditional family to have been not just "relativized" but actually rejected by the gospel. Luke presents the church as replacing, not supporting, marriage and the family.[16]

THE REVELATION OF JOHN

Luke is not the only New Testament author who dreams of an eschatological community in which marriage and the traditional family are replaced by other social formations. The Revelation of John offers a similar vision, though it is also different in significant ways. The most obvious difference lies in the place assigned to women in the two different texts. Whereas the Christian community in Luke-Acts includes women, sometimes even in central roles, John imagines an exclusively male community, a kingdom of male priests and prophets who have "not been defiled by women" (14:4). There is no room in Revelation for actual, human women or for "normal" marriage and family.

John's world is ruled by God, the Pantocrator, the ruler of all, a designation for the Emperor appropriated by Christians for God. Jesus is also the "ruler of the kings of the earth" (1:5), another imperial title. John and his fellow Christians themselves constitute "the kingdom" (1:6). For John, Christians are priests serving God in the kingdom-empire ruled by God and Christ. John's universe is populated mainly by males. In his vision, he meets twenty-four male elders; four male beasts (4:4–7); two male prophets (11:3ff.); and Michael, a male angel who leads an army of apparently male angels (12:7–9). John and his fellow Christians play several different roles in his universe: they are most often designated as fellow slaves with the angels and brothers of one another, but they are also priests, prophets, and even kings (see 20:6). This is an entirely male community: God is father and Jesus is the eldest son, who is also repeatedly portrayed as a huge, vicious, violent, bloody, horned Lamb. The other members of the household are all brothers and fellow slaves—an all-male household.

The first time we encounter a female figure in Revelation is with the appearance of Jezebel, the false prophet who seduces Jesus' "slaves" in the church at Thyatira (2:20). She is depicted as an adulteress and is promised a violent end along with those who have had sex with her, that is, those led astray by her from the strict ascetic Christianity advocated by John. There are only two or three other female figures in Revelation, according to how one counts. The starring role is played by Babylon, the great Whore, Rome, who spreads her legs for any king who wants her (Rev. 18:3, 9). The other two female figures are the woman who gives birth to the male child in Revelation 12 and the Bride of the Lamb, who appears at the end of the book, but some have speculated that these two figures perhaps overlap in the confusing and fluid symbolism of the Apocalypse. At any rate, they are completely passive figures; they are acted upon but scarcely act. The woman of chapter 12 gives birth to a male child (apparently representing Jesus as the Messiah: 12:5), is persecuted by the dragon, and is eventually saved by being put out of the way in "her place" prepared by God for her in the desert (12:14). Unlike her male child, who is snatched up to sit with the male God on the heavenly throne, she apparently doesn't get to go to heaven but spends the rest of the book in "her place" in the desert.

The last female character of Revelation is, of course, the Bride. She is prepared by the father God to marry his son the Horned Lamb (19:7). She is clothed in pure, clean linen, in contrast to the filth and blood and gore of the Whore; in fact, her clothing is actually *composed of* the "righteous deeds of the saints," that is, John and his fellow brother-slaves (19:8). At the end of the vision, we discover that she is the New Jerusalem (21:2, 10), which is of course populated by the male, servile household of God, including the twelve male apostles of the Lamb (21:14) and the twelve tribes of the *sons* of Israel (21:12). Thus, although the Horned Lamb marries a female figure, her body and clothing are actually composed of male deeds and bodies, the population of the divine household, the eschatological city, the finally victorious kingdom and empire.

We see here that although actual sexual intercourse is *supposed* to be absent from the eschatological community, desire and the erotic, especially the erotic of the eye, is everywhere.[17] First, there is the voluptuous though gruesome seductiveness of Jezebel and the Whore—both of whom are depicted as promiscuous and dangerous. But John and his slave-brothers have resisted that seduction. And they have certainly resisted the seduction of normal marriage and family. They have, remember, "not been defiled, or polluted, by women" (14:1–5). The seduction they have apparently not been able to avoid is a certain erotic of homosocial male bonding that pervades the vision. We have the image more than once in

Revelation of God the father and Jesus the Horned Lamb both sitting on the heavenly throne. Jesus also makes this promise to John: "The one who is victorious I will give to sit with me on my throne, as I was victorious and sat with my father on his throne" (3:21; see also 12:5). It is hard to avoid the image, once we actually picture it, of a bunch of men scrambling all over one another and sitting on one another's laps on a huge throne in the sky; perhaps God the father is on bottom, then the Horned Lamb on his lap, and then John and all his slave brothers on their laps. Furthermore, it is curious that although there is a marriage in Revelation between a male and a female, the female's body and clothing are, as we saw, made up of male bodies. John and his brothers, in the person of the Bride herself, actually in the end *do* get to marry the Horned Lamb.

It is as if, for the author of the Apocalypse, there is no room for "normal" marriage and family in his world. The enemy, Rome, is not a "wife" but a whore who has slept around with every important man in the known world. Jesus is the bridegroom who is about to wed his bride. Christians are slave brothers who serve in the great household of God and have no contact with women. In fact, they must not do so since they constitute themselves the body of the bride of the Horned Lamb. They keep themselves pure (and John is obsessed with dirt, filth, and cleanliness, as well as with sex)[18] so they can be properly clean for their nuptial copulation with the Horned Lamb. How, in this universe, could Christians find a place for "normal" marriage and family?

In very different ways, therefore, Luke and John the Seer both envisioned Christian community as displacing marriage and family and replacing them with new eschatological social formations. And they may in fact have been inspired, as we have seen, by the teachings of Jesus himself. I now turn attention, though, to an obvious source for early Christian thinking about marriage and family: Paul and Paulinism.

THE APOSTLE PAUL

I have dealt at length with Paul's own position on sex and marriage elsewhere, so let me briefly summarize those findings here.[19] As we can see from 1 Corinthians 7, Paul was no proponent of marriage or the traditional family. He preferred that all Christians follow his example and remain unmarried. But he believed that some Christians, perhaps even most Christians, would be too weak to avoid the dangers of desire without sexual activity in marriage. So he allowed Christians to be married, in fact encouraged them to be married, if they were too weak to avoid desire otherwise. Note, however, that Paul never gives any indication that he believed marriage was the proper arena for the *expression* of sexual desire. Rather, his language makes it clear, I have argued, that he viewed marriage as the vehicle for the *avoidance* of desire. According to Paul, Christians do not *express* desire by means of marital sex; they *preclude* it. "It is better to marry than to burn" (1 Cor. 7:9). Since "burning" is a reference to sexual passion and desire, and Paul does not say that it is permissible to "burn" just a little, to "simmer," Paul's statement means that he viewed sex within marriage as the technique that would allow Christians to avoid the experience of sexual desire—ironically, from our perspective, through sexual intercourse performed within marriage but devoid of desire.

This interpretation is borne out by a careful examination of what Paul says in 1 Thessalonians 4:3–8. Paul tells the newly converted brothers in the church in Thessalonica (for whatever reason, he addresses only men) that each of them should "possess" or "control" his "thing" or "vessel," probably referring either to their genitalia or their wives, "in holiness and honor, not in the passion of desire like the Gentiles who do not know God" (4:4–5). Sexual passion, for Paul, is something that these Christian men should no longer experience; it is part of the Gentile world they have left behind. Marriage is the arena in which they should be able to have sex but avoid desire.

Whether or not one accepts my admittedly controversial interpretations of these passages, it must be admitted that Paul clearly preferred celibacy to marriage for Christians. He had no interest in the "propagation of the species," making babies, or raising families. He cannot be enlisted as a supporter, certainly in the romantic, modern sense, of marriage and family.

THE "PRO-FAMILY" PAUL

But of course, he has been so enlisted, not least by his disciples and probably not long after his death. The letter to the Colossians, which I take to be pseudonymous, does not actively promote the family, but it does assume it in the so-called "household code" proposed to maintain hierarchy and order in the household (3:18–4:1). Wives are told to submit to their husbands "as is fitting in the Lord"; husbands are told to love their wives and not treat them bitterly. Children are told to obey their parents in everything "for this is pleasing in the Lord"; fathers are told not to provoke their children or render them despondent. In the only admonition that exceeds a couple of phrases, slaves are then addressed with a full paragraph. Basically, they are told to serve their masters as if they were serving Christ, and that any misbehavior on their part will be severely punished not only by their earthly masters but even, it is implied, by Christ himself. Then, in a return to the short phrase, masters are told to treat their slaves equitably, realizing that slave owners themselves have a heavenly master.

Here in the name of Paul, the hierarchy of the ancient patriarchal household is reinforced in a way it never was in the authentic letters of Paul. True, Paul never advocated the abolition of slavery or the true equality of women, but his letters contain nothing really like this.[20] The position of this writer is nonetheless understandable. In the ancient world, if you were going to encourage marriage and the traditional household at all, you did so by placing the household in the structure of the universe, in a descending hierarchy with God on top, then male heads-of-households, then wives, then children, then slaves. The disproportionate attention given here to keeping slaves obedient and submissive works to make their slavery even more secure by inscribing it into their hearts and minds, and into their relation even to God and Christ. When early Christian authors encourage marriage and family, without fail they do so by reinforcing the patriarchal ideology of their society.

The author of Ephesians, writing later and also in Paul's name, elaborates the household code from Colossians. The author of Ephesians, though, makes the male, patriarchal ideology even more insidious by conflating the superior male's role with that of God and Christ in relation to the church. As Christ is head of the church, so the man is head of the woman; as the church is submitted to Christ, so wives must submit to husbands and women to men in everything (5:21–24). Perhaps it should be noted that the Greek terms here for husband and wife are those also for man and woman. We in English have to decide how we will translate them, but we should not forget that the husband-wife hierarchy is but an instance of the universal male-female and man-woman hierarchy. The Greek ambiguity (are we talking about just husbands and wives or all men and women?) nicely preserves the universal ideological "truth" that enforces the household-gender hierarchy.

In the next few verses, the role of the husband is expanded, but significantly the comparison of the husband to Christ ends up allowing Christ and his activity to take over the context: "Husbands, love your wives, just as Christ loved the church and handed himself over for her, in order that he might make her holy, cleaning (her) by the washing of water of the utterance, in order that he may present to himself the glorified church, not having any stain or wrinkle or any such thing, but in order that she might be holy and blameless" (5:25–27). Note how the gendering of dirt is introduced. The gender duality makes the male the active agent: the male brings holiness, cleanness, blamelessness, glory, and spotlessness to the profane, dirty, stained, wrinkled, guilty, *female* principle.

Furthermore, the superior male agent is the *only* active agent. Besides "cleaning up" their wives, husbands also feed them, warm them, and nourish them, as they do their own bodies. Women, on the other hand, don't do much of anything for their husbands except obey and fear them (5:33). Likewise next with the relationship of children to parents. Children are told simply to obey and honor their parents, but fathers (not the parents in general, note) are to nourish, educate, and admonish their children (6:1–4). Women and children are not told to "love" their husbands and fathers, just to obey, honor, and fear them. And they provide nothing for their men, but are themselves provided for. As in all ancient patronal ideology, the superior is the benefactor, the one who supplies the lack experienced by the inferior, whether of cleanliness, holiness, or nourishment. The patriarchal ideology of the ancient world becomes more pronounced and explicit the more the traditional household is encouraged.

This trajectory becomes simply more explicit and pronounced in the later Paulinism of the Pastoral Epistles. The author of 1 and 2 Timothy and Titus (not Paul, but a Christian writing in his name many years later) goes to greater lengths to reinforce and encourage the presence of the ancient family in the church and the structuring of the ancient church itself to resemble the hierarchical household and state. Early in 1 Timothy, for instance, the readers are instructed to pray for "kings and all in authority" (1 Tim. 2:2). (It is hard to imagine John making any such statement in his Apocalypse, just as it is hard to imagine him encouraging marriage and household economy as this author does.) In the Pastorals, women are not even allowed to pray or speak; they must learn "in silence and all submission" (2:11). They may teach younger women, but they are to have no authority over men whatsoever (2:12). This is justified because of their implication in the deception and sin of Eve. Their main role is as childbearers, through which they may be saved if they behave themselves properly (2:15).

Not only is the patriarchal household strengthened within the church; the church itself—no longer a "town meeting"—is forced into the mold of the patriarchal household (3:5). Thus women without husbands become a particular problem for this author. The author, anxious to allow neither young nor old women to escape the confines of the household, urges that the younger women be encouraged to find themselves husbands. For the older women, for whom that would not usually be a practicable solution in the ancient world, the author must figure out some way to insert them into the household of the church. They cannot be allowed to be independent or outside patriarchal authority. They therefore are inscribed in roles within the church family under the authority of its male leaders (5:3–16). It goes without saying that slaves in these letters are similarly dealt with: they are told not to expect any relief from Christianity for their servitude (6:1–2).

The familial highjacking of the apostle Paul, therefore, began early in Christianity. Paul was made to support marriage and the traditional family. But not surprisingly, that meant that Paul became a stronger proponent of social, cosmic, and ecclesiastical patriarchy and hierarchy than he had been in his authentic letters. In the ancient world, to promote marriage and the family necessarily meant to promote patriarchal ideology. And Paul was put to service to that end.

THE "ANTIFAMILY" PAUL

If the canonical disciples of Paul worked to enlist the apostle in their pro-family agenda, other followers of Paul in the ancient church made him their spokesman for an antifamilial Christian message, a message that eventually proved to be more powerful and dominant in the Christianity of late antiquity than the pro-family version. One of the most popular of ancient ascetic tracts was a short document known to modern scholars as *The Acts of Paul and Thecla*.

The story of Thecla recounted in the document is fascinating for the way it appropriates many of the elements of the Greek romantic novel in order to promote a Christian ascetic message. Ancient Greek novels are highly eroticized and romanticized narratives in which two young people struggle throughout the long narrative to consummate their love. The characters are usually separated at the beginning of the story and seek to be reunited. They are placed in all sorts of tragic and traumatic situations of love and danger. They cry about their fate, weep, and mourn. Though their virtue is continually assaulted, they are usually able to remain loyal to one another, and they are eventually reunited and married. The ancient novels actually worked to teach quite conservative notions about the value and eternity of marriage and the traditional, elite Greek household.[21]

The Acts of Paul and Thecla plays on these themes and disrupts them at the same time. The heroine, Thecla, is an upper-class woman who becomes enamored by the ascetic message of the apostle Paul, which teaches young people and women to keep themselves absolute virgins, to avoid sex entirely, to reject marriage, and to devote themselves to complete and pure celibacy. According to Paul in this text, the only way to keep the flesh pure and experience the resurrection and eternal life is to remain virginal and celibate. Thecla's attraction to Paul and his message is narrated in the tones of the desire and passion of the novels: her desire for Paul is provoked simply by hearing his voice or seeing him teaching (§7); like a love-struck heroine, she wastes away when apart from him and is "taken captive" by him (§§8–9); she experiences her love for Paul like a disease (§10). When she is finally allowed to come into his presence, she kisses his fetters and rolls herself around in the dust where he had earlier been sitting (§§18, 20). Throughout the narrative, moreover, the exceptional beauty of Thecla is emphasized; she is even repeatedly portrayed as naked and exposed to the voyeuristic public and authorities (§§33, 34). The emphasis throughout the narrative on the absolute necessity of celibacy is surpassed only by the story's highly charged eroticism. Thus, though the Christianity presented by the text is one of complete sexual renunciation, it is scantily clothed in the obviously erotic rhetoric of the ancient romantic novel.

The ultimate "enemy" of the narrative is the household. Over and over again, the story sets up a conflict between the male heads-of-households—*patres familiae*—along with the male political authorities, on the one hand, and the vast majority of the women, on the other. When Thecla is arrested or condemned to torture, it is the women of the city who pray for her, beg for her release, and bemoan her fate. But interestingly, the wives are not the only ones who side with Thecla against their own husbands. They are joined by the "young men and women" of the towns and cities. And in one scene of torture, a lioness, meant to attack Thecla, ends up siding with her. The lioness attacks the male lion and eventually gives her own life in battle against the *male* beasts in order to save Thecla. Conflict in the story pits male heads-of-households against all other potential members of households—women, girls, and young men—on the other side with Thecla. The men understand perfectly what is at issue: they themselves insist that if Christianity and Thecla succeed, that will mean the destruction of their households (§§10, 15–16).[22]

In the end, Thecla triumphs. She baptizes herself (in a huge vat of killer seals, which are all miraculously killed by a lightning bolt before they can eat Thecla);

she promises to cut her hair like a man's; she dresses herself like a man. At the end of the story, she is given a fortune by a rich widow so that she (and her mother!) can become independent and self-supporting. Thecla no longer needs a man even for financial support. Totally freed from the family and household, financially and spiritually independent, she leaves even Paul, becomes an apostle *like* Paul, and goes off to spread the Christian message of the destruction of the ancient household and to establish alternative communities of erotic Christian ascetics. Traditional marriage is rejected in favor of erotic asceticism.

The Acts of Paul and Thecla appropriates the authority of the apostle Paul to promote a woman-centered, though admittedly androgynous, form of ascetic Christianity set up in direct opposition to the male-dominated, traditional hierarchical household as promoted by other early Christian documents such as the Pastoral Epistles. Though it must be admitted that Thecla plays the really starring role in the narrative, Paul also becomes here a radical opponent of the family. The story seems to recognize what we had surmised when reading the pseudepigraphical Pauline texts: if you want to challenge the male-dominated authority structures of ancient culture, you must reject marriage and the family.

THE JOVINIAN CONTROVERSY

Though there were some early voices, such as the author of 1 and 2 Timothy and Titus examined above, who promoted ancient "family values," the opposite point of view, which valued celibacy over marriage, gradually became the more dominant position in late ancient Christianity, at least among the church's leaders and as portrayed in its writings. As J. N. D. Kelly has put it,

> from the second century onwards a widening stream of such [ascetic] essays [he is here referring first to Jerome's Letter 22, really a treatise denigrating marriage and advising celibacy] had been published by Christian writers. . . . They all draw on a common fund of ideas and expound, though with widely differing nuances, what is essentially the same doctrine. This is that marriage is, on the most favorable interpretation, a poor second best; virginity is the original state willed by God, and sexual intercourse came in only after the Fall. The underlying presuppositions are that the sexual act is intrinsically defiling, and that indulgence in it creates a barrier between the soul and God. If one is married, it is better to abstain from intercourse; a second marriage betokens regrettable carnal weakness.[23]

By the late fourth century, it was difficult to find a church leader with a different opinion.[24]

Difficult, but not impossible. In fact, the issue came to a head in a controversy centered around a Roman Christian named Jovinian, who, sometime around 390, began teaching not the *superiority* of the married state but that those who married and had sex were no worse in the eyes of God than virgins or celibates. Jovinian based his argument on a "high" view of baptism. He taught that all baptized Christians were and would continue to be of equal spiritual and moral status whether they were married, widowed, or virgin. Christians who fast are not superior to those who eat with thankfulness. And at the last judgment, all Christians who have preserved their baptism faithfully will receive equal reward regardless of whether they have been ascetics or not.[25]

Jovinian was quickly and firmly condemned. In probably 393, the bishop of Rome, Pope Siricius, called a synod that promptly rejected Jovinian's views and excommunicated Jovinian and eight of his associates. Siricius announced the excommunication in a letter to Italian bishops, in which he called Jovinian and his friends "the authors of a new heresy and blasphemy." They were, he says, "wounding Catholics, perverting the continence of the Old and New Testaments, interpreting it in a diabolical sense; by their seductive and deceitful speech they have begun to destroy no small number of Christians and to make them allies of their own insanity."[26] David Hunter has noted the historical significance of the letter: "Siricius's letter marked the first time in the history of Christianity that the superiority of celibacy over marriage was officially defined as doctrine, and conversely, that its denial was labeled as 'heresy.'" Though the sentiment had long been held by at least the vocal leadership of Christianity, it had not before been explicitly affirmed as the only permissible Christian view. "Siricius's letter, therefore, marked a distinctive hardening of boundaries in the later fourth century, the moment at which a previously implicit Christian consensus about marriage and celibacy reached a consequential degree of explicitness"—by means, that is, of an explicit statement declaring the inferiority of marriage as doctrine.[27]

In the wake of the condemnation, Jovinian and his friends betook themselves to Milan, but the famous and powerful bishop there, Saint Ambrose, also convened a synod of his own and confirmed both the condemnation of Jovinian's views and the excommunication. Both the pope and one of the most respected of the church fathers had condemned as "heresy" the opinion that the married state could be held to be of equal virtue with celibacy.

The most vocal opponent of Jovinian, however, was Jerome, one of the most prolific and famous of early church fathers and biblical interpreters, who wrote a fairly long treatise refuting Jovinian's claims point by point and besmirching his reputation. Never one to rise above personal invective and misrepresentation, Jerome exaggerates Jovinian's arguments and claims that Jovinian had disparaged celibacy, for which there is absolutely no evidence. Jovinian had simply argued that celibacy was not a *superior* state when compared to marriage.[28] Jerome's main concern is to maintain hierarchy of virtue and reward. He ranks virginity highest, followed by marriage, with fornication ranking below both. Elsewhere, he ranks virginity highest, followed by widowhood, and then marriage. Or he can combine widows and those who avoid sex even though married, and place them above sexually active wives, but below virgins.[29]

Jerome *claims* that he is not condemning marriage or sex completely (e.g., *Against Jovinian* 1.3). When he is careful, he writes that "the Church does not condemn marriage but make it subordinate."[30] But Jerome gets carried away in his disgust for sex and marriage, and many of his readers, ancient and modern, have felt that Jerome does in fact come very close to condemning marriage. Jerome argues that sex is permissible *only* for procreation (*Against Jovinian* 1.20). He argues that since abstaining from sex with one's wife "honors" her, having sex with her is equivalent to "shaming" her (1.7). Throughout, he portrays any kind of sexual activity, even that in marriage, as impure and polluting to the participants: *all* sexual intercourse is "unclean" (1.20). Finally, Jerome also (though he had apparently not by this time heard about the official condemnations of Siricius and Ambrose) calls Jovinian's view of the equality of marriage and virginity "heresy" (2.37).

Saint Augustine somewhat later also came out with publications against Jovinian's view of the "equality" of marriage. Augustine felt Jerome had gone too far, making sex and marriage sound not only "second best" but even sinful. Augustine seems to have altered his views about sex and marriage at different stages of his life. Generally, at any rate, Augustine ended up advocating that marriage was indeed a "good" and that sexual intercourse within marriage should not be condemned if done under the right conditions and with proper attitudes. The main purpose of sex is to produce children, and so sex within marriage should be indulged only for purposes of procreation. Thus, couples should not indulge if the woman is already pregnant.[31] Yet against Jovinian, Augustine affirms the superiority of celibacy: "For this reason it is a good to marry, since it is a good to beget children, to be the mother of a family; but it is better not to marry, since it is better for human society itself not to have need of marriage."[32] Augustine's position would be the one to become *the* view of the church until the Reformation and the beginnings of modernity.

This debate should not be simply ignored as "ancient history." Jovinian's view—and remember that he was advocating simply the *equality* of marriage, not its superiority—was declared heretical by a pope and three of the most honored church "fathers" and saints: Ambrose, Jerome, and Augustine. Whereas Jovinian seems to have been motivated by notions of equality that remarkably resemble modern Christian sensibilities, the "orthodox" Christian leaders were all concerned to maintain strict hierarchies both in this life and in the life to come, hierarchies of virtue and reward in which perpetual virginity occupied the highest position, with celibacy, then abstinence in marriage, then sexual activity in marriage occupying positions of virtue in a descending grade. That was the view that was considered the Christian view for most of Christian history. It is highly ironic that promoters of modern Christian "family values" and the centrality of marriage and family for Christianity portray themselves as the supporters of Christian tradition. In fact, they would be considered heretics by the "orthodox" church fathers.

THE PURITAN REVOLUTION

The long history of the "orthodox" position on marriage and family came under challenge beginning in the sixteenth century and reached a new height with the writings of Anglicans and especially Puritans in the seventeenth century. Some precursors to the Protestant Reformation had already challenged the critical view of marriage and sex of the previous centuries. "Humanist" scholars began proclaiming the superiority of the married state to celibacy. Erasmus may have been influenced by his contact with English humanists in his writing of *Encomium Matrimonii*, in which he praised the married state in comparison to celibacy. The Council of Trent, however, condemned Erasmus's views, and *Encomium Matrimonii* was placed on the index of prohibited books in 1547.[33]

Though the movement was encouraged by the Reformers Luther and Calvin, it was in England, no doubt due to the English Reformation and the abolition there of monasteries and the allowance of clerical marriage, that a change of doctrine became increasingly popular. As Lawrence Stone explains, "the medieval Catholic ideal of chastity, as a legal obligation for priests, monks and nuns and as an ideal for all members of the community to aspire to, was replaced by the ideal of conjugal affection. The married state now became the ethical norm for the virtuous Christian. . . ."[34] The very notion of what constituted a proper Christian churchman changed. In the words of Christopher Hill, "the monasteries, nunneries, friaries and chantries disappeared, and the priest, set apart by his celibacy and mediating the sacraments of the universal Church, yielded place to the parson as good family man."[35]

We must recognize that this was not simply a "reform" of previous corrupt practices or a "purifying" of the church along the lines of acknowledged orthodoxy. It was, rather, a radical *reversal* or *overturning* of previous Christian teaching about the superiority of celibacy over sex and the family.[36] And it was happening among Puritans and Anglicans alike. The theme of "holy matrimony" pervaded Protestant sermons throughout the sixteenth century.[37] Puritans increasingly took the concept further, and it is not difficult to see why: especially after the Restoration of the monarchy and the re-"Establishment" of the Church of England in 1660, Puritans were forced to rely on "separated" churches, and these were constructed as voluntary associations of "pure" and "holy" households. For the Puritans, the separated church made up of pious households replaced the "parish" as the true locus for religious observation.[38]

The seventeenth century saw the publication of many books of advice for the householder, informing him how to arrange and manage his family in a productive and pious manner. But they also sounded the new note of approval for marriage and sex, and explicitly valued marriage over celibacy. William Perkins, at the beginning of the 1600s, provided readers with his sage recommendations on the subject "Of Christian Oeconomie, or Household Government," and though he sounds reserved about marriage compared to the unrestrained encomia of our own day, he insists that it is the superior state: "Mariage of it selfe is a thing indifferent, and the kingdome of God stands no more in it then [sic] in meates and drinkes; and yet it is a state in it selfe, farre more excellent, then the condition of single life."[39] Puritans in the New World read these manuals and wrote their own. They repeatedly insist that God had ordained marriage for everyone, and that sex in marriage was essential.[40]

As we have seen, a few early Christian writers, most notably the author of 1 and 2 Timothy and Titus, offered the household as model for the structure of the church. Puritan authors, in a sense, reversed the direction of influence: in work after work of the sixteenth and seventeenth centuries, they admonish their readers to make their home into "a little church." It is as if the household comes to replace the church as the primary locus of religious activity, certainly as the primary ideological model for piety and observance. The male head of the household assumes the role of priest or pastor. In a commentary on the conversion of the jailor's household in Acts 16:34, Thomas Taylor preached, "Let every Master of Family see to what he is called; namely, to make his house a little Church, to instruct every one of his Family in the feare of God, to containe every one of them under holy discipline, to pray with them, and for them: that there may be a draught or Modell of a Church in his House."[41] In a regularly recurring theme of the entire period, authors told their readers, here in the words of William Gouge in the early seventeenth century, "A family is a little Church, and a little commonwealth."[42] It is not surprising, therefore, that the period, according to Levin Schücking, saw the development of home Bible study as a Protestant invention emphasized even more by Puritans. In fact, the era saw the rise of the "Family Bible" in homes.[43]

Lest this portrait sound too much like the "family" of our own day, we should emphasize that we are speaking here not of the modern, private, nuclear family but of the "household." Though the nuclear family certainly became more visible in this period, perhaps sociologically as well as ideologically, and it may even be true that most Puritans experienced household as predominantly nuclear (that is, it may be that many households *did* include only husband, wife, and immediate children), the kind of household that we see in literary remains of the period, including legal records and the like, was not *presented* mostly as the nuclear family. These advice books, for instance, always have large sections on how to deal with one's servants, sounding as if they *assumed* their presence in any "normal" household. The ideal Puritan household in New England included apprentices and servants, who would live with the family, and sometimes children from other homes who had been "sent out" to live with another family for any number of reasons. Moreover, New England colonies and communities were officially and legally constructed as collections of households, not individuals. Therefore, the authorities made repeated attempts in some locales to keep single adults from living alone or together outside a "normal" household. Single adults, even males, were forced to live within other existing family units. There were, therefore, all sorts of experiments attempting to incorporate "all stray bachelors and maids under the discipline of a real family governor."[44]

Furthermore, there was no expectation in New England communities that the family was "private" or immune from governmental interference or "social engineering." Modern conservatives might argue that "it doesn't take a village to raise a child; it takes a *family*." But their Puritan forefathers were ready to interfere when they felt that a householder was not fulfilling his role properly. The "state," therefore, was in control over who would be a householder and who not, and over their behavior. In the early and mid-1600s, if a householder was not behaving as the governing authorities felt he should, they could disband his household, take away his children and servants, parcel them out to other households, and force him to become a member of another household himself.[45] The Puritan household was a far cry from the nuclear family free from governmental interference so central to modern conservative romance.

The Puritan family was also firmly patriarchal. New England communities did have laws limiting the rights of husbands and providing protection for wives and children. Communities, according to recent studies, did sometimes side with women against their husbands. Some scholars have argued that Puritan women experienced better situations than women of previous eras in Europe. Yet the Puritan household was staunchly hierarchical, with the "master" firmly in charge, at least ideologically.[46] No modern notion of egalitarianism in marriage made its way into the Puritan family. Rather, it is as if what we saw to be the case in early Christianity was true also in Puritanism: the more the family is emphasized, the more patriarchy and hierarchy are strengthened.[47]

Modern Christians, if they paused long enough to look at the actual history rather than their American romanticizing of it, should think twice before calling on their Puritan "forefathers" to support their own ideology of the family. First, they must admit that the Puritan revolution was, by the standards of earlier Christianity, "heresy." When modern gay and lesbian Christians urge the recognition of same-sex marriages in churches, they are actually asking for a change much less radical than that already accomplished by the Reformers and the Puritans, who completely reversed doctrines and ethics of 1,500 years of Christian tradition and made the married state not only equal to singleness but superior to it. In comparison, simply evaluating gay and lesbian relationships on a par with those of their heterosexual neighbors is a modest innovation. Second, modern advocates of "traditional family values" should admit that their notion of the (usually) egalitarian, private, nuclear family is not a true continuation of the Reformation or Puritan household after all. The irony, or rather hypocrisy, of modern appeals to "tradition" or the "religious heritage" of American "forefathers" to support the modern notion of family should be obvious.

THE CHRISTIAN LEGACY OF THE FAMILY

There were certainly voices in ancient Christianity, as throughout its history, that have interpreted the gospel to support and promote traditional family values—of the *ancient household.* But I would argue that the vast majority of the resources of Scripture and Christian tradition until the modern period lend themselves much more readily to a critique of marriage and the family than to advocacy of them. Though the Christianity of the vast sweep of history from the church fathers until the Reformation did not go so far as to condemn marriage outright, it consistently assigned an inferior position to marriage and to those Christians who married. The "higher calling" was most often understood to be the avoidance of marriage, certainly in much of the New Testament and for almost all of late ancient Christianity.

It is thus ironic, though not really surprising, that American Christianity, especially Protestantism, has reversed the traditional valuations of Christianity. Coupled with the obscene emphasis on patriotism and nationalism, the emphasis on the family in American Christianity and popular culture approaches idolatry. "Family values" are practically the only values, along with perhaps nationalism, that seem universally recognized as "Christian values" in American popular culture, including most churches.

One of this chapter's goals is to highlight how wrong modern Christians are when they claim that their own ideology, and idolatry, of the family is simply "the biblical" or "the traditional" position. If they were true to the historical meaning of the texts and the tradition, they would have to admit that their high valuation of marriage and the family runs *counter* to the teachings of Jesus, authors of the Gospels, Paul, other biblical writers, as well as most of the church "fathers," popes, and saints. Furthermore, their own promotion of marriage and their adoration of the family run counter to the longer tradition of Christianity, at least of "orthodox" Christianity, and represent a rather radical and recent innovation in Christian doctrine and ethics. It is simply misleading, perhaps hypocritical, to say that modern family values are simply "the biblical" or "the Christian" view. In fact, there are more resources in Scripture and tradition to *critique* marriage and the family than to support it.

Another goal of this chapter, therefore, is to point out the many texts available to queer Christians that may be used to criticize the modern idolatry of marriage and family. Though I support to some extent the extension of state recognition of same-sex unions on a par with heterosexual marriage—gay and lesbian couples should have all the rights and privileges recognized by the state for heterosexuals—I am deeply ambivalent about pursuing same-sex marriage as a solution to the injustices of homophobia. I believe that both the state and the church should get out of the marriage business.

There are many excellent reasons why people in general and Christians in particular should *not* want to give the state the power to recognize and regulate marriage. When we give the state the right to legitimize one kind of sexual relationship or social formation, we automatically give it the right to render all other relations illegitimate.[48] Surely, the church should never cede its own prerogatives to the state—especially a state as bloodstained and beholden to the interests of the powerful as ours is. But *all* people should realize this: when you marry, you give power to the state over your sexual relations, your person, the most intimate details of your life and body. To agree to marriage is to agree that the modern, violent, bureaucratic state has the right to control your life in its most intimate realms, public and private, personal and sexual, individual and collective. Not to put too fine a point on it, marriage cedes your genitals to the government.

The modern emphasis on marriage and the nuclear family, moreover, fools people into thinking that the modern family can do what it cannot do. The modern family simply cannot bear the weight placed on it; it cannot deliver all the goods demanded of it, whether social, economic, emotional, or psychological. Conservatives and liberals who focus on the family, therefore, are allowing the state to shirk its own responsibilities.[49] They are attempting to push off onto the fragile modern family the responsibilities that only the state in the modern world can really bear: for universal child care and education, health care, care for the elderly and disadvantaged. The state should get out of the marriage business and get to the tasks that are its true responsibilities: caring for its citizens.

But I believe the church should also get out of the marriage business. Marriage is an exclusive and exclusionary technology for control.[50] Modern churches legitimate one kind of social and intimate bonding and therefore declare illegitimate all others. *This* relationship is good—in fact, "divine." All others are bad or at best inferior.

This exclusionary technique can be seen also in the connection of marriage to procreation. Though the stigma and shame associated with births "out of wedlock" have gradually diminished, they are still present—as is proven by the fact that cohabiting couples so often decide to marry when they become or decide to become expectant parents. Marriage legitimates childbirth. But it necessarily therefore declares other births illegitimate. Why should the church want to allow *any* of its children to be thought "illegitimate"? *Our* cry, rather, should be "No bastard children!" Bastard children are not created by the absence of marriage, but by marriage itself. Marriage makes bastards by making the category possible. For these and many other reasons we could give, both the state and the church should get out of the marriage business.

Yet queer Christians need not stop with the simply negative task of critiquing marriage and the family. Another goal of this chapter is to provoke contemporary Christians into thinking about different ways of reading Christian Scripture and tradition. Queer Christians (whose queerness may manifest itself in all sorts of unexpected ways) should use their imaginations to allow Scripture and tradition to inspire new visions of Christian community free from the constraints of the modern, heterosexual, nuclear family. We could imagine traveling bands of erotic followers of Jesus, or spirit-filled "town meetings" sharing things in common, or lively communities of men or women living together, or lively communities of men *and* women living together. We could imagine "households" of new construction, representing in their own adventuresome lives together hopes for new communities of the future. Eschatological communities. Communities in which single people are not second-class citizens, in which there are no "bastards," in which sexual orientation does not in itself stigmatize, in which varieties of households are nurtured. Alternative models to the traditional family are ready-to-hand in rich Christian Scripture and tradition.

The texts of Scripture and tradition I have analyzed bring both problems and possibilities. Some of them offer alternative visions of human community but at the price of an asceticism that renders desire and sex shameful or even sinful, a course we must also reject. Others are built on ideologies that despise the body or women. There will be no resource in Christianity or any other tradition, however, that is not to some extent problematic. All human models are tainted. There are no clean words. But these resources may also be used for retraining our imaginations both to see the inherent evils in the modern idolatry of marriage and family and to develop visions of alternative, eschatological, forward-looking communities. Rather than looking to Scripture and tradition to justify the recognition of same-sex unions and marriage, we should attempt to recover and revise resources from a forgotten Christianity vouchsafed to us in Scripture and premodern traditions: the long and valuable history of the Christian case against marriage.

Chapter 9

The Hermeneutics of Divorce

Less and less do Christians today actually debate the ethics of divorce and remarriage. Most of the time, both seem to be expected, if not accepted, as part of life. This is not to say that the topic is completely uncontroversial. Every once in a while, some Catholic bishop or spokesperson will make headlines by declaring that politicians who are divorced and remarried should be refused communion.[1] But even in those situations, one suspects that the motivating issue is less divorce itself than an attempt by conservative-leaning Roman Catholics to call into question the moral standing of some politician with whom they disagree politically.[2] On the Protestant side, publications address the pastoral issues of divorce and remarriage. But one gets the feeling that the vast majority of Christians, Roman Catholic as well as Protestant, though agreeing that divorce is regrettable and to be avoided if possible, has come to accept for the most part the reality of divorce and remarriage in contemporary society, religious as well as secular.[3]

Yet books and articles are still published on the ethics of divorce and remarriage from a Christian perspective. And when the topic of the ethics surrounding divorce and remarriage comes up among Christians—again including Roman Catholics as well as Protestants—the Bible is almost always taken to play a leading role. Indeed, the rhetoric of "biblical foundationalism" regularly recurs in writings and debates about divorce and remarriage, with very different positions attempting to find justification for their own stances in biblical texts.

Writers who believe that marriage is indissoluble and that divorce and remarriage are absolutely prohibited (except *perhaps* in a situation of adultery) argue that "God's mind" on the matter can be read from Scripture.[4] Recently, some "evangelical" Protestant Christian writers have argued for the allowance of divorce and remarriage in more cases, such as spousal abuse or desertion, but they also believe their positions are in firm agreement with what "Scripture teaches." They thus may speak of "unscriptural divorces" as opposed to "scriptural divorces."[5] Another scholar begins his study of "the biblical design or ideal for marriage" by insisting, "It is indispensably necessary . . . for the biblical guidelines to be brought to bear on the Church and the contemporary scene in which the Church bears its witness."[6] Even Roman Catholics, from whom one might not expect *biblical* foundationalism (though perhaps a foundationalism based on Church teachings or "nature" or some other source of authority), attempt to base their positions on the Bible. One Catholic writer claims, for example, that in spite of some disagreement about exegesis, "scholarship has reached two almost unanimous decisions: (1) the apostolic Church represented in this case by Mark, Luke, and Paul taught clearly the indissolubility of marriage, and (2) this teaching goes back to Jesus himself."[7] Demonstrating the pervasiveness of biblical foundationalism even in the Roman Catholic Church on the issue, another Catholic scholar—advocating the opposite position—finds fault with the Church's "dubious strategy . . . of trying to find in the New Testament teaching the warrant for this later-twelfth-century declaration of marriage's indissolubility."[8]

Authors seldom put the matter as simplistically as saying, "The Bible says it, so we must do it." They often speak of interpretation as involving at least two steps. In the first step one tries to ascertain the "meaning" of the scriptural text in itself, usually understood to mean in its ancient historical context or its "literal meaning." Some authors will then introduce a second step: moving from "what it meant" in the ancient context to "what it should mean" for us Christians today, recognizing that we live in obviously different cultural and historical circumstances.[9] Therefore, we sometimes get the impression that biblical interpretation, at least when it comes to a complicated issue like marriage and divorce, must be done in two stages: first interpreting the text itself, and only then figuring out the proper, modern ethical "application" of the text. This sort of rhetoric tends to give the impression that these two different stages of interpretation constitute actually two different procedures or "methods" of interpretation—first exegesis and then application—and that any responsible theological interpretation of the Bible must proceed in that way and in that order. Moreover, most interpreters assume (if they do not claim outright) that the proper method for ascertaining "what the text *meant*" is historical criticism: one should discern what the original historical author meant or what the meaning of the text would have been in its original historical context. On the basis of that relatively firm foundation (that is, relative to the expected disagreements about how we should *apply* the text today), the task of ethical application of the text's meaning may subsequently proceed.

This chapter has two main purposes. First, I hope to show that it is misleading to portray interpretation as occurring at two different stages, one during which the text of the Bible is "read" and the other during which it is "applied," especially if people assume that the first stage is more "scientific" or "objective" or "exegetical" whereas the second stage, that of "application," is admittedly more "creative" or "imaginative." I want to show how *all* the readings themselves are from the start "creative" interpretations and almost always ethically interested. All readings already have ethical implications.

Second, I hope to expose just how impossible it is to use the Bible as a secure *foundation* for prescriptive ethics. Given the vagaries of interpretation at all levels—from the earliest interpretations by Jesus himself, through the various interpretations by the different Gospel writers, to the interpretations by Paul, and to the different, even conflicting, interpretations of historical critics—the Bible, understood "foundationally," *cannot* provide secure answers for the ethical problems of divorce and remarriage.

THE USE OF HISTORY

Even when people agree that we must use historical research as a beginning for understanding "the New Testament view" of divorce and remarriage, they seldom explicitly point out or agree about which *part* of history, or which "moment" in history, they consider authoritative. Sometimes they sound as if they are looking for what Jesus himself taught about divorce and remarriage.[10] Of course, since we have no immediate access to Jesus in history (we can't travel through time to ask him directly), we have to read the Gospels. And since what we have in each of the Gospels is one particular *presentation* of Jesus, we have to resort to the normal procedures of historiography to ascertain, "behind" the Gospel accounts as it were, what the *historical* Jesus "may" have taught about divorce and remarriage.

Other writers, however, take the locus of authority to be the views of the individual biblical writers. So they work to ascertain what Matthew, Mark, Luke, or Paul (those whose writings address the issue) was trying to say about divorce and remarriage.[11] Still other authors seem to be thinking that the locus of biblical authority lies in the full text of the Bible treated as a whole. In this case, they imagine that "the Bible" is like a person, an agent, whom they can interrogate. Thus, they tend either to emphasize one or another of the *different* teachings about divorce and remarriage from the Bible (and as I will show below, there are very different, even contradictory, teachings about the topic in the Bible), or they homogenize the different accounts to come up with an ethic that is actually one of their own creation, a concoction using ingredients from the different biblical accounts.

Toward the end of this essay I return to this issue: even if we decide that some kind of historical construction of the meaning of the biblical text should be the starting point for ethical discussions about divorce and remarriage, what particular part of "history" do we take to be "authoritative"? The teachings of Jesus of Nazareth? The views of the individual biblical authors? The original "meaning" of "the text itself"? Or a homogenized construction of "the biblical view"? But on the way to raising that question, I first briefly analyze what we can say about the teachings of the historical Jesus and the different biblical authors on divorce and remarriage.

THE HISTORICAL JESUS

Most scholars agree that Jesus of Nazareth probably did teach something about divorce and remarriage. There are three "witnesses" to a saying of Jesus on divorce. Matthew 5:32 is similar in wording to Luke 16:18, leading scholars to believe that Matthew and Luke both took the saying over, with some changes, from a source they held in common (called "Q" by scholars), or that, according to a few other scholars, Luke copied the saying from Matthew, again making some changes along the way.[12] I am content to work with the Q hypothesis, but I don't think it makes much difference for my conclusions. At any rate, the "Q" version of the saying looks like this:

> Every man who divorces his wife [except on an account of *porneia* (sexual immorality)] causes her to commit adultery, and whoever marries a woman who has been divorced commits adultery. (Matt. 5:32)

> Every man who divorces his wife and marries another commits adultery, and whoever marries a woman who has been divorced by her husband commits adultery.[13] (Luke 16:18)

Much could be debated about these sayings, such as which has the better claim to go back to the historical Jesus and whether Matthew's "exception clause" was spoken by Jesus or added. But for now, we may simply note that Matthew and Luke here provide a saying from Jesus on divorce and remarriage.

The similar texts in Mark 10:2–12 and Matthew 19:3–12 relate a "controversy story" in which the Pharisees ask Jesus about divorce and Jesus teaches on the topic. The vast majority of scholars believe that the Gospel of Mark was written before the Gospel of Matthew and that Matthew used Mark as one of his sources. Thus, we probably have here an account that certainly goes back to Mark and may represent a saying of the historical Jesus, an account borrowed and then edited somewhat by Matthew. Several details of the two accounts, in Mark and Matthew, are important, but for the moment I concentrate merely on the main saying about divorce they share.

> Whoever divorces his wife and marries another commits adultery against her, and if she, having divorced her husband, marries another man, she commits adultery. (Mark 10:11–12)

> Whoever divorces his wife [except in the case of *porneia*] and marries another commits adultery. (Matt. 19:9)

Again, there are details here that could draw our attention, but for the time being I note only that Mark 10:11–12 and Matthew 19:9 provide a second piece of evidence for a saying of Jesus on divorce and remarriage.

A third witness to Jesus' attitude toward divorce is found in 1 Corinthians 7:10–11:

> To those who are married I command—not I but the Lord—that the woman must not separate from her husband—if indeed she does separate, let her remain unmarried or be reconciled to her husband—and a man must not put away his wife.

Though scholars believe some of this saying originated with Paul (for instance, the clause about her remaining unmarried or reconciled if she has divorced), Paul attributes the basic prohibition of divorce to "the Lord," which suggests that some form of the saying may go back to the historical Jesus.

Before getting into the interpretation of these different sayings in their textual contexts, we may ask whether any of them may be attributed to the historical Jesus, and if so in what form. First, we should note that none of the versions agrees completely with the others, but that we may reduce the various differences to two basic forms. The saying shared by Matthew 5:32 and Luke 16:18 provides one form, with the wording in the two Gospels at times shared verbatim. The actions of the man are addressed but not those of the woman, whereas in the Mark saying and in Paul the actions of the woman are also addressed. We may call the former the "Q" form of the divorce saying since it is shared by Matthew and Luke but not by Mark. Scholars may debate which version of the saying, that in Matthew or that in Luke, is more likely to go back to "Q" or to the historical Jesus, but other than the "exception clause" of Matthew (which most scholars believe is Matthew's addition, as I explain below), the difference in the versions is not of great importance for my purposes here. I take it that the Luke version has a better claim to be the more "primitive" form (that is, to be closest to what Jesus may have said) and to have read basically, "Whoever divorces his wife and marries another commits adultery, and whoever marries a woman divorced by her husband commits adultery."

As noted above, Matthew 19:3–12 is dependent on Mark 10:2–12, so we may speak of this version of the divorce saying as the Markan version that is taken over and modified by Matthew. Mark's version, though, has an interesting parallel to that passed on by Paul: both Mark and Paul share a dual prohibition, doubling the prohibition against the *man*'s divorcing with a prohibition against the *woman*'s divorcing. For the moment, I will ignore the differences between Paul and Mark's versions. They share almost no words, so Mark cannot here be said to be dependent on Paul's wording, nor can they be found to go back to a common written source. We would want to see verbatim agreements to establish that kind of literary relationship.[14] I believe we have instead two independent witnesses to a saying by Jesus that prohibited both the man and the woman from initiating divorce, and this provides a form of the saying independent from that shared by Matthew and Luke (Q).

Scholars have debated whether the dual prohibition may go back to the historical Jesus, often arguing that it must not because, they claim, it was not possible for a woman to initiate divorce in the Palestinian Jewish context of Jesus' day. The prohibition directed to the woman, therefore, is taken by them to derive from a later Hellenistic church setting. This argument, however, is based on a faulty understanding of the Jewish situation, which was demonstrated many years ago in articles published by Bernadette Brooten, arguments that have been curiously ignored by many scholars. Brooten demonstrated, and other scholars have since supported her conclusions, that Jewish women in first-century Palestine almost certainly could and did initiate divorce on their own.[15] Thus the main argument against the early historicity of the version shared by Mark and Paul collapses, and we must admit that their version could indeed recall a saying of the historical Jesus in Palestine. We cannot, of course, demonstrate that the dual prohibition goes back to the historical Jesus, only that arguments mounted against its historicity are wrong.

To summarize our results so far, we have three independent testimonies that Jesus did teach something about divorce and remarriage: (A) Matthew 5:32 = Luke 16:18; (B) Mark 10:11–12 (adopted with changes by Matt. 19:9); and (C) 1 Corinthians 7:10–11. Moreover, early in the traditions about Jesus two different basic forms of a divorce saying circulated: one that looked like what we find in Mark and Paul with a dual prohibition, and the other like what we find in "Q," or the shared tradition of Matthew 5:32 and Luke 16:18, in which the man's actions only are addressed.

Scholars are mostly in agreement that other details of these sayings are probably secondary; that is, they were added later either by the biblical writers or sources they used. First, the "exception clauses" found in Matthew ("except for *porneia*") are certainly later additions.[16] They are found only in Matthew and therefore are not multiply attested, and they fit Matthew's tendency to "legal," we might even say "casuistic," formulations (compare, for example, Matt. 18:15–17, 21–22 with Luke 17:3–4). Second, Paul's additions to the saying are also clear: "but if she does separate, let her remain unmarried or be reconciled to her husband." Paul adds this clause as needed for the larger point he is making in 1 Corinthians 7 about the superiority of singleness over marriage unless people cannot control their desire. Third, we cannot be confident that the *setting* of the saying in the context of the controversy story of Mark 10 and Matthew 19 is historical. There is no multiple attestation (Matthew could have taken it over from Mark with no independent knowledge). Moreover, some scholars have argued that the controversy story, as a conflict over interpretation of Scriptures with the Pharisees, may better reflect an early church setting than one in Jesus' life (though I am uncertain how much weight to give that argument). In the end,

I content myself with saying that we have not enough evidence to be confident that the controversy story is historical, though it could be.

In spite of these uncertainties, it is highly likely that the historical Jesus did leave behind at least one saying about divorce and remarriage and that Jesus prohibited divorce and remarriage. Though the settings may be secondary, and the "exception clauses" of both Matthew and Paul are later additions, Jesus' prohibition of both divorce and remarriage is almost certainly historical. As W. D. Davies and Dale Allison write, "it has multiple attestation (Mark, Q, Paul), its radicality is characteristic, and, as the history of the tradition shows, the church constantly found the ruling in need of clarification and qualification."[17]

I would go further and say that the Mark version of the saying (though not the whole controversy story) has the best claim to be close to the historical Jesus. The main reason most scholars believe the Mark and Paul versions are later is the inclusion of the wife as one who could divorce; they think this cannot fit a Jewish Palestinian context. Brooten and other scholars have shown them wrong. Moreover, Mark's dual man/woman form is in agreement with Paul. So we have the earliest Gospel (Mark, written perhaps just before or around 70 CE) and Paul (assuming 1 Corinthians to have been written in the 50s) in agreement.

Yet the Pauline version, though from the earliest extant text, uses quite different wording from what must have been in Q as well as Mark. The fact that Luke and Matthew agree on some wording against Mark suggests that the saying was in Q also. Thus we have Mark and Q (or some source independent from Mark) agreeing on some of the basic wording.[18] Thus, my conclusion, in contrast to that of many scholars, is that the "original" wording must be taken as something of a combination of Mark and Paul (the woman included with the man) and Q (some of the wording).

In the end, there is strong evidence that the historical Jesus did provide some teaching on divorce and remarriage and that he forbade both divorce and remarriage outright. The modifications of that teaching came later.

WHY WOULD JESUS PROHIBIT DIVORCE AND REMARRIAGE?

Having decided that the historical Jesus probably did teach against divorce and remarriage, how do we interpret its meaning in a historical Jesus context? One suggestion might be that in this case Jesus was just preserving the status quo, that he was teaching what would have been normal, traditional, conservative Jewish practice. But that certainly is not the case. All sorts of evidence indicate that divorce was generally not forbidden in Jewish Palestine. Different Jewish leaders certainly debated the grounds for legal or moral divorce and remarriage, but to forbid it outright would have been seen as eccentric and perhaps even impossible, as the very controversy story itself indicates. No, if he prohibited divorce and remarriage, Jesus was going against the status quo.[19]

According to another theory, Jesus prohibited divorce because he knew that people divorced almost always for the purposes of remarriage. Jesus' intention was to make the injunction against lust more stringent.[20] Pushing an opposite interpretation, Michael Goulder has argued that the prohibition was *anti-ascetic*: Jesus needed to counteract his disciples' asceticism, in the same way that Paul's use of the saying in 1 Corinthians 7 was in a context in which he was trying to mitigate asceticism more radical than his own.[21] And finally, since the 1970s some have tried to show that Jesus' prohibition of divorce should be seen as an indication of his "pro-woman" gospel: since men but not women had the power of divorce (so the theory goes) and since women were socially disadvantaged more than men by divorce and expulsion from the household, Jesus' prohibition was protective of women.[22] The divorce saying, therefore, relates to the gospel's liberation of women.

Of these different hypotheses, the only one that is compelling is the suggestion that Jesus prohibited divorce in order to encourage asceticism. As to the last mentioned, Bernadette Brooten, again, has convincingly argued against the assumption that Jewish women couldn't initiate divorce in first-century Palestine. Furthermore, she rightly points out that forcing women to remain in marriages could in many contexts have hurt women more than help them.[23] Goulder's suggestion that the prohibition was intended as anti-ascetic is also not likely. For one thing, it ignores other sayings on the part of Jesus that indicate that he may have been an ascetic in sexual matters.[24] Moreover, in order to support his reading, Goulder has to take Matthew 19:10, where the disciples say that *if* divorce is forbidden, then it is better not to marry, as indicating actual hyperasceticism on the part of the disciples.[25] The disciples' comments may not be historical, but in any case there is little evidence otherwise that the disciples were *more* ascetic than Jesus. The suggestion that the divorce sayings were intended as anti-ascetic, therefore, has little support.

In the end, it is difficult to interpret the meaning of the prohibition of divorce and remarriage in the context of the historical Jesus because we have little to go on in reconstructing the possible sexual asceticism of Jesus. Nonetheless, I think the most likely significance of the sayings would have been taken in Jesus' own time to promote sexual asceticism: the common assumption in the ancient world, later monasticism excluded, was that if one divorced it was to pursue someone else. Divorce and remarriage were commonly seen as serving the purposes of gratifying desire. Forbidding divorce and remarriage, therefore, would have been seen as a curb on the free rein too often given to passion. I think it most likely, therefore, that the historical Jesus did forbid divorce and remarriage and that such a prohibition was interpreted along ascetic lines of self-control in expectation of the imminent kingdom of God.

What I find more interesting than historical Jesus speculations, however, is an examination of how each of the early Christian authors presented the divorce and remarriage prohibition, often shaping it so that it ends up becoming something different—sometimes quite different—from what the historical Jesus may have meant.

JESUS AS INTERPRETER OF SCRIPTURE

Before turning to how the different New Testament authors creatively interpreted the sayings of Jesus, let us pause to examine, if only briefly, how Jesus himself interpreted Scripture. I have already admitted that we cannot be confident that the controversy story itself goes back to the historical Jesus, so I will be speaking of the "narrated Jesus," which has, of course, no less claim to "reality" than the "historical Jesus."

Jesus' hermeneutical method is seen more clearly in Mark than in Matthew. Mark has Jesus first ask the Pharisees what Moses had said on the subject, only then to go against Moses' ruling by citing other Scriptures: Genesis 1:27 and 2:24. In Mark's order of the event, it sounds as if Jesus has gotten himself into a bit of a bind: he asks the Pharisees what Moses commanded but then seems unhappy with the result, though he does not dispute their citation of the text. It is clear why Matthew would have reversed the order of the exchange. In Matthew, Jesus takes the initiative and makes his ruling by interpreting Genesis. *Then* the Pharisees counter with another text (Deuteronomy 24), and *then* Jesus gives his reason for allowing one text to trump the other: the text Jesus has cited shows God's will; the text the Pharisees cited shows only a Mosaic concession due to human sin and weakness. The setting of text against text in Matthew's version, therefore, is initiated by the Pharisees, not Jesus. In Mark's version, the fault is clearly Jesus' own, and the clash of texts becomes more obvious.

Jesus quotes one text to nullify another. Jesus quotes God's will to oppose Moses' ruling. Doubtless, this may not be the way "Mark" understood the story. And certainly Matthew would not have taken it that way. But this is obviously the way other early Christians understood it, as exemplified by the second-century *Epistle to Flora* of Ptolemy and, later, Jerome.[26] It is at least fair and reasonable to interpret Jesus' actions as countering one Scripture with another. One text is taken to represent God's will, while another that *could* be taken to contradict it may be interpreted as only human opinion or concession.

Note also that Jesus here breaks one of the cardinal rules of both ancient and modern interpretation theory: one should use the clearer text to interpret the more obscure text; interpret the obscure by appeal to the clear.[27] Here, though, the clearer text, the explicit ruling by Moses in Deuteronomy 24:1–4, which actually *is* about *divorce*, is rejected by appeal to texts (Gen. 1:27 and 2:24) that say *nothing* explicit about divorce at all. Jesus interprets the clear (or rather *rejects* it) by appeal to the obscure.

We may also observe that whereas usually Christians have set text against text to make a "rule" more lenient, Jesus (and Mark and Matthew, as we will see) did just the opposite. In fact, the history of the interpretation of these sayings provides an excellent case in point: Christian interpretation, as we will see, has through the ages taken the more "lenient" version of the divorce and remarriage saying from Matthew, with its exception clause, over the stricter versions of Mark, Luke, and Paul *in order to* render a result more "lenient" and thus more practicable. I return to this point toward the conclusion of this chapter, but I bring it up now to emphasize that most of the history of interpretation of this issue has used the opposite tack from that employed by Jesus in Mark and Matthew.

MARK

As already pointed out, the sayings about divorce and remarriage occur in Mark in the context of a controversy story, when Pharisees ask Jesus whether divorce is ever permissible (Mark 10:2–12). After a brief "back and forth" with the Pharisees, as just discussed above, Jesus first provides his basic answer by quoting Genesis 1:27 and 2:24 (and possibly also 5:2): "Male and female he made them; for this reason a man shall leave his father and mother and be joined to his wife, and the two shall be one flesh." Jesus then adds his interpretation: "So they are no longer two, but one flesh; therefore what God has joined together, let no human being separate" (Mark 10:6–9). Divorce is absolutely and unequivocally prohibited.

Jesus contrasts the actions of God (joining) with the actions of human beings (separating). The dominant idea is not that divorce is wrong for the injustice or harm it brings, but because it is human usurpation of God's prerogatives, or the human overturning of a divine deed. Interestingly, this is a notion that is somewhat at odds both with Markan tendencies and those of, probably, the historical Jesus. We have several indications in the Gospels that God allows human beings a good bit of usurpation of what we might consider "divine" prerogatives, such as casting out demons and abrogating Sabbath observance.[28] Perhaps the saying, therefore, goes back to the historical Jesus since it does not reflect a particularly Markan point of view.

In any case, the context of the divorce saying in Mark 10 provides some indication of how the author interpreted its significance. The surrounding text relates strenuous demands made of people who would be in the kingdom: cutting off one's limbs or organs (9:43–47); becoming like a child (10:15); giving up riches to follow Jesus (10:21–22); leaving houses, brothers, sisters, mother, father, and children (10:29–31; note: no mention of spouses here). Jesus here teaches that it is very difficult for the rich to enter the kingdom of God, though what is impossible with humans is possible with God (10:27). Later in the chapter, Jesus stresses the necessity of suffering and persecutions (10:30, 32–40). All this probably indicates that Mark took the prohibition of divorce as part of the heightening of ethical stringency required of Jesus' disciples. Although recognizing that other Jews permitted divorce in certain circumstances, Mark has Jesus teach that it is absolutely against the will of God and out of character with the stringent demands of the gospel.

MATTHEW

The most significant aspect of Matthew's version of the incident is that he takes a stringent prohibition that he found in Mark and Q, and that probably goes back to the historical Jesus, and turns it into something more lenient, at least somewhat. Apparently, Matthew has added his "exception clause": "except for *porneia*" (that is, some kind of sexual immorality, probably adultery; 19:9). We should note, though, that Matthew first has Jesus forbid divorce outright. Like Mark, he has Jesus quote Genesis 1:27 and 2:24 and then say, "Therefore, what God has joined together, let no human being separate" (19:6). It is only when he is challenged by the counterexample of Moses' permission of divorce that he mentions their "hardness of heart" and then adds, "But I say to you that whoever divorces his wife except for *porneia* and marries another commits adultery" (19:9).

The overwhelming tendency in the history of interpretation has been to take Matthew's "exception clause" as providing a case in which divorce is permitted. Jesus is taken as forbidding divorce unless one of the partners has committed *porneia* (sexual immorality).[29] It is rarely noted that the passage could be read differently.[30] One could interpret Matthew as laying down two separate rules here: he first prohibits divorce in any and all situations. This would be in agreement with Jesus' saying in 19:6: "What God has joined together, let no one separate." The "exception clause" would then be seen as proposing a second, additional "rule" stating that remarriage after divorce is *also* prohibited unless the divorce was due to *porneia* in the first place. In this case, the "exception clause" does not modify the prohibition of divorce; it modifies the prohibition against remarriage. There is nothing in the syntax or grammar of the language that would exclude this reading. The strongest support for it comes from the fact that otherwise Jesus seems to contradict himself, first forbidding divorce outright as against the will of God from creation (19:6), and then permitting it in some cases. If, on the other hand, the exception clause relates to remarriage and not to divorce, there is no contradiction. Matthew in this reading has Jesus forbid divorce but then add that a person will commit a *second transgression*, so to speak, by remarrying after divorce, unless the divorce was prompted by *porneia*.[31]

Does the form of the divorce saying in Matthew 5:32 contradict this interpretation? There, as noted above, the saying takes this form: "Every man who divorces his wife except on an account of *porneia* (sexual immorality) causes her to commit adultery, and whoever marries a woman who has been divorced commits adultery." Since there is no explicit mention of remarriage in this saying, and the exception clause comes immediately after the mention of divorce, one could argue that this provides evidence that the exception relates to divorce itself, thereby perhaps allowing divorce to a man whose wife is guilty of *porneia*.

I would argue that Matthew 5:32 need not be read that way, and in fact that reading it differently allows us to see Matthew as consistent rather than contradicting himself. The quotation says that if a man divorces his wife he causes her to commit adultery unless she was already guilty of *porneia*. The expectation would be that the divorced woman would naturally remarry, given the chance. If she does so, she is an adulterer in relationship to her first partner. By divorcing her, the man becomes an agent in making her an adulterer, unless she had already made herself an adulterer by means of sexual immorality on her part. The sense of the saying is this: If the woman is innocent of *porneia* and her husband divorces her, he will be at fault if she remarries and thus commits adultery against her (first) husband because she was previously innocent of that charge. But if she has committed *porneia* and then marries another, her husband is not at fault for making her an adulterer because she had already made herself one by her own sexual immorality. Thus only if the wife has *not* committed sexual immorality will her husband be culpable for "making her commit adultery" by divorcing her. If he divorces her and she marries another (adultery wouldn't be an issue unless there was "another" involved, which is what provides the clue that remarriage is assumed) he has a hand in making her an adulterer *unless she has already made herself one*. In other words, Matthew 5:32 need not be read as *allowing* divorce in the case of *porneia* but only as teaching that a *second* sin has been committed in remarriage if no *porneia* had already been committed.

Those who read Matt. 5:32 and 19:9 differently, arguing that the verses allow divorce in the case of *porneia*, are left with a clear contradiction in Matthew's text. Matthew has Jesus simply and unequivocally forbid divorce in 19:6. If he then allows an exception to that, he at least appears to be caught in a contradiction. But if Matthew 5:32 and 19:9 are read as I suggest—that divorce is absolutely forbidden, but that remarriage may not constitute a *second sin* if the divorce was due to *porneia*—there is no contradiction: Jesus in Matthew then would be forbidding divorce in all cases, and teaching that a second sin is committed by remarrying unless the divorce was due to *porneia*. In that case, there is no contradiction in Jesus' teachings on divorce in Matthew.

But what would be the *meaning* of the prohibition of divorce in Matthew? The divorce sayings in Matthew can probably be understood by seeing them as part of the "intensification of the Torah" that is an important Matthean theme. This is, in fact, the context of one of his citations of the saying, that in Matthew 5:32, among the other Matthean "antitheses" in which Jesus quotes a ruling of Torah and then teaches an ethic that is even more strict and stringent than the requirements of Torah. We would have another clue about how to understand the divorce saying in Matthew if we knew how to interpret the "eunuch" saying that Matthew adds to the discussion of divorce (19:12). On the one hand, the context suggests eschatological asceticism, but that depends on how we interpret the symbolic significance of "eunuchs." Not everyone in the ancient world would have taken eunuchs to symbolize asceticism or the avoidance of sex. Eunuchs were often seen as particularly lascivious: it was well-known that they *could* indulge in sexual activities and it was often imagined that they did so wildly, precisely because they could more easily get away with it because of no fear of pregnancy.[32] Eunuchs were certainly taken as a symbol of barrenness—that is, the inability to *impregnate*. But that need not have meant the avoidance of sexual intercourse. So the eunuch reference cannot be decisive for how we interpret the divorce saying.

The weight of evidence in Matthew indicates that *he* took the prohibition of divorce to be an intensification of Torah and a move to support eschatological asceticism. It was commonly accepted in the ancient world that divorce was normally sought in order to pursue someone else legally, in order, that is, to gratify desire. Since Matthew elsewhere has Jesus forbid even desiring another man's wife,[33] we may fairly take the motive for the prohibition of divorce to be the curbing of desire also. Yet we must keep in mind that, as mentioned above, along the way Matthew actually makes the prohibition more lenient than had the historical Jesus, Mark, or Q. He modifies his sources to lessen the sting, at least a little, of Jesus' prohibition of divorce—not, perhaps, by allowing for divorce, but at least by allowing for remarriage in limited cases.

LUKE

We face a diametrically opposite position when we turn to Luke. First, we should note that nowhere in Luke is divorce per se explicitly forbidden. Luke 16:18 forbids divorce *and remarriage*. Jesus' words in Luke could easily be taken (if we do not allow ourselves to be influenced by Matthew or Mark) to mean that the *combination* of divorce and remarriage is what is being prohibited in Luke, and that Luke had no intention of presenting Jesus as prohibiting "separation" from one's spouse—if, let us imagine, it is done for the right reasons.[34]

Note that Luke does not use Mark 10:2–12 in his Gospel. It would be hard to do so and not have Jesus forbidding divorce outright. "What God has joined together, let no one separate" (Mark 10:9; Matt. 19:6). The form of the saying Luke quotes is from Q,[35] and in that form Jesus could be taken as forbidding not divorce, but only divorce combined with remarriage. Furthermore, when compared to similar sayings in other Gospels, the "antifamily" sayings are strongest and most radical in Luke. Luke has Jesus speak of himself as a home-breaker, dividing members of households against one another (Luke 12:51–53 parallel to Matt. 10:34–36). In Luke's version of a Q saying (Luke 14:25–27), there occur two important differences compared to Matthew. Whereas Matthew says that one must not *love* father, mother, son, or daughter *more* than Jesus, Luke has the harsher saying that one must "hate" family members. And Luke, unlike Matthew, includes "wife" in the list, along with brothers and sisters. Saying 55 of *The Gospel of Thomas* also has "hate," so perhaps that version has a greater claim to go back to the historical Jesus. But "wives" and "children" are not found in the *Thomas* version, possibly indicating that the mention of wives was Luke's own addition. Note also that Luke's version ends with the statement "None of you who does not give up [*apostassô*] all of his possessions [*hyparchousin*] can be my disciple" (14:33). Family members, including in Luke father, mother, wife, children, siblings, and one's own life, are the possessions disciples are called to forsake.

We may glean similar clues about Luke's special "focus on the family" (or *against* it) from Acts. The ideal eschatological community is romantically portrayed in Acts 2:42–47 and 4:32–37; the disciples give up possessions and live together as a new community set up as an alternative to the traditional household. The antitype to this ideal is represented by Ananias and Sapphira (Acts

5:1–6), who attempt to have it both ways, giving up a portion of their goods, but retaining the rest between them. Is it an accident that Ananias and Sapphira are one of the very few married couples portrayed in Acts and that in their sin they maintain solidarity with one another?[36]

Thus Luke forbids remarriage, but he does not necessarily forbid separation. In fact, Jesus in Luke encourages separation. Lest modern readers assume that divorce and separation are not the same thing, we should remember that most people in the ancient Mediterranean would not have recognized the distinction. Most people in the Roman world would have needed no official ceremony or document to effect a divorce. Even Roman law "recognized" marriage and divorce by reference, ultimately, only to the "will" of the persons involved. If they "willed" that they were married, they were; if they "willed" that they were no longer, they were no longer. Besides the fact that Roman family law would have had little direct jurisdiction (if any) on most of the people living in the Roman Empire, especially most Jews and early Christians living in the east, the different rules and customs of divorce were too varied and unenforced to render much significance to a distinction between divorce and separation.[37] By *urging* separation, Luke was *allowing* divorce. Luke disallows remarriage, but not necessarily divorce since he sees a radically new eschatological community taking the place of the traditional household, including marriage. Luke therefore renders an interpretation opposite that of Matthew: Matthew completely prohibits divorce but permits remarriage in limited cases; Luke allows for divorce but prohibits remarriage completely.[38]

PAUL: 1 CORINTHIANS 7:10–11 IN CONTEXT

The last interpretation of the divorce saying is that by Paul (1 Cor. 7:10–16). First, we may note that Paul quotes the strict version of the prohibition, one without any exception clause: "The woman should not separate from her husband . . . and the man should not divorce his wife" (7:10). And in the beginning of his treatment of the issue, Paul forbids any remarriage except in the form of reconciliation to the original spouse (7:11). We might expect Paul therefore to forbid divorce outright. But Paul then adds material of his own to make the ruling more flexible. First, he allows Christians to agree to a divorce if the unbelieving spouse wants one. The Christian "brother or sister" is not "bound" in such matters (7:15).

But there are still other complications, even confusions, that may make Paul's position more lenient in practice. In fact, the fuller context of 1 Corinthians 7 ends up implicating Paul in inherent contradictions in his teaching on marriage, divorce, and remarriage. Besides modifying "the Lord's" saying that prohibits divorce in order to allow it in certain circumstances, Paul's overall position in 1 Corinthians 7 implicitly works against his explicit prohibition of remarriage—an absolute prohibition he quotes from "the Lord."

As I have pointed out more fully elsewhere, a central problem of 1 Corinthians 7 is the danger of desire.[39] Paul encourages celibacy and the avoidance of sexual intercourse entirely as long as desire poses no threat to the Christian. It is important to see, first, that Paul's *preference* is the avoidance of marriage. But Paul is convinced that for many people in the church desire *will* be a problem. Therefore, he allows sex within marriage for those too weak to avoid the experience of desire. If there is a danger that those within marriages will "burn," they should continue to have sexual relations (7:1–5). If the "virgin" is endangered by "affliction in the flesh," she should marry (7:25–28, 36). And though Paul states his opinion that widows would be better off (in ideal circumstances) remaining single, he allows them to remarry after the deaths of their husbands, as long as they do so "in the Lord" (7:39–40). Since this is the driving strategy of the chapter—that singleness is preferable but that marriage should be entered into if the person is endangered by desire—Paul's position necessarily should have to allow for the remarriage of those who had been divorced by their unbelieving spouses against their will.[40] What about *their* desires and passions? Are they less endangered just because they were made single by an unbelieving ex-spouse? We could take it that Paul's prohibition against remarriage earlier in the chapter was meant to address those situations in which the partners had *willingly* divorced one another. Only in that case would Paul's concession that they may remarry *only one another* make sense. But what about those people, in the same basic situation as widows, whose ex-spouses were no longer available for remarriage and were not under the authority of Paul? If they are not allowed to remarry, isn't there a danger *they* will be consumed by desire? Thus, whether Paul consciously intended it or not, his position, if made at all consistent, would need to allow for remarriage also for those divorced against their will by unbelieving spouses—if, that is, they continued to be threatened by desire. Otherwise, the entire logic of Paul's argument throughout 1 Corinthians 7 collapses. If marriage is preferable to "burning" for single Christians, and if remarriage is preferable to "burning" for widows (7:8–9, see also 39), then surely remarriage rather than "burning" would be preferable for those divorced against their wills.

Thus Paul begins with Jesus' strict prohibition against divorce and remarriage. But Paul makes it more lenient on both accounts, with regard to both divorce and remarriage: he permits divorce if the unbelieving spouse desires it, and he permits remarriage to Christians in certain situations—or at least he must if he is to be consistent with his concerns in 1 Corinthians 7. Paul quotes Jesus but feels free to alter the ruling significantly. Furthermore, Paul's interpretive moves render his text less usable as a "rule" on divorce and remarriage precisely because it contains inherent instabilities and contradictions within itself. Paul's attempt to forbid divorce and remarriage deconstructs itself.

THE RESULTS OF HISTORICAL CRITICISM

Where have we arrived with our survey of the different New Testament texts on divorce? First, it must be admitted that the earliest traditions of teaching forbade divorce entirely and unequivocally. This is most probably what Jesus himself taught, if we attempt to ascertain his teaching by means of the regular methods of constructing "the historical Jesus." It is the teaching passed along in the Gospel of Mark. And it is the teaching Paul passes along from "the Lord"—at least until he begins "massaging" the message a bit to fit his own opinions and situation. Matthew for his part, I have argued, forbids divorce and remarriage entirely but allows an exception *for remarriage* (not divorce!) in the case of sexual immorality on the part of the woman. Paul generally forbids divorce, but allows divorce in one case (when the nonbelieving spouse desires divorce), and I have argued that Paul's position, carried consistently, would seem to have to allow remarriage in such cases also. Finally, Luke, against all the others, allows divorce, even encourages it, but forbids remarriage entirely.

If we were attempting to base our own ethic of divorce on the New Testament read historically, therefore, we would be left with four different positions:

1. No divorce or remarriage, either one and absolutely.
2. No divorce at all, and remarriage allowed after divorce only if the person divorced had committed *porneia*.
3. Divorce forbidden unless the unbelieving spouse requests it, and in that case remarriage may be permitted for the Christian spouse, though only "in the Lord."
4. Divorce is permitted, even encouraged for the sake of "the kingdom," but remarriage is forbidden in all cases.

There we have it: four *very different*, even *contradictory* ethical "rules" for divorce and remarriage from the New Testament—and I have not even considered texts from the Old Testament, which would introduce even more differences.

Of course, others could, and many doubtless will, dispute my readings of the texts. It may be felt that I have pushed Luke, for instance, to a stance that we can hardly imagine any early Christian writer occupying: encouraging divorce "for the sake of the kingdom." But I would insist that I have stuck very carefully precisely to the actual text of the Gospel of Luke, without introducing speculations about "what he must have thought." At any rate, my readings of these texts are thoroughly respectable examples of modern historical criticism and the interpretation of the "literal sense" of the text by contemporary standards. My interpretation of the exception clause of Matthew's text, for instance, is absolutely defensible by the normal standards of reading ancient Greek grammar and syntax. I have refused to harmonize Mark with Matthew so that Matthew's "exception clause" can take precedence over the absolute prohibition of divorce in the Gospel of Mark, and that is a practice (allowing each New Testament document to speak on its own without harmonization with other documents) taught to every seminary student who learns modern historical criticism. One indeed may disagree with my interpretations, but they are perfectly good examples of responsible modern methods. One cannot *disprove* them simply by means of the normal criteria of historical criticism. Thus, if nothing else, my examples should be taken as demonstrating the limits of historical criticism: historical criticism *cannot* in itself provide any secure answer for "what the Bible says" about divorce that could be used as a firm foundation for modern ethics. Historical criticism gives us many and even contradictory "ethics" of marriage and divorce.

MODERN INTERPRETATION: SELF-DELUSION OR HYPOCRISY?

I have argued that the historical Jesus, as best we modern scholars can construe the situation, taught that any divorce or remarriage after divorce was against the will of God. Different biblical authors passed along these traditions differently: Mark retained the absolute prohibitions; Paul altered them to allow for divorce in some cases and perhaps remarriage in some; Matthew forbade divorce but allowed for remarriage in some cases; Luke allowed for divorce but forbade remarriage. What I think is more interesting than this diversity of earliest Christian views, though, is the fact that *no Christian church* has followed the strict interpretation and forbade divorce and remarriage completely and absolutely.[41] *Every* major branch of Christianity—Roman Catholic, Eastern Orthodox, Protestant, liberal, conservative, and evangelical—has figured out some way to permit divorce and remarriage, usually claiming that they are actually following the clear teachings of Scripture on the topic.

Eastern Orthodoxy has always taken a more relaxed, pragmatic—or perhaps one could say "pastoral"—view of divorce and remarriage. Though certainly discouraging divorce and regarding second marriage much less highly than life-long marriage, Eastern Orthodox churches have never attempted to forbid divorce and remarriage entirely.[42] It has been in the Latin Church of the West, with its doctrine of the indissolubility of marriage, that ostensive attempts have been made to forbid divorce and remarriage absolutely.

But those attempts have been inconsistent and unsuccessful. These days it is difficult to pick up a study of divorce among Roman Catholics that does not begin with lamentations about how common divorce and remarriage are among even faithful Catholics, including the admission that Catholics are divorcing and remarrying at about the same rate as Protestants, even though the Roman Catholic Church's official position has been, and still is, that marriage is indissoluble.[43] Traditionally, of course, the means by which the Church recognized what everyone else would call divorce to enable remarriage was the procedure of annulment, in which the Church hierarchy invoked its own authority to declare that the marriage was null or invalid, and therefore not a "real" marriage in the first place. For other Christians (that is, not Roman Catholics), the doctrine and practice of annulment have always looked like sophistry and casuistry run amok at best, and downright hypocrisy and dishonesty at worst. And today, even many loyal Roman Catholics are beginning to say the same. Several recent studies by

Catholic scholars have recorded how Catholics themselves tend no longer to take the annulment process "seriously."[44] Another important study by Catholic scholars, which labels annulment "Catholic divorce" and "deception," quotes even an archbishop as admitting that for many Catholics annulments "border on dishonesty and casuistry of the worst kind."[45] The substantial changes in the past thirty years or so in both the teaching about annulment and the increase in the number of annulments granted at the very least gives the lie to any Roman Catholic claim to consistency in its teaching and practice over the centuries.

The issue of annulment aside, several studies have shown that the Roman Catholic hierarchy has always reserved for itself the authority to dissolve marriages. After a lengthy study of history and canon law, Michael Lawler concludes, "The actual number of marriages the Church holds to be canonically indissoluble is, in reality, very limited."[46] As Kevin Kelly has shown, "the Catholic Church's current teaching and practice with regard to indissolubility has undergone considerable development throughout history. . . . [W]hile it believes in the indissolubility of marriage, it also accepts that most kinds of marriages can be dissolved. In fact, the only kind of marriage which it holds to be absolutely indissoluble is a valid marriage between baptized persons which has been consummated. The Church accepts the possibility of the dissolution of every other kind of marriage."[47] While this still represents a much stricter teaching than we would find in most other churches, it is nonetheless far from conforming to the strict prohibitions of divorce and remarriage we have seen in the New Testament.

One might have thought that biblical foundationalism would play no role for Roman Catholic thinking on the topic. After all, according to Catholic doctrine, the foundation of Catholic teaching lies in the teaching authority of the Church hierarchy itself more than in the text of the Bible—which makes it all the more remarkable how often Roman Catholic arguments about divorce and remarriage (whether on the more conservative or more liberal side of the debate) invoke foundationalist statements about the Bible's teaching.[48] Even moderate Catholic scholars, urging the Church to modify its traditional, strict position, do so by arguing that the strict position is a misrepresentation of the meaning of the biblical text.[49] Thus even Roman Catholic arguments about the ethics of divorce attempt to base their own positions—their diverse and contradictory positions—on a foundationalist notion of Scripture, each claiming to find their own ethics "actually existing" in the text of the Bible.

Protestants, as we would expect, are much more guilty of making foundationalist claims about the "biblical" status of their own positions, and they are usually more anxious to insist that their ethics represent the "true" reading of the text. Of course, some liberal Christian writers will admit that the text, read historically and critically, seems to prohibit divorce and remarriage either absolutely or restrictively, and they will proceed to argue that modern Christians need not or must not treat the Bible as a rule book unaffected by historical context.[50] But even other progressive scholars, urging more leniency on the issue, make biblical-foundationalist claims for their position.[51]

The most interesting instances of biblical foundationalism, though, occur in the writings of "evangelical" or more conservative Protestants who, on the one hand, believe that their ethics must derive from a correct reading of the biblical text (indeed, requiring the historical-critical method in interpreting the text), but who also, on the other hand—compelled by the increasing prevalence of divorce in their own, conservative churches—feel the need to justify more lenience with regard to the ethics of divorce and remarriage. Though there are many examples of this sort of scholarship, I concentrate here on two well-known treatments of the subject by evangelical biblical scholars.

Craig Keener published a study of divorce and remarriage in 1991 that has been welcomed by many conservative Christians precisely because it interprets the Bible as allowing remarriage after divorce in many more cases than conservative churches had previously recognized.[52] Keener affirms the necessity of historical criticism in his approach to the text; that is, he believes that the "meaning" of the text accords with how it would have been understood by its original, first-century readers. The "meaning" of the text is found in the historical reconstruction of the ancient cultural context and what the text would have meant then (ix). Yet Keener is also writing as an "evangelical" (x) and, though he does not use this terminology himself, a biblical foundationalist. For a divorce or remarriage to be "scriptural" it must find warrant in what the Scripture "allows" rather than what it "prohibits."[53] Thus, according to Keener, there are "unscriptural divorces" after which the guilty party or parties are not permitted to remarry. But the "innocent" party in a "scriptural divorce" may remarry without guilt or shame.

The thrust of Keener's study is to allow for divorce and remarriage—again with the claim that this is the *true* meaning of the biblical texts *read historically*—in many different situations. Keener admits, for instance, that the "exception clause" of Matthew was probably added by Matthew himself and did not derive from an explicit teaching of Jesus, but, he contends, "if the exception clause is not original with Jesus, its meaning is implied in his teaching, and Matthew is entirely correct to report it" (27). Keener argues that when Paul says, in 1 Corinthians 7:15, that the Christian who is divorced by her or his partner is "not bound in the matter" Paul means that the Christian is free even to remarry, though the stricter interpretation (and the one I believe is much more likely) would hold simply that Paul was saying that the Christian was not *bound* to insist on continuing the marriage, not that the Christian was then free to remarry (about which Paul says nothing in that immediate context; see 61). Keener repeatedly pushes the interpretation of each passage toward leniency. In fact, in the end Keener goes even further: he believes that physical or sexual abuse or "giving drugs to the kids" are valid reasons for divorce, with the possibility of remarriage for the "innocent" party, even though he admits that these "exceptions" are not in the text of the Bible (106–7). He explains that we may take the exceptions of biblical writers such as Paul and Matthew as providing principles on which we may also make exceptions.

In the end, Keener falls back on his own "common sense" or sense of justice, propriety, and love. I hasten to add that I think such interpretive moves are entirely appropriate: I believe we should try to come up with general principles for loving action based on a reading of Scripture with an end of justice and love in mind—rather than looking to the text as a rule book. But in this regard, Keener is no different, in spite of all his language invoking biblical foundationalism, from the more liberal Christians he elsewhere castigates for accepting "unscriptural divorces" (xi–xii). Where Keener is wrong is in failing to recognize that *his* interpretations are just as creative as those of more liberal Christians, and that such creativity begins with his very *reading* of the text and not merely with the *application* of its meaning to a different situation. His reading of the texts at the base of his interpretive practice is already influenced by his more liberal beliefs about divorce and remarriage, his tendency to avoid the strictest interpretation. To put this point in the terms of foundationalism, Keener's mistake is not in advocating a position more liberal than a historical reading of the text would warrant, but in his insistence that his own ethical conclusion is "based" on a textual foundation itself.

A study by David Instone-Brewer provides a similar example.[54] Like Keener and most other evangelical (conservative) scholars, Instone-Brewer assumes both biblical foundationalism and the necessity of historical criticism. In fact, his entire project is based on a claim that the early church fathers and Christians throughout history have misread the sayings in the New Testament about divorce and remarriage, thinking that the Bible forbids divorce entirely or perhaps allows it only in the case of adultery. This misreading was due to the fact that neither the church fathers nor subsequent Christians knew enough about the Judaism of the time of Jesus and Paul to realize that Jews would have assumed that divorce and remarriage were allowed in many more cases than just adultery. By applying the skills of historical reconstruction, Instone-Brewer is able, he claims, to recover what almost all Jews of Jesus' time would have *assumed* to be valid reasons for divorce, and those assumptions are then used to "fill in the gaps," so to speak, and understand what the earliest hearers of Jesus and Paul *would have understood them to mean* even if they did not *say* it.

Instone-Brewer argues that although both Jesus and Paul "discouraged" divorce "even for valid grounds," they both "affirmed the Old Testament grounds for divorce." The Old Testament allowed divorce in the case of adultery but also for "neglect or abuse," and since these terms are not explicitly defined or clearly delineated, quite a wide window for "valid" divorce is thus opened up. According to Instone-Brewer, "both Jesus and Paul condemned remarriage after an invalid divorce, but not after a valid divorce."[55] The proper way to understand the "biblical teachings" on divorce, therefore, is to see them as allowing divorce and remarriage certainly in the case of adultery, but also in a case of neglect or abuse or failure to keep the marriage "vows," which may include "emotional" abuse or even the withholding of love.[56]

It must be recognized that Instone-Brewer does not believe he is simply taking some general directions on justice and love from his reading of Scripture and seeking to apply them in different situations or novel ways to the particularities of marriage and divorce in our own time. He repeatedly claims that his interpretations about "valid divorce" constitute actually *the* correct interpretation of the text read historically and taken as a foundation for modern ethics. He speaks of "the biblical foundation" of the teaching, "the message of the New Testament," and "the teaching of Jesus and Paul" that must take precedence over "Church tradition."[57] It is therefore rather bizarre that his basic argument is not so much based on what the texts actually say but on what an *ancient Jewish reader must have assumed* the texts meant even if they did not say it. Since almost all Jews would have assumed that there were many legitimate reasons for divorce and remarriage, Jesus, Paul, and the Gospel writers also must have assumed those exceptions to any discouragement of divorce and remarriage. The meaning of the text lies not in the words of the text read literally but in the minds of the reconstructed ancient Jewish hearers and their *assumptions* about what would constitute a legitimate divorce. Yet Instone-Brewer nonetheless claims that this is *the meaning* of the text.

Instone-Brewer admits that many of his arguments are in fact "arguments from silence" (see 184). And they are certainly that: the text of the New Testament includes nothing about what the crowds surrounding Jesus or the first hearers of Paul's letters were *assuming* as they listened. But Instone-Brewer's interpretation goes much further than an argument from silence: it actually denies a more literal reading of the text in favor of an assumption of the early hearers. For as we have seen above, both Jesus' questioners and Jesus himself, as presented in the Gospels of Matthew and Mark, recognize that most people understood Moses and the law to allow divorce. Jesus quotes Genesis to trump Deuteronomy; he cites the intentions of God to deny to his own followers the leniency of Moses. Instone-Brewer claims that Jesus was simply "silent" about different "Old Testament grounds for divorce" (184). But that is a bizarre way of reading either Matthew 19 or Mark 10, where it seems much more correct to say that Jesus quotes one part of Jewish Scripture to make his moral teaching stricter than would be allowed by another part of Jewish Scripture, as I have shown above. Jesus is not at all "silent" about the Old Testament leniency on divorce. He contradicts it explicitly.

If one applied Instone-Brewer's method at all consistently, one would end up with no teaching of Jesus or Paul that would have sounded radical to Jews of their day. In fact, one of the best pieces of evidence against Instone-Brewer's claim that a literal forbidding of divorce and remarriage must not have been what Jesus meant, since that would have been unthinkable to his audience, is that his audience *did* (again, according to the narrative presented by the Gospel writers) find the teaching so radical as to be scarcely comprehensible. In Matthew, remember, the disciples respond in shocked tones, "If that is the case, it is better not to marry!" (Matt. 19:10). Furthermore, the radicalness of Jesus' teaching, forbidding remarriage and divorce altogether, led later Christians, as we have seen above, to alter the position in substantial and different ways.[58] One can't get rid of the radicalness of Jesus' sayings forbidding divorce by simply insisting that it *must* not have been what the sayings meant *because* that would have been too radical.

In the end, we find that one of the main motivations of Instone-Brewer's tendency to deradicalize Jesus' sayings is precisely his recognition that, were the sayings to be taken strictly, the teaching would be "impractical" for direct application to the lives of Christians: "The biggest problem with the interpretation that the NT has no grounds for divorce is that it is totally impractical. It makes no provision for divorce or even separation from adulterous or abusive partners. . . . It is difficult to believe that the Bible can be as impractical as this interpretation implies" (272–73). In other words, Instone-Brewer feels that the text *must* be more lenient than it sounds on first blush *because otherwise modern Christians could scarcely be expected to apply its teachings like a rule book to their lives today.*[59]

Unwittingly, Instone-Brewer has put his finger on one of the problems with biblical foundationalism: it is impractical; it simply doesn't work if a practicable consensus among Christians on ethical issues is sought. One of the reasons it doesn't work, as I have demonstrated, is that Christians often cannot agree about the very *meaning* of the text. But another reason it doesn't work, as this chapter has shown, is that many of the sayings of the New Testament, when taken historically and literally, are too radical to be put into practice by Christians in a consistent way. The Bible, if read historically, doesn't work very well as a rule book. At any rate, my main point here is that Instone-Brewer ignores the wider ramifications of his point about the "impracticality" of the more rigorous interpretation of the text. Instead, he just insists that *his* interpretation of the text must be the right one because it is more "practical" and accords better with modern Christian common sense. Even evangelical and conservative Christians *need* to be able sometimes to divorce and remarry. Instone-Brewer's mistake is that he seems actually to think that this is "what the text means" when interpreted objectively by the lights of historical criticism. On the contrary, Instone-Brewer's interpretation, like that of almost all evangelical scholars who have lately argued for more lenient interpretations of divorce and remarriage in the New Testament, is motivated less by the strictures of good historiography and more by the needs and experiences of contemporary evangelicals, who are divorcing and remarrying but who still want to believe that they are being "true to the Bible."

A MORE RADICAL CONCLUSION

In offering my own interpretation of the sayings on divorce and remarriage, I would like to take my lead from Luke, on the one hand, and from Instone-Brewer, on the other. The Gospel of Luke, as I showed above, parted with the other writings by portraying Jesus as permitting divorce, even encouraging separation "for the sake of the kingdom," but forbidding remarriage. Why would anyone do that? Perhaps it was in order to challenge marriage itself. Instone-Brewer noted just how "impractical" it would be to attempt to forbid divorce entirely. Christians, just like everyone else, will sometimes *need* to divorce. I have also shown that all churches have permitted divorce in some circumstances and by means of some interpretations. And why would they do that? Because any enforced prohibition of divorce entirely would have the ultimate effect of discouraging marriage completely. No institution—church or government—has succeeded in forbidding divorce because to do so would destroy marriage.[60]

And I argue, not historically but theologically, that today we should follow the radicalness of Jesus' own example, both in marriage and in interpreting Scripture. Jesus forbade divorce and remarriage, according to this more radical interpretation, not in order to support traditional marriage and the family, but in order to overturn them. As many of the church fathers thought, the disciples in Matthew's version ironically got it right: if divorce and remarriage are absolutely and completely forbidden it would be crazy to get married in the first place (Matt. 19:10). Again let me stress the point: no human society has ever succeeded in any attempt to get rid of divorce completely—almost none has even attempted it. The complete outlawing of divorce and remarriage would be impossible to enforce and insane to attempt. The history of the interpretation of these texts demonstrates that fact.

Throughout their history, the institutions of Christianity have worked hard to get around Jesus' strict prohibition of divorce and remarriage. They have made exceptions. They have invented "annulment." They have ignored the version provided by Mark in favor of Matthew's version—precisely because it is only in Matthew that they think they have found an "exception" of the prohibition of divorce. And though, as I have argued, one could just as easily read the "exception clause" to apply to remarriage but not to the prohibition of divorce, churches have taken it to provide instead a recourse for legitimate, "valid" divorce. Churches and Christians have chosen which text to read, and they have read their preferred text in a way that provides a "ruling" more likely to maintain the traditional family than to disrupt it. And they have done so for an obvious reason: any strict prohibition of divorce, demanded as radically as Jesus does, would destroy the traditional family. The social institution of marriage could not survive a radical and strictly enforced prohibition of divorce.

And I'm suggesting that was precisely the reason Jesus did so. The true meaning of Jesus' prohibition of divorce and remarriage is to supersede traditional marriage and substitute for it the eschatological family.[61] Jesus forbade divorce in order to destroy marriage. Jesus got rid of divorce and remarriage because he was bringing about radical new notions of community, family, and sexual relations. The history of interpretation, taken firmly into the heart of Scripture itself, reveals the church's continual attempts to subvert any radical notion of eschatological community and sexuality and to substitute for it traditional family values—values Jesus sought to corrupt, not sustain.

Chapter 10

Community-shaped Scripture

In 1989, Richard Hays published what was to become a justly famous book on Paul's methods of interpreting Scripture, *Echoes of Scripture in the Letters of Paul.* In it he meticulously and creatively analyzed how Paul interpreted Jewish Scripture, following and playing off echoes within and among what we may have thought were separated and perhaps even disparate citations. Throughout his study and especially at its conclusion, Hays admitted that Paul's interpretive moves often seem fanciful to us. "Paul's readings of Scripture," Hays wrote,

> are not constrained by a historical scrupulousness about the original meaning of the text. Eschatological meaning subsumes original sense. . . . True interpretation depends neither on historical inquiry nor on erudite literary analysis but on attentiveness to the promptings of the Spirit, who reveals the gospel through Scripture in surprising ways. In such interpretations, there is an element of playfulness, but the freedom of intertextual play is grounded in a secure sense of the continuity of God's grace: Paul trusts the same God who spoke though Moses to speak still in his own transformative reading.[1]

At the end of his book, Hays raises the understandable question as to what extent we ourselves may be allowed to imitate the inventiveness and boldness of Paul's readings of Scripture. Hays argues against others who have backed away from this hermeneutical precipice out of fear that such interpretive freedom will lead to chaos and arbitrary readings. Percy Gardner, from a modern liberal perspective, argues that we moderns know things about texts Paul didn't know, for example that they are historically situated. Interpretation theory, like science or historiography more generally, has progressed since Paul's day.[2] To take textual meaning the way Paul did, Gardner seems to imagine, would be like giving up modern surgery for bloodletting and leech craft. Hays rejects this position as the prejudice and self-delusion characteristic of most appeals to modern "experience" as providing a more secure epistemological foundation than Scripture. Against Richard Longenecker, who holds that we may not follow Paul's example in biblical interpretation too far because Paul was an inspired apostle and we are not, Hays argues that such a position makes us schizophrenic: "We arbitrarily grant privileged status to past interpretations that we deem unjustifiable with regard to normal, sober hermeneutical canons. . . . Longenecker has circumscribed [hermeneutical] freedom for Paul's followers by granting hermeneutical veto power to a modern critical method of which Paul himself was entirely innocent. From the perspective of faith it is not clear why this should be so" (181).

In opposition to the fearful cautiousness of these other New Testament scholars, Hays insists that "only when our interpreters and preachers read with an imaginative freedom analogous to Paul's will Scripture's voice be heard in the church. We are children of the Word," Hays says, "not prisoners" (189). He continues:

> No longer can we think of meaning as something contained by a text; texts have meaning only as they are read and used by communities of readers. Therefore, our normative proposals about the role of Scripture in the community must take account of our own hermeneutical agency. . . . [T]he attempt to separate Paul's hermeneutical freedom from ours cuts off the word at its roots. It is ironically unfaithful, in the most fundamental way, to the teaching of the apostle who insisted that "the word is near you, in your mouth and in your heart."[3]

At the close of this book published in 1989, therefore, Hays issued a clarion call for what we might think of as radical hermeneutical freedom, radical, that is, when judged from the perspective of modernity and historical criticism, which would scarcely give Paul good grades in exegesis class for his methods of interpretation.

A few years later, Hays published another important book, *The Moral Vision of the New Testament.*[4] Here, Hays is concerned to argue that contemporary Christians should read Scripture for guidance about modern ethical dilemmas. There is a lot of language in this book about "listening" to Scripture, about the New Testament "voices" "speaking" (xi), about how the church should "become a Scripture-shaped community" (3, 10). Hays seeks "to clarify how the church can read Scripture in a faithful and disciplined manner so that Scripture might come to shape the life of the church" (3). I have been intrigued by these two calls issued, admittedly at different times, by Hays. We have here an admission of Paul's hermeneutical freedom, his interpretation of Scripture that is unconstrained by the methods of modern historical criticism, along with an assertion that it is perfectly permissible for modern interpreters to follow Paul's lead in such interpretive freedom. But that is followed by a call for modern Christians to allow the biblical text to shape modern Christian identity. We are also, according to Hays, to "become a Scripture-shaped community." It is this combination of proposals—what we may think of as Hays's own hermeneutical and moral vision—that intrigues me. To what extent *may we* imitate the hermeneutics of Paul? And to what extent *did Scripture* shape the Christian identities of Paul's communities of faith? Perhaps the way to pursue these questions is to analyze a few instances of Paul's method of interpretation and its role in the formation of the Christian self among Paul's churches.

Any analysis of Paul's hermeneutical method must pay close attention of course to his letter to the Galatians. Especially Galatians 3 and 4 constitute elaborate arguments using Scripture. And, significantly for my purposes, Paul is here also concerned to define and clarify the identity of the Galatians and their roles in the plan of God, all of which Paul believes can be discerned in Scripture.

GALATIANS 3

We should first note, though, that it is only at Galatians 3:6 that Paul pays explicit attention to interpretation of Scripture. Before that, throughout the first two chapters of the letter, Paul has argued for his point of view—that the Galatians and other Gentiles should not attempt to follow the law as if they were Jews—by invoking several other rhetorical strategies that do not appeal to Scripture in any obvious way. He begins by shaming them: "I am amazed that so quickly you are turning away from the one who called you in the grace of Christ and toward another gospel!" (1:6). He invokes logic: "If I were intent on pleasing human beings, would I pursue an evangelistic strategy that has obviously provoked against me so much opposition?" (paraphrasing 1:10). He points to his apocalyptic calling as legitimating his message, and he narrates his own transformation from preacher of Torah to preacher of Christ. He argues that the central church leaders have not opposed his gospel but have in fact agreed with him. He narrates encounters and debates within other churches to back up his point (though it is none too clear that such stories would have convinced many people who may have had different versions of what had happened). He appeals to Jewish believers' experience: We have ourselves, even as Jews, experienced justification through the faith of Jesus Christ and not through works of law (2:15–16). At the end of chapter 2, he again points to his own experience: "I have died to the law in order that I may live to God" (2:19). And finally he appeals to past facts available to his hearers as well, in combination with reason: "If justification is through the law, then Christ died for nothing" (2:21). It is thus only after appeals to logic, reason, previous experiences of Christians (including his own and the Galatians'), past events, agreements of ecclesiastical bodies and their leadership, and even liberal doses of *pathos* and shaming rhetoric that Paul turns to arguments based on Scripture.

When he does so, he quite clearly reads the Galatians, and all Gentiles, *into* the text of Jewish Scripture. He quotes Genesis 15:6, "Abraham believed God, and it was reckoned to him for righteousness," and then states that everyone who has faith is a son of Abraham. Though we moderns (and Paul's ancient opponents) might wonder where in the text Paul gets this, he confidently claims that Scripture itself *foresaw* that God would justify the Gentiles by faith; Scripture therefore "preevangelized" the message by means of the prophecy that "all the Gentiles will be blessed" *in Abraham*. The Gentiles are written into the body of Abraham by a foreseeing Scripture, which indicated this by placing one clue at Genesis 15:6, another three chapters earlier at Genesis 12:3, and another three chapters later at 18:18.

Paul does not address the question, of course, of whether or not the *author* of Genesis intended these passages to teach that the nations would be justified *by faith*. After all, the text says (one could argue) that *Abraham* was justified by faith, not the nations. And its prediction is simply that the nations will be blessed through Abraham, not specifying *how* they will be blessed (that is, through faith rather than through works of law). It is Paul who finds it acceptable to connect these passages, to claim that "the Scripture" as an agent knew them to be connected, and to teach that the passages together therefore proclaim the inclusion of Gentiles into Abraham's blessing through faith.

There is much more that could be said about Galatians 3, but for the moment let's merely note that the interpretation of Scripture is important for Paul's formation of the Galatians' new identity. Though they are Gentiles, he reads them into the very text of Jewish Scripture. Scripture foresaw what God would do with them, and Scripture therefore wrote them into the body of Abraham and indicated long ago that they would be included among the sons of Abraham on the basis of faith rather than law, just like Abraham. We should also note, though, that Paul does *not* (perhaps surprisingly?) interpret all this to mean that the Galatians are no longer Gentiles. We might think that Scripture was indicating that the Galatians were Jews after all: if they were in the body of Abraham, certainly they are as much "Israel" as Paul himself. But Paul does not take that step. Indeed, it is precisely *as Gentiles* (as "the nations") that they are blessed in Abraham (3:8). We will see this puzzling inconsistency elsewhere in Paul's letters.

We should also remember, though, that Paul begins invoking Scripture only after appealing to several other kinds of arguments and "sources" of knowledge, including his own and the Galatians' *experiences*.

GALATIANS 4

But for the moment, let us continue with Paul's argument in Galatians. In the next chapter, Galatians 4, Paul again does not *begin* with an argument from Scripture. Rather, he uses common analogies drawn from the social experience of his hearers: they all know that a child is legally little better than a slave until the age of maturity (4:1–2). Paul cites the particularly Christian experiences of his hearers (4:3–7), especially invoking, again, their reception of the spirit as proof that they are already sons of God (4:6). Then he argues on the basis of shared rationality and the avoidance of contradiction: you were freed from slavery to the *stoicheia* of the universe, weren't you? Why do you want to submit to it again, which is exactly what would be happening if you began attempting to manipulate or appease the *stoicheia* by abiding by the rules of law (4:8–11)?[5]

The next point, contained in 4:12–20, is more than anything an appeal to *pathos* (that is, to their emotions) and the history Paul shares with the Galatians. He reminds them of their love and care for him and then implies that if they reject his point of view here, they are also rejecting him personally (none of which they need acknowledge themselves, of course). He points to his own use of "frank speech," *parrhêsia* ("Have I become your enemy suddenly by speaking truth to you?" 4:16). Then he uses invective against his rivals (4:17–18). He returns to emphasize his connection to the Galatians, this time appropriating even a maternal image to portray himself as their mother who suffered in bringing them into the world (4:19). And finally he appeals to their sympathy by admitting that he is at such a loss that he can't even figure out how to talk to them, so he wishes he were present with them in order to be able to change his tone to suit their mood (4:20).

It is only at 4:21 that he turns to scriptural interpretation to make his point. And to many people—certainly modern but probably ancient hearers as well—Paul's interpretation presented here (of the Sarah and Hagar stories) may seem counterintuitive. First, we should note that Paul sets up the entire interpretation as teaching the fundamental opposition of "promise" and "flesh," and he signals at the beginning that he will interpret allegorically, though he does so by claiming not that his *interpretation* is an allegory, but that the scripture *spoke* allegorically (4:24). At first, Paul sets out on what could be a rather normal and unsurprising allegory: the two women, Sarah and Hagar, will represent two covenants, one linked to "slavery" and the other to "promise." But then Paul says, "Now Hagar is Mount Sinai in Arabia, which corresponds to the present Jerusalem, for she is in slavery with her children" (4:25). His allegory quickly seems to go awry since Sinai, as the place of the giving of the Torah, might be expected to signify the Jews. Sinai, we might have thought, should be linked to Sarah, not Hagar. In fact, it no doubt occurs to Paul to connect Hagar with Sinai precisely because he intends to make a point about the Jews. And it would be natural to connect "Arabia" with the Gentiles; after all, Paul had already mentioned Arabia as his first destination after his "call" to preach to the Gentiles (1:17). One certainly might expect, therefore, that when Paul mentions Arabia in chapter 4 it would be as a reference to Gentiles. But it is not. By the connection of Sinai to Arabia, Paul connects Arabia, the place of "non-Israel," to Israel, the Jews. The mother of the Arabs (and by extension of the allegory, of all Gentiles) becomes rather the mother of the "now" Jews.

The ruling trope of the allegory is the dichotomy free/slave. Since Paul already has insisted that the law enslaves, then the law, earthly Jerusalem, and most of the Jews must be on the Hagar side of the dichotomy. Paul therefore is forced to come up with another "Jerusalem" that can be the home of the law-free believers in Christ: "The above Jerusalem is free, which is our mother" (4:26). The "Jerusalem above" is invented in order to signify freedom, Paul and his converts, and Sarah. Geography, history, and ethnic identity are all subsumed under the stronger rubric that dichotomizes Christ and freedom on one side and law and slavery on the other. The allegory is necessary so that Paul can wrest Abraham, Sarah, the covenant of freedom, and the "real" Jerusalem from the grip of the current Torah-observant Jews.

Later in the chapter, Paul will provide an equally bold allegory, claiming that the story of Ishmael's mistreatment of Isaac prefigures the current mistreatment of Christ-believers at the hands of Jews. (It need not concern us here the extent to which Paul's depiction of such persecution is accurate or the extent to which it was a reality at all; he assumes its reality in order to make his point.) Paul points to the *experience* of "persecution" by Jews of Gentile believers as another piece of evidence that *the Gentiles* (rather than the Jews) *are* "Isaac." The Gentile believers *become* Isaac in their experience of persecution. Again, things are reversed from what we would expect: the Jews are Ishmael, and the Gentiles are Isaac, though the only "proof" that Paul is able to offer to back up his interpretation is the "fact" that the Jews were actually "persecuting" Gentile believers, and not vice versa.

In other words, the reason for interpreting Isaac as representing the Gentiles rather than the Jews is the *social fact* of Jewish "persecution" of Gentile believers. Social experience provides the impetus for a particular interpretation of Scripture. To argue otherwise—that Paul simply begins with Scripture and attempts to mold the Galatians' identity and experience in accordance with Scripture—would not take seriously the counterintuitive nature of Paul's interpretations of Scripture in Galatians, interpretations that would have been just as counterintuitive to ancient readers—especially any Jews whom we may imagine listening in on Paul's exegesis.

Just as Paul had written the Galatian Gentiles into the body of Abraham, so now he has written them into the body of Isaac. Paul's interpretation of Scripture is certainly important for his attempt to define new identities for himself and his converts. But it would be misleading for us to describe that process as any sort of *secondary* formation of Christian identity or community by means of a *primary* reading of Scripture. Of course, since Paul would probably not take the situation in the way we moderns likely do, in our tendency to separate out Scripture, tradition, experience, ecclesiastical authority, nature, science, and so on, as different "sources" or "foundations" of knowledge, Paul may himself have assumed that Scripture *did* form the identity of Christians. But from our perspective, we can see that such a description of the procedure will be true only if we allow Paul his rather "fanciful" exegesis. Looking at it from the outside, it appears as if Paul rather takes first the experience of faith, reception of the spirit, adoption as children of God, hearing of the gospel, and then interprets Scripture to fit those known facts. The story of what God has done in Christ and then in believers in Christ is much more "foundational" for Paul than "listening to Scripture" in anything like the sense meant by modern New Testament scholars. Thus, it is more accurate to say that the conversion experiences of the early Christians create their identity, and then that identity causes them to interpret Scripture in certain ways to match the truth of those experiences. Their identity is set by God and the Spirit, which is confirmed in their reading of Scripture.[6]

FIRST CORINTHIANS 10 AND THE CONFUSING IDENTITY OF THE GENTILES

I mentioned above, at the end of my discussion of Galatians 3, that there is something of an inconsistency in Paul's placement of the Gentiles. On the one hand, he writes them into the bodies of Abraham and Isaac; he writes them into the story of Israel by reading the Scriptures of Israel as being, in the end, just as much about them as about the Jews. On the other hand, Paul does not take what we would think would be the next logical step and *make* the Gentiles Jews or "Israel." The one place where he might be taken as having made just such a statement would be Galatians 6:16, where Paul pronounces a blessing on "everyone who lives according to this guide (canon)."[7] He concludes with "peace and mercy on them and on the Israel of God." It is tempting to take his reference to "the Israel of God" to include the Gentiles, but since he also says "on them," we certainly must admit that "the Israel of God" *may* be limited to Jews. Therefore, we are left with this problem: Paul so eagerly writes the Gentiles into the bodies and Scripture of Israel and yet holds back from making them "Jews" or explicitly calling them "Israel" (as in "you Gentiles are now Israel").

This can be seen in another of Paul's hermeneutical adventures, this time his interpretation of the story of the golden calf in 1 Corinthians 10:1–14. At the beginning of the chapter, Paul does apparently inscribe the Corinthian Gentiles into the ancient people of Israel. He begins by saying, "Our fathers were all under the cloud and all passed through the sea" (10:1). Our? Paul could be using the first-person-plural pronoun to refer only to himself and his fellow Jews, but I think that less likely than that he intends to include the Corinthians in the "our" also. But if so, this is a striking inclusion of Gentiles into the *ethnos* (the "people" or "nation") of Israel: there are few ways of signaling ethnicity and selfhood in the ancient world more clearly than by invoking common paternity.

Yet it is then a bit surprising that the ancient Israelites become not a type for imitation or continuity but rather a negative example of behavior the Corinthians are to avoid. The Israelites are the "fathers" of the Corinthian Gentiles, but only as a negative type meant to contrast with what Paul hopes will be their own more righteous, harmonious behavior. Paul points to the Israelites in order to shape the Corinthian self, but only as a negative model which the Corinthian self-formation must avoid.

And far from attempting to pour the Corinthians' selves into the mold provided by the scriptural story, Paul rather pours the story into the mold of the Corinthians' experience. The passing under the cloud and through the sea are baptism. The people of Israel were baptized into Moses—presumably prefiguring the baptism of the Corinthians into Christ. The rock from which the Israelites drank was Christ, about whom the Corinthian Gentiles admittedly have much more direct knowledge. And is Paul adding to the text of Scripture when he writes that Christ was the rock that followed the ancient Israelites through the desert?

One has to say that although Paul has inscribed the Corinthian Gentiles into the people of Israel ("our fathers"), he has actually (from the modern point of view anyway) interpreted the Scripture to fit the experience of himself and his converts. He does of course want to influence their behavior on the basis of the moral example provided by the text. But the Scripture provides a *negative* example of idolatrous behavior that Paul insists the Corinthians avoid. The ancient people of Israel are a negative example but still a *typos* (a "type" or "figure") for the Corinthians. Thus, Paul does use the Scripture to influence the behavior of the Corinthians, but he also uses their experience as Christians (here especially baptism and eucharist) as the key for reading the text. Experience shapes reading, and then the reading is offered to shape behavior. But if we had to say where the emphasis lies in the creation of Christian identity, whether it comes from the text or more from some other source, we would have to say that their experience shapes the meaning of the text rather than the other way around. It is certainly not true that Paul *simply* inscribes them into the world of the text. It is truer that Paul interprets the text by means of their experiences as new Christians.

SCRIPTURE-SHAPED COMMUNITY OR COMMUNITY-SHAPED SCRIPTURE?

Thus my confusion with Hays's and other scholars' calls for the modern church to be a "Scripture-shaped community," especially if such calls are combined with a frank admission of Paul's hermeneutical creativity combined with a claim that modern Christians may imitate the methods of interpretation represented by biblical interpreters themselves. One problem with this combination, as I have briefly tried to illustrate, is that *if* we take Paul's hermeneutics as a model for our own, we will be more likely to allow ourselves to shape the meaning of the text rather than only allowing the text (understood from a modern perspective) to shape the meaning of our *selves*. Paul's interpretive method could better be described by invoking a term such as "the community-shaped Scripture" than "the Scripture-shaped community."

Of course, such dichotomies are always misleading. Paul *did* use Scripture to form his own identity: he saw what many have called his "conversion" as a prophetic "call" along the lines of the ancient Hebrew prophets brought to him from the pages of Scripture. And by writing his Gentile converts into the texts of Israel, he attempted to mold their identities by means of scriptural interpretation. But when we pay attention to his methods of interpretation, we see that he just as easily can be said to have molded the meaning of Scripture by reading it in light of his and his churches' experiences. The community shaped Scripture at least as much as (I would say more than) Scripture shaped the community.

THE "EXPERIENCE/SCRIPTURE" FALLACY

Actually, I do not want ultimately to press the notion that Paul used experience more to shape the meaning of Scripture than he used the meaning of Scripture to shape Christian experience. I believe the dualism itself is problematic and has caused more harm and confusion than good. Yet Hays and other conservative scholars have precisely criticized other Christians for, in their view, relying too much on "experience" rather than the "voice of Scripture" in making ethical decisions and arguments. Hays explicitly criticizes Elisabeth Schüssler Fiorenza because her method, according to Hays, "does not appeal to the Bible as its primary source but begins with women's own experience and vision of liberation." He faults her for appealing to women's experience and "critically scrutinizing" the Bible "in its light."[8] Similarly, N. T. Wright, though allowing experience some kind of role in ethical discussion, insists that it does not provide a reliable enough foundation to equal Scripture: "'Experience' is far too slippery for the concept to stand any chance of providing a stable basis sufficient to serve as an 'authority,' unless what is meant is that, as the book of Judges wryly puts it, everyone should simply do that which is right in their own eyes. And that, of course, means that there is no authority at all. Indeed, the stress on 'experience' has contributed materially to that form of pluralism, verging on anarchy, which we now see across the Western world."[9] Wright believes that experience is too subjective and open to interpretation: "If 'experience' is itself a *source* of authority, we can no longer be *addressed* by a word which comes from beyond ourselves" (102). Both Hays and Wright, along with many others, believe that the text of the Bible can "speak" and therefore provide a source of knowledge *outside ourselves*. What they are actually seeking is a source of ethical information that is not subject to the vagaries of our own interpretive activities. They set up experience as somehow a separate source for knowledge that compares unfavorably with the Bible because the text is supposed to be more stable than unreliable experience.

The fact is, it is misleading to act as if Scripture can be set up as an independent source for knowledge apart from experience. Every time we read a text we are experiencing. Readings of texts are part of our human experience, not something separate from it that can then serve as a control over experience. What we are as human beings, how we experience our lives and surroundings, is altered, at least slightly, by our experiences of readings. We can never encounter the text "outside" experience. Reading and interpretation *are* experience, though of course not all of experience or our only experience.

Scholars who wish to stress Scripture over against experience may simply mean that we should allow our *experience of reading Scripture* greater weight in our lives and ethics than we allow our *experiences of doing other things or reading other texts*. But they do not put it that way. And I believe they do not because it seems rhetorically more powerful for them to use language that implies that the text of the Bible can somehow influence us independently of the very messy process of the *experience of interpretation*. After all, they are trying to convince people that the text of the Bible is a more reliable foundation or basis for ethical knowledge than "mere" human experience. By putting it that way, they misleadingly imply that the text can serve as an independent source of knowledge that is somehow more secure and reliable and somehow not "tainted" by the messiness of human experience. But precisely because we can never have access to a text without the precarious experience of human interpretation, the dichotomy between "Scripture" and "experience" offers false hopes and only a deceptive promise of a more secure source for knowledge or ethics.

This conservative strategy of holding up Scripture as a counterweight to experience is part of a wider tradition of opposing "Christ" to "culture." Supposedly, liberals are those people who succumb to the truth claims of culture, while conservatives eschew dependence on culture by going to the Bible or Christ for their values and knowledge. Christ-against-culture rhetoric has been a staple in the "culture wars" over ethics and the Bible, usually—though not exclusively—appropriated by conservatives against more progressive positions on topics from sex to divorce to "family values," and many others. Those Christians advocating a change in ethics for sexuality, in this portrait, are supposedly abandoning Christian values and giving in to dominant secular, or Enlightenment, or just "popular" ideas. Culture is set up as something negative or dispensable, and opposed to "Christ" or "Christian values."

I have criticized this kind of rhetoric more fully in chapter 2. Briefly put, Christians can no more extricate ourselves from culture than can any other human being. Our knowledge of Christ is entirely mediated by *something* that is cultural: language, images, symbols, signs. Culture necessarily shapes *all* our experiences and anything we are able to *say* about Christ whatsoever. Since all language is cultural, and we can say nothing about Christ without language, *everything* we say about Christ is culture. Scripture is not a separate source we have access to apart from cultural experience. It is part of experience.

Rather than appealing to experience to trump Scripture or to Scripture to trump experience, Christians must recognize that our experiences, if we are Christians, are *already* shaped by influences from readings of Scripture familiar to us in some cases from our earliest memories. Many of us Christians cannot experience our experiences purified from influence from readings of Scripture. And, on the other side, there is no reading of Scripture that is not experience. The entire dualism should be jettisoned, especially when used as rhetoric to dismiss other people's experiences or readings of Scripture in order to privilege only our own. Not only is such rhetoric deceptive; it is also immoral and self-serving.

LIBERATING HERMENEUTICS

We may indeed take a lesson from Paul's own interpretive practices. Especially in Galatians, Paul appealed to the experiences of his readers to convince them of his points. In opposition to those who, quite naturally, could have appealed to Scripture to justify circumcising the Galatians—if you want to be children of Abraham, allow yourselves to be circumcised *as were Abraham's children*—Paul rather asks, "How did you receive the Spirit? Through works of the law or through faithful hearing?" (Gal. 3:2). It is certainly not a methodological leap to make a similar point for modern Christians: Did you gay and lesbian Christians come to know the fullness of the Spirit, the joy of love, the peace of God when you were fearfully living in the closet and desperately trying to deny your own feelings of love? Or did you experience the Spirit when you embraced your sexuality as a gift from God? The experience of the Spirit in the lives of Christians attempting to follow the leading of the Spirit *is* a valid means for Christian ethical reasoning, and it imitates the model of ethical reasoning and scriptural interpretation practiced by the apostle Paul.

A similar argument has been advanced by New Testament scholar Jeffrey Siker.[10] Siker notes that the early Christian leaders as portrayed in the Acts of the Apostles faced a similar decision as do modern churches when debating whether fully to accept lesbian and gay Christians in their communities. Every suggestion of Scripture they were familiar with taught that the proper way to be one of the people of God was by keeping the law, becoming circumcised, following Jewish dietary restrictions, and keeping the Sabbath. Centuries of tradition had held that if Gentiles wished to become united with the people of Israel, the children of Abraham, they had to be circumcised and keep the law. Scripture and tradition seemed clear and united. Yet the argument advanced by Peter, James, and some others of the leaders was that, in spite of Scripture and tradition, God had demonstrated his acceptance of the Gentiles *as Gentiles* by giving them the experience of the reception of the Spirit. As Siker puts it, "the experiences of Peter and Paul led them, and eventually many others, to the realization that even as a Gentile one could come to know God, to worship God, and to receive and show the Spirit of God. . . . Peter and Paul called the Jewish Christian church in their day to move beyond the marginal toleration of Gentile Christians to welcome their full inclusion. Similarly, in our day we in the heterosexual Christian church are being called by God to move beyond our marginal toleration of homosexual Christians to welcome their full inclusion."[11]

Siker's argument has of course not convinced everyone.[12] But it really cannot be denied that the shape of reasoning between the two situations is comparable and even close to identical. The evidence that God had accepted the Gentiles was their possession of the Spirit given from God. The *social fact* that they were members of the family of God even though they had not obeyed the command to be circumcised was taken as evidence enough of their acceptance by God *as they were*. And the church's leaders felt that their only recourse was also to accept them as they were.

We gay and lesbian Christians have repeatedly borne witness to our own inclusion in the family of God and our experience of the Spirit and grace of God. Our experiences have confirmed, at least to our satisfaction and to the satisfaction of millions of other Christians, that we are full members of the body of Christ as gay and lesbian people. This is not to ignore or reject Scripture. It is to follow the example of Paul, Peter, and James in interpreting Scripture by the leading of the Spirit from slavery to freedom.

Chapter 11

Conclusion

The Space of Scripture, the Risk of Faith

Throughout this book, I have addressed a variety of issues in biblical interpretation: homosexuality, sex and desire, gender equality, the singleness of Jesus, the family, divorce, and Paul's own interpretations of Scripture. The different chapters have all been driven by common goals: to explain what I label as "textual foundationalism" and demonstrate its inadequacies; to show how historical criticism, even when practiced diligently and professionally, *cannot* provide predictably ethical readings of the Bible; and to encourage more imaginative and creative thinking about the interpretation of Scripture. Repeatedly, I have critiqued rhetoric that has falsely ascribed "agency" for creating textual meaning to the "text itself" or to a "method" for reading the text, thus masking the agency *of the interpreters themselves* in the creation of meaning. I have shown that "texts don't mean; people mean with texts."

It should be clear that I am *not* arguing that the Bible is irrelevant for modern Christians, though that will probably be what some of my critics will charge. In this case, the charge would be false. I firmly believe that Christians should read Scripture and make it relevant to our lives. But I also believe that we need new ways of thinking about *how* we read Scripture. We need to move beyond the false claims of modernism that looked to the text of the Bible as a reliable and objective "source" for knowledge or as a "foundation" for ethics. We need to think about Scripture more theologically and with fresh imaginations. Far from urging the irrelevance of the Bible, I am advocating a more robust use of the Bible and a more sophisticated and adequate theology of Scripture.

POSTMODERN CHRISTIAN HISTORICISM

If I were to identify the method I have employed in these chapters, though I'm sure no such identification is necessary, I might call it "postmodern Christian historicism." My approach has certainly been some sort of "historicism." I am trained as a historical critic of the New Testament, and I use those tools. One of the questions I ask about a text, though not the only question, is; "What would this text have meant for its original author and readers, insofar as I, as a historian, can construct that?" I use word studies of the original languages. I compare the language and ideas to those of the ancient Greco-Roman world more broadly, including Judaism. I attempt to avoid "anachronism" (when I am working *as* a "historical critic"). That is, I avoid attributing to the text a meaning that would not be believable in its ancient context. I attempt to interpret Paul's letters or the individual Gospels by reference mainly to that particular document and avoid "harmonizing" the texts with those of other early Christian writers, thus allowing the diversity of early Christianity to come out in my interpretations. These are all practices of modern historical criticism that scholars learn even in the first years of university or seminary training. I am a historical critic and use historical methods.

But I call my method "historicism" rather than simply "history" to hint that my uses of modern historiography are not based on the assumption that those methods will give me "the true" meaning of the text, much less "the only" meaning. I do not assume that the historical-critical method is objective or nonbiased.[1] Nor do I believe that its conclusions will provide a reliable foundation even for knowledge of the past, much less for doctrine or ethics. Thus, though I practice the research and writing of history in a modern manner, I do not have the confidence in its results that modernists anticipated. Moreover, I advocate the use of historical criticism as one among several possible methods of reading the Bible, and not as the single privileged one. My approach may thus be labeled "postmodernist." It uses the methods of modernism without the confidence in the "knowledge" produced by modernism.[2]

My method, though, may also be identified as "Christian." Actually, when I am making a point about the "historical meaning" of the text, I try to keep my Christian beliefs at bay. I believe that what I say about the life of Jesus of Nazareth, or the authorial intentions of Paul, or the ancient meanings of the text of Revelation or the *Acts of Paul and Thecla* could usually be said by a non-Christian, a Jewish scholar, an atheist, or agnostic. In that case, I see myself as a responsible historian, attempting to describe what I take to be historically probable by the normal, public methods of modern historiography. Yet in many of these essays I have not stopped there. I have gone on to press the issue: "What may be a *Christian* reading of these texts?"

In my view, the text of the Bible is not Scripture *in itself.* It is Scripture when it is *taken* to be Scripture—holy writing, the "word of God," "inspired"—by the church, the community of Christians, the communion of the saints. One goal of my work over the past several years has been to show how much modern scholarship is inadequate for the *Christian* use of this text as Scripture; I have attempted to nod in new directions for imagining *how we may think* of the text as Scripture in better ways. Thus my method in these chapters: it is postmodern because it denies the epistemological foundations of modernism; it is Christian because in the end it is interested in the Christian reading of the text; and it is "historicism" because it uses the methods of modern historiography yet without a full commitment to the philosophical assumptions of modern historiography.

SCRIPTURE IS ABOUT SCRIPTURE

One of the problems of many modern notions about Scripture has been the assumption that we can discern, at least if we use the proper methods, what Scripture says "about" different things: doctrinal disputes, history, morality, or whatever. The commonsense assumption has been that the truth of Scripture is something to which the text of Scripture "points" or "refers." I have already mentioned the modern tendency to take the "referent" of Scripture to be historical events in themselves. Hans Frei, among others, traced the development of this tendency in the modern period: Scripture came to be less and less about the narrative of the activities of God and Jesus Christ and was taken to be about "what really happened," some kind of historical referent to which the text was simply a witness. The locus of Christian authority shifted from being Scripture itself to the historical Jesus, or the consciousness of Jesus, or the consciousness of early Christians. Frei called this "the eclipse of biblical narrative" since the *narrative* of Scripture—its story about Jesus Christ—became "eclipsed" by the supposed history "lying behind" the narrative of Scripture. The theological problem with this way of thinking is that once the *history* was thought to be "recovered," the narrative became dispensable. "History," understood to be "what the text referred to," could then displace Scripture itself as the locus of Christian attention. Scripture lost its "authority" to be replaced by the ("reconstructed" though actually *constructed*) "historical referent" of the text. Frei insisted, rightly, that what was Scripture for the church was not the history "lying behind" the text, but the text itself.[3]

I have made a similar point about authorial intention in a couple of the chapters herein. When scholars make the author's intention rather than the text itself the locus of authority, they in effect displace Scripture from the central location of Christian attention and substitute for it a modern scholarly construction of an ancient author's mental processes. And this is theologically wrong. Some scholars may answer that the *meaning* of the text is itself identical with the author's intention, but as I demonstrated in the introduction, and as many theorists have demonstrated many times, that is simply incorrect: we readers *may* sometimes entertain notions of the original author's intention, but we typically *do not identify* the "meaning" of the text with the human author's intention. This has been especially true in the history of Christian theology, except insofar as faith has said that *the author is considered God or the Holy Spirit.* Christian theology has typically resisted identifying the meaning of Scripture—even the "literal sense" of Scripture—with the intentions of the original *human* author. Again, when we shift the meaning of Scripture away from the text itself to the author's intention we in effect displace Scripture and substitute "something else" in its place.

I would go further and sound a note of caution also about suggestions from "narrative theology" in the past several years that Scripture is "about" the narrative of salvation history, a particular story about what God has done with Israel and through Jesus Christ. This move often invokes the work of Hans Frei, whom I have already mentioned. Granted, talking about the narrative of God and Jesus Christ as what Scripture is "about" is an improvement over thinking that Scripture is "about" the history to which it refers or the historical author's intentions thought to lie "behind" it. But even to say that Scripture is "about" the story of Jesus Christ is, in my view, dangerous. The tendency may then be to relate that narrative and think that by telling that particular story we have captured the meaning of Scripture. Of course, Scripture is legitimately read to tell stories, to narrate the "acts of God." But Scripture may legitimately be read to be much more than narrative: it also is poetry, rules, parables, letters, apocalypses, prophecy, philosophy (of a sort). The possible literary readings of Scripture are certainly not *exhausted* by invoking the category of "narrative." It is moreover questionable whether we should make "narrative" the dominant and controlling generic category for all our readings of Scripture. Again, I want to insist that Scripture is not "about" a narrative—whether that exemplified by the Apostles' Creed, the Nicene Creed, the Gospel of Luke and the Acts of the Apostles, or any "story" thought to be implied by the entire canon. Scripture is about itself.

Of course, it is legitimate to say that Scripture is about God or the identity of Jesus Christ, and that has been a theological claim made often in Christian history. But once we attempt to distill the terms "God" or "Jesus Christ" in the previous sentence into some particular *proposition about* God or Christ, we have again overstepped the appropriate bounds: we are then substituting some proposition for the irreducible nature of Scripture. Since the "content" of what we mean by "God" and "Jesus Christ" is precisely what we go to Scripture to figure out, it may be theologically correct to say that Scripture is "about" God or Christ, but it is also circular. We should not think we can distill the meaning of Scripture into anything but Scripture. The meaning of Scripture is Scripture, or God, or Jesus Christ, but not some propositional, historical, or ethical statement about truth.

We should leave behind the modernist idea that we read Scripture in order to distill from it some propositional, doctrinal, or ethical truth statement, and think of the meaning of Scripture as residing in the reading of Scripture itself. In fact,

I find it helpful to think of the meaning of Scripture as residing in the *performance* of scripture. We *are* accessing the meaning of Scripture when we attempt to read it in faith, when we read it aloud in church, when we sing it in hymns, when we perform it in music, when we dance it, when we enact it in a procession, when we stage it in the stations of the cross or the Easter Vigil, when we construct it in stained glass or paintings or statuary. This is again not to say that we should replace Scripture itself with any of these particular activities. It is just to make the point that the meaning of Scripture resides more than any place else in the *enacting* of Scripture in particular practices. The "meaning of Scripture" is not something outside Scripture to which Scripture "points." The "meaning of Scripture" is in the performance of Scripture, in the reading of Scripture itself—in the varied and unending ways in which we may imagine "reading" taking place.

DOWN WITH LOVE?

So how do we judge which readings are better? In some of the chapters in this volume I have invoked an ethic of love as a ruling guide for our interpretations of Scripture. To those who know recent debates in theological ethics, this may have sounded naïve on my part. Several theologians and ethicists have pointed out problems with a too-easy appeal to compassion or love as a guide for Christian ethics.[4] One classic expression of this position was made by Stanley Hauerwas in an essay titled "Love Isn't All You Need."[5] Reacting mainly to "situation ethics" as it was debated in the 1960s and 1970s, Hauerwas argued that "love" is "insufficient" as a guide for Christian ethics.[6] Part of Hauerwas's argument is that too often "love" is turned into an "abstraction" (*Vision and Virtue*, 116–17) and that its application is too often "sentimental." But, as Hauerwas explains, "even if love is freed from its sentimental perversions, it is still not an adequate principle, policy, or summary metaphor to capture the thrust of the Gospel for the Christian's moral behavior. . . . The Christian is thus better advised to resist the temptation to reduce the Gospel to a single formula or summary image for the moral life. Christian ethics and the Christian moral life are as rich and various as the story we hold and the life we must live to be true to it" (120).

Though I sympathize with Hauerwas's concerns, I believe his argument is weak in significant aspects, and I find it less than compelling as a dismissal of love in ethical discourse. In the first place, Hauerwas too readily slips into an easy but deceptive rhetoric that denigrates "love" until it becomes little more than a lax and lazy "tolerance" or "inclusivity." Ethicists and theologians who make the "down with love" kind of argument almost invariably slip into degrading love and making it sound like nothing more than the avoidance of confrontation.[7] This is a false caricature. When other Christians invoke "love" as an ethical guide they do *not* regularly turn it into nothing more than an "anything goes" lack of ethical rigor. People who emphasize the centrality of love for the gospel know that it is difficult, demanding of sacrifice, and will *not* avoid confrontation or judgment *when appropriate for the ends of love*. Christian talk about love always includes reference to the cross, and few authors, in my view, have forgotten that, in spite of the insinuations of their critics. Hauerwas and his followers cheapen the discourse of love by employing the rhetoric of mere sentimentality or tolerance.

Second, Hauerwas's rhetoric rightly notes that a principle of love cannot be "sufficient" to capture all the complexities of the gospel and "the depth and heights of the world we must see to be worthwhile and substantive moral beings" (117). But Hauerwas comes dangerously close to implying that there is *something else* that is a more adequate guide for Christian ethics, such as "virtue," or "character," or "justice," or the "story" of the gospel itself. Hauerwas's position is much better than that of many others who make the "down with love" kind of argument because, in the end, Hauerwas rejects other foundationalisms also, finally arguing that there is no "principle" or "idea" that in itself can serve as an adequate guide. He thus usually emphasizes the need for proper Christian communities that may nurture the proper Christian virtues and create Christian character that will lead to moral choices and behavior. But as long as one is not making any kind of foundationalist claim about love—not claiming, that is, that "love" can serve as a dependable and predictable source for ethical knowledge—Hauerwas's arguments against appealing to love become much weaker.

Though Hauerwas's rhetoric, I believe, has too often implied a foundationalism of "the community" and "the story," Hauerwas for the most part has attempted to avoid epistemological foundationalism. Others have not been so careful. Richard Hays follows Hauerwas in arguing that "love" cannot suffice as "a unifying theme for New Testament ethics."[8] But Hays's language reveals the foundationalism, especially the textual foundationalism, I criticize in chapters 1 and 2. Hays argues against appeals to love on several grounds. First, Hays argues that "love" is not found in all parts of the Bible, so focusing on it would leave out of consideration many parts of the text. Of course, this implies that the three "focal images" Hays chooses in place of "love" ("community, cross, and new creation") *do* occur in all parts of the New Testament, and that is not true. Second, Hays claims that "love" is "not an image" but a "conceptual abstraction." Again, one need not agree: "love" may just as easily be treated as an "image," and Hays's preferred "images" (community, cross, and new creation) can just as easily become "conceptual abstractions." Third, Hays follows Hauerwas in noting that love "can cover a multitude of sins." What Hays does not acknowledge is that *any* concept, principle, or "focal image" may also "cover a multitude of sins." Any word or principle may be used to unethical ends. Finally, Hays makes the point (also made by others) that love is not "sufficient." Love "might produce more distortion than clarity in our construal of the New Testament's ethical witness" (203). But Hays doesn't recognize that nothing is "sufficient" *in itself* to capture the fullness of the gospel or Scripture—*including* Hays's own suggested method for arriving at ethical interpretations of Scripture, nor can anything else guarantee a lack of "distortion." None of the "images" or principles advocated by Hays himself can serve as a "sufficient" foundation for ethics—because *nothing can*. Hays demands from love a standard of "sufficiency" or "adequacy" for prescriptive ethics that no concept, word, principle, image, or method can meet.

Hauerwas, Hays, and most other scholars who dismiss appeals to love in ethical debate usually invoke, in the end, some notion of Christian "community" as the way to guard against the unethical application of Christian notions, including "love." Yet here again, the regular invocation of "community" by Hauerwas and many of his students can be subjected to the same criticisms turned against "love." No one can identify in our physical world this idealistic moral "community" to which they refer. All actual Christian communities are just as prone to sin and self-deception as is any ethicist advocating "love." The invocation of Christian "community" may appeal to those who have experienced Christian groups as open-minded, loving, and benevolent. But to many of us—most lesbian, gay, and other "nonstraight" Christians—Christian communities have just as often been a source of hatred and sin.

This realization came home to me with something of a shock while reading a book on the ethical use of the Bible written by two scholars who also take their lead from Hauerwas's work, Stephen E. Fowl and L. Gregory Jones. To illustrate the importance of Christian community and identity, Fowl and Jones tell a story. A woman and her husband are hunting in the mountains of Colorado. She becomes separated from him and lost in the forest. As night falls and the cold increases in the wilderness, she becomes more and more lost and frightened. "Finally, through the trees she sees some lights in a secluded cabin. She has no idea what might happen to her if she knocks on the door, and she is very anxious. A person opens the door, and the woman says urgently, 'Please help me—I'm lost.' The people in the house comfort her and tell her, 'It's OK. You're safe. We'll take care of you. We are Christians here.'"[9]

Doubtless, Fowl and Jones intend the story as one of reassurance. I assume they expect the reader to breathe a sigh of relief at the last line. But when I first read the story a chill ran up my spine, and when I have recounted the story to audiences of "people like me"—gay men, lesbians, bisexuals, and other "sexual minorities"—the chill was felt throughout the room, often accompanied by gasps. For many of us, the story sounds like the beginning of a horror movie. Why did the couple so quickly blurt out their religion? Were they members of some kind of self-consciously separated sect? After all, this is supposed to take place in the mountains of Colorado, the home of virulently homophobic institutions such as "Focus on the Family" and the American Air Force Academy, not to mention countless other right-wing groups, hate groups, and disturbed individuals living in the hills. Are we supposed to assume that the couple helped the woman *only because they were Christians*? Are Fowl and Jones implying that ordinary Coloradans who *didn't* wear their Christianity "on their sleeve" would harm the woman? For many of us, identifying this couple as "Christian" says nothing reassuring about their ethics at all. The mere label "Christian" does not carry the same value for many of us that it apparently does for Fowl and Jones. We've experienced some of the greatest hate from Christians.

The recent popular appeal to Christian community, therefore, is not only less than satisfactory for most of us lesbian and gay Christians. We find the easy appeal to "community" not only too facile but even threatening without more emphasis on a demand that those communities practice, *towards us*, love.

Admittedly, love as a mere principle or "abstract concept" is not "sufficient" as a foundation for reliable knowledge about ethics. But nothing is. And that realization need not lead to a rejection of the demand that Christian interpreters defend their interpretations by demonstrating that they render loving practices. The appeal to love will not solve all our problems or settle all our disagreements. But demanding that interpreters demonstrate that their condemnations of lesbian and gay Christians are "the loving thing to do" is at least preferable to the simple statement that something is true just because "the Bible says so" or because it is "the will of God." A debate about love and its demands is preferable to simplistic and deceptive claims about "what the Bible says."

This proposal has the added benefit, as I mentioned already in chapter 3 (p. 49), of being precisely that test of interpretation advocated by other "greats" in Christian tradition, not least St. Augustine. Of course, Augustine probably believed he was simply building on a reading of the New Testament itself. The Gospels famously present Jesus as teaching the priority of the command to love God and our neighbor (Mark 12:29–31; Matt. 22:36–40; Luke 10:25–28; see also John 13:34). The apostle Paul went even further: in Romans 13:9 he taught that *all* commandments are fulfilled by the one commandment to love the neighbor, even leaving out any reference to the commandment to love God. This is of course not to say that Paul would have rejected or ignored the commandment to love God, but it could certainly be argued that Paul was here teaching that love of God would itself have no meaning without love of neighbor and that the love of God must never be interpreted as separable from or ignoring the love of neighbor.[10]

St. Augustine followed the same path. As I noted in chapter 1, for Augustine the test for whether a text is to be taken "literally" or "figuratively" is love: if a text of Scripture seems to advocate actions that do not promote the love of God and neighbor, it should be interpreted figuratively. If it advocates love, it is literal.[11] When we are confronted with things that seem like foreign cultural practices to us, we should not despair, imagining that there is no universal justice, "that all peoples view their own conventions as just." Rather, we should evaluate such cultural differences by the criterion of love, because, as Augustine puts it, "the command 'what you would not want done to yourself, do not do to another' can in no way be altered by the differences among nations."[12] In fact, since for Augustine the true meaning of Scripture is love, Scripture for Augustine is, in the words of James Callahan, "practically dispensable."[13] Augustine writes, "Therefore a person strengthened by faith, hope, and love, and who steadfastly holds on to them, has no need of the scriptures except to instruct others."[14] At the very least, the suggestion that all interpretations of Scripture should be called before the tribunal of love has compelling precedent in Christian tradition. [15]

I urge not that we assume that love will provide a reliable foundation for knowledge but that we nonetheless keep the requirements of love of neighbor foremost in our interpretations of Scripture. We should consider, for example, love to be a *necessary* criterion (a *minimum*) when defending an interpretation of Scripture even if it cannot be a *sufficient* criterion that will guarantee ethical interpretation. Though love may not work as a foundation for knowledge, I propose that we learn to assume something like a "stance" of love. I take this notion of a stance from philosopher of science Bas van Fraassen. In his book *The Empirical Stance*, van Fraassen demonstrates how the modern foundationalist philosophies of empiricism eventually collapsed under the pressure of skepticism.[16] "Old-fashioned" modernist empiricism believed that science could replicate the reality of nature by disciplined observation. But the very demand for an absolutely solid foundation for knowledge itself led to the collapse of the optimism of empiricism as a philosophy of knowledge.[17] Many philosophers gradually gave up the older idea that we may "find" reliable, objective truth about nature if we just observe it carefully enough and without bias. In place of the older confidence of modern empiricism, van Fraassen advocates that we assume a more modest and open-ended point of view, a "stance." We must regularly remind ourselves that the world around us may surprise us; we constantly realize that we could be wrong; we regularly test our beliefs by recourse to the "facts," realizing of course that "facts" are themselves constructed with hard work and may change; and we compare our beliefs with those of others. As van Fraassen puts it,

> stances do involve beliefs and are indeed inconceivable in separation from beliefs and opinion. The important point is simply that a stance will involve a good deal more, will not be identifiable through the beliefs involved, and can persist through changes of belief. . . . All our factual beliefs are to be given over as hostages to fortune, to the fortunes of future empirical evidence, and given up when they fail, without succumbing to despair, cynicism, or debilitating relativism.[18]

Van Fraassen's way of thinking about empiricism in a postfoundationalist environment is informative for how we may think about holding onto the centrality of love as a guide to ethical interpretation of Scripture in the absence of textual or other ethical foundations. Recognizing that unfortunate mistakes and even terrible atrocities have been committed in the name of love, we nonetheless should nurture a "stance of love." We are always to be on our guard that our interpretations of Scripture do not harm but actively promote what is truly good for our neighbor. Whether an interpretation is finally Christian will still not be predictable ahead of time, but one central test by which we attempt to make that determination, a test for the Christian ethical value of an interpretation, will be more than anything whether it promotes the love of the other. Not a secure foundation for knowledge, by any means, but certainly a much needed attitude: the "stance of love."

SCRIPTURE AS SPACE: MUSEUM

The chapters in this volume have all tried to demonstrate that we need to move beyond thinking of Scripture as a foundation for knowledge, as a rule book, a constitution, or an owner's manual. In spite of assumptions propagated by the "self-help" culture that infects so much of contemporary American Christianity, the Bible is not a self-help book or owner's manual. If it were an owner's manual, it would be a bad one. For one thing, there are no illustrations. There's no place where we are clearly shown that "tab A" goes into "slot B," even though that is precisely how many conservative Christians attempt to read the Bible sexually. One of the best arguments against taking the Bible as a constitution, rule book, or owner's manual is that it makes a lousy one.

I believe we must educate our imaginations in new ways to think about Scripture differently. And this is a work of the imagination.[19] There is no one answer for how we should interpret Scripture. There is no workable prescription for arriving at ethically valid readings of the Bible. But I do believe we may begin by learning to think differently about what Scripture *is* and *does*. I myself have experimented with thinking of Scripture as space: we should think of Scripture as "sanctuary space" and interpretation as moving through complex and ever-expanding hypertext systems.[20] In the next section of this chapter I focus on imagining Scripture as the sanctuary space of a church or cathedral. But first I would like to invoke another kind of sanctuary space: an art museum. What can we learn about interpreting Scripture in a nonfoundationalist way by imagining Scripture as a museum?

First, consider how we think about a building "communicating." Does a building "communicate"? Does a building tell us what to think of it? The answer could be "yes"—*if* we assume that the viewer has been socialized to read its signs. But the answer would certainly be "no" if we take the question as more than metaphor. A building cannot force an interpretation of itself on me. In fact, the human designers and builders of the building cannot do so either. We may read a book in which the builders tell us what they *wanted* to communicate by means of the building. But that need not constrain my own experience of the building. Insofar, though, as the designers and builders use common social signs and conventions, they *may* be able to influence my experience of the building quite strongly.

Thus, even a postmodernist nonfoundationalist may say, "What is this building saying?" But to do so as a nonfoundationalist is to keep the question from fooling us into thinking that the building itself (apart from our socialization and interpretive activities) is dispensing its meaning and controlling our experience of it. That is to say, it is perfectly legitimate to debate the meaning of a building even if we don't believe there is some "place" to go finally to adjudicate potential disagreements. Just appealing to "the building itself" will not settle the issue—without, that is, the need for more elaborate persuasion. I think we would all agree that asking about the architect's "intention," though a possible strategy of persuasion, would not on its own settle any debate about what a building communicates. We often disagree with the architect's "intention"; we may believe, for instance, that "it didn't work" despite "the best of intentions." So history and authority *may* play roles in interpretation. They just don't get to *decide* the issues.

A museum, of course, is more than its building. It is more than anything its collection and display. And as I have found the "meaning" of the building stimulating for new imaginations about the "meaning" of Scripture and interpretation, so I find a museum with its collection stimulating for reimagining what Scripture is.

To some people, it may seem inappropriate to compare Scripture to a museum. Museums have been thought of as places for old things that have outlived their original use. Museums contain "relics." Furthermore, historians have often noted the rise of the museum in modern culture and the way museum culture can be seen as removing objects from their original, "natural" environment (a painting in a home or church, for instance) and placing them in an artificial, secondary, even "false" environment in which they no longer serve the purpose for which they were originally created but are commodified for the gaze of the consumer of the "museum market." To compare Scripture to a museum or the objects in a museum may imply to some people, therefore, that Scripture is a relic from the past that no longer lives a productive life. I think this sentiment, though, suffers from a naïve notion of "authenticity." I love museums and experience them as living, changing, interesting, and inspiring environments. The anxiety over "authenticity" is a tired old worry, about as interesting as teenage boys arguing over which garage band is truly "authentic" and which has "sold out." If we don't bother too much about popular misconceptions concerning museums and art, I think we may find the comparison of Scripture to a museum a fruitful one.

Museums are obviously "secondary" constructions in which artifacts, or at least many of them, are placed in a context different from that of their creation. Other than modern art that is constructed for its position in a museum—sometimes even for the precise place in the particular museum where we encounter it—most objects in a museum are displayed in ways their creators may never have intended or ways their original viewers may never have imagined. Likewise, historical criticism has drilled it into our heads that the different books of the Bible weren't created to be books of the Bible, at least not in the conscious intention of their human authors. These different texts, and even parts of the different texts, served very different functions originally than they now serve as parts of Scripture.

Which brings up another point: Scripture is a collection, like a museum. Moreover, it is a collection whose selection involved important value judgments. Think also of the amazing variety of objects included in a modern art museum. But once an object is included in the collection, whether that of a museum or of the canon, its new context determines to some extent its interpretation and the appropriate "rules" by which it will be interpreted.

Furthermore, just as a museum contains a diversity of objects and increasingly a diversity of kinds of objects, so also is there a diversity, in fact a *hierarchy*, of interpreters and interpretive expertise, from the child to the adult to the docent to the art professor—and all positions in between. The docent's interpretation probably will be "ruled" by that of the art professor. But neither of them may legitimately rule the interpretations of the child or even of the "tourist" adult. After all, good docents often begin by asking the viewer, "What do *you* see in this work?" The idea that the expert should be allowed to constrain the interpretations of others rightly offends our sensibilities about museums and art. It ought to offend us just as much when applied to Scripture.

I have also argued, following contemporary theologians, that there is no *property* inherent in the text of the Bible that *makes* it Scripture. It is Scripture because the church (according to faith led by the Holy Spirit) *takes* the text to be Scripture. This is quite like the way "art" is established *as art* in a museum. There are many things in museums that *could* be art but that we do not take as art: say, an elevator door, a stairway, or a metal panel on a wall that may remarkably resemble a piece of abstract, modern art. Some art on display is actually "found art," pieces of everyday material—sand, magazines, rope, old tires—*made into art* by being placed by an "artist" in a certain manner in a museum. My point is that context and social agreement (even if not explicit or conscious) determine whether something is or is not art. I would argue that there is nothing intrinsic in the work of art itself that makes it art. It is the placement of the piece in a particular kind of setting that defines it as art, and the kinds of settings that make something art are themselves constituted by either explicit or implicit social consensus. In the same way, the different texts that make up Scripture need not be thought of as containing within themselves any quality or property that makes them Scripture. They are Scripture because they have been taken to be Scripture by particular communities of people. In all their variety, the texts that make up Scripture do so because of the explicit and implicit social consensus of a people.

Finally, an important way in which museums and Scripture are alike is that in both contexts notions of "truth" are neither *excluded* nor the sole determining issue. We would be foolish to exclude questions about truth when discussing museums or works of art. But we would be perhaps even more foolish if we thought that questions of truth were the only ones that really mattered in such discussions. I return to this question later.

Just as I have used the museum to think about interpretation of Scripture, so I want to offer an interpretation of a painting in order to think about how we may interpret texts.[21] When I was living in Copenhagen one fall, on research leave and working at the University of Copenhagen, I enjoyed visiting the Statens Museum for Kunst, the national art gallery of Denmark. On my first visit I was taken by surprise when I rounded a corner and came before a large painting by Carl Bloch, a Danish painter. The painting (dated 1863) is called "Samson and the Philistines." It is a huge painting depicting Samson struggling as he turns a treadmill. He is guarded by a Philistine taskmaster and watched by three other Philistine men.[22]

When I first saw the painting in Copenhagen I experienced a case of "memory shock." Although I couldn't have said who the painter was, I knew the painting immediately. I have distinct memories of staring at a reproduction of

Samson and the Philistines, 1863, Carl Bloch

this painting in my childhood—not from a book of art history, but from some kind of religious literature: perhaps the painting illustrated some Sunday school materials from my childhood church, or maybe I had seen it as an illustration in a Bible. I don't remember. But the painting had an impact on me even as a child, and that memory washed over me suddenly as I looked again at the painting in the museum in Copenhagen. What did it mean to me and why? What *does* it mean?

We could interpret the painting formally, concentrating on issues of color, balance, composition of images in the painting, or even the technique of the artist. Or we could provide rather traditional interpretations of the subject matter and composition. We might focus, for example, on Samson's blue, filigreed robe, of which only scraps remain, partly lying on the ground and partly serving as Samson's loincloth. We could focus on such details along with the biblical story and say that the painting was about more than Samson's story. It is rather more broadly about "human nature" and the fleeting quality of power and prosperity. The painting is a moral story meant to warn us all about the transience of strength; we look at Samson's fate and learn humility.

We could also pursue a less romantic (or less "nineteenth-century") interpretation and focus on the "orientalism" of the painting—the tendency in literature and scholarship to portray people of "the East" as exotic but also a bit barbaric.[23] We then see the painting as implicating Carl Bloch in Western European colonialist prejudice as he depicts the Philistines in typical caricatures of oriental barbarism and despotism. The painting portrays the helplessness of submission to fatalism so like the East and unlike the self-determination and humanism of the West. We recall from the biblical story that even though Samson regains his strength, in the end he can use it only to seal his own fate in the destruction he finally brings upon the Philistines. He and they seemed fated for destruction no matter what they do. Bloch's painting, showing the growing strength of Samson in the midst of those he will destroy, is a portrait of oriental fatalism.

But I want to offer an interpretation of the painting that is more personal, one that springs from my remembrances of the painting from my childhood. Because I do remember the image. I remember studying it, lingering over it, being aroused by it—sexually aroused. You see, the painting does not just depict Samson toiling; it depicts him as a young, muscular, almost naked man. His exposed buttock is foremost in the center of the painting.

Even as a small boy, without knowing what "homosexual" meant, much less the term "gay," which was scarcely common in my circles at that time, I knew two things for certain: that I was sexually aroused by other males, and that I wasn't supposed to be. I knew both about my desires and the shame they were supposed to entail. And here in my Bible or Sunday school book was a stimulating image of a beautiful, erotic, muscular male body. The temptation was being presented to me in the folds of holiness. Though the thought would never have occurred to me then, I now can say that it was as if the "sin" was being offered to me by the very hand of God. But my musings provoke the question, Was I misinterpreting the painting as a child—do I misinterpret it now—because it seems to me so clearly to communicate male homoerotic desire?

Perhaps, then, I should give an account, as an adult and even a scholar, for why I, decades and much "sophistication" later, still see the painting as conveying male homoeroticism. First, of course, is the near nakedness of Samson and his beautiful body. He needn't have been depicted that way, of course. He could have been clothed in sufficient rags that we needn't gaze upon his flexing triceps, his tensed calves, his taut hamstrings, his quivering thighs, his arching back, and last but certainly not least, his soft and rounded buttocks.

Mr. Bloch could even have made him ugly. But he didn't. Mr. Bloch unveiled for us, exposed for us, this beautiful body, as hairless and smooth-skinned as any depilated model in a gay porn magazine. Of course, Mr. Bloch probably knew his business well. So, like any caterer to the voyeuristic interest, he left the most strategic parts of Samson covered. Try as I might as a young boy, I couldn't turn the page fast enough to get a glimpse under Samson's loose, hanging, almost-falling-off loincloth. I knew there had to be treasures in the darkness of that shadow, but I couldn't turn the page to the light enough to see. And whenever I visited the painting in the museum, I couldn't seem to scoot around the side of the frame fast enough to see what I wanted to see. But this is the result of tried and true techniques in the production of desire.

It is not just Samson's body, though, that makes the subject of the painting male homoeroticism. I also remember studying the expressions of the men who gleefully watch Samson work. There are three of them off in the shadows, though we can see the full faces of only two. They grin. They stare. They are delighted. Someone could say that they are merely gloating that their enemy is now in chains, doing a beast's labor for their benefit. They are gloating in their sudden and unexpected triumph over Samson. But as a little boy, I saw something else in their eyes: arousal. They hunch their shoulders in a tinge of sexual guilt; they giggle; they turn to go but cannot help stealing another lurid glance. The man in back is even too ashamed to come completely into the room, but he can't help looking at the beautiful muscle man. Beauty—even subjugated beauty—for some people, *especially* subjugated beauty—is irresistible. Even their uniformly long noses, given what we know from Freud and older folk knowledge, give them away. Their phalluses on their faces are stiff as they gaze upon Samson slaving away. The slave driver sitting on the mill is himself not uninterested or bored. He gleefully pokes Samson with his long, stiff rod. He obviously enjoys being on top.

There are other details we could take as supplementing the erotic nature of the painting. Behind and to the left of the mill from our perspective are the smoldering red-hot coals of a fire, signifying the embers of desire. And at the top of the painting, close to the right-hand corner, is a lone lamp burning, signifying night, the time of bedding down and lovemaking—and this even though there *needn't* be a lamp there: we can tell from the reflections and shadows cast by the light coming from a source off the canvas to our left that it is daytime, and the candle seems to be doing nothing to illuminate the room. It therefore must have a symbolic purpose. All these details provide, I believe, more than sufficient justification for seeing the painting as depicting the subject of male homoerotic desire and even voyeurism.

Or am I reading into the painting what I want to see? I don't think that would be a fair accusation. Certainly as a young boy years ago I did not "want" to see any such thing—at least not consciously. And can we really speak of "wanting" something of which a person is completely unaware? Perhaps "needing" or "lacking," but not "wanting." I insist that my boyhood viewing was at least an "innocent" (that is, uncontrived) response to the painting. And even now, I believe that the interpretation of the painting I have offered pays enough careful attention to the details of the work to justify itself as a legitimate interpretation.

But how do we evaluate such interpretations? If we could find out what Bloch "intended," would that be sufficient or even allowable as a "test"? Or how about examining the painting's nineteenth-century viewers? If I could demonstrate that *they* saw it as treating the subject of male homoeroticism, would that settle the matter? Or should we interpret the painting by reference to the text of Judges it depicts? Certainly we *may* do so, but *must* we? I argue that any such "intertextual" interpretation (connecting the painting to the biblical story or even the art-historical comparison of other depictions of Samson) is quite allowable. But we certainly wouldn't judge the painting or painter negatively if we decided that his painting did not "match" the Bible. Or perhaps only a "Philistine" would. Without denying that the biblical text might enrich our viewing of the painting, we must certainly resist any attempt to allow that text to *constrain* our viewing of the painting—as I think just about everyone would agree. Likewise for the "historical meaning" of Samson, or the painter's intentions, or the nineteenth-century viewers' interpretations.

My point is that it is the *plurality* of resources, intertexts, and methods that *should* be employed in an ever-broadening interpretation of the painting. And that the same kind of plurality of method, intertexts, and resources may—should—be used in interpreting Scripture. Bloch's "Samson and the Philistines" "means" many things—as many as there are viewers and views of it: the "historical" referent, the "historical reconstruction," the textual narratological "character," the story, the history of interpretation, the history of art, Bloch's goals, the painting's nineteenth-century viewers, and yes, my boyish homoerotic reaction and my mature homosexual interpretation. No one of these interpretations has the right to force the others to submit to its adjudication—unless *we* give it that right. And I am arguing that we should not.

How would we describe what I've been doing in all my interpretations of this piece of art? Free association? Just blathering about my "feelings"? I have raised issues of intentionality, historicity, social context, and location. I haven't, but I could, raise issues of "influence" and "originality." I have also raised questions about the perceptions of both historical and contemporary (to ourselves) viewers. But has there been a *method* at work here? I would say that one *could* distill my practices down to a "method"—but that doing so wouldn't get us very far if our goal is to come up with a method that would render dependable, "true," or "good" interpretations when applied prescriptively.

And that, I argue, is precisely the situation we find ourselves in when interpreting Scripture in a postmodern, nonfoundationalist environment. Issues such as the author's intention or the historical meaning of the text, like the art, certainly need not be excluded. But each must serve as one approach among many others. We have impoverished our readings of Scripture because we have narrowed our methods of interpretation. We need to retrain our imaginations about what Scripture is and how we may interpret it. Thinking about Scripture as a museum, and interpretation of a text as similar to interpretation of an artwork, may be one way to expand that imagination.

SCRIPTURE AS SPACE: CATHEDRAL

My goal here is not to say anything profound about museums or art but to prod our imaginations in new directions with regard to how we think about the nature of Scripture and its interpretation. So perhaps an even more appropriate "sanctuary space" for thinking about Scripture would be a cathedral or a church.

The architecture of a sanctuary is obviously intended to communicate. Its height and loft, its pointing to the heavens, lift our gaze. We can't look at a cathedral without looking up. Its parts literally point to the sky. In the classic Gothic cathedral, the height of the walls, the shimmering of the glass, and the very need of flying buttresses to hold the thing up speak of the transcendence of the divine. The building itself moves our gaze in the direction of God.

The open doors of a church invite passersby to enter. At times, people off the street, often with no connection to that particular church, cautiously and silently enter an open door of a chapel or church to feel the peace or sense the beauty of the place. They may have little or no faith, but the church itself, the door, seem to entice them in. And once inside, there are things to see and contemplate.

For one thing, there is the multiplicity of spaces. Space is different in different places; it feels different. Entering provides one experience; moving through different areas provides another; standing at the back, or in the center, or at the altar looking up or back—all are somewhat different from one another. The architecture communicates—height, light, openness, or darkness. Arches, columns, colors. The deep reds and whites of my own Episcopal church in New Haven, Christ Church, soothe but also evoke images of royalty or luxury. In Christ Church the consciously imitative medieval architecture and decoration connect us to a long and rich history: the communion of the saints, the catholic church universal and ancient. The very building and its contents communicate the extension of our community through time, and the architecture is one of those ways we learn who we are.

The medieval church, when able, often incorporated its message in the easily readable medium of stained glass. In an era when most people could not read, telling the stories of Scripture through images, especially the shining and eye-catching images of stained glass, was a most effective means of communicating the biblical stories and messages. The distance between text and visual art, therefore, is especially bridged by the medieval communicative technology of stained glass.

The extension through time, the "telescoping" of centuries, comes out especially in stained-glass depictions. The art form was developed before the advent of modern historical consciousness, so the settings of the scenes are usually those not of ancient Palestine and the Middle East, but of medieval Europe. The architecture portrayed in the windows of Christ Church, New Haven, as in many stained-glass depictions, looks like northern Italy or rural England, not ancient Israel. The people are dressed in medieval European fashions, not those of the ancient Jews. The current building housing Christ Church in New Haven was built in the 1890s, yet the architecture and the windows self-consciously imitate English Gothic style. The windows, though constructed at the end of the nineteenth century in an industrial town of New England, portray the figures in medieval dress and the settings as something like medieval England. To the modernist historical imagination, this is anachronism, that dreaded boogeyman or horror of historical criticism. But it may also be seen as *delightful* anachronism, a conscious and determined anachronism, again invoking the transhistorical nature of Christian faith: here twenty-first-century Christians worship surrounded by glittering images of people in medieval costume and landscape, depicting scenes that are supposed to have taken place in first-century Palestine. The worshipers in the church are surrounded by movement through time, the communion of saints dead and alive.

The move through time is not limited, moreover, to the Christian era. In Christ Church, the narrative in the glass begins with the expulsion of Adam and Eve from the garden, appropriate for one thing because this is "Christ Church," and the coming of Christ was to redeem us from the separation from God depicted in that expulsion. That window is appropriately situated in the chapel to Mary at one corner of the nave, appropriate because Mary has been interpreted through centuries as the counterpoint to Eve: through Mary's acceptance of God's will, she brings us with her back into the purity of God's presence. Then the windows, almost all of them, tell the story of Jesus Christ, beginning with "Hail Mary, full of grace," and "Blessed art thou amongst women." The gospel then continues around the walls in the glass, with depictions of healings, miracles, feedings, betrayals, and suffering.

In Christ Church, the centrality of the passion of Christ is emphasized by the location, all around the walls of the church, of the stations of the cross carved in white stone. The passion surrounds the Christians as they pray and celebrate. But of course the gospel does not end with the crucifixion, and the iconography of the church, like the narrative of Scripture, leads the viewer through the rest of the story: the resurrection and appearances, the recognition of Christ in his breaking of the bread. At the rear of the church, to the west so that the setting sun sets it ablaze, is a great window depicting the last judgment, the defeat of evil, and the final salvation of the world.

It is easy to see how stained-glass windows tell the story of Scripture, even to the point sometimes of having the text inscribed in the window itself. But just as Scripture does more than tell a linear narrative—it contains poems and songs, wisdom sayings, rules and commands, prophecies, and stories of several different types—so does a cathedral communicate in many different ways, by alluding to all sorts of saints, figures, symbols in art, statues, images.

In many cathedrals, the architecture itself is designed to lead the worshipers, as they proceed forward to receive the eucharist at the altar rail, in a symbolic journey from the world to the presence of God, from earth to heaven. Passing through the rood screen from the nave to the choir, from the congregation to the chancel, symbolizes the passing into the presence of God in order to receive the body and blood of Christ. Often, the chancel is designed to evoke the glory and beauty of heaven, to lift the worshiper up from the frustrations and perhaps disappointments of the week, and to promise relief, joy, light, music, and beauty. After receiving the eucharist, the worshiper symbolically moves back into the world.

The space of a cathedral feels a certain way when entered alone, and the same space takes on different meanings when filled by the congregation. There is nothing inappropriate about an empty church, even if we admit that it speaks one meaning when empty and another when bustling with the movements and noise and music and smells of the liturgy. Just as we read Scripture both alone and together, so one can experience the gospel communicated through a sanctuary by a solitary visit, by slipping in to pray or just to look, or in congregation, in public worship and liturgy (*leitourgia*, "service") to God. When we read Scripture alone at home or by a lake, that is like entering a sanctuary in the quiet alone, letting that space guide our meditations and prayers. But we also read Scripture with others, in community. And the space of a cathedral, like Scripture, *feels* different, communicates differently, *means* differently when experienced with others.

We may learn new ways of reading Scripture if we think about it in terms of how the sanctuary space of a cathedral communicates. Reading Scripture, I urge, should not be like consulting a rule book or owner's manual. It should be like entering a space, a cathedral, moving around in its communicative richness, allowing our imaginations, our very selves, to be changed by the experience. It is not simply "learning a truth" that is propositional or derived linearly. But it *is* making meaning.

COMMENTARY AS HYPERTEXT: VIRTUAL CATHEDRAL

I have asked that we imagine reading the Bible to be like entering a cathedral, a sanctuary. Fortunately, we are at the beginning of new technology that appropriates notions of space to present all sorts of textuality that were once presented only in the linear, solid form of the printed text on paper. I refer, of course, to the Internet and the medium of hypertext. Briefly, I would like to urge us to think about the model of the Internet hypertext as the future of biblical commentary.[24]

In fact, what I have been doing is something like hypertext. We have moved from image to image almost by suggestion and association rather than strict linear logic or referentiality. I have asked the reader to accompany me to different spaces—museums and churches, inside and outside—just as a hypertext document on a computer, like a video game, takes us into different spaces. I have been suggesting that we think about different media of communication—texts, painting, music, sculpture, architecture—the way hypertexts eclectically combine and sometimes surprisingly juxtapose different media. Could this point toward the biblical commentary of the future?

Let us imagine that we have a hypertext commentary of the Bible. We click on the icon of the Bible and select a page, say the creation story from Genesis 1, or the story of the transfiguration from the Gospel of Luke. When we move the cursor over the text, words light up if there is something there to pursue. We click on a word, or perhaps a verse, and are taken to another place where we may access word studies, find out what the Greek or Hebrew is and its range of meanings. We see links to commentaries on the word or text, certainly modern commentaries, but also premodern commentaries, to read what Meister Eckhart, or Julian of Norwich, or Augustine, or Jerome, or Origen said about the text. In the modernist world of biblical scholarship, premodern interpretation has often been considered irrelevant. We certainly don't usually encounter patristic exegesis in academic courses in biblical studies, captured as they are by historical criticism, with its disdain of anything not done under the rubric of modern historiography. But the hypertext commentary has the advantage of bringing in premodern interpretation without throwing out historical criticism and modern commentary.

Another link, though, might take us to sermons people have preached on this text, again from the ancient period to today. Another takes us to art galleries, where we may study and derive inspiration from the ways artists have depicted the scene, perhaps with commentary on the paintings or sculpture or abstract art itself. Another link brings us to a music room, where we may select from a menu of musical compositions based on or related to the particular biblical text we are studying. We listen to the music while browsing through the paintings. Another link takes us to literature: Milton, Shakespeare, Bunyan, T. S. Eliot, Flannery O'Connor, whichever literary sources might help us think about this particular biblical text in a new and challenging way. We could go on to suggest other possible links: perhaps to plays and theater, films, black American spirituals, and folklore.

We are standing on the edge of what could be a new era in the study and teaching of the Bible. We now have the technology to move biblical commentary out of the narrow confines of textual comments on the "original historical meaning" of the text or the "author's intention" and outward to an expanding vista of ever-newly built rooms, links, evolving commentary. The meaning of the biblical text grows outward, into the whole world and all of history, and inward, into the depths of history, literature, art, and music—and into the infinity of our minds, the limits of which we cannot reach. Why don't we teach biblical studies this way? Wouldn't hypertext be a truer, more theologically defensible model for biblical interpretation than the more "archeological" image of just digging up "the" true and "single" meaning of the text, the image of biblical studies that has held hegemonic sway over modern biblical studies? And isn't it time to end the hegemony over biblical interpretation that historical criticism has exercised in most of our seminaries and divinity schools for the past hundred years?

FLOATING ON A SEA OF FAITH

But how do we know our interpretations of Scripture will not be misinterpretations? How can we guard against unethical uses of the Bible? Are there no standards, methods, or safeguards against misuse of Scripture?

Unfortunately, the truest answer is, "No." There are no absolutely dependable criteria or methods that can assure us that we will read Scripture rightly.[25] There are, of course, ways we can attempt to interpret Christianly. As Augustine and so many other church fathers and Christian theologians have advocated, we should be on our guard to interpret Scripture so that it accords with correct doctrine and the love of God and neighbor. But as I have already admitted, those safeguards are not foolproof or absolutely solid. Even when attempting to interpret the Bible in a loving way, we may fool ourselves or be fooled by others and mistake paternalism or sentimentality or self-interest for love. And the church, all churches, have too often changed what they consider "orthodox doctrine" to allow us to believe, if we really know our history well, that just appealing to "orthodoxy" or "correct doctrine" or "Christian tradition" will provide a constant and reliable interpretation. As I demonstrated in the chapters herein, the church's stand on sex, marriage, celibacy, effeminacy, divorce, and many other issues has changed over the past two thousand years in fundamental ways. To assume that what was "orthodox" or accepted tradition in previous centuries will necessarily be God's will for us would be deliberately to close our eyes to the facts of history and willfully believe a lie, which is a dire sin in itself. Correct doctrine and the love of God and neighbor may serve as guidelines in interpretation, but they cannot provide predictably reliable foundations or guarantees for interpretation.

When asked these questions by students or audiences, I have often appealed to those theologians who urge contemporary Christians to read Scripture in community with other Christians. The reading of Scripture *in the church* should always, I agree, be used by individual Christians as one means of avoiding merely self-interested and idiosyncratic interpretations.[26] But as I have argued herein, communities can be just as sinful as individuals, and the advice to read Scripture in communion with others (those living and those dead whose readings live on in our traditions and books), though good advice, should also not be taken as a reliable guarantee for faithful and ethical interpretations. In the end, there is *no* method or principle that we can be assured will deliver good interpretations. We simply must be diligent, attempt to interpret in love, pray that we are led by the Holy Spirit, listen to one another and all others, and interpret in faith.

But isn't that the nature of Christian life—living without absolute foundations but with faith that the Holy Spirit will lead us and that God will save us, even in spite of ourselves? One man who spent almost his entire life making that argument was Søren Kierkegaard (1813–1855). Writing at a time when modern historiography was just beginning to make its powerful influence felt on Christian faith and theology, Kierkegaard struggled to define the relationship between "certain knowledge," history, and faith. Like modern apologists for the historical-critical method discussed in chapter 1, Kierkegaard noted that the center of Christian faith was an event that had happened in time. It was, to cite one term he used, a "moment" and happened in a certain man who existed at a particular time: "the eternal itself came into the world at a moment of time. . . . The historical assertion is that the Deity, the Eternal, came into being at a definite moment in time as an individual man."[27]

Yet unlike modern scholars who use this observation to insist on the *necessity* of historical criticism, Kierkegaard argued that the conclusions of historiography can have *nothing absolutely essential* to say about the meaning of that moment or event. After making his point about the incarnation as a moment in history, Kierkegaard dismisses any need for historical details about the moment: "Whether this particular man is a servant or an emperor is neither here nor there."[28] Note how odd this statement would be if made by a historian! For Kierkegaard, it is important that the incarnation happened "in time" and in a particular man, but all the details that "real" historians would want to know are considered by Kierkegaard completely irrelevant: "We see at once that the historical in the more concrete sense is a matter of indifference; we may suppose a degree of ignorance with respect to it, and permit this ignorance as if to annihilate one detail after the other, historically annihilating the historical; if only the Moment remains, as point of departure for the Eternal, the Paradox will be there."[29] Or as he puts it later in the same work, "As long as the Eternal and the historical are external to one another, the historical is merely an occasion."[30] The very nuts and bolts of historiography, such as whether the man was a "servant" or an "emperor," the details of his life, where he was born, precisely how he died, what he said and did—as those "facts" would be established by modern historical methods—are irrelevant. We see, therefore, that when Kierkegaard speaks of the Moment happening in "history" he does *not* mean by "history" the established results of modern historical criticism.

History *as a modern "scientific" discipline* represented for Kierkegaard the *opposite* of faith, not its foundation or a necessary factor in its interpretation. Kierkegaard recognized that historical research could never rise above the level of *possibility*, or, in his term, "approximation":

> Nothing is more readily evident than that the greatest attainable certainty with respect to anything historical is merely an *approximation*. . . . It is impossible in the case of historical problems to reach an objective decision so certain that no doubt could disturb it. This also serves to show that the problem ought to be put subjectively, and that it is precisely a misunder-

> standing to seek an objective assurance, thereby avoiding the risk in which passion chooses and continues to live, reaffirming its choice.[31]

Kierkegaard realized that the quest of historiography was certainty, "facts," secure knowledge, but he also realized that by its very nature historiography could never arrive at anything more than an "approximation." Faith, in Kierkegaard's mind, was itself a "passion" and therefore could never take as its foundation the "possibilities" or even "probabilities," the "approximations" of historical research. Therefore, although Kierkegaard recognized the "historical nature" of Christianity, he did not allow that to confuse him into believing that the methods of modern historiography were therefore *necessary* for ascertaining its meaning.

But another reason Kierkegaard rejected the necessity of modern historiography for Christian interpretation is that he viewed the *nature of faith* itself as something that *rejected* the need for secure, objective "knowledge." For Kierkegaard, "faith is itself a miracle." He contrasts "faith" with the "knowledge" promised by modern science and historiography: "By way of contrast it now becomes easy to see that belief is not a form of knowledge, but a free act, an expression of will."[32] In answer to the question "How do we *know* our opinions are true?" Kierkegaard would have answered, "You can't; and to demand that you *know* is a betrayal of faith itself." One should never confuse knowledge with faith, says Kierkegaard, because faith is a "passion":

> While faith has hitherto had a profitable school master in the existing uncertainty, it would have in the new certainty [by which Kierkegaard means modern scientific and philosophical methods inspired by the Hegelianism popular in his time] its most dangerous enemy. For if passion is eliminated, faith no longer exists, and certainty and passion do not go together.[33]

It should be noted here that part of what Kierkegaard means by "passion" also includes "suffering" (a key meaning of the term in ancient Greek and Latin), which is the central passion of Christianity, at least in *Concluding Unscientific Postscript*, from which this quotation is taken. For Kierkegaard, "passion" therefore includes the "suffering" of *uncertainty* in which faith must live.

Kierkegaard's criticism of the positivism of modern historiography is part of his suspicion of sense perception in general, which he takes from the ancient philosophy of Skepticism: "The certainty afforded by sense-perception is a deception, as one may learn from a study of the Greek sceptics, and from the entire treatment of this subject in the writings of modern idealism, which is very instructive. The positiveness of historical knowledge is illusory, since it is approximation-knowledge; the speculative result is a delusion."[34] Kierkegaard, therefore, had he possessed the vocabulary, would have rejected *all* forms of "foundationalism" for knowledge, whether that of the modern "science of nature" or the modern "science of history."[35]

For Kierkegaard, the only foundation for Christianity is faith. And that is admittedly dangerous. Yet, "without risk there is no faith." In fact, "the greater the risk the greater the faith."[36] Kierkegaard offers no secure grounds for Christian knowledge. One central image suggested by Kierkegaard for what faith is like is the image of a person lying out in the middle of the sea, floating on 70,000 fathoms of water:

> Spiritual existence, especially the religious, is not easy; the believer continually lies out on the deep, has 70,000 fathoms of water beneath him. However long he lies out there, this still does not mean that he will gradually end up lying and relaxing onshore. He can become more calm, more experienced, find a confidence that loves jest and a cheerful temperament—but until the very last he lies out on 70,000 fathoms of water.[37]

I have found this image incredibly helpful for reimagining faith without secure epistemological foundations. Many of us have experienced the tinge of terror when swimming or floating far out in the ocean, where no land is in sight and we sense the miles of deep water beneath us. Simply the unknown beneath us and the sense of nothing firm for miles below can prompt a feeling of unease or even panic. To avoid panic or fear, we tell ourselves that we are floating just fine, that we do not *need* to stand on firm ground, that we *can* float and swim over the vast depth of water. For me, it is helpful to remind myself: that is what faith is like.

Moreover, according to Kierkegaard, floating over 70,000 fathoms need not inspire only anxiety; we must learn to float and accept the risk with joy. And we *can* learn to do so. Arguing against the idea that we must have total security to experience joy, Kierkegaard says, "The question is whether one has not become joyful in the wrong place; and where is the right place? It is—in danger. To be joyful out on 70,000 fathoms of water, many, many miles from all human help—yes, that is something great!"[38] Instead of promising secure knowledge and firm foundations to those we love, promises we could not deliver anyway, we should instead coax them out into the deep, where they will certainly experience anxiety, but where they may also learn the only true happiness. After coaxing our loved ones out into the deep, we challenge them by shouting, "If you do not become happy now, then know this, know that it is your own fault."[39] That is the invitation, the demand, of faith.

And that kind of faith—indeed, even that kind of *knowledge*, knowledge that is *not* firmly based on indisputable foundations—is sufficient, in spite of the anxieties induced by the modernist quest for certainty. We modern people have been deceived into thinking that we should be anxious unless we can know what we know with absolute certainty. We actually do not need that kind of certainty. For example, I cannot be absolutely certain that when I get out of bed tomorrow my left leg will hold me up. I could have developed a disease during the night that paralyzed my leg. Or my leg could simply have "fallen asleep" and become numb, and I will stumble and fall when attempting to put weight on it. Or the nature of physics could have changed radically during the night, and legs would suddenly go through floors. There is no way to be *certain* that none of those scenarios could happen. But that will not keep me from getting out of bed tomorrow.

I have enough confidence in what I think I "know" to live perfectly well with my legs, floors, and physics as I believe them to be. That is also, I believe, something of what faith is like: the willingness to live and even live joyfully with confidence that God will take care of us, even if we do make mistakes and fall. To demand more than that—to demand more certainty than that in our interpretations of Scripture—is to allow ourselves to be deceived and to abandon faith.

The possibility offered to us now—with the collapse of confidence in scientific or historical or textual foundationalisms and the rise of antifoundationalist philosophies and theologies—is to learn to live faithfully without foundations—or without any other foundation than faith in Jesus Christ. The chapters in this volume have variously attempted to demonstrate that historical criticism *cannot* offer the firm foundation it promised many years ago—nor can any other method of interpreting the Bible. We should accept that realization not with fear and anxiety but as a challenge to our imaginations and an invitation to faith without foundations. Floating on a sea of faith.

Notes

Chapter 1

1. For a good, accessible introduction to "foundationalism" and "nonfoundationalism," see John E. Thiel, *Nonfoundationalism* (Minneapolis: Fortress, 1994); see also A. K. M. Adam, *What Is Postmodern Biblical Criticism?* (Minneapolis: Fortress, 1995). J. Wentzel van Huyssteen, *Essays in Postfoundationalist Theology* (Grand Rapids: Wm. B. Eerdmans, 1997), 2–3 also supplies a good definition of *foundationalism*. See also the Introduction by Nancey Murphy in Stanley Hauerwas, Nancey Murphy, and Mark Nation, eds., *Theology Without Foundations: Religious Practice and the Future of Theological Truth* (Nashville: Abingdon, 1994), esp. 9–12.
2. This sort of "scientific foundationalism" has been sufficiently critiqued by philosophers, but it still holds sway, certainly in much popular thought and even among some scientists. The most famous critique of foundationalism in philosophy and science is Richard Rorty, *Philosophy and the Mirror of Nature* (Princeton, NJ: Princeton University Press, 1979); see esp. 315–56 for discussion of philosophy of science.
3. Besides the critique of this way of thinking provided by Rorty, *Philosophy and the Mirror of Nature*, see also the compelling critique of assumptions about scientific "empiricism" by Bas C. van Fraasen, *The Empirical Stance* (New Haven, CT: Yale University Press, 2002).
4. See the description of "experiential-expressivism" in George Lindbeck, *The Nature of Doctrine: Religion and Theology in a Postliberal Age* (Philadelphia: Westminster, 1984).
5. The classic and most accessible texts on reader-response criticism are Stanley Fish, *Is There a Text in This Class? The Authority of Interpretive Communities* (Cambridge, MA: Harvard University Press, 1980); idem, *Doing What Comes Naturally: Change, Rhetoric, and the Practice of Theory in Literary and Legal Studies* (Durham, NC: Duke University Press, 1989); Jane P. Tompkins, ed., *Reader-response Criticism: From Formalism to Post-structuralism* (Baltimore: Johns Hopkins University Press, 1980). For an excellent introduction to how these theories impact on biblical studies and theology, see A. K. M. Adam, *Making Sense of New Testament Theology: "Modern" Problems and Prospects* (Macon, GA: Mercer University Press, 1995). After referring to Jonathan Culler's discussion of how people might "make sense" of the phrase "Colorless green ideas sleep furiously" (a statement deliberately contrived to be "nonsense"), Adam rightly notes, "Hypothetical senses of the sentence could be multiplied indefinitely, but the point is that an interpreter can make sense of even a deliberately nonsensical and self-contradictory statement. In short, sense is something *ascribed to* the text, not a property that the text *has*" (171; his emphasis).

6. I hasten to add that there is nothing wrong with methodological discussions or attempts to be methodologically rigorous or consistent in interpretation. The recent book by Charles H. Cosgrove, *Appealing to Scripture in Moral Debate: Five Hermeneutical Rules* (Grand Rapids: Wm. B. Eerdmans, 2002), is a fine and honest attempt at methodological clarity by making explicit different "rules" we often use in debates about interpretation. Cosgrove provides a good rhetorical description of the kinds of arguments people do tend to advance in debates. But as even his "sample argument" demonstrates (perhaps unknowingly?), Cosgrove's rules are *descriptive* and not sufficiently *prescriptive* as a method that can confidently produce true, good, or ethical interpretations—precisely because each of the rules can be applied in other ways for other ends (for the "sample argument," see 187–91).
7. Irenaeus, *Against the Heresies* 1.14.6; see also 1.15.1; 1.26.1. For an English translation, see Alexander Roberts and James Donaldson, eds., *The Ante-Nicene Fathers: Translations of the Writings of the Fathers Down to A.D. 325*, vol. 1 (Grand Rapids: Wm. B. Eerdmans, 1978). See also St. Irenaeus of Lyons, *Against the Heresies*, trans. and annotated by Dominic J. Unger, with further revisions by John J. Dillon, vol. 1, book 1, Ancient Christian Writers 55 (New York: Paulist, 1992), 209n39.
8. For one introduction to "adoptionists," see Bart D. Ehrman, *Lost Christianities: The Battles for Scripture and the Faiths We Never Knew* (New York: Oxford University Press, 2003), 15, 101, 221–23, and "Adoptionists" in the index.
9. See Ehrman, *Lost Christianities*, 216, 221–23, for some of the texts fought over by "adoptionists" on the one side and those Christians Ehrman calls "proto-orthodox" on the other. Both sides could appeal to New Testament texts to support their Christologies.
10. New Testament historical critics have sometimes attempted to defend their idea that the text *has* its own meaning and "voice" and that the good interpreter's job is to "listen," but their arguments are without exception weak and usually beg the question by simply *assuming* or *stating* that the text "speaks" without demonstrating that it does. Kevin J. Vanhoozer, for example, gives a fairly good review of the different kinds of reader-response theory, yet when he gets to his own position, his arguments against reader-response theory are easily refuted. See "The Reader in New Testament Interpretation," in *Hearing the New Testament: Strategies for Interpretation*, ed. Joel B. Green (Grand Rapids: Wm. B. Eerdmans, 1995), 301–28. First, Vanhoozer simply states that the text *has* "intentions" of its own and that the interpreter, in order to be "just," must "heed its voice" (315), none of which can be proven. Then he makes further mistaken arguments, such as (1) that otherwise there would be no way to evaluate different readings at all; (2) that otherwise we must assume that individuals would be able to use language in totally idiosyncratic ways (this is the "Humpty-Dumpty" argument, along with the famous quotation from *Through the Looking-Glass*); and (3) the accusation that otherwise readers are doing "violence" to the text. Argument 1 is obviously not true: as I demonstrate in several chapters in this book, I regularly make judgments about better or worse interpretations on several different criteria without believing that the text itself is communicating its meaning. Point 2, in spite of being repeated regularly, ignores those reader-response theorists who have reminded us (the point has been known since classical times, but modern scholars regularly forget it) that language is *social* not *individual*, and that readers almost always interpret within "reading communities." Though the *text itself* cannot establish its meaning, "communities of readers" obviously can, and they can also put pressure (either acknowledged or not) on other readers to constrain or control interpretations. Argument 3 is a misuse of a

metaphor that begs the question being debated. It assumes that the text is a person or sentient being who can suffer pain from violence. The text has no "feelings." We may believe and try to persuade one another that it is an act of social violence to interpret a text in a certain way, but then we will be back into a discussion of how we should interpret *for ethical ends*. Talk about "violence against texts" is a false personification and just confuses the issue. It is good pathos but bad theory. Vanhoozer makes similar, and fallacious, arguments in "The Spirit of Understanding: Special Revelation and General Hermeneutics," in *Disciplining Hermeneutics: Interpretation in Christian Perspective,* ed. Roger Lundin (Grand Rapids: Wm. B. Eerdmans; Leicester: Apollos, 1997), 131–65. Again, Vanhoozer argues that if the meaning is not there in the text, it is simply the reader's projection and solipsism is inevitable. Again, this ignores the aspect of the *social* or *communal* that has been emphasized by reader-response theorists.

11. Note the way this misunderstanding about *what textual interpretation is* influences so much of biblical scholarship. Joel B. Green, for instance, in a book with the telling title *Hearing the New Testament* (as if the text spoke), initially writes as if *all* interpretation of the Bible is like a communication of one person to another, like a conversation in a coffee shop. See Green, "The Challenge of Hearing the New Testament," in Joel B. Green, ed., *Hearing the New Testament: Strategies for Interpretation* (Grand Rapids: Wm. B. Eerdmans, 1995), 1–9, esp. 2. Green admits that in the case of biblical interpretation we readers actually do not have the "addresser" present so that we can interrogate him or her about the "correct meaning" of the statements. And he concedes that there are other factors that complicate his model of communication, such as differences in culture and language. Finally, when he comes to discuss reader-centered approaches to interpretation, Green grants that "interpretation is not foremost the passing on of objective information from text to reader"(8). But he still offers only this one model for what we do when we read Scripture, demonstrating, I believe, how "commonsensical" this assumption is among most biblical scholars. This is a misrepresentation of textual interpretation, which may be diagrammed as the passing of information from one person to another, but *need not be*. We actually interpret texts in different ways that do not fit that dialogical model: we read poems more creatively than that; we read novels by "entering their world," not worrying about what the "author" intended to "communicate"; and throughout Christian history, people have read Scripture not simply to discern the intentions of the human author, but to enter into communion (*not* simply "communication" in the sense of the passing of information) with the Trinity. The dialogical model proposed by Green is simply too limiting to represent all the various ways we human beings read texts. It is especially too narrow for thinking about how we should read Scripture. See the conclusion to this book in chapter 11.
12. Even apart from the theoretical points made here, other scholars have shown how the idea of "recovering" the "original text" (even from a text-critical point of view) or the "original authorial intention" does not sufficiently appreciate the complexity of historical research itself and the fact that its results are not, after all, "stable." See, for instance, Eugene Ulrich, "Our Sharper Focus on the Bible and Theology Thanks to the Dead Sea Scrolls," *Catholic Biblical Quarterly* 66 (2004): 1–24; D. C. Parker, *The Living Text of the Gospels* (Cambridge: Cambridge University Press, 1997); Bart D. Ehrman, *Misquoting Jesus: The Story Behind Who Changed the Bible and Why* (San Francisco: HarperSanFrancisco, 2005).
13. A recent book that makes this point particularly well for premodern Christianity is James Callahan's *The Clarity of Scripture: History, Theology and Contemporary Literary Studies* (Downers Grove, IL: InterVarsity, 2001), see esp. 24, 193–202.

14. It is actually debated whether one may talk about Paul or other New Testament authors as being "Trinitarians" or not. One of the best known attempts of a contemporary to find the Trinity in Paul's letters is that by Gordon D. Fee; see "Paul and the Trinity: The Experience of Christ and the Spirit for Paul's Understanding of God," in *The Trinity: An Interdisciplinary Symposium on the Trinity*, ed. Stephen T. Davis et al. (Oxford: Oxford University Press, 1999), 49–72, and even in his case he must admit that we find only a "latent Trinitarianism" in Paul. I am not convinced by Fee's arguments.
15. As Callahan explains, to make the author's intention the locus of the meaning of Scripture in fact displaces Scripture itself as the actual "authority," locus of revelation, or center of meaning: "The notion of an author's intention implies the belief that there exists something against which the text can be measured, can be clarified by knowing or discerning. . . . [T]he effort to pursue the human author's intention for a text illustrates the effective displacement of the text itself" (Callahan, *Clarity of Scripture*, 193, 194).
16. The now-classic study of this shift is Hans W. Frei, *The Eclipse of Biblical Narrative: A Study in Eighteenth and Nineteenth Century Hermeneutics* (New Haven, CT: Yale University Press, 1974); see also the description of the modern shift in Brevard Childs, "The Sensus Literalis of Scripture: An Ancient and Modern Problem," in *Beiträge zur alttestamentlichen Theologie: Festschrift für Walther Zimmerli zum 70. Geburtstag*, ed. Herbert Donner et al. (Göttingen: Vanderhoeck & Ruprecht, 1977), 80–93.
17. "Yahwist" and "Elohist" here refer to a modern theory of authorship of the Pentateuch, the first five books of the Bible. Scholars beginning in the nineteenth century noticed that some texts in these books call God "Yahweh" (or actually just the consonants: YHWH), whereas other texts called God "Elohim." Thus one group of texts is cited as the "Yahweh" source, and others as the "Elohim" or "Elohist" source.
18. More on the "literal sense" below.
19. For discussion of how historical criticism arose out of the modern anxiety over the instability and unpredictability of interpretation, see Walter Brueggemann, *Texts Under Negotiation: The Bible and Postmodern Imagination* (Minneapolis: Fortress, 1993), 1–6; L. William Countryman, *Biblical Authority or Biblical Tyranny? Scripture and the Christian Pilgrimage* (Valley Forge, PA: Trinity Press International; Cambridge, MA: Cowley, 1994), 70–71; Wayne A. Meeks, *Christ Is the Question* (Louisville, KY: Westminster John Knox, 2006), chapter 2; Adam, *Making Sense of New Testament Theology*, esp. 53, but the entire book is excellent for illustrating the history of historical criticism and its inadequacies, and as an introduction to biblical interpretation in a nonfoundationalist mode.
20. Chapter 2 in this volume is one concerted effort to demonstrate this fact, though the point is made in most of these chapters. See also Luke Timothy Johnson and William S. Kurz, *The Future of Catholic Biblical Scholarship: A Constructive Conversation* (Grand Rapids: Wm. B. Eerdmans, 2002), 14–15.
21. A point made also by Stephen E. Fowl, *Engaging Scripture: A Model for Theological Interpretation* (Oxford: Blackwell, 1998), 36.
22. N. T. Wright, *The Last Word: Beyond the Bible Wars to a New Understanding of the Authority of Scripture* (San Francisco: HarperSanFrancisco, 2005), 109.
23. See, for instance, Beryl Smalley, *The Study of the Bible in the Middle Ages* (Oxford: Clarendon, 1941), 2, 20, 22, 27, 29, passim.
24. Charles M. Wood, *The Formation of Christian Understanding: An Essay in Theological Hermeneutics* (Philadelphia: Westminster, 1981), 43; see also Wayne Meeks, *Christ Is the Question*, chapter 5.

25. Augustine, *De doctrina christiana*, ed. and trans. R. P. H. Green (Oxford: Clarendon, 1995) 3.84 (27.38). The first numbers given are those of Bulhart used for the CSEL edition of *De doctrina christiana* prepared by W. M. Green. The second reference numbers, given in parentheses, reflect an older system of reference but are still found in some works.
26. *De doctrina christiana* 3.86 (28.39).
27. Thomas Aquinas, *Summa theologiae* 1a. 1, 10. For Latin and this English translation, see *Summa theologiae*, Latin text and English trans. Thomas Gilby (Cambridge: Blackfriars, 1964), 1:39.
28. James Samuel Preus, *From Shadow to Promise: Old Testament Interpretation from Augustine to the Young Luther* (Cambridge, MA: Harvard University Press, 1969), 68–69. On Nicholas, see also Stephen E. Fowl, ed., *The Theological Interpretation of Scripture: Classic and Contemporary Readings* (Cambridge, MA: Blackwell, 1997), 114–28.
29. See also Preus, *From Shadow to Promise*, 90–91: Paul of Burgos (fifteenth century) insisted that the "literal sense" could not oppose church doctrine because the Holy Spirit, as the author of Scripture, led the church. Faber Stapulensis (died 1536): the *sensus literalis* is *not* the *sensus historicus*; rather it is what the Holy Spirit intends (138–39). And for Luther, "the interpreter does not place himself with the Old Testament writer in time" (164).
30. Hans W. Frei, "The 'Literal Reading' of Biblical Narrative in the Christian Tradition: Does It Stretch or Will It Break?" in *The Bible and the Narrative Tradition*, ed. Frank McConnell (New York: Oxford University Press, 1986), 36–77, at 68.
31. George Lindbeck, "The Story-shaped Church: Critical Exegesis and Theological Interpretation," in *Scriptural Authority and Narrative Interpretation*, ed. Garrett Green (Philadelphia: Fortress, 1987), 161–78, at 164.
32. Kathryn E. Tanner, "Theology and the Plain Sense," in Green, ed., *Scriptural Authority and Narrative Interpretation*, 59–78, at 62–64.
33. For example, Wright, *The Last Word*, 110.
34. This usually has occurred in Christian self-serving attempts to distinguish the stories of the Bible as "historical," because of having happened "once for all," from "myths," which are said to be "cyclical" or not as having "actually occurred" at all. See Jonathan Z. Smith, *Drudgery Divine: On the Comparison of Early Christianities and the Religions of Late Antiquity* (Chicago: Chicago University Press, 1990), 105. For other insightful analyses showing that there is more confusion than clarity in assertions that Christianity is a "historical" religion or that the Bible is "history-like" and thus demands the use of historical criticism, see Maurice Wiles, *Maurice Wiles*, Explorations in Theology 4 (London: SCM, 1979), 53–65, originally published as "In What Sense Is Christianity a 'Historical' Religion?" *Theology* 81 (1978): 4–14; James Barr, *The Scope and Authority of the Bible* (Philadelphia: Westminster, 1980), 6–17, 30–51; Frances Young, "Allegory and the Ethics of Reading" in Francis Watson, ed., *Open Text: New Directions for Biblical Studies?* (London: SCM, 1993), 103–20, at 105: "[I]t was by no means clear what it meant to claim that Christianity was a historical religion. In the claim a number of different elements were confused." It is unfortunate that although Wiles and Barr long ago pointed out how confused were biblical scholars' appeals to the "historicity of Christianity" to underwrite the necessity of historical criticism, the claim is still repeatedly made with no increase in sophistication or clarity.
35. Contemporary philosophies of history have struggled to maintain a distinction between the two notions of something designated as "past" and something as "history"—the latter referring to the historiographically constructed *account* of

the "past," which is not immediately observable or truly "recoverable." See Elizabeth A. Clark, *History, Theory, Text: Historians and the Linguistic Turn* (Cambridge, MA: Harvard University Press, 2004), 156, passim. See "Past, status of" in the Index. For an accessible introduction to this as well as other issues in modern historiography and theory, see Keith Jenkins, *Re-thinking History: With a New Preface and Conversation with the Author by Alun Munslow* (London: Routledge, 2003).

36. Richard Hays makes similar claims with regard to the incarnation and Jesus' mental states. See *New Testament Ethics: The Story Retold* (Winnipeg, MB: CMBC, 1998), 48. In this context, however, Hays does not exactly say that scholars *must* use historical criticism in their interpretations of Jesus (though elsewhere he makes such assertions), but only that the historicity of Jesus of Nazareth means that we *may* investigate Jesus' life using historical methods. I would not disagree with that explicit statement, but I would insist that we *need not* use history to establish truths about Jesus. Modern historiography may be used as one method among others, but it is not necessary for a Christian reading of Scripture.
37. Ibid., 46.
38. I wouldn't grant to Hays the claim that the Gospels are "history-like narratives." I don't believe "history-like narratives" use miraculous interventions to move the plot along or explain the motivations of characters. Modern novels, for instance, are "history-like" precisely because they usually reject such techniques, which premodern or postmodern fiction may employ without apology or compunction.
39. I take the example of Hamlet from George Lindbeck, though he did not use it as I have. See "Toward a Postliberal Theology," in *The Return to Scripture in Judaism and Christianity: Essays in Postcritical Scriptural Interpretation*, ed. Peter Ochs (New York: Paulist, 1993), 83–103, at 95. Lindbeck is referring to the *character* of Hamlet and comparing that to the *character* of Jesus Christ: in each case, their *title* ("Son of the God of Abraham, Isaac, and Jacob," on the one hand, and "Prince of Denmark," on the other) takes its meaning from the wider narrative and "irreplaceably rather than contingently identifies the bearer of the name." The *identities* of Jesus and Hamlet are a function of their roles in a narrative. What makes Lindbeck's statements correct and Hays's wrong is that Hays has confused a quality of narrative and characterization with the relationship of that narrative or character to what exists *outside the narrative in a (presumed) historical nature*, and Hays's mistaken notion that *if* the narrative is "history-like" *then* historical criticism must be necessary to understand its meaning. Lindbeck makes neither mistake.
40. The sentiment is so common in scholarship that it would be impossible to provide even a modest survey of expressions of it. But for examples one may see Gerald Bray, *Biblical Interpretation: Past and Present* (Downers Grove, IL: InterVarsity, 1996), esp. 101–3; Wright, *The Last Word*, 69. The poststructuralist insistence that texts cannot control their own meanings or do not "possess" their meanings is often, apparently, misunderstood. Gregory J. Laughery, for instance, repeatedly assumes that if texts do not contain their meaning inherently in themselves, we will be left with "autocratic chaos" and that readers will see "only a textual mirroring of themselves." See *Living Hermeneutics in Motion: An Analysis and Evaluation of Paul Ricoeur's Contribution to Biblical Hermeneutics* (Lanham, MD: University Press of America, 2002), 150. Laughery, like Vanhoozer mentioned above, thus leaves out of consideration the *social* constraints on "normal" interpretation highlighted by reader-response theorists such as Stanley Fish. Theorists who stress "textual indeterminacy" recognize that "autocratic chaos" actually does *not* occur, but the reasons are *social*, not some kind of mythological agency exercised by the text itself.

41. A point well made by Adam, *Making Sense of New Testament Theology*, see esp. 181.
42. Wayne A. Meeks, "A Nazi New Testament Professor Reads His Bible: The Strange Case of Gerhard Kittel," in Hindy Najman and Judith H. Newman, eds., *The Idea of Biblical Interpretation: Essays in Honor of James L. Kugel* (Leiden: E. J. Brill, 2004), 513–44.
43. See Willard Swartley, *Slavery, Sabbath, War, and Women: Case Studies in Biblical Interpretation* (Scottdale, PA: Herald Press, 1983); Wayne A. Meeks, "The 'Haustafeln' and American Slavery: A Hermeneutical Challenge," in Eugene H. Lovering Jr. and Jerry L. Sumney, eds., *Theology and Ethics in Paul and His Interpreters: Essays in Honor of Victor Paul Furnish* (Nashville: Abingdon, 1996), 232–53; J. Albert Harrill, *Slaves in the New Testament: Literary, Social, and Moral Dimensions* (Minneapolis: Fortress, 2006), 165–92.

Chapter 2

1. For a similar attempt at a taxonomy of different strategies of argumentation on the issue, see D. J. Good, "Reading Strategies for Biblical Passages on Same-Sex Relations," *Theology and Sexuality* 7 (1997): 70–82. See also, for another analysis that speaks of "rules" of argument and interpretation we commonly use, Charles H. Cosgrove, *Appealing to Scripture in Moral Debate: Five Hermeneutical Rules* (Grand Rapids: Wm. B. Eerdmans, 2002). For something a bit different—in this case a *biblical* scholar surveying the ways different Christian *ethicists* use the Bible—see Jeffrey S. Siker, *Scripture and Ethics: Twentieth-Century Portraits* (Oxford: Oxford University Press, 1997).
2. The works I cite in this section certainly do not represent anything like a comprehensive survey of recent interpretations of Romans 1. I cite these merely as examples known to me. I should also note that my survey was made easier by the annotated bibliography supplied as an appendix in Bernadette J. Brooten, *Love Between Women: Early Christian Responses to Female Homoeroticism* (Chicago: University of Chicago Press, 1996), 363–71. (One should, of course, consult the actual books and articles and use Brooten's summaries with caution.) Simply reading through the different arguments about Romans 1 paraphrased by Brooten gives a remarkable sense of the wide variety of possible interpretive strategies, rhetorics, and conclusions even by scholars applying the same general method: basic historical criticism.
3. Kathleen E. Corley and Karen J. Torjesen, "Sexuality, Hierarchy and Evangelicalism," *Theological Students' Fellowship Bulletin* 10, no. 4 (March–April 1987): 23–27; Wolfgang Stegemann, "Paul and the Sexual Mentality of His World," *Biblical Theology Bulletin* 23 (1993): 161–66; Brooten, *Love Between Women*, passim but esp. 302; Michael McIntyre, "Gay Texts of Terror?" *Christian Scholar's Review* 26 (1997): 413–34 (McIntyre's entire article provides a good illustration of how historical criticism can lead to widely different conclusions; he surveys much scholarship and fairly represents other scholars' views, yet the different ideas of what the texts mean wildly vary).
4. L. William Countryman, *Dirt, Greed, and Sex: Sexual Ethics in the New Testament and Their Implications for Today* (Philadelphia: Fortress, 1988); see also McIntyre, "Gay Texts of Terror?" 426–27.
5. A. M. J. M. Herman van de Spijker, *Die gleichgeschlechteliche Zuneigung: Homotropie: Homosexualität, Homoerotik, Homophilie—und die katholische Moraltheologie* (Freiburg: Walter, 1968), 81–86; Victor Paul Furnish, *The Moral Teaching of Paul: Selected Essays*, 2d ed. (Nashville: Abingdon, 1985), 72–81; Furnish, "Homosexual Practices in Biblical Perspective," in *The Sexuality Debate in*

North American Churches, 1988–1995: Controversies, Unresolved Issues, Future Prospects, ed. John J. Carey (Lewiston, NY: Edwin Mellen, 1995), 253–73, at 263; Letha Scanzoni and Virginia Ramey Mollenkott, *Is the Homosexual My Neighbor?* (San Francisco: Harper & Row, 1978), 62–63; Robin Scroggs, *The New Testament and Homosexuality: Contextual Background for Contemporary Debate* (Philadelphia: Fortress, 1983), esp. 115–18, 126–29; Jeffrey S. Siker, "Homosexual Christians, the Bible, and Gentile Inclusion: Confessions of a Repenting Heterosexist," in Siker, ed., *Homosexuality in the Church: Both Sides of the Debate* (Louisville, KY: Westminster John Knox, 1994), 178–94; Abraham Smith, "The New Testament and Homosexuality," *Quarterly Review* 11:4 (1991): 18–32.

6. For example, Martti Nissinen, *Homoeroticism in the Biblical World: A Historical Perspective,* trans. Kirsi Stjerna (Minneapolis: Fortress, 1998), 111, 124–25; Victor Paul Furnish, "The Bible and Homosexuality: Reading the Texts in Context," in Siker, ed., *Homosexuality in the Church,* 18–35; Else Kähler, "Exegese zweier neutestamentlicher Stellen," in Th. Bovet, ed., *Probleme der Homophilie in medizinischer, theologischer und juristischer Sicht* (Bern: Paul Haupt, 1965), 12–43, see esp. 31–32. See also, for somewhat different but similar arguments related to cultural placement of Paul, George R. Edwards, *Gay/Lesbian Liberation: A Biblical Perspective* (New York: Pilgrim, 1984), esp. 98–99.
7. Throughout this essay I use the admittedly problematic terms "conservative" and "liberal" (or "progressive"). Recognizing that these terms may mean many different things to different people, I have tried to come up with others, but I have found no particular terms that would be clearer or less misleading, and I could hardly substitute lengthy circumlocutions on each occasion. By "conservative" I simply mean those people who believe God and Scripture oppose homosexuality, and by "liberal" I mean those who advocate the complete acceptance of gay and lesbian people in the full life of the church with no negative judgment against homosexuality itself. I recognize that some scholars may not wish to appropriate these labels for themselves. (I, for example, do not think of myself as a "liberal"; I would more likely identify myself as a "leftist" politically and perhaps even as a "radical" in the current climate when it comes to issues of sexuality and politics.)
8. Richard B. Hays, "Awaiting the Redemption of Our Bodies: The Witness of Scripture Concerning Homosexuality," in Siker, ed., *Homosexuality in the Church,* 3–17; originally published in a shorter version in *Sojourners* 20, no. 6 (July 1991): 17–21; I cite the more recent, complete version; Hays, *The Moral Vision of the New Testament: Community, Cross, New Creation: A Contemporary Introduction to New Testament Ethics* (New York: HarperCollins, 1996), 398; see some similar statements by Robert A. J. Gagnon, *The Bible and Homosexual Practice: Texts and Hermeneutics* (Nashville: Abingdon, 2001), esp. 430–32.
9. This is a bit different from Richard Hays's use of the "sexual orientation" argument. He notes that many modern scholars observe that "sexual orientation" is a modern notion, an invention of the nineteenth or twentieth century; therefore, John Boswell is wrong in saying that Paul is condemning not homosexuals having sex with one another, but heterosexuals engaging in homosexual sex. Since Paul couldn't have known about "heterosexuals" in this sense, Boswell's interpretation anachronistically retrojects the category into the ancient context. Hays's is a strange appropriation of "sexual orientation," since in the end he insists that the notion should have no real bearing on ethical decisions about the lives of gay and lesbian Christians. But *if* sexual orientation *is* what many modern people believe it to be—a core constituent of the self and not in itself "evil"—that certainly should be taken into account in any comprehensive ethic of sexuality that makes any attempt to be compassionate.

10. Jürgen Becker, "Zum Problem der Homosexualität in der Bibel," *Zeitschrift für evangelische Ethik* 31 (1987): 36–59, connects Paul's attitude to homosexuality with Jewish traditions and Scripture, but insists that the church must not accept homosexual relationships. See also Peter Coleman, *Christian Attitudes to Homosexuality* (London: SPCK, 1980), 92–93.
11. David L. Bartlett, "A Biblical Perspective on Homosexuality," *Foundations* 20 (1977): 133–47. Klaus Wengst, "Paulus und die Homosexualität," *Zeitschrift für evangelische Ethik* 31 (1987): 72–79, notes that Paul's connection of homosexuality with idolatry is a particularly Jewish practice, which is then used to argue that the church should not take it as binding for modern Christians.
12. As David Bartlett noted many years ago, the "encultured nature" of the biblical writers also means that attempts to separate "truth" from "culture" are doomed to fail: "There is no pure, distilled Paul, who can be freed of cultural impurities and allowed to preach eternal truths. Everything Paul said was affected by his culture" ("Biblical Perspective," 143). This is of course *not* to say that Paul and his letters are meaningless for Christians; just that Christians will have to try to discern the will of God *within* culture rather than *apart* from it.
13. For a brief discussion of "culture" see my introduction to *The Cultural Turn in Late Ancient Studies: Gender, Asceticism, and Historiography*, ed. Dale B. Martin and Patricia Cox Miller (Durham, NC: Duke University Press, 2005), 1–25. For a fuller discussion, see Kathryn Tanner, *Theories of Culture: A New Agenda for Theology* (Minneapolis: Fortress, 1997).
14. Kenneth Grayston, for example, supplements the point from Genesis that sexual intercourse is God's provision for procreation with reference to the Song of Solomon, which could be read to suggest that sexuality is also for erotic enjoyment; he likewise urges that texts such as Romans 1 must be read in wider context of Christian Scripture and reason: "Adultery and Sodomy: The Biblical Sources of Christian Moral Judgment," *Epworth Review* 15 (1988): 64–70; Michael McIntyre, "Gay Texts of Terror?" *Christian Scholar's Review* 26 (1997): 413–34, argues that the text is about honor, shame, and purity, but that Christians should listen to other "voices" of Scripture, such as those of the prophets advocating justice and compassion; thus we "make our stand not on our own, but with Isaiah" (427).
15. McIntyre, "Gay Texts of Terror?" 427.
16. Elizabeth A. Clark, *Reading Renunciation: Asceticism and Scripture in Early Christianity* (Princeton, NJ: Princeton University Press, 1999), esp. 128–34, but examples occur throughout the book.
17. See the fuller discussion of Jesus' interpretive practices in chapter 9, "The Hermeneutics of Divorce," in this volume.
18. This is one part of my treatment of the passage in chapter 4, "Heterosexism and the Interpretation of Romans 1:18–32," in this volume; see also Bartlett, "Biblical Perspective," 140–41; Wengst, "Paulus und die Homosexualität"; Robert Goss, *Jesus Acted Up: A Gay and Lesbian Manifesto* (San Francisco: HarperSanFrancisco, 1994), 92–93.
19. James B. Nelson, "Homosexuality: An Issue for the Church," in *Theological Markings* 5 (1975): 41–52, at 43; Bartlett, "Biblical Perspective," 140.
20. Hans-Georg Wiedemann, "Homosexualität und Bibel," in *Die Menschlichkeit der Sexualität: Berichte, Analysen, Kommentare ausgelöst durch die Frage: Wie homosexuell dürfen Pfarrer sein?* ed. Helmut Kentler (Munich: Chr. Kaiser, 1983), 89–106.
21. Wengst, "Paulus und die Homosexualität." Of course, this is one more use, though for the "liberal" side, of the problematic "nature vs. culture" dichotomy I criticize above.

22. John Boswell, *Christianity, Social Tolerance, and Homosexuality: Gay People in Western Europe from the Beginning of the Christian Era to the Fourteenth Century* (Chicago: University of Chicago Press, 1980); a similar argument had been made before by various scholars, but Boswell argued it most thoroughly and famously; see John J. McNeill, *The Church and the Homosexual* (Kansas City: Sheed Andrews & McNeel, 1976), 55–56; Nelson, "Homosexuality," 42–43.
23. For one example of this kind of argument see Joseph A. Fitzmyer, *Romans: A New Translation with Introduction and Commentary* (New York: Doubleday, 1993), 286–87, though Fitzmyer is not addressing the issue of homosexuality.
24. It is also interesting that *both* Gagnon and Brooten contradict themselves, stating in places that the text *does* "explicitly" condemn female same-sex activity, and then admitting elsewhere that the condemnation is *not* "explicit": Gagnon, *The Bible*, 229, 298; Brooten, *Love Between Women*, 216, 240. Paul's text reads, "Their women exchanged natural use for unnatural" (Rom. 1:26). One may *think* that *Paul was thinking* about female same-sex intercourse, but that is not the "explicit" reading of the text. Other scholars have argued, persuasively, I believe, that female "unnatural use" of sex, as understood more generally in the ancient world, may have included female same-sex intercourse, but would have meant, for most ancient readers, all sorts of activities, including masturbation, oral sex, and the woman being the "insertive partner" in heterosexual sex. In any case, it is wrong to say that the text "explicitly" names female same-sex intercourse, as both Gagnon and Brooten eventually have to admit, in spite of their initial claims.
25. Gagnon in particular is confused about the issue. Against my statement that "the *Scripture* for the church is traditionally the text, not a historically reconstructed authorial intention" (see chapter 3, "*Arsenokoitês* and *Malakos,*" in this volume, at p. 206n39), Gagnon claims that the statement "makes no sense" to him (324n122). He also implies that because in other works I myself work with a notion of authorial intention, I am merely inconsistent. Gagnon insists, "To the extent that authorial meaning is recoverable, it must be recovered. Otherwise, one might as well forget about exegeting the meaning of a text." Gagnon's confusion shows a lack of basic knowledge about interpretation history and theory. As I show elsewhere in this book, authorial intention is a construction of the reader, not a property of the text or anything that exists elsewhere "in nature." Moreover, it is not at all a self-contradiction to believe that authorial intention is itself a construction of the reader and still to be willing to use it at times as a reading strategy. The point is that "the meaning of the text" isn't *identical* to that constructed "authorial intention." And if Gagnon cannot imagine interpreting a text (especially *Christian* interpretation of Scripture) without concentrating on authorial intention, he simply does not know the vast history of interpretation in Christianity, which *could* use "authorial intention" but never *identified* the meaning of the text with the "author's intention." The majority of Christian interpreters throughout history have not limited themselves to the historically constructed authorial intention to ascertain "the meaning" of the text. See the fuller discussion of these issues in the introduction to this volume.
26. Thomas Laqueur, *Making Sex: Body and Gender from the Greeks to Freud* (Cambridge, MA: Harvard University Press, 1990).
27. See my fuller discussion of Robert Gagnon's use of this argument below. For two brilliant critiques of the tendency of modern scholars to read the creation stories as *necessarily* "about" the gender and therefore sexual complementariness of men and women, see Ken Stone, *Practicing Safer Texts: Food, Sex, and Bible in Queer Perspective* (London: T. & T. Clark, 2005), chapter 1; and Diana Swancutt, "Sexing the Pauline Body of Christ: Scriptural 'Sex' in the Context of the American Christian Culture War," in *Toward a Theology of Eros: Transfiguring Passion*

at the Limits of Discipline, ed. Virginia Burrus and Catherine Keller (New York: Fordham University Press, 2006).

28. Siker, "Homosexual Christians, the Bible, and Gentile Inclusion." I discuss Siker's article more fully in chapter 10.
29. See the suggestion by Hendrik Hart, "Romans Revisited," *The Other Side* 28, no. 4 (July–August 1992): 56–62; and the debate between Hart and Albert Wolters, which demonstrates nicely just how difficult it is to establish consensus of interpretation on whether something is a "quotation" or the actual view of the author: Wolters, "Hart's Exegetical Proposal on Romans 1," *Calvin Theological Journal* 28 (1993): 166–70; Hart, "Reply to Wolters," *Calvin Theological Journal* 28 (1993): 170–74.
30. This sort of comment from William S. Kurz is typical of the shaming rhetoric used by many scholars: "Much of what is authoritative in Scripture is apparent to any reasonably intelligent and literate reader and believer" (Luke Timothy Johnson and William S. Kurz, *The Future of Catholic Biblical Scholarship: A Constructive Conversation* [Grand Rapids: Wm. B. Eerdmans, 2002], 118). Kurz's readers who disagree with his own beliefs about "what is authoritative in Scripture" must be simply unintelligent or illiterate.
31. Compare two books written for a popular audience, both based on foundationalist notions of textual meaning and commitments to the historical-critical method as the means for arriving at that meaning. Daniel A. Helminiak, *What the Bible Really Says About Homosexuality* (San Francisco: Alamo Square, 1994), depends heavily on the work of some of the scholars I have mentioned above to argue that the Bible does not condemn homosexuality itself, but rather oppression, ethics based on notions of pollution, or other issues. Harold E. Brunson, *Homosexuality and the New Testament: What Does Christian Scripture Really Teach* (San Francisco: International Scholars, 1998), just as confidently uses word studies and historical criticism to come to *opposite* conclusions, claiming objectivity: "I have attempted to deduce my conclusions through a careful linguistic analysis to discover exactly what the biblical text says without infusing my presuppositions and opinions into the text" (xv). That Brunson is not as objective as he thinks he is can be demonstrated by noting that the book is rabid in its homophobia, advocating that homosexual people, and even merely effeminate men, should be completely shut off from all human society, especially churches. The book is full of language of abomination and disgust. For another excellent example of how precisely the same methods of historical criticism arrive at diametrically opposite "meanings," this time not about sexuality, see Daniel Patte's discussion of the issue in *Ethics of Biblical Interpretation: A Reevaluation* (Louisville, KY: Westminster John Knox, 1995), 27, 35n35, and 58–59. See also Johnson and Kurz, *Future of Catholic Biblical Scholarship*, 14–15.
32. Terry Eagleton wonderfully illustrates how all readers *must* fill in gaps in texts. See the chapter introducing reader-response theories in his *Literary Theory: An Introduction* (Minneapolis: University of Minnesota Press, 1983).
33. I expand on these points in the conclusion of this volume.
34. See also Gagnon, *The Bible,* 168–69: the fact that semen is effective for procreation only when it encounters an egg in a woman's womb "is clear and convincing proof of God's exclusive design in nature for heterosexual intercourse." Gagnon does not explain why, if this is such "clear and convincing proof," so many of us are not convinced. Apparently we, but not he, are just too biased and prejudiced to see "clear and convincing proof." Elsewhere he insists, "Nature is material creation, visible to the naked eye, to the extent that it is not distorted or corrupted by the fall" (392). This does hint that Gagnon suspects that arguments from "nature" may be unreliable. Homosexual Christians, for instance, may point

to our own sexuality as evidence from "nature" that there is nothing "unnatural" about homosexuality. (The obvious answer to that conservative quip "God made Adam and Eve, not Adam and Steve," is "Well then, who made Steve?") Gagnon may also fear that appeals to "nature" could just as easily be used to justify violence, since there are few things more "natural" about human beings than our capacity for violence. But Gagnon would apparently reject such appeals to "nature" by insisting that "nature" in the case of the actual existence of homosexuality or violence is "fallen" and "distorted." But again, that just proves that appeals to "nature" cannot provide reliable knowledge about either nature or God.

35. Gagnon, much later in *The Bible*, admits the problem: "In the contemporary context, one hears repeatedly the objection that not all sexual activity involves penetration by a phallus, even in heterosexual relationships. Why, then, should the absence of such penetration in homoerotic relationships (particularly lesbian) deny their legitimacy?" But Gagnon responds simply by insisting, "Yet that misses the point. The point is not that sexual intimacy must always and only involve phallic penetration . . . but rather that the fittedness of the penis and vagina provide clues as to how God desires sexual pairing to be organized by gender" (365). But it is Gagnon who "misses the point." *If* the anatomy of penis/vagina and the process of procreation are taken as "clear and convincing" evidence for *the* meaning of sex, *why should it not then also mean* that all other forms of sexual activity are *also* against God's will, rather than just homosexuality? Gagnon's logic *should* lead him to affirm the Roman Catholic position, which does argue against artificial birth control, for one thing, precisely by the sort of logic Gagnon here employs. But Gagnon wants to have it both ways: to take procreation and male-female anatomy to mean the *exclusion* of homosexuality, but *not* the exclusion of other heterosexual activities that are neither procreative nor involve penis-vagina penetration. Gagnon's logic is flawed, self-contradictory, and self-serving.
36. This also relates to another favorite rhetorical device employed by Gagnon: his manipulation of analogy. He repeatedly rejects the analogies urged by others who suggest that the church should think about homosexuality and the Bible in ways analogous to slavery, or the roles of women, or the inclusion of the Gentiles: just as the church has come to read the Bible differently in those cases, so perhaps it should see other possibilities for treating homosexuals in its midst. Gagnon responds by insisting that such analogies are not perfect parallels to homosexuality (what analogy is?), but he uses analogies of his own that are no more perfect than those he rejects (such as comparing homosexuality with alcoholism). For a good discussion of the use of analogy and how complicated (and unpredictive) it *always* is, see Charles H. Cosgrove, *Appealing to Scripture in Moral Debate: Five Hermeneutical Rules* (Grand Rapids: Wm. B. Eerdmans, 2002), 85. If one is a firm foundationalist, it is near impossible to see the "interestedness" of one's own "readings" in the same way one is able to identify the "biases" of others. The sense of security provided by foundationalism makes self-critical awareness unlikely.
37. Speaking about the "unity" of the New Testament or its "moral coherence," Hays says, "We cannot escape acknowledging that any synthetic account of the unity of the New Testament's moral vision will be a product of our artifice, an imaginative construct of the interpreter—or, perhaps better, since interpreters do not form their readings in isolation—of the interpretive community." Yet that claim of modesty seems undermined by the rhetoric in the following paragraph, which again inscribes the reader not as a "construer" of meaning but a "perceiver" of it: "We proceed by trial and error, testing various synthetic intuitions against the evidence"; and Hays hopes to offer "ground rules" and suggestions that "enable us to perceive significant unity among the New Testament's witnesses." The "unity" is *there in the text.* We may be able to "perceive" it if we read sensitively

and by correct methods. Elsewhere, Hays argues that the stances he takes on different ethical issues are not pronouncements "ex cathedra" but are offered as "readings" open to disagreement and dialogue, yet, in the end, his rhetoric again suggests that what should decide any disagreement will be positions that persuade others "on biblical grounds" (315). It is precisely the nature of the existence of "biblical grounds" that I am questioning; I do not believe the foundationalist image ("ground") is inconsequential. For another critique of *Moral Vision*, noting that Hays does not use his own method consistently and also criticizing the idea that the text can furnish "an adequate source for Christian moral discourse," see Luke Timothy Johnson, "Why Scripture Isn't Enough," *Commonweal* 124, no. 11 (June 6, 1997): 23–25. I made similar arguments in my review of *Moral Vision*: see the *Journal of Biblical Literature* 117 (1998): 358–60.

38. See also Hays, *Moral Vision*, 228–29. But Hays's anxieties about the instability of interpretation and the dangers of hermeneutical insecurity pervade the book.
39. A point well made by Anthony C. Thiselton, "Can Hermeneutics Ease the Deadlock? Some Biblical Exegesis and Hermeneutical Models," in *The Way Forward? Christian Voices on Homosexuality and the Church*, ed. Timothy Bradshaw (London: Hodder & Stoughton, 1997), 145–96, see esp. 150–51.
40. Elisabeth Schüssler Fiorenza's interpretation of *ekklêsia* in democratic terms is invalidated, according to Hays, by appeal to what the original New Testament authors *would have thought* about the term (274). Here as in other contexts, Hays uses the term *exegesis* as equivalent to historical criticism. Apparently, exegesis *must* be historical critical. (Literally, the word *exegesis* means simply "interpretation.")
41. At *Moral Vision*, 235, Hays faults Karl Barth for not paying enough attention to the "individual theological perspectives" of the different Gospel writers. Hays does not point out that he himself has offered no theological rationale for *insisting* on this relatively recent criterion.
42. In a later publication, Hays more explicitly defends the *necessity* of historical criticism for establishing the foundational sense of the text. See Hays, *New Testament Ethics: The Story Retold* (Winnipeg, MB: CMBC, 1998), 46–48, and see also my criticism of his position in the introduction to this volume.
43. Richard B. Hays, *Echoes of Scripture in the Letters of Paul* (New Haven, CT: Yale University Press, 1990), 156.
44. I provide a fuller account of these issues in chapter 10.
45. Francis Watson, *Paul, Judaism and the Gentiles: A Sociological Approach* (Cambridge: Cambridge University Press, 1986).
46. Francis Watson, ed., *The Open Text: New Directions for Biblical Studies?* (London: SCM, 1993).
47. Watson, ed., *Open Text*, 1–12.
48. "Liberating the Reader: A Theological-Exegetical Study of the Parable of the Sheep and the Goats (Matt. 25.31–46)," in Watson, ed., *Open Text*, 57–84, at 66.
49. Francis Watson, *Text, Church and World: Biblical Interpretation in Theological Perspective* (Grand Rapids: Wm. B. Eerdmans, 1994).
50. Francis Watson, *Text and Truth: Redefining Biblical Theology* (Grand Rapids: Wm. B. Eerdmans, 1997), 112.
51. For texts as the necessary factor in "mediating reality" to human beings, see Watson, *Text, Church and World*, 293; *Text and Truth*, 1.
52. See also statements from Watson, *Agape, Eros, Gender: Towards a Pauline Sexual Ethic* (Cambridge: Cambridge University Press, 2000) that texts *give us* their meaning and that the task of the interpreter is to discern the "intentions" of the biblical writer, in this case Paul: ix, 43, 55, 89, 131. This may be somewhat surprising since Watson in this particular book reads the Pauline texts synchronously with writings of church fathers (from centuries later) and even modern authors

such as Virginia Woolf, Luce Irigaray, and Sigmund Freud. Yet Watson's readings of Paul are indeed informed mostly by historical criticism. Others of us certainly do *not* feel that Watson has simply "let the texts speak for themselves" nor "discerned" Paul's intentions. Watson's construal of the biblical texts makes Paul's ethic of sex proheterosexual, promarriage, and pro-procreation, which others of us historical critics would say is an ideological misconstrual of Paul's texts, done to support modern conservative Christian practices and ideology. Elizabeth A. Clark voiced some of these criticisms in a public review of Watson's book at the Annual Meeting of the Society of Biblical Literature (presentation to the Romans through History and Cultures Seminar, November 18, 2001, Denver, Colorado).

53. It should be noted that when Watson speaks of "authorial intention" in *Text and Truth* he is not thinking about the intentions of the historical author, but about something he believes is *in the text itself* and discernible by the reader. "A determinate communicative intention is embedded in the text" (11). Moreover, this is taken to constitute "the literal sense": "The literal sense is the sense intended by the author in so far as this authorial intention is objectively embodied in the words of the text" (115, see also 118). But if this is true (and I don't think it is), the point just leads us back circularly to an interpretation of the text. Since "intention" can be found only by an interpretation of the text, it ends up being more an "attitude" or a "stance" *we as interpreters decide to take* with the text, not some outside control over our interpretation of the text. Watson is here under the sway of E. D. Hirsch, and the same arguments that have shown the inadequacy of Hirsch's theories suffice for Watson's arguments. Moreover, an empirical analysis of Watson's own interpretation demonstrates how unconvincing his theory is. After quoting Mark 1:9, where Jesus is said to have left Nazareth and gone to the Jordan, being there baptized by John, Watson says, "Despite the apparent openendedness of the words [the text does not explicitly *say* that Jesus left Nazareth *with the goal* of baptism at the hands of John], the text does not in fact leave open the possibility that Jesus left Nazareth for some quite other reason, and that, on reaching the Jordan and seeing what was happening, he made a sudden decision to submit to baptism. . . . The text can only mean that Jesus left Nazareth *with the intention* of getting himself baptized by John" (*Text and Truth*, 104; emphasis in original). This is so baldly false as to make one wonder if Watson is attempting to play a joke on his readers. *Of course* and "in fact" the text *cannot* close off some such reading. The text cannot keep someone from reading that verse and thinking that *perhaps* Jesus had other reasons for leaving Nazareth and *later* decided to be baptized by John. Even if we all agree that it is a faulty interpretation of the text, that fact cannot preclude the possibility that *someone somewhere* might indeed interpret the text that way. The text literally cannot reach out and force someone *not* to interpret it in this or any other way. And Watson's statement that the text "can only mean" one thing? Every Christian reader of Scripture before the beginning of the modern period, and most since, would find that absurd (it is impossible to imagine Origen, Jerome, Augustine, Ambrose, or even Thomas Aquinas *not* being baffled—perhaps offended—by the statement).

54. Francis Watson, "Spaces Sacred and Profane: Stephen Moore, Sex and the Bible," *Journal for the Study of the New Testament* 25 (2002): 109–17; Stephen D. Moore, *God's Beauty Parlor, and Other Queer Spaces in and around the Bible* (Stanford, CA: Stanford University Press, 2001); *God's Gym: Divine Male Bodies in the Bible* (New York: Routledge, 1996).

55. Watson assumes that what *is* the issue in Paul's texts, even Romans 1, is the "Jewish scriptural 'nature' of Gen. 2, in which male and female are created to belong together and not to turn away from the other towards the same, as they do in the

Pauline passage." Watson sees his modern notion of "gender complementarity" all over the place, even in a context, Romans 1, that does not quote or mention Genesis 2, and even when the emphasis in Genesis seems to be placed more on the *sameness* of Adam and Eve ("bone of my bone, flesh of my flesh") rather than on their *difference*. People who think they are simply "hearing" the text or "seeing" what is "in" it are inevitably "seeing" things there that many other people don't see. For some of us, such interpreters curiously *rewrite* Genesis in order to make it about *difference* rather than *sameness*.

56. L. William Countryman, *Interpreting the Truth: Changing the Paradigm of Biblical Studies* (Harrisburg, PA: Trinity Press International, 2003).
57. See ibid., 58, for another reference to "the voice of the text."
58. Ibid., 19. Countryman is speaking here in particular of texts from another historical period, but the basic point about his attribution of *agency* to the text remains whether speaking about historical or contemporary texts. And that is the aspect of his statement I am criticizing.
59. The interpretation in question is Jeffrey L. Staley, *Reading With a Passion: Rhetoric, Autobiography, and the American West in the Gospel of John* (New York: Continuum, 1995). In the same context, Countryman also misunderstands or misrepresents "constructionism." He tries to prove that "reality" does "communicate" to us by pointing out that we "bump into" reality all the time and thereby alter our understandings of reality. But constructionism never said that there is *nothing* "out there," as if a stubbed toe could convince "constructivists" of their error. It rather insists that there is no "meaning" of reality for human beings (discursive meaning, interpretation) without cultural construction. A stubbed toe would have no *discursive* meaning for someone who had no symbolic structures with which to *think* about it. Even a stubbed toe cannot *interpret itself*. That is what is meant by "cultural construction." For a good refutation of the commonsense *assumption* that "reality" itself communicates to us, see Merold Westphal, "Post-Kantian Reflections on the Importance of Hermeneutics," in *Disciplining Hermeneutics: Interpretation in Christian Perspective*, ed. Roger Lundin (Grand Rapids: Wm. B. Eerdmans, 1997), 57–66; Westphal makes the point that interpretation is *always* necessary: "The real world is a virtual reality" (64).
60. Countryman is also mistaken by using the word "largely" here. Whether the text "does" what Countryman wants it to do is *completely*, not largely, dependent on how it is interpreted.
61. Stanley Fish, *Is There a Text In This Class? The Authority of Interpretive Communities* (Cambridge, MA: Harvard University Press, 1980); Fish, *Doing What Comes Naturally: Change, Rhetoric, and the Practice of Theory in Literary and Legal Studies* (Durham, NC: Duke University Press, 1989).
62. Another problem, in my view, comes with Countryman's arguments that historical criticism is indispensable for biblical interpretation (see, e.g., 57). He never, however, provides a real theoretical or theological defense of that position. For a counterargument, see my discussions of "historicism" and appeals to "history" in the introduction and conclusion to this volume.

Chapter 3

1. For a similar ideological analysis of modern interpretations of Romans 1 and homosexuality, see chapter 4, "Heterosexism and the Interpretation of Romans 1:18–32."
2. So most of the commentaries. See also Else Kähler, "Exegese zweier neutestamentlicher Stellen (Römer 1.18–32; 1 Korinther 6.9–11)," in *Probleme der*

Homophilie in medizinischer, theologischer, und juristischer Sicht, ed. Th. Bovet (Bern: Paul Haupt, 1965), 33; Jürgen Becker, "Zum Problem der Homosexualität in der Bibel," *Zeitschrift für evangelische Ethik* 31 (1987): 51.

3. William F. Orr and James Arthur Walker, *I Corinthians* (Garden City, NY: Doubleday, 1976), 199. While not tying *arsenokoitês* to *malakos* directly, Wolfgang Schrage says that the former should not be taken to refer to pederasty alone but to all homosexual relations, this on the basis of Romans 1 (*Der erste Brief an die Korinther* [Zurich: Benziger, 1991], 1:432). Of course, unless we can be certain that *arsenokoitês* refers simply to homosexual relations in general, an appeal to Romans 1 is irrelevant.
4. "Practicing homosexuals" was suggested several years ago for a Catholic lectionary translation. I do not know if the suggestion was finally adopted or published. The arguments by John Boswell (*Christianity, Social Tolerance, and Homosexuality* [Chicago: University of Chicago Press, 1980]), while useful as a corrective to many overly confident claims that *arsenokoitês* "of course" means a "male homosexual," are, I believe, flawed by overstatement and occasional interpretive errors. On the other hand, some of those arguing against Boswell seem not completely to understand his arguments, make textual mistakes of their own, and operate from uncritical linguistic assumptions (e.g., David F. Wright, "Homosexuals or Prostitutes? The Meaning of ARSENOKOITAI [1 Cor. 6:9, 1 Tim. 1:10]," *Vigiliae christianae* 38 [1984]:125–53; see my comments on Wright in following notes). To enter into a detailed tit-for-tat with Boswell, Wright, or other individual treatments of the issue would result in a quagmire. I will, instead, offer my reading with an occasional note on those of others.
5. The history of the invention of "homosexuality" as a psychological, indeed medical, category is now well known. See, e.g., Michel Foucault, *The History of Sexuality I: An Introduction* (New York: Random, 1978); and David M. Halperin, *One Hundred Years of Homosexuality* (New York: Routledge, 1990); for a comparison with ancient concepts see Martha Nussbaum, "Therapeutic Arguments and Structures of Desire," *Differences* 2 (1990): 46–66, esp. 49.
6. See note 2 and William L. Petersen, "Can ARSENOKOITAI Be Translated by 'Homosexuals'?" *Vigiliae christianae* 40 (1986): 187–91.
7. Wright, "Homosexuals or Prostitutes?" 129; Robin Scroggs, *The New Testament and Homosexuality* (Philadelphia: Fortress, 1983), 85–86.
8. See James Barr, *The Semantics of Biblical Language* (London: Oxford University Press, 1961), 107–10.
9. Anton Vögtle, *Die Tugend- und Lasterkataloge im Neuen Testament* (Münster: Aschendorffschen Buckdrockerei, 1936), 13–18; for comparative texts, see Ehrhard Kamlah, *Die Form der katalogischen Paränese im Neuen Testament* (Tübingen: Mohr/Siebeck, 1964).
10. The dates for the document and its different sections are uncertain. This section of the oracle quotes Pseudo-Phocylides (excepting those verses in parentheses). See comments by John J. Collins in *The Old Testament Pseudepigrapha*, ed. James H. Charlesworth (Garden City, NY: Doubleday, 1983), 1:330.
11. Dio Chrysostom, *Orations* 46.8; Philostratus, *Life of Apollonius* 1.15.
12. Wright argues (136–38) that since Pseudo-Phocylides elsewhere shows his disapprobation of homosexual conduct, the term must here be a reference to homosexual conduct. Of course the second point does not proceed from the first.
13. Section 36; for this English translation, see Wilhelm Schneemelcher, ed., *New Testament Apocrypha*, rev. ed., English trans. ed. R. McL. Wilson (Philadelphia: Westminster, 1991).

14. I use the edition by Robert M. Grant: *Ad Autolycum* (Oxford: Clarendon, 1970). Wright's quotation of this passage (134–35) has a different order for the vices because he is relying on the Greek text of Gustave Bardy, Théophile d' Antioche, *Trois Livres a Autolycus,* Sources chrétiennes 20 (Paris: du Cerf, 1948). There seems to be no textual evidence for Bardy's version—at least he gives none in the apparatus, and no edition I have examined suggests any textual variation here among the manuscripts. Bardy admits he is mainly following the edition by J. C. T. Otto: Theophili Episcopi Antiocheni, *Ad Autolycum, libri tres.* Corpus Apologetarum Christianorum Saeculi Secundi 8 (Wiesbaden: Martin Sändig, 1969; reprint of 1861). It is not clear, therefore, why he gives a different order for the vice list from that of Otto and the other modern editions. Perhaps Bardy altered the order to conform more nearly to that of 1 Cor. 6:9, or he carelessly placed *arsenokoitês* after *pornos* because he *assumed* it belonged with the "sexual sins." If the latter is the case, it provides interesting evidence that the order of vices in the lists is important.
15. The term *pornos* would have been understood most often to refer to a male prostitute. See Jeffrey Henderson, *The Maculate Muse: Obscene Language in Attic Comedy* (New Haven, CT: Yale University Press, 1975); Scroggs, *The New Testament and Homosexuality,* 40. Eva Cantarella takes it as such even in its occurrence in 1 Tim. 1:10 (*Bisexuality in the Ancient World* [New Haven, CT: Yale University Press, 1992], 192–94). *Pornos* also seems to have become, at least in Jewish and Christian circles, a more general term for all sorts of persons considered "sexually immoral."
16. This reading may find support even from the position of the term in 1 Tim. 1:10, if *pornoi* there is taken to be a reference to male prostitutes rather than "fornicators" or sexually immoral persons in general (see Scroggs, *The New Testament and Homosexuality,* 118–21). Since Cantarella *does* read *pornoi* in 1 Tim. 1:10 as referring to male prostitutes and the term following *arsenokoitês* as a reference to people who enslave other people in order to prostitute them (*andrapodistai*), I am puzzled by her insistence that *arsenokoitês* in the same passage cannot refer to prostitutes but must instead be a reference to male-male sex in general (see *Bisexuality,* 192–94). If, on the other hand, we read *pornoi* as referring to prostitutes, the list supports my reading of *arsenokoitês,* occurring as it does between two other terms that refer to sex and economic injustice.
17. *Preparation for the Gospel* 6.10.25; *Die Fragmente der griechischen Historiker,* ed. Felix Jacoby (Leiden: E. J. Brill, 1969), vol. 3C fr. 719.
18. Ibid.; see also *Die Pseudoklementinen II Rekognitionen in Rufins Übersetzung,* rev. ed. Bernard Rehm, earlier ed. Georg Strecker (Berlin: Akademie, 1994), 284–87.
19. I do not discuss other occurrences of the term mentioned by Boswell and Wright because I see no possibility that they shed light on the first-century meaning of *arsenokoitês.* Its meaning in a ninth-century inscription, for example, is unclear, in spite of Wright's overconfident interpretation; besides, the usage is very late (*Greek Anthology* 9.686; see Boswell, *Christianity, Social Tolerance, and Homosexuality,* 344n22; Wright, "Homosexuals or Prostitutes?" 130). The meaning in the sixth-century "Penitential" of (perhaps) John the Faster (see Boswell, *Christianity, Social Tolerance, and Homosexuality,* 363–65) is equally unclear. Though Wright accuses Boswell of "irrepressible resourcefulness" and "desperate reasoning" in this case (139–40), I find Wright's exegesis no less fanciful or strained. Such late and opaque uses of the term should be set aside until we have clearer evidence about their meaning and relation to first-century usage.
20. This is certainly true of the later translations of the Greek into other languages. But later translations provide little reliable evidence for the meaning of the term in a first-century Greek context.

21. See my *The Corinthian Body* (New Haven, CT: Yale University Press, 1995), 32–34, 222, 230–31, 241–42.
22. Some scholars define *malakos* as simply a synonym for *kinaedos*, citing texts where the two terms occur together. See, for example, Gaston Vorberg, *Glossarium Eroticum* (Rome: L'Erma, 1965), s.v. Vorberg's citations do not support his definition; in every such case, *kinaedos* is better interpreted as constituting a subcategory within the larger category of *malakoi* (Diogenes Laertius, *Lives*, 7.173) or simply another vice in a list of vices (Plutarch, *Moralia* 88C; Vettius Valens, *Anthologiae* 2.37.54 [ed. David Pingree, 108, 1.3]; Appendix 1.173 [384, 1.11]). I take *arrêtopoios* in Vettius Valens to be a reference not to homosexual sex but to oral sex—which could, of course, be performed on a man or a woman (see Artemidorus, *Dream Handbook* 1.79). No text I have found equates *malakos* with *kinaedos* or defines one term by the other. Note the list of terms for "fucked men" from Attic comedy: Henderson, *Maculate Muse*, 209–15, 222; *malakos* is not among them.
23. Plutarch, *Gaius Gracchus* 4.4; *Cicero* 7.5; Athenaeus, *Deipnosophistae* 565E. Scroggs (*The New Testament and Homosexuality*, 42n45) misuses such references to argue that dressing like a *malakos* would signal that someone was a *kinaedos*, and therefore *malakos* meant an "effeminate call boy." This ignores the fact that *malakos* more often occurs where neither homosexual sex nor prostitution per se is involved.
24. *Hellenica* 3.4.19; 6.1.6; *Apology* 19; *Memorabilia* 1.2.2. Note that in this last case, the reference to *malakos* relates to work, and it follows a reference to sex (*aphrodisiôn akrateis*); *malakos* here has nothing to do with sex.
25. Epictetus, 3.6.9; 4.1.25; "Epistle of Crates" 19 (*The Cynic Epistles: A Study Edition*, ed. Abraham J. Malherbe [Missoula, MT: Scholars, 1977], 68); "Epistle of Diogenes" 29 (Malherbe, 126): in both cases, sleeping and eating too much are important.
26. Dio Cassius, *Roman History* 58.4.6; Plutarch, *Pericles* 27.4; Josephus, *War* 6.211, *Antiquities* 19.197.
27. Xenophon, *Hiero* 1.23; Plutarch, *Moralia* 831B; 136B; *Pericles* 27.4; Athenaeus, *Deipnosophistae* 12.536C; 543B. In one of Philo's condemnations of decadence, he includes remarks about penetrated men as being thus made effeminate (*Abraham* 133–36). The term *malakos*, however, is used of this entire process of degenerating decadence and effeminacy due to luxurious living—including the effeminacy of *heterosexual* sex. The aspects of homosexual sex play only one part.
28. In Dionysius Halicarnassus, *Roman Antiquities* 7.2.4, people cannot tell whether a ruler earned the sobriquet *malakos* because he had allowed himself to be penetrated as a young man or because he possessed an exceptionally mild nature.
29. The "softness of the Lydians" (*ta Lydôn malaka*) is reflected in their luxurious living, gourmet food, use of too many *female* prostitutes, and lots of indiscriminate sex with men *and* women (Athenaeus, *Deipnosophistae* 12.540F). Plutarch relates the "Lydian mode" in music to softness and general decadence: *Moralia* 83F.
30. Note a similar assumption mentioned by Athenaeus; the Syracusans are reported as forbidding women to wear gold or colorful clothing unless they confess to being prostitutes; similarly, men were not allowed to "dress up" unless they admitted to being either adulterers or *kinaedoi* (*Deipnosophistae* 12.521b). Dressing up was considered effeminate, but that could mean an attempt to attract either men or women.
31. The suitors of a young girl arrive at her door adorned with long hair styled prettily (Athenaeus, *Deipnosophistae* 528d, citing Agathon, *Thyestes*). This entire section of Athenaeus is instructive for the ancient concept of effeminacy; it usually is related to luxurious and decadent living in general and is expressed far more

often here by heterosexual activities than homosexual. For example, the Lydians, according to Clearchus, expressed their effeminacy by laying out parks with lots of shade, gathering the wives and virgins of other men and raping them, and then finally adopting "the manner of life of women," whatever that means (*Deipnosophistae* 12.515e–516a). There is no mention here of homosexual sex.

32. This point was made by John Boswell (*Christianity, Social Tolerance, and Homosexuality*, 340) but generally ignored by biblical scholars, who continue naively to assume that any concern about effeminacy would involve at least an unconscious anxiety about homosexuality. Thus, Paul's concerns about long hair on men in 1 Corinthians 11 must harbor a concern about homosexuality. See Robin Scroggs, "Paul and the Eschatological Woman," *The Text and the Times* (Minneapolis: Fortress, 1993), 88n38; originally in *Journal of the American Academy of Religion* 40 (1972): 283–303; Scroggs, *The New Testament and Homosexuality* (Philadelphia: Fortress, 1983), 53–55, 62–65; Jerome Murphy-O'Connor, "Sex and Logic in I Corinthians 11:2–16," *Catholic Biblical Quarterly* 42 (1980): 482–500.
33. For a character in Achilles Tatius's novel *Clitophon and Leucippe*, male love is natural, frank, real, and lacking in any softness or effeminacy (2.38; *ou malthassei*). Even Dio Chrysostom, no advocate of male-male love, knows that love of a woman is liable to be thought excessively feminine (7.151–52).
34. Noted also by Scroggs, *The New Testament and Homosexuality*, 46–48.
35. The degradation of the female comes to be a theme of asceticism in general, especially but not exclusively in Jewish and Christian writers. Philo praises women who give up sex entirely, thereby becoming "manly," and Thecla, through celibacy, becomes masculinized and saved. See Philo, *On the Contemplative Life* 40–64; see Richard A. Baer Jr., *Philo's Use of the Categories Male and Female* (Leiden: E. J. Brill, 1970), 99–100. For English translations of the *Acts of Paul and Thecla*, see Schneemelcher, *New Testament Apocrypha*, 2:239–46; or J. K. Elliott, *The Apocryphal New Testament* (Oxford: Clarendon, 1993), 364–72; reproduced in Bart D. Ehrman, *Lost Scriptures: Books That Did Not Make It Into the New Testament* (Oxford: Oxford University Press, 2003), 113–21.
36. A common practice among New Testament scholars has been to define *malakos* as the "passive partner" due to its proximity to *arsenokoitês*, which is taken to be the "active partner" (see, e.g., Gordon Fee, *First Epistle to the Corinthians* [Grand Rapids: Wm. B. Eerdmans, 1987], 243–44). But this is circular reasoning. The meaning of *arsenokoitês* is famously problematic, and there is no evidence that it was a special term for the "active" partner in homosexual sex (even if one concedes, which I do not, that it is a reference to "men who sleep with men"). Furthermore, while there is no evidence that *malakos* was considered a special ("technical") term for the "passive" partner (as Fee admits), its general meaning as "effeminate" independent of sexual position or object is easily demonstrated. To define *malakos* by *arsenokoitês* is to define something already clear by something that is obscure.
37. Every text cited by Scroggs in support of this reading, in his terminology "effeminate call boy" (*The New Testament and Homosexuality*), is better read as I have: by being penetrated, a boy shows his effeminacy, but *malakos* refers to the effeminacy, not the penetration; there were many other signs, many heterosexual, that could also reveal "effeminacy."
38. The list, of course, could be expanded. This is taken mainly from H. Herter, "Effeminatus," *Reallexikon für Antike und Christentum* (Stuttgart: Hiersemann, 1959), 4.620–50; for the associations of hair with effeminacy and decadence, see also Pseudo-Phocylides, *Sentences*, 210–12, and the commentary by P. W. van der Horst, *The Sentences of Pseudo-Phocylides* (Leiden: E. J. Brill, 1978), 250; Hubert

Cancik, *Untersuchungen zur lyrischen Kunst des P. Papianus Statius,* Spudasmata 13 (Hildesheim: Olms, 1965), 58. For masturbation as evidence of *malakia,* see Vorberg, *Glossarium Eroticum* s.v.

39. I say this to forestall one possible objection to my method. One *might* argue that although *malakos* and *arsenokoitês* did not mean, in the common linguistic currency, the "passive" and "active" partners in homosexual sex, that was surely what Paul intended by his use of the terms. The goal of translation, however, is to translate the text, not some guessed-at authorial intention. See Ferdinand Deist, "Presuppositions and Contextual Bible Translation," *Journal of Northwest Semitic Languages* 19 (1993): 13–23, esp. 19–20. Furthermore, contrary to some assumptions of modernist historiography, the *Scripture* for the church is traditionally the text, not a historically reconstructed authorial intention. Thus we translate and interpret not what Paul meant to say but what he said (or at least as close as we can ascertain what that was).

Chapter 4

1. Patricia Beattie Jung and Ralph F. Smith, *Heterosexism: An Ethical Challenge* (Albany: SUNY Press, 1993), 13–14.
2. Thus, my approach here differs from those scholars offering a more "pro-gay" reading of Paul, such as John Boswell, *Christianity, Social Tolerance, and Homosexuality: Gay People in Western Europe from the Beginning of the Christian Era to the Fourteenth Century* (Chicago: University of Chicago Press, 1980). My approach is perhaps closer to that of Klaus Wengst, "Paulus und die Homosexualität: Überlegungen zu Röm, 1, 26f.," *Zeitschrift für evangelische Ethik* 31 (1987): 72–81.
3. Richard B. Hays, "Relations Natural and Unnatural: A Response to John Boswell's Exegesis of Romans 1," *Journal of Christian Ethics* 14 (1986): 184–215, at 189.
4. Hays, "Relations Natural and Unnatural," 190; Robin Scroggs, *The New Testament and Homosexuality* (Philadelphia: Fortress, 1983), 110.
5. Hays, "Relations Natural and Unnatural," 191, 200.
6. Helmut Thielicke, *The Ethics of Sex* (New York: Harper & Row, 1964), 282–83; for similar views, see also H. Kimball-Jones, *Toward a Christian Understanding of the Homosexual* (London: SCM, 1966), 77; William Muehl, "Some Words of Caution," in *Male and Female: Christian Approaches to Sexuality,* ed. Ruth Tiffany Barnhouse and Urban R. Holmes III (New York: Seabury, 1976), 167–74, at 174; Richard B. Hays, "Awaiting the Redemption of Our Bodies: The Witness of Scripture Concerning Homosexuality," in *Homosexuality in the Church: Both Sides of the Debate,* ed. Jeffrey S. Siker (Louisville, KY: Westminster John Knox, 1994), 3–17 (originally published in an edited version in *Sojourners* 20, no. 6 [July 1991]: 17–21; I cite the more recent, complete version); P. Michael Ukleja, "The Bible and Homosexuality, Part 2: Homosexuality in the New Testament," *Bibliotheca sacra* 140 (1983): 350–58; S. Lewis Johnson Jr., "God Gave Them Up," *Bibliotheca sacra* 129 (1972): 124–33; D. S. Bailey, ed., *Sexual Offenders and Social Punishment* (Church Information Board for Church of England Moral Welfare Council, 1956), 76, quoted in D. J. Atkinson, *Homosexuals in the Christian Fellowship* (Grand Rapids: Wm. B. Eerdmans, 1979), 62.
7. So also K. Wengst, "Paulus und die Homosexualität," 74. The most famous argument that Romans 1 refers to Adam is M. D. Hooker, "Adam in Romans I," *New Testament Studies* 6 (1959–60): 297–306; see also her "A Further Note on Romans I," *New Testament Studies* 13 (1966–67): 181–83. For refutations of Hooker's arguments, see Joseph A. Fitzmyer, *Romans* (Garden City, NY: Dou-

bleday, 1993), 274; and Stanley K. Stowers, *A Rereading of Romans: Justice, Jews, and Gentiles* (New Haven, CT: Yale University Press, 1994), 86–94.

8. See Louis Ginzberg, *Legends of the Jews,* 7 vols. (Philadelphia: Jewish Publication Society of America, 1909–66), 1:123–24; 4:306; 5:150n53, 151n54; for Christian explanations of the origins of idolatry, see 5:150n54.
9. Stowers, *A Rereading of Romans,* 85, 97–100. Stowers provides many parallels of such "decline narratives" and their hortatory use in Greek, Roman, and Jewish contexts. As Stowers points out, the particularly Jewish modifications of the commonplace are the condemnation of idolatry in particular as a degenerate and late invention of Gentile peoples and the blame placed on idolatry and polytheism for the other degenerate aspects of heathen civilization, such as rampant sexual immorality, warfare, pharmacology, and cosmetics.
10. This part of the narrative is one piece of evidence that Paul is not here referring to any rejection of knowledge of God by Adam and Eve nor to the Israelite sin of idolatry with the "golden calf." The particular description of the *kind* of idolatry here evident would evoke images not of Jewish rebellion but of the polymorphous polytheism of Gentile culture as depicted by contemporary Jews.
11. The Greek *para physin,* usually translated "contrary to nature" or "unnatural," more exactly means "beyond nature," the significance of which I explain below.
12. For a convincing argument that Paul is addressing a Gentile (rather than Jewish) moralist in Rom. 2:1–16, see Stowers, *A Rereading of Romans,* 100–109.
13. For example, Ukleja, "Bible and Homosexuality," 356.
14. Hays, "Relations Natural and Unnatural," 195.
15. Hays notes (at 195 and 200) that Paul is referring in Romans 1 to "pagan gentiles" and "the whole *pagan* world" (emphasis added); he alters his language in several places, however, to take the passage as referring actually to the universal human condition: 189, 190, 191, 195, 200, 207, 211. See also "Awaiting the Redemption," 8–9, where Hays, in spite of realizing that Paul's initial subject is idolatry, continually slips into rhetoric about "the underlying sickness of humanity as a whole, Jews and Greeks alike," "the universal fall of humanity," "human fallenness," and "humanity's tragic confusion and alienation from God the Creator." It may be true that Paul's argument takes idolatry to be one expression of the fallenness of humanity, an expression particular to Gentiles. In that case, however, homosexual activity, as an example of the depravities caused by idolatry, would be a subset of a set: homosexual sex came from idolatry, which came from the fall. But this is a long way from using homosexuality itself as a special symptom of the universal fallenness of human nature, which Hays takes Paul to do.
16. The classic critique of this practice is Krister Stendahl, "The Apostle Paul and the Introspective Conscience of the West," *Harvard Theological Review* 56 (1963): 199–215.
17. Stowers labels Paul's portrait an "ethnic caricature" of non-Jewish civilization (*A Rereading of Romans,* 95), and "what moderns would call an ethnic cultural stereotype" (109). The redundancy (in Paul's thought) of "gentile sinners" comes naturally to Paul's pen (Gal. 2:15).
18. Thielicke, *Ethics of Sex,* 282–83.
19. Bailey, ed., *Sexual Offenders,* 75–76, quoted in Atkinson, *Homosexuals,* 62.
20. Hays, "Relations Natural and Unnatural," 208.
21. Note Martha Nussbaum's succinct description of the difference between ancient and modern notions: "There was for the ancient Greeks no salient distinction corresponding to our own distinction between heterosexuality and homosexuality: no distinction, that is, of persons into two profoundly different kinds on the basis of the gender of the object they most deeply or most characteristically desire. Nor is there, indeed, anything precisely corresponding to our modern concept of

'sexuality'—a deep and relatively stable inner orientation towards objects of a certain gender" ("Therapeutic Arguments and Structures of Desire," *Differences* 2 [1990]: 46–66, at 49). Among the many treatments of the modern invention of homosexuality, perhaps the most famous are Michel Foucault, *The History of Sexuality,* vol. 1: *An Introduction* (New York: Random House, 1978); Foucault, *The History of Sexuality,* vol. 2: *The Use of Pleasure* (New York: Random House, 1985); David M. Halperin, *One Hundred Years of Homosexuality* (New York: Routledge, 1990); see also the collection of essays, written from a social-constructionist point of view, in David M. Halperin et al., eds., *Before Sexuality: The Construction of Erotic Experience in the Ancient Greek World* (Princeton, NJ: Princeton University Press, 1990). See also John Boswell's response to those critics who label him an "essentialist": "Concepts, Experience, and Sexuality," *Differences* 2 (1990): 67–87. For an excellent account of "constructionism," "history," and the problem of knowledge, see Eve Kosofsky Sedgwick, *Epistemology of the Closet* (Berkeley: University of California Press, 1990), esp. 1–63.

22. This is the necessary implication of Hays's connection of an admission of sexual orientation in perhaps 10 percent of the population (a figure he yet questions without providing contrary evidence) to his statements that Paul would respond to such information by pointing to it as "evidence" for "the wrath of God." See also "Awaiting the Redemption," 12, where Hays imagines Paul responding to "sexual orientation" as proof that "the power of sin is rampant in the world" (see also Atkinson, *Homosexuals,* 58.) Hays admits that he himself accepts the reality of "homosexual orientation" (14). It is baffling to me that Hays can admit such an important difference between his own beliefs and Paul's (that there is such a thing as "sexual orientation") and then act as if the difference is irrelevant. For an excellent theological critique of both progressive and conservative assumptions of the modernist "sexed identity" (which includes the modern notion of sexual orientation), see Mary McClintock Fulkerson, "Gender—Being It or Doing It? The Church, Homosexuality, and the Politics of Identity," *Union Seminary Quarterly Review* 47 (1993): 29–46.
23. See, for example, Victor Paul Furnish, "The Bible and Homosexuality: Reading the Texts in Context," in Siker, ed., *Homosexuality in the Church,* 18–35, at 27. I disagree, however, with Furnish's claims that in the Greco-Roman world "it was universally presupposed that anyone who sought intercourse with a partner of the same sex was willfully overriding his or her own 'natural' desire for the opposite sex" (26; see also 31). As I explain below, ancient persons considered same-sex eroticism to be simply one expression of "desire" in general—perhaps taken to an undue extreme, but not different in kind from opposite-sex eroticism. In fact, one *reason* the ancients had no conception of homosexual orientation in the modern sense is that they did not differentiate the different sexual activities into a bimorphic dichotomy framed by two different *kinds* of desire. They considered same-sex desire completely "natural," even if they did sometimes consider same-sex *intercourse* "unnatural."
24. Apuleius, *The Golden Ass,* book 16, contains a famous fictitious account of a noblewoman's insatiable lust. See the parallel story in (Pseudo?-) Lucian, *Lucius, or the Ass,* 51.
25. Dio Chrysostom 7:151–52; see 7:135 for Dio's remark indicating that he took male-female intercourse within the family to represent sex "according to nature" (*kata physin*). Since I will presently compare notions of "natural" sexual activity with "natural" use of food, it is interesting that, just after his quotation as given above, Dio compares insatiable appetites in sex to those in wine drinking: "His state is like that of men who are addicted to drinking and wine-bibbing, who after long and steady drinking of unmixed wine, often lose their taste for it and create

an artificial thirst by the stimulus of sweatings, salted foods, and condiments" (7:152). Importantly, Hays knows and even quotes this passage from Dio; I am puzzled that he does not perceive the radical difference between the ancient logic of the "natural" and the modern.

26. Victor Paul Furnish, "The Bible and Homosexuality," in *Homosexuality: In Search of a Christian Understanding,* ed. Leon Smith (Nashville: Discipleship Resources, 1981), 6–21, at 13; see also Furnish's comments in "The Bible and Homosexuality," 18–35, esp. 26–28. Hays, it should be noted, knows of this material (see "Relations Natural and Unnatural," 193). I generally offer as examples ancient texts known to Hays himself; Hays's failure to discern the radical difference between his and Paul's notions about "nature" and "desire" is due not to ignorance of the ancient sources but ideological misconstrual or elision of the ancient logics of sex and desire.
27. John Chrysostom, *Homily IV on Romans.* This translation is by Boswell, in *Christianity, Social Tolerance, and Homosexuality,* 361. An English translation of the homilies is also available in *The Homilies of S. John Chrysostom,* 3d ed. rev. (Oxford: James Parker, 1877), and in the Nicene and Post-Nicene Fathers series.
28. Interestingly, as Jeff Siker reminded me in personal conversation, the heterosexist inclination to compare homosexual orientation with a propensity towards alcoholism (which Hays in particular does, see "Awaiting the Redemption") has more in common with the ancient notion that "unnatural" action springs from a basically "natural" activity taken to an extreme. Also interestingly, however, modern scholars do not label alcoholism "unnatural."
29. Importantly, commentators on Romans 1 writing in the nineteenth century do *not* look to the passage as providing an etiology of homosexual desire. Much more akin to ancient conceptions, they generally assume that same-sex *desire* is an extension of desire in general, not a different *kind* of sexuality. They offer not an etiology of homosexual desire but an etiology of homosexual *sex* that is assumed to spring from lust in general, given too much latitude. This makes perfect sense once we realize that they were writing before the common currency of the concepts of "homosexuality" as opposed to "heterosexuality" in terms of orientation or personhood. See, for example, Albert Barnes, *Notes, Explanatory and Practical, on the Epistle to the Romans* (New York: Leavitt, Lord, 1835), 40–42; M. F. Sadler, *The Epistle to the Romans, with Notes Critical and Practical* (London: George Bell, 1888), 22–23; William G. T. Shedd, *A Critical and Doctrinal Commentary on the Epistle of St. Paul to the Romans* (Grand Rapids: Zondervan, 1967 [1879]), 25–29; Moses Stuart, *A Commentary on the Epistle to the Romans* (Andover: Flagg and Gould, 1832), 104, 108. Martin Luther also does not speak of homosexual *desire* as different; it is simply excessive indulgence in lust in general: *Commentary on the Epistle to the Romans,* trans. J. Theodore Mueller (Grand Rapids: Zondervan, 1954), 31. According to one study, the culture of colonial New England also knew of no particular *kind* of "homosexual" desire; see Jonathan Ned Katz, "The Age of Sodomitical Sin, 1607–1740," in *Reclaiming Sodom,* ed. Jonathan Goldberg (New York: Routledge, 1994), 43–58, originally published, in a longer version, in Katz, *Gay/Lesbian Almanac* (New York: Harper & Row, 1983), 31–65.
30. See Aristotle, *Nichomachean Ethics* 1148b15–9a20; [*Problemata*] 4.26; Kenneth J. Dover, *Greek Homosexuality* (Cambridge, MA: Harvard University Press, 1978), 168–69.
31. In female-female intercourse, it was generally assumed that one of the women would have to penetrate the other, and the "penetrating woman" was more than an oxymoron; she was a monster—contrary to nature. Descriptions and analyses of the importance of gender hierarchy for Greco-Roman sexuality are now quite numerous. For starters, see Michel Foucault, *The History of Sexuality,* vol. 3: *The*

Care of the Self (New York: Pantheon, 1986), 18–20, 84–88, passim; Halperin, *One Hundred Years of Homosexuality,* 22–24, 130; Boswell, "Concepts, Experience, and Sexuality," 72–73; John J. Winkler, *The Constraints of Desire* (New York: Routledge, 1990), 39–40, 51, passim (see index under "penetration"). I deal at length with the subject of gender hierarchy, penetration, and the construction of the feminine in my *The Corinthian Body* (New Haven, CT: Yale University Press, 1995), esp. 177, 240, 247–48. Penetration framed in terms of gender hierarchy is of course not limited to the Greco-Roman world. For comparison with similar situations from anthropological studies, see Gerald W. Creed, "Sexual Subordination: Institutionalized Homosexuality and Social Control in Melanesia," in *Reclaiming Sodom,* 66–94 (originally published in *Ethnography* 23 [Pittsburgh: Department of Anthropology, University of Pittsburgh, 1984]: 157–76); J. W. M. Whiting, *Becoming a Kwoma* (New Haven, CT: Yale University Press, 1941), 51; S. Brandes, "Like Wounded Stags: Male Sexual Ideology in an Andalusian Town," in *Sexual Meanings: The Cultural Construction of Gender and Sexuality,* ed. S. Ortner and H. Whitehead (Cambridge: Cambridge University Press, 1981), 216–39, at 232–33. I do not mean to imply that *all* homosexual relations were rigidly constructed along the lines of dominance/subordination; only that that was the way sexual relations in general were ideologically constructed. For the variety of possible constructions of homosexual relations, see John Boswell, *Same-Sex Unions in Premodern Europe* (New York: Villard, 1994); it is not hard to imagine that in many cases same-sex relations provided opportunity for more equality between lovers than opposite-sex ones. I also do not wish to imply that our modern society is free from the misogynous tendency to degrade the person penetrated. Common derogatory language and insults no longer even considered obscene by most people ("This sucks!") derive their meaning from assumptions about the despised role of the penetrated in intercourse, implicating therefore the feminine in the inferior.

32. *Laws* 636a–c; 836c–e.
33. *Moralia* 751d.
34. *Special Laws* 3:43; see also 3:37.
35. *Abraham* 133–36.
36. See also *Special Laws* 1:325; *The Contemplative Life* 59–62.
37. Although agreeing with many points made by David L. Bartlett, "A Biblical Perspective on Homosexuality," *Foundations* 20 (1977): 133–47, my position on the nature of desire in Paul's thought puts me at odds with his statement that Paul condemns homosexual *lust* rather than homosexual love in Romans 1 (140). I would say, rather, that Paul considers *any* homosexual activity necessarily to spring from lust in general (that is, the "lust" is the same thing whether directed towards persons of the same or opposite sex). This does not mean, however, that Paul had some other notion of desire that would be appropriate—either homosexual or heterosexual.
38. This constitutes an important difference between Paul's position and that of most others of his time who wrote on desire and sex. Philosophers and physicians, for example, believed that "moderate" desire and passion were necessary for sexual activity; some "burning" was necessary to induce sex and provide the semen for ejaculation. Their moralism extended only to urging people to moderate their passion. Paul, on the other hand, never gives "moderated passion" as a possible solution to the problems of desire (see further, Martin, *Corinthian Body,* chap. 8).
39. See also Col. 3:5. In Galatians *pathêma* is linked with *epithymia* in a context that refers to various sexual "impurities" as "works of the flesh" that have no place among Christians (Gal. 5:16, 19, 24).
40. See Martin, *Corinthian Body,* 209–17.

41. Significantly, most early Christian commentators on Romans take the references to women to refer *not* to lesbian activity but to heterosexual intercourse considered "unnatural" due to the female's assumption of the "male" role. Again, the concern is about "natural" gender hierarchy—in these cases related to heterosexual rather than lesbian sex. See Bernadette J. Brooten, "Patristic Interpretation of Romans 1:26," in *Studia Patristica XVIII,* ed. Elizabeth A. Livingstone (Kalamazoo, MI: Cistercian, 1985), 1:287–91.
42. In *Corinthian Body,* 229–49, I offer a fuller argument that Paul is reinforcing, rather than challenging, an assumed Greco-Roman gender hierarchy.
43. Some have tried to interpret vv. 11–12 to depict Paul as backing off a rigid hierarchy and providing an opening for egalitarian mutuality. In the ancient world, however, interdependence (whether economic, social, or sexual) did not in any way imply equality. See, further, Martin, *Corinthian Body,* 229–49.
44. Wengst, "Paulus und die Homosexualität," 75. Joseph Fitzmyer recognizes that Paul's comment about "nature" in 1 Cor. 11:14 "creates a problem" for an uncritical acceptance of Paul's argument from "nature" in Romans 1. In an astonishing instance of double-speak, however, he insists that the reference to nature in 1 Cor. 11:14 is actually a reference to culture and that it has, in any case, no relevance for the function of Paul's argument from nature in Romans 1: "In this instance [1 Cor. 11:14], *phusis* hardly refers to the natural order of things, but the social convention. That use of *phusis,* however, is said to be 'of no theological significance' [citing the *Theological Dictionary of the New Testament,* 9:273]; but it is a problem for the interpretation of 1 Corinthians. Yet what is meant there has little relevance for this context in Romans" (*Romans,* 286–87). Fitzmyer never explains *why* the only other instance of a Pauline argument "from nature" is irrelevant for the interpretation of the same kind of argument in Romans 1. Having noted, correctly, that appeals to "nature" are actually appeals to social constructions, Fitzmyer does not seem to realize that "nature" is *always* socially constructed—or, put differently, that "culture" is always "natural." At this point, it seems to make little difference which option one takes; the real objective should be to dispense with the modernist culture/nature dichotomy as an explanatory, hermeneutical trick. See, for example, Bruno Latour, *We Have Never Been Modern* (Cambridge, MA: Harvard University Press, 1993). It should come as no surprise that "nature" in Paul's world may differ radically from "nature" in ours (assuming, perhaps too rashly, that there is an "us" that *has* a common construction of nature).
45. Hays, "Awaiting the Redemption," 4, 9; "Relations Natural and Unnatural," 200.
46. Hays, "Relations Natural and Unnatural," 204.
47. For various discussions of heterosexism, homophobia, and the problematics of such terminology, see Warren J. Blumenfeld, ed., *Homophobia: How We All Pay the Price* (Boston: Beacon, 1992).
48. Hays, "Awaiting the Redemption," 3–4, 15.
49. For the full text, see Ramsey Colloquium, "The Homosexual Movement: A Response by the Ramsey Colloquium," *First Things* 41 (March 1994): 15–20. An excerpt appeared in *The Wall Street Journal* on 24 February 1994. I quote from the *First Things* article. For the reference to the fall, see p. 18.
50. Ibid., 18.
51. The article, as is typical in heterosexist literature, nowhere explains exactly what is meant by calling heterosexuality "normal" or "the norm." This could conceivably be rather innocuous (though it seldom, if ever, is) if it means no more than that most people are straight rather than gay, just like most people are right-handed. One may believe, that is, that it is "normal" to be right-handed without believing that there is anything "wrong" with left-handed people or that society

or right-handedness is threatened by the availability of commodities like left-handed scissors or drinking cups. It is, in my opinion, heterosexist but not necessarily homophobic to consider heterosexuality "the norm." I believe, in other words, that it is heterosexist in our *current* cultural situation to hold up heterosexuality as "normal" even if one does not mean by that that homosexuality should be prohibited. What is homophobic is the belief or fear that the very existence of homosexuality or gay men and lesbians threatens the existence of heterosexuality or the social structures supporting it.

52. Ramsey Colloquium, "Homosexual Movement," 19.
53. This should not be taken as a claim that I have offered here a completely sufficient and final "explanation." Having granted that these interpretations are instances of cultural homophobia, one might then pose the further question "So why does homophobia exist in our culture?" My suggestions, however, may perhaps be useful for introducing new directions for discussion and analysis.

Chapter 5

1. I have offered a fuller argument on these issues in Martin, *The Corinthian Body* (New Haven, CT: Yale University Press, 1995), 198–228.
2. Ibid., 212–14.
3. G. D. Collier, "'That we might not crave evil.' The Structure and Argument of 1 Corinthians 10:1–3," *Journal for the Study of the New Testament* 55 (1994): 55–75, at 71 (emphasis in original).
4. See my argument in chapter 4, "Heterosexism and the Interpretation of Romans 1:18–32" (esp. pp. 56–60) that the ancient world, and Paul as part of it, did not differentiate sexual desires by the gender of the object desired. Whereas Paul does condemn same-sex intercourse, he has no notion of a particular desire (homosexual) that was a different *kind* of desire from "normal" desire (heterosexual).
5. For one account of the cultural specificity of "common sense," see Clifford Geertz, *Local Knowledge: Further Essays in Interpretive Anthropology* (New York: Basic Books, 1983), 73–93.
6. Martin, *Corinthian Body*, 146–53, 216–17.
7. Fragments of Rufus's text are found in the collection of medical texts made in late antiquity by Oribasius. Greek: Oribasius, *Oribasii collectionum medicarum reliquiae*, ed. Ioannes Raeder (Amsterdam: Adolf M. Hakkert, 1964), 4:106–9. Greek with French translation: Oribasius, *Oeuvres*, ed. and trans. C. Daremberg and U. C. Bussemaker (Paris: Impr. Nationale, 1858).
8. See, for example, Soranus, *Gynecology* 1.7.31 and 1.8.33. Greek: Soranus, *Sorani Gynaeciorum libri IV. De signis fracturarum, de fasciis, vita Hippocratis secundum Soranum*, ed. Johannes Ilberg, Corpus medicorum graecorum 4 (Leipzig: Teubner, 1927). English: Soranus, *Gynecology*, trans. Owsei Temkin (Baltimore: Johns Hopkins University Press, 1956).
9. Plutarch, *De tuenda sanitate praecepta* 125B; Aristotle, *Nichomachean Ethics* 3.11.1, 1118b8; 7.2.6, 1146a10.
10. Plutarch, *De tuenda sanitate praecepta* 129F; see also 129E; 125D.
11. As noted, this is an unremarkable representation of the traditional Aristotelian view. It seems to have been quite widespread among physicians and moral philosophers, though other, more rigorous views were also known. Aristotle believes that too much sex is damaging, but in moderation healthy; see for example his remarks about sex and young people: *Historia animalium* 581b9; 581b24–30.
12. Martha C. Nussbaum, *The Therapy of Desire: Theory and Practice in Hellenistic Ethics* (Princeton, NJ: Princeton University Press, 1994).

13. *Epistles* 116.5; see also Cicero, *Tusculan Disputations* 35.75; 4.11.25–27.
14. Fragment of Seneca, *De matrimonia*, quoted by Jerome. See F. Haase, *L. Annaei Senecae, Opera quae supersunt*, vol. 3 (Leipzig: Teubner, 1872).
15. Diogenes Laertius, *Lives of Philosophers* 7.85; another term used for this "urge" is *orexis*; see Nussbaum, *Therapy of Desire*, 86.
16. This picture is taken mainly from *Therapy of Desire*, 5–6, where Nussbaum criticizes Foucault.
17. Charles Taylor identifies these two different uses of *rationality* (not, however, in reference to Nussbaum) as the use of the term to refer to *procedure*, on the one hand, and *content*, on the other: *Sources of the Self: The Making of the Modern Identity* (Cambridge, MA: Harvard University Press, 1989), 86. I agree with Taylor's claim that the use of *rationality* to refer to particular beliefs (content) is more ancient than modern, whereas the use of the term to refer to *how* someone thinks (procedure) is more modern than ancient. Furthermore, the modern stress on "procedural rationality" is bound up with the "allegiance to modern freedom," that is, the Kantian notion that a truly moral choice (one that is "rational") must be made free from the constraints of authority (such as that of religion or culture) or contingency.
18. See for example Nussbaum, *The Fragility of Goodness: Luck and Ethics in Greek Tragedy and Philosophy* (Cambridge: Cambridge University Press, 1986), note on 11; and *Therapy of Desire*, 148.
19. Nussbaum *Therapy of Desire*, 6.
20. Martin, *Corinthian Body*, 153–59.
21. Jan Nicolaas Sevenster, *Paul and Seneca* (Leiden: E. J. Brill, 1961), 113–15.
22. Aristotle, *Politics* 1.1.4, 1252a25–30: the very root of community, in its simplest form male-female bonding, is in Aristotle's political theory *anagkê*, "necessity, need."
23. See the discussion of this issue, and suggestions about how to interpret apparent inconsistencies in Aristotle's own writings, in the footnote to Aristotle, *Historia animalium*, by D. M. Balme in the Loeb Classical Library edition, book 10: 487–89. For Galen's arguments against the Aristotelian view, see his *On Semen* 1.9.15; 2.1; 2.4.5. Greek and English: Galen, *On Semen*, ed. Phillip de Lacy, Corpus medicorum graecorum 3/1 (Berlin: Akademie-Verlag, 1992).
24. For a further analysis of the ideology of sexual control in upper-class Greeks and Romans, see Dale B. Martin, "Contradictions of Masculinity: Ascetic Inseminators and Menstruating Men in Greco-Roman Culture," in *Generation and Degeneration: Literature and Tropes of Reproduction*, ed. Valeria Finucci and Kevin Brownlee (Durham, NC: Duke University Press, 2001), 81–108.
25. See Paul's frank admission, indeed celebration, of the utter *lack* of self-sufficiency in 2 Cor. 1:8–11. For one instance of "overabundance" (*hyperperisseuô*) see 2 Cor. 7:4.
26. Martin, *Corinthian Body*, 131–32, 170–74, 176–77, 190–97.
27. That is, although Paul can, of course, speak of choices, one cannot imagine him making the same sort of claims as Epictetus, who can say to the tyrant, "My leg you may bind, but my free will [ability to choose, *prohairesis*] even Zeus is not able to conquer!" (1.1.23; trans. mine).
28. For a stronger questioning of their view of self-sufficiency, see Nussbaum, *Fragility of Goodness*, 3.
29. Nussbaum, *Therapy of Desire*, 7. Indeed, when culture and society make appearances in the book they are usually placed in simple opposition to other things taken as more "real" or "true." For example, reason and the individual represent the "rational" side of a dichotomy whose "mere convention" side (irrational) is represented by culture and society (*Therapy of Desire*, 328, 334); elsewhere

"nature" is opposed to "the social" (497; we know from other statements that "nature" is "rational": 160–63; 501).

30. Among the few studies that spring quickly to mind are the following: Douglas R. Hofstadler, *The Mind's I: Fantasies and Reflections on Self and Soul* (New York: Basic Books, 1981); Gilles Deleuze and Félix Guattari, *Anti-Oedipus: Capitalism and Schizophrenia* (Minneapolis: University of Minnesota Press, 1983); Elaine Scarry, *The Body in Pain: The Making and Unmaking of the World* (New York: Oxford University Press, 1985); Richard Rorty, *Contingency, Irony, and Solidarity* (Cambridge: Cambridge University Press, 1989), esp. chapter 2; Daniel C. Dennett, *Consciousness Explained* (Boston: Little, Brown, & Co., 1991); and of course the entire work of Foucault, against which Nussbaum is directing much of her fire. I believe Nussbaum is still too implicated in Kantian assumptions about ethics, the will, and rationality that, in my view, deserve the deconstruction to which they have already been subjected by other scholars. For one critique of the Kantian emphasis on radical freedom of the will from authority and contingency, a critique that I believe should also be turned against Nussbaum's views, see Alasdair C. MacIntyre, "How Moral Agents Became Ghosts or Why the History of Ethics Diverged from that of the Philosophy of Mind," *Synthese* 53 (1982): 295–312.
31. For more criticism of biblical *and* historicist "foundationalism" in Christian ethical discussion, and what precisely I mean by the term, see the introduction and chapter 2, "The Rhetoric of Biblical Scholarship," in this volume.

Chapter 6

1. A quotation of Albert Einstein is apropos: "Common sense is nothing more than a deposit of prejudices laid down in the mind before you reach eighteen," quoted in E. T. Bell, *Mathematics, Queen and Servant of the Sciences* (New York: McGraw-Hill, 1951), 42.
2. Krister Stendahl, *The Bible and the Role of Women: A Case Study in Hermeneutics* (Philadelphia: Fortress, 1966), 33. This little book, more exactly a pamphlet, is an English translation of a Swedish work published in 1958.
3. Mary Hayter, *The New Eve in Christ: The Use and Abuse of the Bible in the Debate about Women in the Church* (London: SPCK, 1987), 134; Stanley E. Porter, "Wittgenstein's Classes of Utterances and Pauline Ethical Texts," *Journal of the Evangelical Theological Society* 32 (1989): 85–97, at 94. For other liberationist readings of Paul and women, see Robin Scroggs, "Paul and the Eschatological Woman," in *Journal of the American Academy of Religion* 40 (1972): 283–303 (Gal. 3:28 teaches "equality" but retains "distinction" between the sexes: 288, 293), who cites both Stendahl and Else Kähler, *Die Frau in den paulinischen Briefen* (Zürich: Gotthalf, 1960) as important influences on his interpretation; Constance F. Parvey, "The Theology and Leadership of Women in the New Testament," in Rosemary Radford Ruether, ed., *Religion and Sexism: Images of Woman in the Jewish and Christian Traditions* (New York: Simon & Schuster, 1974), 117–49; Gerhard Dautzenberg, "Da ist nicht männlich und weiblich. Zur Interpretation von Gal 3:28," *Kairos* 24 (1984): 181–206; and D. Wenham, "Whatever Went Wrong in Corinth?" *Expository Times* 108 (1997): 137–41.
4. Elisabeth Schüssler Fiorenza, *In Memory of Her: A Feminist Theological Reconstruction of Christian Origins* (New York: Crossroad, 1983). Schüssler Fiorenza also calls Gal. 3:28 the *locus classicus* of Christian equality (205). For other references to the "equality" of the verse, see 210, 213, 218, and 235. Schüssler Fiorenza rejects Stendahl's proposal that Gal. 3:28 represents a "Pauline breakthrough." It rather reflects a pre-Pauline, broad, social fact of early Christianity. Women were

only gradually excluded from important roles in early Christianity. In Paul's letters we may discern the beginnings of this decline that becomes dominant only in the post-Pauline, institutional church. (See 199 for an explicit rejection of Stendahl's account; see also 251, 279.) Even those scholars who reject other aspects of Schüssler Fiorenza's account usually agree with her arguments that Pauline Christianity was relatively egalitarian with regard to women's roles and that Gal. 3:28 reflects that egalitarianism.

5. See also Charles B. Cousar, *Galatians* (Atlanta: John Knox, 1982); Stephen Motyer, "The Relationship Between Paul's Gospel of 'All One in Christ Jesus' (Galatians 3:28) and the 'Household Codes,'" *Vox Evangelica* 19 (1989): 33–48. Robert Jewett argued that Paul's letters could be assigned to three chronological phases in which Paul becomes increasingly egalitarian and liberating with regard to women over time. "Contradictions" are explained as coming from different times. The last stage is the "consistent-equality stage" (see "The Sexual Liberation of the Apostle Paul," *Journal of the American Academy of Religion Supplement* 47, no. 1 [1979]: 55–87). For a brief survey of some attempts to make sense of the "contradiction" between the egalitarian vision of Gal. 3:28 and the hierarchical passages in Paul, see Nicholas Taylor, "Paul for Today: Race, Class, and Gender in the Light of Cognitive Dissonance Theory," *Listening* 32 (1997): 22–38, at 31–32. Günter Röhser argues that Paul's egalitarian statement of Gal. 3:28 was meant to apply to the Christian community; there may be tension within Paul's writings, but no real contradiction ("Mann und Frau in Christus. Eine Verhältnesbestimmung von Gal 3, 28 und 1 Kor 11, 2–16," *Studien zum Neuen Testament und seiner Umwelt* 22 [1997]: 57–78).
6. G. G. Findlay, *The Epistle to the Galatians* (New York: A. C. Armstrong & Son, 1893), 235.
7. Joseph Agar Beet, *A Commentary on St. Paul's Epistle to the Galatians*, 4th ed. (London: Hodder & Stoughton, 1893), 100.
8. George S. Duncan, *The Epistle of Paul to the Galatians* (New York: Harper & Brothers, no date, but probably around 1935), 123–24.
9. Donald Guthrie, *Galatians* (London: Nelson, 1969), 116.
10. So also Josep Moncho Pascual, "La asimetría principio rector de la sociedad antiqua," *Cuidad de Dios* 210 (1997): 473–93, at 493. This exegetical position is also advocated by people who apparently nonetheless support full social equality for women. Madeleine Boucher, for example, argued against Stendahl's interpretation that Gal. 3:28 suggested equal roles for men and women in Paul's churches. She still took Gal. 3:28 to be about equality, but not necessarily *social* equality: "Thus the ideas of equality before God and inferiority in the social order are in harmony in the New Testament. To be precise, the tension did not exist in first-century thought, and it is not present in the texts themselves. The tension arises from *modern man's* inability to hold these two ideas together." "Some Unexplored Parallels to 1 Cor 11, 11–12 and Gal 3, 28: The New Testament on the Role of Women," *Catholic Biblical Quarterly* 31 (1969): 50–58, at 57 (emphasis in the original). See also Elaine Pagels's critique of Robin Scroggs's liberationist reading: "Paul and Women: A Response to Recent Discussion," *Journal of the American Academy of Religion* 42 (1974): 538–49; and Averil Cameron, "Neither Male Nor Female," *Greece and Rome* 27 (1980): 60–68, esp. 64.
11. Elizabeth Cady Stanton, *The Woman's Bible* (Boston: Northeastern University Press, 1993 [1895]), 21; see also the comments by Ellen Battelle Dietrick, 130.
12. W. M. Ramsay, *A Historical Commentary on St. Paul's Epistle to the Galatians* (London: Hodder & Stoughton, 1899), 387.
13. C. B. Hock Jr., "The Role of Women in the Church: A Survey of Current Approaches," *Grace Theological Journal* 8, no. 2 (1987): 241–51; cited in Stephen

D. Lowe, "Rethinking the Female Status/Function Question: The Jew/Gentile Relationship as Paradigm," *Journal of the Evangelical Theological Society* 34 (1991): 59–75.

14. Judith M. Gundry-Volf, "Male and Female in Creation and New Creation: Interpretations of Galatians 3:28C in 1 Corinthians 7," in *To Tell the Mystery: Essays on New Testament Eschatology in Honor of Robert H. Gundry*, ed. Thomas E. Schmidt and Moisés Silva (Sheffield: Sheffield Academic Press, 1994), 95–121, at 101.
15. See also Gundry-Volf, "Gender and Creation in 1 Corinthians 11:2–16: A Study in Paul's Theological Method," in *Evangelium Schriftauslegung Kirche: Festschrift für Peter Stuhlmacher zum 65. Geburtstag*, ed. Jostein Ådna et al. (Göttingen: Vandenhoeck & Ruprecht, 1997), 151–71, where Gundry-Volf, without further explanation, refers to "the equality proclaimed in Galatians 3:28" (169).
16. Miroslav Volf, *Exclusion and Embrace: A Theological Exploration of Identity, Otherness, and Reconciliation* (Nashville: Abingdon, 1996), 175, 184; see also 182–83. Perhaps I should point out that "evangelical" is not simply my designation for Volf; not long after the publication of his book Volf used the term for himself in a lecture at Duke Divinity School (in the spring of 1998) and in private conversation.
17. Harold O. J. Brown, "The New Testament Against Itself: 1 Timothy 2:9–15 and the 'Breakthrough' of Galatians 3:28," in *Women in the Church: Fresh Analysis of 1 Timothy 2:9–15*, ed. Andreas J. Köstenberger et al. (Grand Rapids: Baker Books, 1995), 197–208.
18. Robert W. Yarbrough, "The Hermeneutics of 1 Timothy 2:9–15," in Köstenberger et al., eds., *Women in the Church*, 155–96, at 179n116 and192–193.
19. John Jefferson Davis, "Some Reflections on Galatians 3:28, Sexual Roles, and Biblical Hermeneutics," *Journal of the Evangelical Theological Society* 19 (1976): 201–8.
20. Grant R. Osborne, "Hermeneutics and Women in the Church," *Journal of the Evangelical Theological Society* 20 (1977): 337–52, at 349.
21. I differentiate "dichotomy" from "polarity" for good reasons. One might imagine that male and female occupied opposite "poles" of a continuum or spectrum and that different human beings might fall anywhere along that continuum without those in the "middle" appearing problematic to anyone. One person, say, might be perceived as 95 percent male and 5 percent female while another would be 50 percent of both, and neither person would be perceived as "odd" or "unnatural." Modern Western culture, however, mostly construes male and female in a dichotomous relation: one is *either* male *or* female, or there is something amiss.
22. Wayne A. Meeks, "The Image of the Androgyne: Some Uses of a Symbol in Earliest Christianity," *History of Religion* 13 (1974): 165–208, at 208. I should note that Meeks has changed his mind; he has informed me in private conversations that he no longer takes ancient androgyny to have promoted egalitarianism in Pauline Christianity.
23. Ingvild Saelid Gilhus, "Male and Female Symbolism in the Gnostic *Apocryphon of John*," *Temenos* 19 (1983): 33–43; Dennis Ronald MacDonald, "Corinthian Veils and Gnostic Androgynes," in *Images of the Feminine in Gnosticism*, ed. Karen L. King (Philadelphia: Fortress, 1988), 276–92. See also Jorunn Jacobsen Buckley, "An Interpretation of Logion 114 in *The Gospel of Thomas*," *Novum Testamentum* 27 (1985): 245–72.
24. See, for example, the different notions of androgyny assumed by several different authors in *"Femininity," "Masculinity," and "Androgyny": A Modern Philosophical Discussion*, ed. Mary Vetterling-Braggin (Totowa, NJ: Rowman & Littlefield, 1982). Though different notions of androgyny are proposed in the book, all of

them give rather equal weight to the "male" and the "female" sides of an accepted duality.

25. Thomas Laqueur, *Making Sex: Body and Gender from the Greeks to Freud* (Cambridge, MA: Harvard University Press, 1990).
26. I say "predominant" because I want to leave open the possibility that some ancient text may imply a more "equal" kind of androgyny. Aristophanes' myth in Plato's *Symposium*, for instance, which is incidentally the best-known ancient text portraying androgyny, seems to allow for a more "equal" and dichotomous kind of androgyny.
27. F. Gerald Downing, "A Cynic Preparation for Paul's Gospel for Jew and Greek, Slave and Free, Male and Female," *New Testament Studies* 42 (1996): 454–62, suggests a Cynic background for the theme. Downing argues that even if the *source* for Paul's saying cannot be proved as Cynic, if Christians actually *acted on* the destruction of these distinctions, their behavior would have been interpreted by others as "Cynic." Downing does not note that in most of the cases he cites the "male" characteristics are the ones praised and emulated. The woman who affects Cynicism in Lucian's satire *Runaways*, for example, is "masculine" looking (§27). Male Cynics weren't famous for trying to appear feminine!

   Some scholars have rejected the "androgyny" interpretation of Gal. 3:28, in my view, because they are thinking about androgyny only in the modern sense, that is, as something like "bisexuality" or the presence of equal male and female aspects. Ben Witherington, for example, notes that Paul speaks of a masculine "one" rather than a neuter "one" (the Greek term is masculine rather than feminine or neuter) and that male and female become "one" *in Christ* (male). He reasons that this precludes androgyny. But if the dominant *ancient* way of conceiving of the reunification of male and female was precisely as I have described it here, then Witherington's objections do not dispense with the "androgynous" interpretations of the verse. See "Rite and Rights for Women—Galatians 3.28," *New Testament Studies* 27 (1981): 593–604.

   Other scholars reject the androgynous interpretation of Paul's language in Gal. 3:28, claiming that such interpretations of the phrase arose later, in Gnostic circles and in the writings of some of the church fathers I mention below. But these scholars, in my view, provide no counterproposals or evidence. They simply *state* that Gal. 3:28 is not about androgyny without giving some other ancient context by which its language could be understood. Schüssler Fiorenza insists that the phrase suggests not androgyny (the combination of two different sexes) but something like a "presexual" state, like that imagined for children (*In Memory of Her*, 212, 218; incidentally, I think this reflects a modern notion of the nonsexuality of children; I find no evidence that ancient cultures thought of children as nonsexual). But she does not point to other contexts in which the phrase "no male and female" is so interpreted in the ancient world. Likewise, Robert Grant, after quoting interpretations like those of Clement of Alexandria (see my treatment below) that take the phrase as referring to androgyny, writes, "Such expressions, like Gnostic notions about hermaphrodites or women becoming men, do not necessarily indicate the context Paul may have given his idea. As Marie Delcourt pointed out, Paul refers to a being raised above sexuality, not a bisexual one" ("Neither Male nor Female," *Biblical Research* 37 [1992]: 5–14, at 8–9; referring to Marie Delcourt, "Hermaphrodit," in *Reallexikon für Antike und Christentum* [Stuttgart: Anton Hiersemann, 1988], 14.649–82). But if we do not *expect* to find "bisexuality" in ancient "androgyny" we will not be puzzled by its absence in Gal. 3:28. Grant also provides no *demonstration* for his opinion (for example, by outlining what such "transcendence" of sexuality would look like in the ancient world apart from the male-oriented "androgyny" of precisely those Gnostic and other early Christian interpreters). Simply stating that Paul must not be referring to ancient androgyny does not make it so.

It may well be that we should dispense with the term "androgyny" in this regard, especially if it is taken necessarily to refer to a being that has both male and female parts, like a hermaphrodite statue—and even more especially if those parts are expected to be in equal proportion. But we will be mistaken if we think we can come up with some other, more exact, ancient term. As Wendy Doniger O'Flaherty and Mircea Eliade insist, "It must be noted that although androgynes are popularly supposed to stand for a kind of equality and balance between the sexes, since they are technically half male and half female, they more often represent a desirable or undesirable distortion of the male-female relationship or a tension based on an unequal distribution of power" ("Androgynes," in *The Encyclopedia of Religion*, 2d ed. [New York: MacMillan/Thomson Gale, 2005], 1.337–42, at 337). Ancient "androgyny" took different forms, anywhere from an "equal parts" kind of hermaphroditism to a swallowing up of one side by the other, as when, for example, Zeus swallows up Metis in order then to give birth to Athena. But if we understand "androgyny" to refer generally to the unification of what were previously two separate entities—male and female—then all these different unifications could be called "androgyny," even those that end up representing the perfected male form that has swallowed up the imperfect female.

28. Kari Vogt, "'Becoming Male': A Gnostic and Early Christian Metaphor," in *The Image of God: Gender Models in Judaeo-Christian Tradition*, ed. Kari Elisabeth Børresen (Minneapolis: Fortress, 1995), 170–86.

29. Lone Fatum, "Image of God and Glory of Man: Women in the Pauline Congregations," in *Image of God*, 50–133, at 63–64. See also Fatum, "Women, Symbolic Universe and Structures of Silence: Challenges and Possibilities in Androcentric Texts," *Studia Theologica* 43 (1989): 61–80; see especially 78n21 for a list of the liberationist interpretations against which Fatum is reacting. According to a note on p. 61, this is an earlier version of the argument offered with more exegetical thoroughness in "Image of God and Glory of Man." I do not agree with Fatum's tendency in these articles to blame negative views of femaleness or women on "Judaism," "rabbinic Jewish tradition," or Paul's identity as a "conservative Jewish Christian" (see 70, 72). In fact, I suspect that Fatum has changed her mind on these points since first publishing these articles. There was no more misogyny in Judaism than in any other ethnic culture in antiquity, as far as I can tell. There were plenty of negative attitudes toward the "female" to go around in the ancient male-dominated world without blaming early Christianity's attitudes or Paul's on Judaism in particular.

For arguments that dispute the older view that women experienced much less freedom and lower status in Jewish circles than in Greek or Roman, see the studies by Bernadette J. Brooten, "Jüdinnen zur Zeit Jesu: Ein plädoyer für Differenzierung," *Theologische Quartalschrift* 161 (1981): 280–85; "Zur Debatte über das Scheidungsrecht der jüdischen Frau," *Evangelische Theologie* 43 (1983): 466–78; *Women Leaders in the Ancient Synagogue: Inscriptional Evidence and Background* (Chico, CA: Scholars, 1982).

30. Against those scholars who claim that the later Christian writers were misinterpreting Paul by reading Gal. 3:28 as "androgynous" (see my comments on Grant, Schüssler Fiorenza, and Witherington above), I insist that the ancient interpreters were closer to his cultural location than we, and that if we want to dispute their reading of Gal. 3:28, we must provide more evidence that Paul meant something radically different and, in his time, practically unheard of: the complete equality, though distinction, of male and female.

31. Hippocrates, *The Nature of Man* 2. For the Greek and English text, see *Hippocrates*, vol. 4, trans. W. H. S. Jones, in the Loeb Classical Library (Cambridge, MA: Harvard University Press, 1931).
32. For English translations of the homilies of John Chrysostom, see *The Homilies of S. John Chrysostom,* 3d ed. rev. (Oxford: James Parker, 1877), and the Nicene and Post-Nicene Fathers series. See also similar treatments by Gregory of Nyssa, *On Virginity* 20; *De opificio hominis* 16.7, 9. Desire is part of the irrational. Gender division brings with it irrationality. The Platonic precursors to all this occur in, among other texts, *Timaeus* 90–91; and *Symposium*189D–193D. See the discussion of the Platonic texts in Roy Bowan Ward, "Why Unnatural: The Tradition Behind Romans 1:26–27," *Harvard Theological Review* 90 (1997): 263–84.
33. Clement of Alexandria, *Stromateis* 3.13.92–93; I have modified the English translation by John Ferguson, *The Fathers of the Church*, v. 85. See also *2 Clement* 12:2; *Gospel of Thomas* 37, 22b.
34. See, for example, Schüssler Fiorenza, *In Memory of Her*, 230–31. See also now the discussion in Jorunn Økland, *Women in Their Place: Paul and the Corinthian Discourse of Gender and Sanctuary Space* (London: T. & T. Clark, 2004), 149–52.
35. So also Halvor Moxnes, "Social Integration and the Problem of Gender in St. Paul's Letters," *Studia theologica* 43 (1989): 99–113, at 107.
36. The most famous ancient example is Aristotle's theorizing of the master-slave relation. See, for example, *Politics* 1.2.4, 1253b.
37. Note the way Leslie Heywood and Jennifer Drake, in their delightful collection of third-wave essays by several younger feminists, characterize "first" and "second" wave feminisms: "Early, 'first wave' feminists, for example, worked for abolition, voting rights, and temperance causes. Second wave feminists concentrated on the ERA [Equal Rights Amendment] and wage equity [note the emphasis on equality], developed 'gender' and 'sexism' as key categories of analysis, criticized beauty culture, and often worked in black, gay, and New Left movements" (*Third Wave Agenda: Being Feminist, Doing Feminism* [Minneapolis: University of Minnesota Press, 1997], 23). One of the reasons this is a favorite third-wave book for me is because these younger authors avoid condescension or criticism of previous feminist scholarship and politics. They see themselves as doing work that is somewhat differently structured but not contrary to second-wave feminism, building on but not putting down or disavowing previous feminist movements. They explicitly reject the term "postfeminist" for their work because they see that as a label appropriated by reactionary critics of second-wave feminists, and they explicitly mention Katie Roiphe, Rene Denfield, and Naomi Wolf as representing the more "conservative" reaction from which they disassociate themselves. Another positive (nonreactionary and nonsupersessionist) example of third-wave feminism is the anthology *"Bad Girls"/"Good Girls": Women, Sex, and Power in the Nineties*, ed. Nan Bauer Maglin and Donna Perry (New Brunswick, NJ: Rutgers University Press, 1996).
38. Heywood and Drake characterize third-wave feminism simply as a combination of the liberation-egalitarian politics of first- and second-wave feminisms with poststructuralist and "cultural studies" emphasis on theory, reading strategies, a plurality of feminisms, and multiply structured identities. Third-wave feminism assumes the postmodernist emphasis on hybridity and contingency. Contradiction, if seen in the context of perspective or point-of-view, is embraced. Contrary to some critiques that accuse poststructuralist feminists of abdicating political struggle, some self-described third-wave feminists consider themselves quite politically active but in new ways, using "language and images that account for multiplicity and difference, that negotiate contradiction in affirmative ways, and

that give voice to a politics of hybridity and coalition" (see Heywood and Drake, *Third Wave Agenda*, 3, 7, 9).

It should be pointed out that Schüssler Fiorenza does not fit neatly into one or the other of these categories if her entire work is taken into account. She does speak of her own work as representing "second-wave" feminism (see, for example, *Sharing Her Word: Feminist Biblical Interpretation in Context* [Boston: Beacon, 1998], 2, 4, 60), and I do not recall any explicit claim by her to be part of "third-wave" feminism. On the other hand, she has recently insisted that her work never assumed the "essentialism" of "woman" that characterized much of second-wave feminism, at least in North America in the 1970s, and that has been critiqued by more recent feminist work. It is true that Schüssler Fiorenza has been critical of several aspects of poststructuralist theory and postmodernism (see, for example, "Text and Reality—Reality as Text: The Problem of a Feminist Historical and Social Reconstruction Based on Texts," *Studia theologica* 43 [1989]: 19–34), and her work has been taken by some others as representative of modernist feminism that postmodernist feminists critique, but for her part Schüssler Fiorenza rejects such readings of her work. For one "postmodern" response to Schüssler Fiorenza's criticisms of poststructuralist feminist scholarship, see The Bible and Culture Collective, *The Postmodern Bible* (New Haven, CT: Yale University Press, 1995), 260–267. For Schüssler Fiorenza's defense and counterattack, see *Sharing Her Word*, 15–21.

39. See also Fatum, "Women, Symbolic Universe and Structures of Silence," 62.
40. Heywood and Drake, *Third Wave Agenda*, 8. As this quotation suggests, it should be clear that "queer theory" arose out of the combination of feminism and poststructuralism, just as the gay liberation movement arose out of the civil rights and feminist movements. I make no attempt to define "queer theory" at this time. (One could think of it, on analogy with third-wave feminism as described above, as gay and lesbian studies and historiography that has read a lot of poststructuralist theory.) For starters, one may consult the anthology *The Gay and Lesbian Studies Reader*, ed. Henry Abelove et al. (New York: Routledge, 1993). In my own mind, the seminal works that led to the development of "queer theory" (as differentiated from gay and lesbian historiography or studies)—or at least were the most influential for me—are Eve Kosofsky Sedgwick, *Epistemology of the Closet* (Berkeley: University of California Press, 1990), esp. chap. 1; Judith Butler, *Gender Trouble: Feminism and the Subversion of Identity* (New York: Routledge, 1990); and the entire work of Michel Foucault, especially *History of Sexuality*, vol. 1 (New York: Random House, 1978; French: *La Volenté de savoir*, 1976). For an anthology of gay, lesbian, and queer studies related to religion, see Gary David Comstock and Susan E. Henking, *Que(e)rying Religion: A Critical Anthology* (New York: Continuum, 1997).
41. It should be clear that I am here rejecting the second-wave feminist differentiation between "gender" (which is taken to be culturally constructed) and "sex" (which is taken as rooted in biology or "nature"). In my view, it may sometimes be helpful, perhaps even necessary, to speak in terms of "biology" and "culture," but we should not take those terms as referring to different *kinds* of *things*. I insist that biology *is* cultural, and that culture *is* biological. For humans, what could be more natural than culture? And any human portrait of nature must be cultural. I prefer to dispense with these dichotomies, especially if one side is used as the "foundation" (the more "real" usually being understood as "nature") for the second-order (epiphenomenal) construction of the other ("culture"). For the problematics of "nature" and "culture," see Bruno Latour, *We Have Never Been Modern* (Cambridge, MA: Harvard University Press, 1993; French: 1991).

Chapter 7

1. The motion picture was produced by Barbara De Fina, directed by Martin Scorsese, and released in 1988 by Universal Pictures and Cineplex Odeon Films. *The Last Temptation of Christ* (trans. P. A. Bien; New York: Simon & Schuster, 1960) is the English translation of *Ho Teleutaios Peirasmos* by Nikos Kazantzakis.
2. Dan Brown, *The Da Vinci Code: A Novel* (New York: Doubleday, 2003). Much of the popularity of the novel, quite probably, is due to the false assertions made by the author that some of its most controversial claims are actually based on historical "fact" and good scholarship. That so many of these "facts" are easily refuted by any real scholar of history has meant that a virtual growth-industry of books debunking Brown's claims has also sprung up in the past few years. For a more "literary" fictional version of Jesus' heterosexual "fulfillment" that predates both Kazantzakis and Brown, see the novella by D. H. Lawrence, *The Man Who Died* (previously titled *The Escaped Cock* . . . really!) (London: Martin Secker, 1931). In Lawrence's imagination, the crucified Jesus awakes in the tomb, escapes, travels around, and eventually has a sexual relationship with a young woman in a precinct of the goddess Isis, finally finding in heterosexual union the fulfillment he had always sought.
3. The appearance of Terrence McNally's *Corpus Christi: A Play* (New York: Grove Press, 1988) was greeted by protests. For descriptions of the play, the protests, and other similar events, see Robert E. Goss, *Queering Christ: Beyond Jesus Acted Up* (Cleveland: Pilgrim, 2002), 138–39, 171–76.
4. The film *Jesus Christ Superstar*, produced by Robert Stigwood and Norman Jewison and directed by Norman Jewison, was a 1973 motion picture based on the rock opera of the same name from the book by Tim Rice.
5. I don't mean by this to imply that most more conservative, pious Christians assume Jesus was sexual. As the conservative backlash against different popular treatments of Jesus' sexuality demonstrate, many more traditional Christians are dismayed, and sometimes react violently, when Jesus' sexuality is raised, even objecting when someone points out that Jesus "had a penis." See Robert Williams, *Just As I Am: A Practical Guide to Being Out, Proud, and Christian* (New York: Crown, 1992). An interesting counterpoint to this is Leo Steinberg's argument that Renaissance artists emphasized the sexuality of Jesus, even "pointing" to Jesus' genitals in paintings precisely in order to highlight his humanness and even sex. See Leo Steinberg, *The Sexuality of Christ in Renaissance Art and in Modern Illusion* (New York: Pantheon Books, 1983). It should be admitted, though, that not everyone has been convinced by Steinberg's interpretations. Increasingly, in any case, a few voices are calling for Christians to consider the sexuality of Jesus (his sexual desires and capabilities at least, and sometimes actual sexual activity): see, for example, Joan H. Timmerman, "The Sexuality of Jesus and the Human Vocation," in *Sexuality and the Sacred: Sources for Theological Reflection* (ed. James B. Nelson and Sandra P. Longfellow; Louisville, KY: Westminster John Knox, 1994), 91–104; Robert Beckford, "Does Jesus Have a Penis? Black Male Sexual Representation and Christology," *Theology and Sexuality* 5 (September 1996): 10–21.
6. This is precisely the argument H. W. Montefiore put forward many years ago, apparently greeted by controversy: not only that Jesus' humanity meant that he must have been a sexual being but also that we must at least entertain the possibility that homosexual inclinations explain his apparent celibacy. See H. W. Montefiore, "Jesus, the Revelation of God," in *Christ for Us Today: Papers Read at the Conference of Modern Churchmen, Somerville College, Oxford, July 1967*, ed. Norman Pittenger (London: SBM, 1968), 101–16, esp. 109. The point about Jesus'

full humanity is also made by Nancy Wilson, who argues for a bisexual Jesus using arguments similar to those of Montefiore: "*It is very important to deshame the fact that Jesus, as part of his humanness, part of the concept of incarnation, was sexual*" (Nancy Wilson, *Our Tribe: Queer Folks, God, Jesus, and the Bible* [San Francisco: HarperSanFrancisco, 1995], 147; emphasis in original).

7. John P. Meier, *A Marginal Jew: Rethinking the Historical Jesus*, vol. 1 (New York: Doubleday, 1991), 332. I find it interesting that when members of the Jesus Seminar were polled about the sexuality of Jesus, according to a report by Robert Funk, Roy Hoover, and the Jesus Seminar, a majority of them said that Jesus was probably not celibate: "They regard it probable that he had a special relationship with at least one woman, Mary of Magdala." See Robert Funk, Roy W. Hoover, and the Jesus Seminar, *The Five Gospels: The Search for the Authentic Words of Jesus* (New York: Macmillan, 1993), 220–21. I find it telling that heterosexuality was the majority assumption. I also wonder whether this may be one indication (along with others, such as their tendency to deeschatologize the historical Jesus and their faith in abilities to plumb the different historical layers of the hypothetical document "Q" and its "community") that the Jesus Seminar may not be representative of the guild of biblical scholars as a whole.
8. William E. Phipps, *The Sexuality of Jesus: Theological and Literary Perspectives* (New York: Harper & Row, 1973); *Was Jesus Married? The Distortion of Sexuality in the Christian Tradition* (Lanham, MD: University Press of America, 1986).
9. Phipps, *Sexuality of Jesus*, 11.
10. For another such argument that Jesus must not have taught celibacy because that would have been unthinkable in Judaism of his day, which commanded marriage, see the work of a journalist (not a biblical scholar): Marcello Craveri, *The Life of Jesus* (London: Panther, 1969), 260.
11. Meier, *Marginal Jew*, 338–39. Meier notes other sources that may shed light on the motivations or meanings of Jesus' own singleness. He mentions Jewish prophets such as Jeremiah, John the Baptist, and others who molded themselves on "the recycled Moses figure," all of whom may have avoided sexual relations as a result of experiencing a "radical alteration" of their lives due to reception of divine revelation: "The alteration, this being set apart by and for God's Word, is embodied graphically in the rare, awesome, and—for many Jews—terrible vocation of celibacy." Or put differently, "an all-consuming commitment to God's word in one's whole life precludes the usual path of marriage and child-rearing" (341).
12. Moreover, Meier thinks it likely that Jesus was motivated by "his total, all-consuming commitment to proclaiming and realizing the kingdom of God" (Meier, *Marginal Jew*, 342).
13. Dale C. Allison, *Jesus of Nazareth: Millenarian Prophet* (Minneapolis: Fortress, 1998). Pointing out that asceticism may often be found in movements motivated by eschatological fervor, both in the modern world and the ancient, Allison surmises that certain apparently ascetical statements attributed to Jesus are likely authentic and that Jesus taught sexual asceticism as part of his eschatological message. Jesus praises those who are eunuchs "for the sake of the kingdom [Matt. 19:12] because the approach of the kingdom requires of them a service that they might otherwise not be able to fulfill. Jesus and other celibates like him . . . have chosen their uncommon condition because, as heralds and servants of the approaching order, it is their primary duty to prepare people for its coming. There can be no time for marriage and children, no time for those consuming responsibilities. This is why, when Jesus calls others to the full-time job of fishing for people, he calls them to abandon their jobs, families, and money." In Mark 12:18–27, moreover, where he speaks of the resurrection, Jesus explains that res-

urrected persons will be like the angels and therefore not marry. So it would be sensible if Jesus and some of his disciples adopted celibacy as present participation in the imminent eschatological state. As Allison concludes, "Indeed, such an individual might, as did so many Christian celibates later on, interpret his or her forswearing of sex in terms of realized eschatology: if one can make do without intercourse then this might be understood as one way of making present an eschatological circumstance" (189).

14. Religious celibacy reflects and reinforces "estrangement from the normal structures of society" (ibid., 204).
15. Ibid., 206.
16. Their actions were intended as "a warning that the normal course of things was about to change" (ibid., 208).
17. "Jesus understood chastity as a replay of paradise and thus an anticipation of eschatological existence, in other words, as a proleptic recovery of 'the glory of Adam'" (ibid., 208).
18. One factor usually ignored by scholars is the question of the normal age of marriage for men in the ancient Mediterranean. Contrary to modern assumptions, men in the ancient world often did not marry until around the age of thirty, for several reasons. First, most demographics of antiquity conclude that there were probably fewer eligible females than males of marriageable age. Men tended to marry much younger females, often even girls. Men of lesser means may have simply lost out in the competition for the fewer eligible females. Moreover, men sometimes put off marriage for financial reasons. In any case, if the Christian traditions about Jesus beginning his ministry around the age of thirty are true, we probably should not expect a man of his age to be already married. For age of marriage, see W. K. Lacey, *Family in Classical Greece* (Ithaca, NY: Cornell University Press, 1968), 106, 162, 284n38, 294n27; Keith Hopkins, "The Age of Roman Girls at Marriage," *Population Studies* 18 (1965): 309–27; Brent Shaw, "The Age of Roman Girls at Marriage: Some Reconsiderations," *Journal of Roman Studies* 77 (1987): 30–46; Richard Saller, *Patriarchy, Property and Death in the Roman Family* (Cambridge: Cambridge University Press, 1994), 25–41. These studies are of Greek and Roman practices, but I know of no evidence that Jewish practices regarding age of marriage were substantially different.
19. I use the term "queer" as has become popular in "queer theory" since the 1990s. See, for example, the collection *Que(e)rying Religion: A Critical Anthology*, ed. Gary David Comstock and Susan E. Henking (New York: Continuum, 1997).
20. Though "Clement" insists in his letter that certain words said by the Carpocratians to be in the text—"naked man upon [or next to, or with] naked man"—were not in the authentic version of the secret Gospel, "Clement's" version itself is quite homoerotic enough.
21. Morton Smith, *Clement of Alexandria and a Secret Gospel of Mark* (Cambridge, MA: Harvard University Press, 1973); *The Secret Gospel: The Discovery and Interpretation of the Secret Gospel According to Mark* (New York: Harper & Row, 1973). There have been very few other authors who have at least appropriated historical arguments to present a Jesus who is erotic with men (they sometimes even use the term "gay"). See, for some examples, Williams, *Just As I Am*, 116–23; Goss, *Queering Christ*, 114–22, 134–39.
22. Steven D. Fraade, "The Nazirite in Ancient Judaism (Selected Texts)," in *Ascetic Behavior in Greco-Roman Antiquity: A Sourcebook*, ed. Vincent Wimbush (Minneapolis: Fortress, 1990), 213–23.
23. In spite of the misnamed "cleansing of the Temple" incident in the Gospels, I believe we can produce no firm evidence that Jesus was concerned to reform the Temple service.

24. See, e.g., Augustine, *On the Good of Marriage* 21(26).
25. It sometimes does happen. Tertullian, for example, cites both Christ and Paul, though briefly, as examples to demonstrate the "preference for continence"(*On Monogamy* 3). Gregory of Nazianzus speaks of both Christ and Basil as personal examples of virginity as well as promoters of it (*Panegyric on Basil* 62). But even though Jesus is used (rather oddly, sometimes) as a model, he seldom occurs as a model for Christian celibacy among the "orthodox" fathers.
26. *Lecture* 13.23; 4.24. Jesus is also offered as an example that Christians should follow the proper "order of things": 3.14.
27. *On the Spirit (De spiritu sancto)* 15.35.
28. Tertullian, *On Fasting* 8.
29. See Augustine, *De sancta virginitate.*
30. See, for example, Susanna Elm, "*Virgins of God": The Making of Asceticism in Late Antiquity* (Oxford: Clarendon, 1994), 118–20.
31. Tertullian, *On Monogamy* 5.
32. See Brother Casimir, "Saint Gregory of Nyssa: PERI TELEIOTHTOS—On Perfection," *Greek Orthodox Theological Review* 29 (1984): 349–79; esp. 354–55, 376.
33. For just one example, see Tertullian, *De sancta virginitate.* Interestingly in this document, given our attention to the way Christ's celibacy is used or not used as a model for Christian behavior, Tertullian treats Christ's virginity as basically the *only* one of his traits that all Christians do *not* imitate! Tertullian makes an important exception to a general *imitatio Christi* with regard to celibacy: see 27–28. For Origen, see references in John Ernest Leonard Oulton and Henry Chadwick, eds., *Alexandrian Christianity: Selected Translations of Clement and Origen, with Introduction and Notes,* Library of Christian Classics, vol. 2 (Philadelphia: Westminster, 1954), 34–35.
34. In Mark he is just a man; in Matthew 19:20, he is said to be young; in Luke 18:18, he is said to be a ruler; only Mark has the part about Jesus loving him. The "rich young ruler" is a conflation of all of them.
35. And thus, as pointed out above, the remarkable popularity of Brown's *Da Vinci Code.*
36. The Hebrew word for "feet" was also a euphemism for "genitals."
37. For a clear and brief introduction to "nonfoundationalism" and its relation to theology, see John E. Thiel, *Nonfoundationalism* (Minneapolis: Fortress, 1994) and the introduction in this volume.

Chapter 8

1. Rodney Clapp notes that the church may be called "the last great stronghold of family idolatry"; see *Families at the Crossroads: Beyond Traditional and Modern Options* (Downers Grove, IL: InterVarsity, 1993), 12; see also Janet Fishburn, *Confronting the Idolatry of Family: A New Vision for the Household of God* (Nashville: Abingdon, 1991), esp. 107. The idolatry of the family can be seen by a careful analysis of one study that argues that "the healthy family as we know it today would not exist but for the profound influence of religion, especially Christianity, through the ages" (Anthony J. Guerra, *Family Matters: The Role of Christianity in the Formation of the Western Family* [St. Paul: Paragon House, 2002], xi). Guerra states that the most important factor promoting the "healthy family" is religion (xxi–xxiii). He also insists that no one religion "has a monopoly" on the value he attributes to religion in general to promote and protect "family values" (xii–xiii). Since there is no belief or doctrine that *all* "religions" hold in common (not even monotheism or the belief in "God" at all), the *only* thing all "religions" must hold

in common (in Guerra's construction) is the promotion of the family. But that is what Guerra is highlighting as the fundamental value of Christianity. Unwittingly perhaps, Guerra has substituted "family values" for all other doctrines, beliefs, and practices as *the* central aspect of Christianity of any importance. The theological word for that is "idolatry." (Incidentally, the "healthy family" for Guerra is only the modern, nuclear family consisting of a heterosexual couple, only once married, and their immediate children; see xii–xiii, xiv, xvi, xvii.)

2. See Kathy Rudy, *Sex and the Church: Gender, Homosexuality, and the Transformation of Christian Ethics* (Boston: Beacon, 1997), 119.
3. On the novelty and *aberration* of the 1950s ideal family when compared to most of human history and most cultures, see Stephanie Coontz, *The Way We Never Were: American Families and the Nostalgia Trap* (New York: Basic Books, 1992), 25–29.
4. Byron R. McCane, "'Let the Dead Bury Their Own Dead': Secondary Burial and Matt. 8:21–22," *Harvard Theological Review* 83 (1990): 31–43.
5. T. W. Manson, *The Sayings of Jesus* (Grand Rapids: Wm. B. Eerdmans, 1957), 131; François Bovon, *L'Évangile selon Saint Luc (9,51–14,35)* (Geneva: Labor et Fides, 1996), 471.
6. "Q," from the German word *Quelle,* which means "source," is the designation given to a hypothetical document many scholars believe was used by both Matthew and Luke in the writing of their own Gospels. If they both used it, it obviously would represent a source earlier than their own texts.
7. Elizabeth A. Clark, *Reading Renunciation: Asceticism and Scripture in Early Christianity* (Princeton, NJ: Princeton University Press, 1999), 242–50.
8. Or that of Thomas in the precise sense. Thomas has a man excuse himself in order to arrange the wedding of someone else (*Gospel of Thomas* 64).
9. François Bovon, *Luke: A Commentary on the Gospel of Luke 1:1–9:50* (Minneapolis: Fortress, 2002), 1:114.
10. I take it that Barnabas is not married because no wife or family is ever mentioned for him; he travels around with Paul, likewise unmarried, without a family; and he is mentioned in this capacity by Paul in 1 Cor. 9:6. Though the precise verse in which Barnabas is mentioned refers to working for a living rather than living off contributions from the churches, the context also includes "traveling around with a sister-wife" as had Peter and other apostles. I take it that Paul then includes Barnabas with himself as someone who has not taken advantage of that "right."
11. Commentators generally note that Barnabas serves as a positive example and Ananias and Sapphira as negative examples of the communalism expected of early Christians in Acts. See, e.g., C. K. Barrett, *A Critical and Exegetical Commentary on the Acts of the Apostles* (Edinburgh: T. & T. Clark, 1994), 2:257–271; Joseph A. Fitzmyer, *The Acts of the Apostles* (New York: Doubleday, 1964), 315.
12. They aren't "normal" for several reasons. They have no children, nor a "stable" household, but rather are themselves fairly itinerant; Prisca (or Priscilla, as in Acts) is often mentioned first, implying higher status for her, at least for the author, than her husband; their "household" is permeable enough to include Paul in it at times. Paul moves in with them, works with them, and relocates with them. Their relationship, in any case, cannot be made into a "nuclear family," and neither does it look like the traditional extended family of antiquity.
13. For the activities of Satan in Luke-Acts, see Susan R. Garrett, *The Demise of the Devil: Magic and the Demonic in Luke's Writings* (Minneapolis: Fortress, 1989).
14. The "togetherness" of Ananias and Sapphira "violated the togetherness of the Christian community" (Ben Witherington III, *The Acts of the Apostles: A Socio-Rhetorical Commentary* [Grand Rapids: Wm. B. Eerdmans, 1998], 218). Ananias and Sapphira

represent a "counter-community . . . over against the spirit-community that shares its possessions" (Luke Timothy Johnson, *The Acts of the Apostles*, Sacra Pagina Series, vol. 5 [Collegeville, MN: Liturgical, 1992], 87, see also 89).

15. For most people in the Greco-Roman world, separation *meant* divorce, even legally. According to Roman family law, which may not have even applied to non-Roman Christians and Jews, divorce was effected simply by one of the partners "willing" to be no longer married. Abandonment was almost always sufficient for divorce. Moreover, without marriage laws to regulate the daily lives of most inhabitants of the Greco-Roman world (Roman family law applied only to Roman citizens), "divorce" would have most normally been effected simply by "separation."
16. I take the language of "relativization" mainly from Stephen C. Barton, *Discipleship and Family Ties in Mark and Matthew* (Cambridge: Cambridge University Press, 1994), passim. Though Barton is dealing with Mark and Matthew rather than Luke, I believe he, even for those contexts, is too eager to downplay any possible "anti-familial" message in the texts. Referring to Mark 10:1–31, for instance, he claims, "Nevertheless, it should be pointed out that this material reflects no animosity to family and household *per se*, something we had cause to observe in relation to earlier pericopae, as well. Instead, their significance is made relative to cross-bearing discipleship for the sake of Jesus and the gospel" (107; see also 122). It is hard to evaluate such a claim, which is repeated several times in one form or another in Barton's study, because Barton never really explains what "animosity" means or what "*per se*" covers. Certainly it would be stretching the evidence to say that it shows that Jesus had some *personal, psychological hatred* ("animosity") to the family *in the abstract* ("*per se*"). But it is just as unlikely that the texts make *only* the point—similar to modern Christian piety—that Jesus and the gospel are to demand "relatively" more loyalty than one's household. Rather, the statements teach the replacement of the traditional household by the eschatological community of God initiated by Jesus. There is nothing "psychological" or "abstract" going on here; it is rather a radical challenge of the "normal family" by the kingdom of God.
17. Tina Pippin, *Death and Desire: The Rhetoric of Gender in the Apocalypse of John* (Louisville, KY: Westminster/John Knox, 1992), 57–86.
18. References to pollution: 14:1–5; filth or dirt: 22:11; "abomination" (*bdelygma* = *bdelyssô*, meaning "rot" or "stink"; 21:8, 27); see also 7:14; 16:13; 17:4; 18:2; 19:2. One can also discern the obsession by noting the many references to fire and sulphur, i.e., "purifying" substances.
19. See Dale B. Martin, *The Corinthian Body* (New Haven, CT: Yale University Press, 1995); and "Paul without Passion" in this volume.
20. I have elsewhere shown that modern attempts to read Paul as a "gender egalitarian" do not stand up to scrutiny, though such claims do continue to be made, presumably by those wishing to "save" Paul from his fairly obvious, and natural for his time, hierarchical view of gender. See, e.g., Martin, *Corinthian Body*, 230–33; and chap. 6, "The Queer History of Galatians 3:28: 'No Male and Female,'" in this volume. Contrast James D. G. Dunn, "The Household Rules in the New Testament," in *The Family in Theological Perspective*, ed. Stephen C. Barton (Edinburgh: T. & T. Clark, 1996), 55.
21. See R. P. Reardon, *Collected Ancient Greek Novels* (Berkeley: University of California Press, 1989); Judith Perkins, *The Suffering Self: Pain and Representation in the Early Christian Era* (London: Routledge, 1995), 44–76.
22. See Andrew S. Jacobs, "A Family Affair: Marriage, Class, and Ethics in the Apocryphal Acts of the Apostles," *Journal of Early Christian Studies* 7 (1999): 105–38.

23. J. N. D. Kelly, *Jerome: His Life, Writings, and Controversies* (New York: Harper & Row, 1975), 102.
24. David Hunter provides a collection of early church writings on marriage: David G. Hunter, ed., *Marriage in the Early Church* (Minneapolis: Fortress, 1992). It is telling that though Hunter clearly attempted to balance out the "negative" views with the few available "positive" views of marriage, the book is rather thin. There just aren't enough "positive" views in early Christianity to balance out the "negative" ones.
25. For brief introductions to the controversy, see Kelly, *Jerome*, 181–82; Peter Brown, *The Body and Society: Men, Women and Sexual Renunciation in Early Christianity* (London: Faber & Faber, 1989), 359–62. For the original texts: Wilhelm Haller, ed., *Iovinianus: Die Fragmente seiner Schriften, die Quellen zu seiner Geschichte, sein Leben und seine Lehre* (Leipzig: J. C. Hinrich, 1897). The best and most up-to-date research on the Jovinian controversy is contained in articles by David G. Hunter; see esp. "Resistance to the Virginal Ideal in Late-Fourth-Century Rome: The Case of Jovinian," *Theological Studies* 48 (1987): 45–64; "Helvidius, Jovinian, and the Virginity of Mary in Late Fourth-Century Rome," *Journal for Early Christian Studies* 1 (1993): 47–71; and "Rereading the Jovinianist Controversy: Asceticism and Clerical Authority in Late Ancient Christianity," *Journal of Medieval and Early Modern Studies* 33 (2003): 453–70; reprinted in *The Cultural Turn in Late Ancient Studies: Gender, Asceticism, and Historiography*, Dale B. Martin and Patricia Cox Miller, eds. (Durham, NC: Duke University Press, 2005). John Gavin Nolan's earlier study (see *Jerome and Jovinian* [Washington, DC: Catholic University of America Press, 1956], an abstract of his Catholic University dissertation) is too biased towards Jerome and against Jovinian to be reliable. Nolan often takes Jerome's obvious exaggeration and misrepresentation at face value—with regard, for instance, to Jovinian's alleged lack of education.
26. These translations are from Hunter, "Rereading the Jovinianist Controversy," 453; for the Latin, see Siricius, *Epistolae* 7.4–6 (Corpus Scriptorum Ecclesiasticorum Latinorum 82/3:301).
27. Hunter, "Rereading the Jovinianist Controversy," 453.
28. Hunter, "Resistance to the Virginal Ideal."
29. Jerome, *Against Jovinian*, 1.7; 2.35; and 1.33, respectively; trans. W. H. Fremantle, with G. Lewis and W. G. Martley, *The Principal Works of St. Jerome*, Nicene and Post-Nicene Fathers, 2d ser. (Grand Rapids: Wm. B. Eerdmans, 1979), vol. 6.
30. Ibid., 1.40.
31. See, e.g., Augustine, *The Good of Marriage* 6. For the English of this as well as other excerpts from Augustine's relevant writings, and including an excellent introduction, see Elizabeth A. Clark, *St. Augustine on Marriage and Sexuality* (Washington, DC: Catholic University of America Press, 1996). See also Elizabeth A. Clark, "'Adam's Only Companion': Augustine and the Early Christian Debate on Marriage," *Recherches Augustiniennes* 21 (1986): 139–62; Philip Lyndon Reynolds, *Marriage in the Western Church: The Christianization of Marriage during the Patristic and Early Medieval Periods* (Leiden: E. J. Brill, 1994), 259.
32. Augustine, *The Good of Marriage* 9; trans. Clark, *St. Augustine on Marriage and Sexuality*, 51.
33. Edmund Leites, *The Puritan Conscience and Modern Sexuality* (New Haven, CT: Yale University Press, 1986), 80–83.
34. Lawrence Stone, *The Family, Sex and Marriage In England 1500–1800* (London: Weidenfeld and Nicolson, 1977), 135.

35. Christopher Hill, *Society and Puritanism in Pre-Revolutionary England* (New York: Schocken Books, 1964), 453.
36. Guerra, *Family Matters*, 30.
37. Stone, *Family*, 136.
38. Ibid., 141.
39. William Perkins, *Works* (Cambridge: Cantrell Legge, 1618), 3:671. Perkins goes on to say that had the fall not occurred, the single life should have no place in the world at all, but because of the exigencies of existence after the fall, *some* people, no doubt only a few, may do better to remain single *if* they "have the gift of continence."
40. Edmund S. Morgan, "The Puritans and Sex," in *The American Family in Social-Historical Perspective*, 2d ed., ed. Michael Gordon (New York: St. Martin's, 1978), see esp. 364, 371.
41. Thomas Taylor, *Works* (London: Printed by T. R. & E. M. for J. Bartlet the elder and J. Bartlet the younger, 1653), 190.
42. William Gouge, *Of Domesticall Duties: Eight Treatises* (London: John Haviland, 1622), 18.
43. Levin L. Schücking, *The Puritan Family: A Social Study from the Literary Sources*, 2d ed. (New York: Schocken Books, 1969), 65–66.
44. Edmund S. Morgan, *The Puritan Family: Essays on Religion and Domestic Relations in Seventeenth-Century New England* (Boston: Boston Public Library, 1944), 85.
45. Morgan, *Puritan Family*, 86–89; Guerra, *Family Matters*, 43.
46. Morgan, *Puritan Family*, 9–14; Schücking, *Puritan Family*, 67; Hill, *Society and Puritanism*, 458–62.
47. For other Christian ethical critiques of the Puritan family model, see Lisa Sowle Cahill, *Family: A Christian Social Perspective* (Minneapolis: Fortress, 2000), 51.
48. Much of my point here is dependent on Michael Warner, *The Trouble with Normal: Sex, Politics, and the Ethics of Queer Life* (New York: Free Press, 1999).
49. The focus on the family is ultimately *antisocial*. It is politically quietistic, opposed to social reform, and "tolerant of economic injustice." The "private family" is therefore socially *irresponsible*. See Coontz, *The Way We Never Were*, 97–98. Or as Jessie Bernard has put it, "Marriage is a cheap way for society at large to take care of a lot of difficult people. We force individuals—a wife or a husband—to take care of them on a one-to-one basis" (*The Future of Marriage* [New Haven, CT: Yale University Press, 1982], 161; quoted and affirmed by Brian W. Grant, *The Social Structure of Christian Families: A Historical Perspective* (St. Louis: Chalice, 2000), 147.
50. Even an author intent on affirming the normativity of marriage for Christians (though she does suggest that it should be now balanced with "a favourable account of celibacy") admits that "the 'Christian family' makes plenty of people feel excluded, not strengthened" (Helen Oppenheimer, *Marriage* [London: Mowbray, 1990], 87, 110).

Chapter 9

1. See, for example, Julia Duin, "Politics Cloud Kerry's Easter Plans," *Washington Times*, April 5, 2004, http://www.washtimes.com/national/20040405-125311-9075r.htm; Daniel J. Wakin, "The Nation: Abortion to Annulment; Communion Becomes a Test of Faith and Politics," *The New York Times*, March 9, 2004, sec. 4, 3; Iver Peterson, "Bishop Installed Amid Dust-up Over Stand on Governor's Divorce," *New York Times*, May 1, 2004, sec. B, 1; Kenneth L. Woodward, "A Political Sacrament," *New York Times*, May 28, 2004, sec. A, 21; Ian Fisher,

"Catholic Bishops Again Reject Married Priests," *New York Times*, October 23, 2005, sec. A, 12.

2. This suspicion is supported by the fact that it has been almost overwhelmingly those more "moderate" or "liberal" politicians, rather than those more conservative or Republican politicians, who have been targeted with such calls—and the issues have been overwhelmingly abortion and divorce. Moreover, few Catholic bishops, if any, have called on churches to refuse communion to politicians who support the death penalty or who voted to support the manifestly "unjust war" (using the term in its technical sense as recognized by the Roman Catholic Church) against Iraq. If the issue were really simply one of upholding the Roman Catholic Church's position on divorce as a moral issue, one would expect similar pronouncements on the equally important moral issues of capital punishment and war.
3. Many contemporary Christian studies of divorce and remarriage begin by admitting that the acceptance of both has become the norm among most Christians, Roman Catholic as well as Protestant. See, for example, Gerald D. Coleman, *Divorce and Remarriage in the Catholic Church* (New York: Paulist, 1988), 5; Robert H. Vasoli, *What God Has Joined Together: The Annulment Crisis in American Catholicism* (New York: Oxford University Press, 1998), 4, 201; Pierre Hegy and Joseph Martos, eds., *Catholic Divorce: The Deception of Annulments* (New York: Continuum, 2000); Timothy J. Buckley, *What Binds Marriage? Roman Catholic Theology in Practice* (London: Continuum, 2002), 3–16; Michael G. Lawler, *Marriage and the Catholic Church: Disputed Questions* (Collegeville, MN: Liturgical, 2002), 92.
4. See Andrew Cornes, *Divorce and Remarriage: Biblical Principles and Pastoral Practice* (Grand Rapids: Wm. B. Eerdmans, 1993); the reference to "God's mind" is at 80. Biblical foundationalist statements are found throughout the book, but see especially 215, 217. See also the conservative but nonetheless harmonizing interpretation of the New Testament passages by Gordon J. Wenham and William E. Heth, *Jesus and Divorce*, updated ed. (Carlisle, Australia: Paternoster, 2002). Wenham and Heth are Protestant foundationalists: "Unless a practice or doctrine can be demonstrated from the Bible itself it should not bind the Christian conscience. This Protestants have always affirmed" (20).
5. This terminology comes from Craig S. Keener, *And Marries Another: Divorce and Remarriage in the Teaching of the New Testament* (Peabody, MA: Hendrickson, 1991), see ix–xii. I discuss Keener's book at more length below.
6. Alex R. G. Deasley, *Marriage and Divorce in the Bible and the Church* (Kansas City, MO: Beacon Hill, 2000), 10–11.
7. A. L. Descamps, "The New Testament Doctrine on Marriage," in *Contemporary Perspectives on Christian Marriage: Propositions and Papers from the International Theological Commission*, ed. Richard Malone and John R. Connery (Chicago: Loyola University Press, 1984), 217. Not only is this statement notable for sounding almost Protestant in its emphasis on biblical foundationalism, it is also, at least now, inaccurate. There is no such consensus about the "indissolubility of marriage" being the universal position in ancient Christianity nor that the notion goes back to the historical Jesus. In his defense, the situation may have been different in the early 1980s, when Descamps was writing, and he may have been thinking only of Roman Catholic scholars.
8. Theodore Mackin, *Divorce and Remarriage* (New York: Paulist, 1984), 1. Even more liberal Protestants, who advocate more leniency on divorce and remarriage, often sound like biblical foundationalists. Myrna Kysar and Robert Kysar, in a study published in 1978, when the issue was a bit more debated among "mainline" Protestant denominations than it is now, urged, "The Biblical teachings

upon which the church depends for guidance do not necessitate that the church add its condemnations to that of society" (*The Asundered: Biblical Teachings on Divorce and Remarriage* [Atlanta: John Knox, 1978], 12). And though they believe that Christian ethics cannot be simplistically based on "what the Bible says," they still talk like biblical foundationalists at times: "The rise in divorce rates in America may in part be due to an ignorance or rejection of the Biblical teachings. Perhaps many do not understand or know the basis of the Biblical prohibition against divorce—what God intended marriage to be" (69). An aside: it is almost quaint to see that Kysar and Kysar could refer, in 1978, to a *general societal* condemnation of divorced persons which churches, they believed, should resist. In our day and society, one is hard-pressed to find any stigmatizing of divorced persons *except* in conservative church circles.

9. The classic expression is Krister Stendahl, "Biblical Theology, Contemporary," *Interpreter's Dictionary of the Bible* (Nashville: Abingdon, 1962), 1:418–432. See alsoWerner G. Jeanrond, *Text and Interpretation as Categories of Theological Thinking* (New York: Crossroad, 1988), 6, 75. For an excellent historical contextualization and critique of the position, see A. K. M. Adam, *Making Sense of New Testament Theology: "Modern" Problems and Prospects* (Macon, GA: Mercer University Press, 1995), esp. 76–86.
10. To cite only a few examples picked almost at random: Descamps, "New Testament Doctrine of Marriage," 217; David Instone-Brewer, *Divorce and Remarriage in the Bible: The Social and Literary Context* (Grand Rapids: Wm. B. Eerdmans, 2002), ix, 276; Michael Goulder, "Devotion, Divorce and Debauchery," in *Tro og historie: Festschrift til Niels Hyldahl i anledning af 65 års fødselsdagen den 30. december 1995*, ed. Lone Fatum and Mogens Müller (Copenhagen: Copenhagen University, Museum Tusculanums, 1996), 107–17, at 107; Cornes, *Divorce and Remarriage*, 204.
11. As usual, I use the names "Matthew, Mark, and Luke" for convenience to represent the views of the authors of those texts. I do not assume, in fact I doubt, that these Gospels were actually written by those historical persons. I take all the canonical Gospels to have been anonymous.
12. The debate about the existence of "Q" has not completely disappeared. Many studies questioning the existence of Q could be cited, but perhaps two of the most important are E. P. Sanders and Margaret Davies, *Studying the Synoptic Gospels* (Philadelphia: Trinity Press International, 1989); and Mark S. Goodacre, *The Case Against Q: Studies in Markan Priority and the Synoptic Problem* (Harrisburg, PA: Trinity Press International, 2002). For the purposes of this chapter, I assume the Q hypothesis, but my treatment does not stand or fall on that assumption. I could just as easily argue that Luke altered the text as he found it in Matthew.
13. I put the "exception clause" in brackets just to indicate that it is an important part of the saying that is *not* held in common by Matthew and Luke. It is not part of the "common" saying.
14. I reject the suggestion by Robert G. Olender that Paul was actually dependent on Gospel sources for his teachings on divorce and remarriage. See Olender, "Paul's Source for 1 Corinthians 6:10–7:11," *Faith and Mission* 18, no. 3 (Summer 2001): 60–73. The reasons given by Olender for direct literary borrowing by Paul from the Gospels are unconvincing, invoking stretched readings of allusions in Paul to wording in Matthew and Mark. The "allusions" are almost all better explained as simply common ways of speaking or oral traditions about teachings of Jesus. Olender can offer nothing approaching the kind of quotation we would need to establish literary dependence.
15. Bernadette Brooten, "Konnten Frauen im alten Judentum die Scheidung betreiben? Überlegungen zu Mk 10, 11–12 und Kor 7, 10–11," *Evangelische The-*

ologie 42 (1982): 65–80; Brooten, "Zur Debatte über das Scheidungsrecht der jüdischen Frau," *Evangelische Theologie* 43 (1983): 466–78; Michael L. Satlow, *Jewish Marriage in Antiquity* (Princeton, NJ: Princeton University Press, 2001), 214; Instone-Brewer, *Divorce and Remarriage*, 85–90, 151–52; William Loader, *Sexuality and the Jesus Tradition* (Grand Rapids: Wm. B. Eerdmans, 2005), 113–14, and especially 113n144 for extensive and up-to-date bibliography on the question.

16. *Porneia* could mean any of a number of sexual actions considered immoral by Jews. I am unconvinced by scholarship that has tried to pin down the meaning more specifically than "sexual immorality." For discussion, see Keener, *And Marries Another*, 29–30; Instone-Brewer, *Divorce and Remarriage*, 275–76; Allen R. Guenther, "The Exception Phrases: Except *porneia*, Including *porneia* or Excluding *porneia*? (Matthew 5:32; 19:9)," *Tyndale Bulletin* 53 (2002): 83–96; Loader, *Sexuality and the Jesus Tradition*, 68–76. I believe the precise meaning of *porneia* is simply uncertain given the lack of evidence we have; see, for example, W. F. Albright and C. S. Mann, *Matthew*, Anchor Bible Commentary (Garden City, NY: Doubleday, 1971), 226. On the secondary character of the "exception clauses" in Matthew, see Albright and Mann, *Matthew*, 226 ("Commentators have generally taken the position that these words are not part of the saying as originally uttered, but are a community regulation later inserted into the text. It certainly appears to be inconsistent with vs. 6."). John P. Meier notes that it is the "common, not to say nearly universal view" that the exception clause does not go back to Jesus: "The Historical Jesus and the Historical Law: Some Problems Within the Problem," *Catholic Biblical Quarterly* 65 (2003): 52–79, at 78n59. There are scholars who take the exception clause either to have been spoken by the historical Jesus or rightly to be implied in Jesus' sayings or intention, but usually these are scholars who want to read the texts and the historical Jesus as more lenient than traditionally construed. See, for example, Keener, *And Marries Another*, 27; Instone-Brewer, *Divorce and Remarriage in the Bible*, 276.
17. W. D. Davies and Dale C. Allison Jr., *A Critical and Exegetical Commentary on the Gospel According to Saint Matthew* (Edinburgh: T. & T. Clark, 1997), 3:19.
18. Both Mark, on the one hand, and the combination of Matthew and Luke, on the other, use the same root word (*apoluô*) for divorce, though the form of the word differs. All agree in the wording of "his wife." They all use the same root word for the verb for committing adultery or making her an adulterer (though again, Luke and Matthew agree in some significant details against Mark). Mark and Luke agree (against Matthew) in the wording "and marries" (though again the actual form of "marries" is different, a verb in Mark and a participle in Luke). Mark and Matthew also agree in some details of wording against Luke (the use of *ean* in one place, and the wording for "marries" and "commits adultery" at the end of the saying). These agreements in details are more notable when we compare the sayings with Paul's, where different wording in general is used (Paul uses entirely different words for "separate" and "divorce"). If we are working with the hypothesis of "Q," these details would suggest that both Mark and Q are witnesses to wording that may go back to the historical Jesus, providing independent attestation from two early sources.
19. Meier, "Historical Jesus and Historical Law," 78–79.
20. John Nolland, "The Gospel Prohibition of Divorce: Tradition History and Meaning," *Journal for the Study of the New Testament* 58 (1995): 19–35.
21. Goulder, "Devotion, Divorce and Debauchery."
22. For example, Kysar and Kysar, *The Asundered*, 43–44, but many such examples from that time could be cited.
23. See Brooten's works cited in note 15 above.

24. See my discussion in chapter 7, "Sex and the Single Savior," in this volume, pp. 96–97, and chapter 8, "Familiar Idolatry," pp. 104–6.
25. Though some church fathers read the text this way, almost all modern scholars attribute their interpretation to the Fathers' tendency to "hyperasceticize" the Bible whenever possible. See Elizabeth A. Clark, *Reading Renunciation: Asceticism and Scripture in Early Christianity* (Princeton, NJ: Princeton University Press, 1999), 142, 243.
26. Ptolemy's *Epistle to Flora* may be found in English translation in Bentley Layton, *The Gnostic Scriptures* (Garden City, NY: Doubleday, 1987), 306–15; see 33.4.4–10 (309–10) for the discussion of Matthew 19:6–8. See also Jerome, *Commentaire sur S. Matthieu*, ed. Emile Bonnard, Sources Chrétiennes, no. 259 (Paris: Éditions du Cerf, 1979), 2:68.
27. Augustine, *De doctrina christiana* 3.83 (26.37); Duncan S. Ferguson, *Biblical Hermeneutics: An Introduction* (Atlanta: John Knox, 1986), see, e.g., 161. One doesn't usually come across an explicitly stated rule like this in modern handbooks on interpretation, but to get an idea of how common it still is in Christian "guidelines" in interpretation, one may simply search the Internet for the phrase "interpret the obscure by the clear." Many sites come up using the phrase when speaking about interpreting Scripture.
28. Mark 2:23–28; 3:15; 6:7–13; 11:23–24. Note also the "binding and loosing" motif from Matt. 18:18.
29. On the meaning of *porneia*, see note 16. I have nothing of substance to add to the debate on the meaning of the term here, though I think it is most defensible *not* to attempt to narrow down the meaning to some particular aspect of "sexual immorality," such as "incest." The word clearly had a wide range of semantic meaning in first-century Jewish contexts, and that wide range should be allowed by any responsible translation or interpretation.
30. Indeed, some interpreters, mainly more conservative Anglicans and Roman Catholics, have argued that Matthew forbids divorce entirely and that the "exception clause" should not be interpreted as an "out" permitting divorce. See, for example, Cornes, *Divorce and Remarriage*: "So it seems that Jesus differed from the Jewish legal authorities in that while they said that husbands *must* divorce adulterous wives; [sic] he merely said that they *may* do so. The reason for Matthew's exception is to exculpate the husband—given the current legal situation—from sin when he divorces his wife for adultery. But this is not Jesus' ideal . . ." (204). Furthermore, Cornes argues that the "exception clause" is not intended to permit remarriage after even a legitimate divorce (Wenham and Heth, *Jesus and Divorce*, 198). Wenham and Heth, though, harmonize the other Gospel accounts to Matthew's and use that to argue that Jesus prohibited divorce and remarriage entirely.
31. Willoughby C. Allen long ago took the exception clause to relate to divorce, not remarriage, but then had to admit that this involves Matthew in a self-contradiction, which Allen says Matthew is led into by his attempt to use Mark as a source but add an exception clause to the simpler absolute prohibition of divorce. See *A Critical and Exegetical Commentary on the Gospel According to Matthew*, 3d ed. (Edinburgh: T. & T. Clark, 1912), 202. Most commentators do not even recognize that Matthew does seem to contradict himself; they simply conflate the different prohibitions and allow the exception clause to relate to Jesus' position overall.
32. For extensive, recent research on eunuchs and social perception about them in the ancient Mediterranean, see Mathew Kuefler, *The Manly Eunuch: Masculinity, Gender Ambiguity, and Christian Ideology in Late Antiquity* (Chicago: University of Chicago Press, 2001). For sexual activities of eunuchs, see esp. 32–35, 96–102.

33. Matthew 5:27–28. Some translate the Greek *epithymeô* as "lust after," which would imply a stronger state of passion than the translation "desire." But I believe we should go with the more usual translation of "desire" and allow that Matthew again may be more stringent than some modern Christians would prefer. He is having Jesus say that even looking at another man's wife with the purpose of desiring her (sexually, of course) is itself forbidden.
34. Note a similar suggestion in Eric K. C. Wong, "The Deradicalization of Jesus' Ethical Sayings in 1 Corinthians," *New Testament Studies* 48 (2002): 181–94, at 184.
35. Or if one doubts the existence of Q, we could assume that Luke is quoting the saying from Matthew, but in either case Luke makes his own, important, editorial decisions about it.
36. For a fuller discussion of the marriage and family in Luke-Acts, see chapter 8, "Familiar Idolatry and the Christian Case against Marriage," in this volume.
37. As many other scholars have noted, the later Christian approval of "separation from bed and board" while remaining married was unknown in either Jewish or Roman law. See, for example, Mackin, *Divorce and Remarriage*, 82. Augustine may have entertained the idea of separation without divorce. See Clark, *Reading Renunciation*, 244; Augustine, *Commentary on the Sermon on the Mount* 1.14.39; English: *Nicene and Post-Nicene Fathers of the Christian Church*, ed. Philip Schaff [Grand Rapids: Wm. B. Eerdmans, 1979], 6:17; Latin: *Corpus Christianorum Series Latina* [Turnholt: Brepols, 1967], 35:42–43. But Augustine's situation was completely different. In a Roman situation separation would *normally* have necessarily meant divorce. The later church's attempt to make that distinction, in order to maintain the indissolubility of marriage while still allowing for separation, is anachronistic if retrojected into the situation of the first century. Interestingly, Gerald L. Borchert argues that the Greek term for "putting away" is not the same as "divorce," thus differentiating separation from divorce, but he does so in order to *allow* divorce: the biblical text, in his reading, forbade husbands from "putting away" their wives in order to take other women but without allowing their wives the ability to remarry by means of a divorce. Thus, the text does not, according to Borchert, forbid divorce. See "1 Corinthians 7:15 and the Church's Historic Misunderstanding of Divorce and Remarriage," *Review and Expositor* 96 (1999): 125–29. Borchert's argument is vitiated by the fact that he is interpreting the New Testament Greek words by appeal only to two different *Hebrew* words, and he fails to take into account the ancient social and legal contexts. Separation without divorce was not really an option in the ancient world, or at least it was almost never considered.
38. My reading of Luke on this certainly represents a minority position among scholars, but I am not alone. See also Goulder, "Devotion, Divorce and Debauchery," 114.
39. See Martin, *Corinthian Body*, 198–228; and chap. 5, "Paul without Passion," in this volume.
40. Some authors even go so far as to say that this is what Paul *must have meant* and therefore what the text *must mean*. Theodore Mackin, for instance, argues, "Paul is taken to mean not only that the Christian husband or wife is not obligated to continue cohabitation with the unbelieving spouse, but that he or she is no longer bound in and by the marriage, and is free to marry again. This interpretation [known especially in Catholic circles as "the Pauline privilege"] is reinforced by the contrasting instructions wherein Paul insists (in verse 11) that if the two spouses who separate are both Christians, they must either remain single or be reconciled, but where (in verse 15) the separation is of a non-Christian from a Christian spouse, he omits this insistence" (9). My interpretation differs from Mackin's in that I argue that there is an inconsistency in the literal reading of

Paul's text which allows *us* to note that *for his position to be consistent* he should allow for remarriage; but I do not attempt to argue that that was Paul's intention or the "literal" meaning of the text.

41. By "no Christian church" I mean to refer to the main, recognized branches, traditions, or denominations of Christianity: Roman Catholic, Eastern Orthodox, and all the major representatives of Protestantism, whether conservative or liberal, "mainstream," "evangelical," or "fundamentalist." I do not mean to deny that there may have existed some *congregation* of Christians who attempted to forbid divorce and remarriage entirely.
42. See Peter L'Huillier, "The Indissolubility of Marriage in Orthodox Law and Practice," in *Catholic Divorce: The Deception of Annulments*, ed. Pierre Hegy and Joseph Martos (New York: Continuum, 2000), 108–26.
43. For example, Timothy J. Buckley, *What Binds Marriage? Roman Catholic Theology in Practice* (London: Continuum, 2002), 3–16; Michael G. Lawler, *Marriage and the Catholic Church: Disputed Questions* (Collegeville, MN: Liturgical, 2002), 92; Robert H. Vasoli, *What God Has Joined Together: The Annulment Crisis in American Catholicism* (New York: Oxford University Press, 1998), 4; Gerald D. Coleman, *Divorce and Remarriage in the Catholic Church* (New York: Paulist, 1988), 5–6.
44. Buckley, *What Binds Marriage?* 192.
45. Hegy and Martos, *Catholic Divorce: The Deception of Annulments*; see 9 for the quotation from Rembert Weakland, *America* 18 (1998): 13. One finds such sentiments also among Roman Catholic writers who are *bemoaning* the relaxation of strict prohibitions of divorce and urging the Church to return to less-lenient practices. See, for example, Vasoli, *What God Has Joined Together*, 213.
46. Lawler, *Marriage and the Catholic Church*, 98; see the fuller discussion at 98–99.
47. Kevin T. Kelly, *Divorce and Second Marriage: Facing the Challenge*, 2d ed. (expanded) (London: Geoffrey Chapman, 1996), 21. See also Mackin, *Divorce and Remarriage*, 11–16, for examples of the ways the Roman Catholic Church reserves for itself the power to dissolve marriages.
48. See the quotations from Descamps and Mackin cited at the beginning of this chapter.
49. See Lawler, *Marriage and the Catholic Church*, 94; Buckley, *What Binds Marriage?* 29, 34.
50. See, for instance, Mary Rose D'Angelo, "Remarriage and the Divorce Sayings Attributed to Jesus," in *Divorce and Remarriage: Religious and Psychological Perspectives*, ed. William P. Roberts (Kansas City, MO: Sheed & Ward, 1990), 78–106.
51. See, for example, the reference above (note 8) to Kysar and Kysar, *The Asundered*. For "foundationalist" statements, see 12–13, 69; for statements that argue for a more qualified use of the Bible (not as a legalistic text), see 14–15, 58.
52. Keener, *And Marries Another*. Reviews by evangelical or conservative scholars have generally been positive about Keener's book, even if they are occasionally a bit wary of his more-lenient conclusions. See reviews by Rodney Clapp, *Christianity Today* 36 (May 18, 1992): 75–76; John A. Witmer, *Bibliotheca sacra* 151 (April–June 1994): 250; Ronald Fuller, *Journal of Evangelical Theological Society* 38 (1995): 277–78.
53. The use of language of agency for Scripture runs throughout Keener's study, but for a couple of specific instances using these particular terms, see xii and 109.
54. It is difficult to avoid the impression that Instone-Brewer's study has been well-received among certain circles precisely because he provides a biblical foundationalist argument for more leniency on divorce and remarriage. For a not-untypical

review, see that by W. Eugene March in the *Journal of Family Ministry* 17 (2003): 74–75. For more critical reviews, which I believe are on target, see Earl C. Muller's in *Catholic Biblical Quarterly* 65 (2003): 470–72; and Mary E. Shield's review in *Review of Biblical Literature* (2003), http://www.bookreviews.org.

55. Most quotations in this paragraph are taken from Instone-Brewer, *Divorce and Remarriage,* ix.
56. See for example, ibid., 308–9.
57. See, for instance, ibid., ix, xi, 314. For "searching for the biblical basis" for divorce and remarriage, see 268. But the language of biblical foundationalism occurs throughout the book.
58. John Meier notes just how odd Jesus' absolute prohibition of divorce would have been in the ancient world, but Meier nonetheless believes the historical Jesus did forbid it: "With Qumran and the Mishna out of the picture, Jesus' prohibition of divorce seems to come out of nowhere in Judaism and to go nowhere in Judaism. Even its reception in Christianity is ambiguous, where Paul, in 1 Corinthians 7, makes history in first-generation Christianity by being the first to create some 'wiggle room' around the prohibition" ("Historical Jesus and the Historical Law," 79).
59. A similar inconsistency occurs in the study by Wenham and Heth, *Jesus and Divorce* (cited in note 4 above). In spite of their firm belief that marriage is indissoluble and no divorce is permitted, they in the end say that Christians who have been remarried after divorce should not separate from their current spouses, even though according to their own logic such Christians would be living in an adulterous relationship. Their reasons for this are ultimately based on "pastoral" motivations: "To act otherwise and seek to return to your former partner may or may not succeed, but it will surely bring great grief to your second partner" (201). Wenham and Heth don't even mention the possibility that a Christian might separate from the second partner and simply remain single (as the Fathers, even according to Wenham and Heth's demonstration, would have urged). Again, modern conservative Christian scholars, though insisting that their views match the "foundation" of Scripture, end up more lenient than the strict reading of Scripture *as they recognize the impracticality of the absolute prohibition.*
60. For interesting examples of the ways even Christian emperors and governments were forced to regulate divorce and remarriage more liberally than the church leaders desired, demonstrating once again that no human society can succeed in completely excluding divorce and remarriage, see John T. Noonan Jr., "Novel 22," in *The Bond of Marriage: An Ecumenical and Interdisciplinary Study,* ed. William W. Bassett (Notre Dame, IN: University of Notre Dame Press, 1968), 41–96. As Bruce Vawter noted years ago, "Christian tradition, earlier and later, has honored the ideal of indissoluble monogamous marriage as a decree of its Lord, and Christian tradition, earlier and later, has never hesitated to compromise this ideal by adapting it to human realities" ("Divorce and the New Testament," *Catholic Biblical Quarterly* 39 [1977]: 528–42, at 541).
61. For more on this, see chap. 8, "Familiar Idolatry and the Christian Case against Marriage."

Chapter 10

1. Richard B. Hays, *Echoes of Scripture in the Letters of Paul* (New Haven, CT: Yale University Press, 1989), 156.
2. Percy Gardner, *The Religious Experience of Saint Paul* (New York: G. P. Putnam's Sons, 1913), 215.

3. Hays, *Echoes of Scripture*, 189; referring to David H. Kelsey, *Uses of Scripture in Recent Theology* (Philadelphia: Fortress, 1975), 215–16.
4. Richard B. Hays, *The Moral Vision of the New Testament: Community, Cross, New Creation: A Contemporary Introduction to New Testament Ethics* (San Francisco: HarperSanFrancisco, 1996).
5. The Greek term *stoicheia* is difficult to translate with just one word. It referred to the "elements" that made up the cosmos (such as air, fire, earth, and water in one ancient theory), or it could refer to other "components" of nature. It was also used to refer to the superhuman beings (understood by most Jews and Christians to be demonic) who lived in the atmosphere and opposed attempts by human beings to rise to greater physical heights by means of greater heights of virtue—or magic. Though I have my own opinions about the meaning of the term here, they would make no difference to the current context.
6. So also Stephen E. Fowl, *Engaging Scripture: A Model for Theological Interpretation* (Oxford: Blackwell, 1998), 70, 98, 138–42. Significantly, in *Echoes of Scripture* Hays also notes that Paul interprets Scripture by making "the biblical text pass through the filter of his experience of God's action" (102); the "community's corporate experience of the Spirit and of the miracles wrought in their midst" (107) affect their interpretation of the text; Paul opts for the "hermeneutical priority of Spirit-experience" (108). I do not believe, however, that Hays has allowed these observations adequately to correct his more generally one-sided position in his later writings that our own churches should be "Scripture-shaped communities" rather than that we allow our "experiences" to shape directly our interpretations of Scripture.
7. The term translated here as "guide (canon)" is the Greek word *kanôn*, from which we derive the English "canon." The word could refer to a measuring rod or metaphorically to any standard, device for measuring or evaluating, or even to a "rule of thumb." Paul is probably calling his immediately previous statement ("For there is neither circumcision nor uncircumcision, but new creation") a "rule" or "standard" the Galatians should follow.
8. Richard B. Hays, *New Testament Ethics: The Story Retold* (Winnipeg, MB: CMBC, 1998), 13.
9. N. T. Wright, *The Last Word: Beyond the Bible Wars to a New Understanding of the Authority of Scripture* (San Francisco: HarperSanFrancisco, 2005), 101. See also Kathryn Greene-McCreight, "The Logic of the Interpretation of Scripture and the Church's Debate Over Sexual Ethics," in David L. Balch, ed., *Homosexuality, Science, and the "Plain Sense" of Scripture* (Grand Rapids: Wm. B. Eerdmans, 2000), 242–60, esp. 260.
10. See also Luke Timothy Johnson, "Debate and Discernment, Scripture and the Spirit," *Commonweal* (January 1994): 11–13, reprinted in *Virtues and Practices in the Christian Tradition: Christian Ethics after MacIntyre*, ed. Nancey Murphy, Brad J. Kallenberg, and Mark Thiessen Nation (Harrisburg, PA: Trinity Press International, 1997), 215–20.
11. Jeffrey S. Siker, "Homosexual Christians, the Bible, and Gentile Inclusion: Confessions of a Repenting Heterosexist," in Siker, ed., *Homosexuality in the Church: Both Sides of the Debate* (Louisville, KY: Westminster John Knox, 1994), 178–94, at 187 and 188.
12. Hays takes note of it in *Moral Vision of the New Testament*, 395–96, calling the analogy "richly suggestive" and deserving of "careful consideration." But he finally rejects the conclusions, again by appealing in a foundationalist way to what "the text requires," that is, in his view, the condemnation of homosexuality. Again, the *text* is made into an *agent* whose "requirement" trumps an appeal to "experience."

Chapter 11

1. For an excellent introduction to debates about philosophy of history and challenges to the theories of knowledge underwriting modern historiography, see Elizabeth A. Clark, *History, Theory, Text: Historians and the Linguistic Turn* (Cambridge, MA: Harvard University Press, 2004).
2. For another interesting attempt to use historical criticism but in a postmodernist way, and to counter antihomosexual uses of Romans 1 with a reading of the text that treats homoeroticism positively, see Teresa J. Hornsby, "Paul and the Remedies of Idolatry: Reading Romans 1:18–24 with Romans 7," in A. K. M. Adam, ed., *Postmodern Interpretations of the Bible: A Reader* (St. Louis: Chalice, 2001), 219–232.
3. Hans W. Frei, *The Eclipse of Biblical Narrative: A Study in Eighteenth and Nineteenth Century Hermeneutics* (New Haven, CT: Yale University Press, 1974).
4. Much of the rejection of making love the central ethical focus has been a reaction to the hugely influential ideas of Paul Ramsey, as expressed especially in his *Basic Christian Ethics* (New York: Scribner, 1950). See, for example, the fairly recent critique by Robert W. Tuttle, "All You Need Is Love: Paul Ramsey's *Basic Christian Ethics* and the Dilemma of Protestant Antilegalism," *Journal of Law and Religion* 18 (2002–2003): 427–57. In my view, Tuttle's criticisms are to a great extent vitiated because he collapses "love" into mere uncritical "acceptance" of others and a lax "tolerance." He complains, for instance, that we cannot "discuss unchastity or infidelity" or teach against abortion because we are not supposed to make the other "feel guilty and thus unwelcomed" (443). This is a remarkably weak concept of love, and one certainly Ramsey or others who emphasize the centrality of love would reject.
5. "Love Isn't All You Need," originally published in the journal *Cross Currents*, can be found in Stanley Hauerwas, *Vision and Virtue: Essays in Christian Ethical Reflection* (Notre Dame, IN: Fides, 1974). It is to that publication that the page numbers I cite correspond.
6. Joseph F. Fletcher, *Situation Ethics: The New Morality* (Philadelphia: Westminster, 1966).
7. Note how Hauerwas turns "love" into a simple "living together" without confrontation: 120–22.
8. Richard B. Hays, *The Moral Vision of the New Testament: Community, Cross, New Creation: A Contemporary Introduction to New Testament Ethics* (San Francisco: HarperSanFrancisco, 1996), 200–203.
9. Stephen E. Fowl and L. Gregory Jones, *Reading in Communion: Scripture and Ethics in Christian Life* (Grand Rapids: Wm. B. Eerdmans, 1991), 72. I should point out that Fowl and Jones *do* repeatedly note that there can be devised no *method* of reading that will dependably deliver ethical interpretations. They nonetheless repeatedly fall back on "community" as a safeguard against bad interpretations in a way I see as naïve and sanguine, especially in light of the overwhelming *immorality* of so many contemporary churches' treatment of homosexual people. Also close to my own position, yet with too much confidence in "community," is Stephen E. Fowl, *Engaging Scripture: A Model for Theological Interpretation* (Oxford: Blackwell, 1998).
10. This is of course debatable, but quite defensible. See the interesting discussion of the passage by someone who is not a New Testament scholar but a Jewish philosopher: Jacob Taubes, *The Political Theology of Paul*, Aleida Assmann et al., eds. (Stanford, CA: Stanford University Press, 2004), 53. In any case, attempts by Christians throughout centuries to commit unloving acts against their fellow human beings under the excuse of "love of God" might be made much more difficult to defend if Paul's expression of the commandment were kept foremost.

11. Augustine, *De doctrina christiana*, ed. and trans. R. P. H. Green (Oxford: Clarendon, 1995), 3.33–34 (10.14).
12. *De doctrina christiana* 3.52–53 (14.22), my translations in this case. The "negative" version of the command quoted here by Augustine recalls Tobit 4:15. Of course, we need not be as sanguine as Augustine about the universality of notions of love and justice, even here. My point is simply that Augustine himself appealed to the universality of love to mitigate the problems raised by (what we would call) cultural relativism.
13. James Callahan, *The Clarity of Scripture: History, Theology and Contemporary Literary Studies* (Downers Grove, IL: InterVarsity, 2001), 96.
14. *De doctrina christiana* 1.93 (39.43), trans. R. P. H. Green.
15. For another discussion of the rule of love, emphasizing the long history and commonality of its use in adjudicating different interpretations of Scripture, see Charles H. Cosgrove, *Appealing to Scripture in Moral Debate: Five Hermeneutical Rules* (Grand Rapids: Wm. B. Eerdmans, 2002), 158–61. Cosgrove quotes also recent denominational statements approving the use of the rule of love in biblical interpretation.
16. Bas C. van Fraassen, *The Empirical Stance* (New Haven, CT: Yale University Press, 2002).
17. As van Fraassen puts it, in a nice phrase, "the search for a rock-solid foundation for knowledge was precisely the rock on which empiricism foundered" (*The Empirical Stance*, 117). See a similar invocation of van Fraassen, though to a somewhat different purpose, in my essay "The Promise of Teleology, the Constraints of Epistemology, and Universal Vision in Paul," in *St. Paul Among the Philosophers: Subjectivity, Universality, and the Event*, ed. John Caputo (forthcoming).
18. Van Fraassen, *Empirical Stance*, 62–63.
19. Some good studies in the past several years have emphasized the importance of training the imagination for Christian thinking and living. See for example, David J. Bryant, *Faith and the Play of Imagination: On the Role of Imagination in Religion* (Macon, GA: Mercer, 1989); Garrett Green, *Imagining God: Theology and the Religious Imagination* (Grand Rapids: Wm. B. Eerdmans, 1998); Green, *Theology, Hermeneutics, and Imagination: The Crisis of Interpretation at the End of Modernity* (Cambridge: Cambridge University Press, 2000); Walter Brueggemann, *Texts Under Negotiation: The Bible and Postmodern Imagination* (Minneapolis: Fortress, 1993).
20. A similar suggestion for imagining Scripture as space, in this case as a "city," is made by Luke Timothy Johnson, in Johnson and William S. Kurz, *The Future of Catholic Biblical Scholarship: A Constructive Conversation* (Grand Rapids: Wm. B. Eerdmans, 2002), 123–25. I disagree with Johnson, however, in his insistence that historical criticism is still *essential* for reading Scripture (8 passim), and his language implying that it is the text itself that "imagines" (123–25). It is not the text that "imagines" but the Christian who "imagines" when reading the text. For a rather different attempt—this one inspired by Hans Georg Gadamer and continental phenomenology—to bring the creativity of the interpreter and the imagination to bear on theories of biblical interpretation, see Thomas W. Ogletree, *The Use of the Bible in Christian Ethics: A Constructive Essay* (Philadelphia: Fortress, 1983), esp. 176.
21. For another suggestion that reading Scripture should proceed as "art" see Ellen F. Davis, "Teaching the Bible Confessionally in the Church," in Ellen F. Davis and Richard B. Hays, *The Art of Reading Scripture* (Grand Rapids: Wm. B. Eerdmans, 2003), 9–26; see also xvi.
22. The catalog number is KMS 830, Statens Museum for Kunst, Copenhagen, Denmark.

23. The seminal treatment of "orientalism" is Edward W. Said, *Orientalism* (New York: Pantheon, 1978).
24. For studies using hypertext technology as a way to think about interpretation more generally, see George P. Landow, *Hypertext 2.0* (Baltimore: Johns Hopkins University Press, 1997); Landow, ed., *Hyper/text/theory* (Baltimore: Johns Hopkins University Press, 1994). For one example of the use of hypertext to think about religious meaning and experience, see Jonathan Rosen, *The Talmud and the Internet: A Journey Between Worlds* (New York: Farrar, Straus, & Giroux, 2000).
25. So also Douglas Harink, *Paul Among the Postliberals: Pauline Theology Beyond Christendom and Modernity* (Grand Rapids: Baker, 2003), esp. 20–22.
26. See especially Fowl and Jones, *Reading in Communion.*
27. Søren Kierkegaard (pseudonym: Johannes Climacus), *Concluding Unscientific Postscript*, trans. David F. Swenson and Walter Lowrie (Princeton, NJ: Princeton University Press, 1941), 505 and 512; see also Kierkegaard, *Philosophical Fragments or A Fragment of Philosophy*, trans. David Swenson, trans. revised Howard V. Hong (Princeton, NJ: Princeton University Press, 1936, 1962), 26. *Concluding Unscientific Postscript* announces itself as basically a commentary (a long one, at that) on the shorter *Philosophical Fragments.*
28. Kierkegaard, *Concluding Unscientific Postscript*, 528.
29. Kierkegaard, *Philosophical Fragments*, 73.
30. Ibid., 75.
31. Kierkegaard, *Concluding Unscientific Postscript*, 25 and 41, emphasis in the original; see also 509, 511, where the same point is made, sometimes in even the same wording.
32. Kierkegaard, *Philosophical Fragments*, 81 and 103.
33. Kierkegaard, *Concluding Unscientific Postscript*, 30.
34. Ibid., 75. See also Kierkegaard, *Stages on Life's Way: Studies by Various Persons*, ed. and trans. with introduction and notes by Howard V. Hong and Edna H. Hong (Princeton, NJ: Princeton University Press, 1988), 445: "The religious seeks no foothold in the historical. . . ."
35. Note the comments by Alastair Hannay, *Kierkegaard: A Biography* (Cambridge: Cambridge University Press, 2001), 280–81: "The case against resorting to the Holy Word to decide Christian doctrine is that it runs afoul of the problem of historical uncertainty, so that however honourable a discipline historical philology may be, its results, excellent in themselves, can still at best always only approximate the truth of what was written, and when, and can therefore never provide the basis for an eternal happiness. The problem here appears to be the inaccessibility of the basis of one's belief, but Climacus keeps on interjecting that this whole way of relating to Christianity as something 'out there' is wrong in any case. Approximation is a quantitative affair, a matter of accumulation (of evidence) or removal (of reasons for doubt) as if in the end the facts, ideally at least, could lie bare before us. Nor is what is inappropriate about this simply that waiting for someone else's expert judgment on such things takes away the opportunity to make faith one's own; even if the facts were delivered on a plate they still would not suffice as a basis for an eternal happiness." Hannay goes on to explain how the Grundtvigian notion that posits the church as the foundation will also not work according to Kierkegaard, mainly because one can't be sure that the contemporary church is "the apostolic church" (281–82).
36. Kierkegaard, *Concluding Unscientific Postscript*, 182, 188.
37. Kierkegaard, *Stages on Life's Way*, 444; see also 443–45, 470.
38. Ibid., 470; see also 471. I hasten to add that I would not want to appropriate *all* of Kierkegaard's ideas. (Of course, I would not want to take over uncritically all the ideas of *any* writer or theologian, whether Thomas Aquinas, Augustine, or

even the apostle Paul.) Kierkegaard's emphasis here on individualism, a common theme in Kierkegaard's work, should be corrected by an emphasis on community, especially the need for the Christian to exist in Christian community. The individualism of Kierkegaard, which admittedly was one feature that contributed to the success of his reception in the twentieth century, especially as an inspiration to "existentialism," has been rightly rejected in more recent theologies. Another aspect of Kierkegaard's thought that I would reject is the idea that "knowledge" is something different *in kind* from "belief." Postmodern philosophies have successfully deconstructed the firm differentiation between "knowledge" and "belief," pointing out that, in important senses, even what we call "scientific knowledge" is still the acceptance of "beliefs" for which we can have no *absolute, indisputable, universal, incontrovertible proof.* See, for example, Barbara Herrnstein Smith, *Belief and Resistance: Dynamics of Contemporary Intellectual Controversy* (Cambridge, MA: Harvard University Press, 1997). Postmodernists would also say that we do not *need* that kind of "proof" to have completely *adequate* knowledge.

39. Kierkegaard, *Stages on Life's Way*, 471.

Bibliography

Abelove, Henry et al., eds. *The Gay and Lesbian Studies Reader.* New York: Routledge, 1993.

Adam, A. K. M. *Making Sense of New Testament Theology: "Modern" Problems and Prospects.* Macon, GA: Mercer University Press, 1995.

———. *What Is Postmodern Biblical Criticism?* Minneapolis: Fortress, 1995.

Albright, W. F., and C. S. Mann. *Matthew.* Anchor Bible Commentary. Garden City, NY: Doubleday, 1971.

Allen, Willoughby C. *A Critical and Exegetical Commentary on the Gospel According to Matthew.* 3d ed. Edinburgh: T. & T. Clark, 1912.

Allison, Dale C. *Jesus of Nazareth: Millenarian Prophet.* Minneapolis: Fortress, 1998.

Atkinson, D. J. *Homosexuals in the Christian Fellowship.* Grand Rapids: Wm. B. Eerdmans, 1979.

Augustine. *De doctrina christiana.* Ed. and trans. R. P. H. Green. Oxford: Clarendon, 1995.

Baer, Richard A., Jr. *Philo's Use of the Categories Male and Female.* Leiden: E. J. Brill, 1970.

Barnes, Albert. *Notes, Explanatory and Practical, on the Epistle to the Romans.* New York: Leavitt, Lord, 1835.

Barr, James. *The Scope and Authority of the Bible.* Philadelphia: Westminster, 1980.

———. *The Semantics of Biblical Language.* London: Oxford, 1961.

Barrett, C. K. *A Critical and Exegetical Commentary on the Acts of the Apostles.* 2 vols. Edinburgh: T. & T. Clark, 1994.

Bartlett, David L. "A Biblical Perspective on Homosexuality." *Foundations* 20 (1977): 133–47.

Barton, Stephen C. *Discipleship and Family Ties in Mark and Matthew.* Cambridge: Cambridge University Press, 1994.

Becker, Jürgen. "Zum Problem der Homosexualität in der Bibel." *Zeitschrift für evangelische Ethik* 31 (1987): 36–59.

Beckford, Robert. "Does Jesus Have a Penis? Black Male Sexual Representation and Christology." *Theology and Sexuality* 5 (September 1996): 10–21.

Beet, Joseph Agar. *A Commentary on St. Paul's Epistle to the Galatians.* 4th ed. London: Hodder & Stoughton, 1893.

Bell, E. T. *Mathematics, Queen and Servant of the Sciences.* New York: McGraw-Hill, 1951.

Bernard, Jessie. *The Future of Marriage*. New Haven, CT: Yale University Press, 1982.

Bible and Culture Collective. *The Postmodern Bible*. New Haven, CT: Yale University Press, 1995.

Blumenfeld, Warren J., ed. *Homophobia: How We All Pay the Price*. Boston: Beacon Press, 1992.

Borchert, Gerald L. "1 Corinthians 7:15 and the Church's Historic Misunderstanding of Divorce and Remarriage." *Review and Expositor* 96 (1999): 125–29.

Boswell, John. "Concepts, Experience, and Sexuality." *Differences* 2 (1990): 67–87.

———. *Christianity, Social Tolerance, and Homosexuality: Gay People in Western Europe from the Beginning of the Christian Era to the Fourteenth Century*. Chicago: University of Chicago Press, 1980.

———. *Same-Sex Unions in Premodern Europe*. New York: Villard, 1994.

Boucher, Madeleine."Some Unexplored Parallels to 1 Cor 11, 11–12 and Gal 3, 28: The New Testament on the Role of Women." *Catholic Biblical Quarterly* 31 (1969): 50–58.

Bovon, François. *L'Évangile selon Saint Luc (9, 51–14, 35)*. Geneva: Labor et Fides, 1996.

———. *Luke: A Commentary on the Gospel of Luke 1:1–9:50*. Minneapolis: Fortress, 2002.

Brandes, S. "Like Wounded Stags: Male Sexual Ideology in an Andalusian Town." In *Sexual Meanings: The Cultural Construction of Gender and Sexuality*, ed. S. Ortner and H. Whitehead, 216–39. Cambridge: Cambridge University Press, 1981.

Bray, Gerald. *Biblical Interpretation: Past and Present*. Downers Grove, IL: InterVarsity, 1996.

Brooten, Bernadette J. "Jüdinnen zur Zeit Jesu: Ein plädoyer für Differenzierung." *Theologische Quartalschrift* 161 (1981): 280–85.

———. *Love Between Women: Early Christian Responses to Female Homoeroticism*. Chicago: University of Chicago Press, 1996.

———. "Patristic Interpretation of Romans 1:26." In *Studia Patristica XVIII*, ed. Elizabeth A. Livingstone, 1:287–91. Kalamazoo, MI: Cistercian Publications, 1985.

———. *Women Leaders in the Ancient Synagogue: Inscriptional Evidence and Background*. Chico, CA: Scholars, 1982.

———. "Zur Debatte über das Scheidungsrecht der jüdischen Frau." *Evangelische Theologie* 43 (1983): 466–78.

Brown, Dan. *The Da Vinci Code: A Novel*. New York: Doubleday, 2003.

Brown, Harold O. J. "The New Testament Against Itself: 1 Timothy 2:9–15 and the 'Breakthrough' of Galatians 3:28." In *Women in the Church: Fresh Analysis of 1 Timothy 2:9–15*, ed. Andreas J. Köstenberger et al., 197–208. Grand Rapids: Baker Books, 1995.

Brown, Peter. *The Body and Society: Men, Women and Sexual Renunciation in Early Christianity*. London: Faber & Faber, 1989.

Brueggemann, Walter. *Texts Under Negotiation: The Bible and Postmodern Imagination*. Minneapolis: Fortress, 1993.

Brunson, Harold E. *Homosexuality and the New Testament: What Does Christian Scripture Really Teach*. San Francisco: International Scholars Publications, 1998.

Bryant, David J. *Faith and the Play of Imagination: On the Role of Imagination in Religion*. Macon, GA: Mercer, 1989.

Buckley, Jorunn Jacobsen. "An Interpretation of Logion 114 in *The Gospel of Thomas*." *Novum Testamentum* 27 (1985): 245–72.

Buckley, Timothy J. *What Binds Marriage? Roman Catholic Theology in Practice*. London: Continuum, 2002.

Butler, Judith. *Gender Trouble: Feminism and the Subversion of Identity*. New York: Routledge, 1990.

Cahill, Lisa Sowle. *Family: A Christian Social Perspective*. Minneapolis: Fortress, 2000.

Callahan, James. *The Clarity of Scripture: History, Theology and Contemporary Literary Studies*. Downers Grove, IL: InterVarsity, 2001.
Cameron, Averil. "Neither Male Nor Female." *Greece and Rome* 27 (1980): 60–68.
Cancik, Hubert. *Untersuchungen zur lyrischen Kunst des P. Papianus Statius*. Spudasmata 13. Hildesheim: Olms, 1965.
Cantarella, Eva. *Bisexuality in the Ancient World*. New Haven, CT: Yale University Press, 1992.
Casimir, Brother. "Saint Gregory of Nyssa: PERI TELEIOTHTOS—On Perfection." *Greek Orthodox Theological Review* 29 (1984): 349–79.
Charlesworth, James H. *The Old Testament Pseudepigrapha*. 2 vols. Garden City, NY: Doubleday, 1983–1985.
Childs, Brevard. "The *Sensus Literalis* of Scripture: An Ancient and Modern Problem." In *Beiträge zur alttestamentlichen Theologie: Festschrift für Walther Zimmerli zum 70. Geburtstag*, ed. Herbert Donner et al., 80–93. Göttingen: Vanderhoeck & Ruprecht, 1977.
Clapp, Rodney. *Families at the Crossroads: Beyond Traditional and Modern Options*. Downers Grove, IL: InterVarsity, 1993.
———. Review of Keener, *And Marries Another*. *Christianity Today* 36 (May 18, 1992): 75–76. See Craig Keener.
Clark, Elizabeth A. "'Adam's Only Companion': Augustine and the Early Christian Debate on Marriage." *Recherches Augustiniennes* 21 (1986): 139–62.
———. *History, Theory, Text: Historians and the Linguistic Turn*. Cambridge, MA: Harvard University Press, 2004.
———. *Reading Renunciation: Asceticism and Scripture in Early Christianity*. Princeton, NJ: Princeton University Press, 1999.
———. *St. Augustine on Marriage and Sexuality*. Washington, DC: Catholic University of America Press, 1996.
Coleman, Gerald D. *Divorce and Remarriage in the Catholic Church*. New York: Paulist, 1988.
Coleman, Peter. *Christian Attitudes to Homosexuality*. London: SPCK, 1980.
Collier, G. D. "'That we might not crave evil.' The Structure and Argument of 1 Corinthians 10:1–3." *Journal for the Study of the New Testament* 55 (1994): 55–75.
Comstock, Gary David, and Susan E. Henking. *Que(e)rying Religion: A Critical Anthology*. New York: Continuum, 1997.
Coontz, Stephanie. *The Way We Never Were: American Families and the Nostalgia Trap*. New York: Basic Books, 1992.
Corley, Kathleen E., and Karen J. Torjesen. "Sexuality, Hierarchy and Evangelicalism." *Theological Students' Fellowship Bulletin* 10, no. 4 (March–April 1987): 23–27.
Cornes, Andrew. *Divorce and Remarriage: Biblical Principles and Pastoral Practice*. Grand Rapids: Wm. B. Eerdmans, 1993.
Corpus Christianorum: Series latina. Turnholt: Brepols, 1954–.
Cosgrove, Charles H. *Appealing to Scripture in Moral Debate: Five Hermeneutical Rules*. Grand Rapids: Wm. B. Eerdmans, 2002.
Countryman, L. William. *Biblical Authority or Biblical Tyranny? Scripture and the Christian Pilgrimage*. Valley Forge, PA: Trinity; Cambridge, MA: Cowley, 1994.
———. *Dirt, Greed, and Sex: Sexual Ethics in the New Testament and Their Implications for Today*. Philadelphia: Fortress, 1988.
———. *Interpreting the Truth: Changing the Paradigm of Biblical Studies*. Harrisburg, PA: Trinity Press International, 2003.
Cousar, Charles B. *Galatians*. Atlanta: John Knox, 1982.
Craveri, Marcello. *The Life of Jesus*. London: Panther, 1969.
Creed, Gerald W. "Sexual Subordination: Institutionalized Homosexuality and Social Control in Melanesia." In *Reclaiming Sodom*, 66–94. See Jonathan Goldberg; originally published in *Ethnography* 23 (1984): 157–76.

D'Angelo, Mary Rose. "Remarriage and the Divorce Sayings Attributed to Jesus." In *Divorce and Remarriage: Religious and Psychological Perspectives,* ed. William P. Roberts, 78–106. Kansas City, MO: Sheed & Ward, 1990.

Dautzenberg, Gerhard. "Da ist nicht männlich und weiblich. Zur Interpretation von Gal 3:28." *Kairos* 24 (1984): 181–206.

Davies, W. D., and Dale C. Allison Jr. *A Critical and Exegetical Commentary on the Gospel According to Saint Matthew*. Edinburgh: T. & T. Clark, 1997.

Davis, Ellen F. "Teaching the Bible Confessionally in the Church." In *The Art of Reading Scripture,* ed. Ellen F. Davis and Richard B. Hays, 9–26. Grand Rapids: Wm. B. Eerdmans, 2003.

Davis, John Jefferson. "Some Reflections on Galatians 3:28, Sexual Roles, and Biblical Hermeneutics." *Journal of the Evangelical Theological Society* 19 (1976): 201–8.

Deasley, Alex R. G. *Marriage and Divorce in the Bible and the Church*. Kansas City, MO: Beacon Hill, 2000.

Deist, Ferdinand. "Presuppositions and Contextual Bible Translation." *Journal of Northwest Semitic Languages* 19 (1993): 13–23.

Delcourt, Marie. "Hermaphrodit." In *Reallexikon für Antike und Christentum,* 14.649–682. Stuttgart: Anton Hiersemann, 1988.

Deleuze, Gilles, and Félix Guattari. *Anti-Oedipus: Capitalism and Schizophrenia*. Minneapolis: University of Minnesota Press, 1983.

Dennett, Daniel C. *Consciousness Explained*. Boston: Little, Brown & Co., 1991.

Descamps, A. L. "The New Testament Doctrine on Marriage." In *Contemporary Perspectives on Christian Marriage: Propositions and Papers from the International Theological Commission,* ed. Richard Malone and John R. Connery, 217–73. Chicago: Loyola University Press, 1984.

Dover, Kenneth J. *Greek Homosexuality*. Cambridge, MA: Harvard University Press, 1978.

Downing, F. Gerald. "A Cynic Preparation for Paul's Gospel for Jew and Greek, Slave and Free, Male and Female." *New Testament Studies* 42 (1996): 454–62.

Duin, Julia. "Politics Cloud Kerry's Easter Plans." *Washington Times,* April 5, 2004, http://www.washtimes.com/national/20040405–125311-9075r.htm.

Duncan, George S. *The Epistle of Paul to the Galatians*. New York: Harper & Brothers, no date.

Dunn, James D. G. "The Household Rules in the New Testament." In *The Family in Theological Perspective,* ed. Stephen C. Barton, 43–63. Edinburgh: T. & T. Clark, 1996.

Eagleton, Terry. *Literary Theory: An Introduction*. Minneapolis: University of Minnesota Press, 1983.

Edwards, George R. *Gay/Lesbian Liberation: A Biblical Perspective*. New York: Pilgrim, 1984.

Ehrman, Bart D. *Lost Christianities: The Battles for Scripture and the Faiths We Never Knew.* New York: Oxford University Press, 2003.

———. *Lost Scriptures: Books That Did Not Make It Into the New Testament*. Oxford and New York: Oxford University Press, 2003.

———. *Misquoting Jesus: The Story Behind Who Changed the Bible and Why*. San Francisco: HarperSanFrancisco, 2005.

Elliott, J. K. *The Apocryphal New Testament*. Oxford: Clarendon, 1993.

Elm, Susanna. *"Virgins of God": The Making of Asceticism in Late Antiquity*. Oxford: Clarendon, 1994.

Fatum, Lone. "Image of God and Glory of Man: Women in the Pauline Congregations." In *The Image of God: Gender Models in Judaeo-Christian Tradition,* ed. Kari Elisabeth Børresen, 50–133. Minneapolis: Fortress, 1995.

———. "Women, Symbolic Universe and Structures of Silence: Challenges and Possibilities in Androcentric Texts." *Studia theologica* 43 (1989): 61–80.

Fee, Gordon D. *First Epistle to the Corinthians*. Grand Rapids: Wm. B. Eerdmans, 1987.

———. "Paul and the Trinity: The Experience of Christ and the Spirit for Paul's Understanding of God." In *The Trinity: An Interdisciplinary Symposium on the Trinity*, ed. Stephen T. Davis et al., 49–72. Oxford: Oxford University Press, 1999.

Ferguson, Duncan S. *Biblical Hermeneutics: An Introduction*. Atlanta: John Knox, 1986.

Findlay, G. G. *The Epistle to the Galatians*. New York: A. C. Armstrong & Son, 1893.

Fiorenza, Elisabeth Schüssler. *In Memory of Her: A Feminist Theological Reconstruction of Christian Origins*. New York: Crossroad, 1983.

———. *Sharing Her Word: Feminist Biblical Interpretation in Context*. Boston: Beacon, 1998.

———. "Text and Reality—Reality as Text: The Problem of a Feminist Historical and Social Reconstruction Based on Texts." *Studia theologica* 43 (1989): 19–34.

Fish, Stanley. *Doing What Comes Naturally: Change, Rhetoric, and the Practice of Theory in Literary and Legal Studies*. Durham, NC: Duke University Press, 1989.

———. *Is There a Text in This Class? The Authority of Interpretive Communities*. Cambridge, MA: Harvard University Press, 1980.

Fishburn, Janet. *Confronting the Idolatry of Family: A New Vision for the Household of God*. Nashville: Abingdon, 1991.

Fisher, Ian. "Catholic Bishops Again Reject Married Priests." *New York Times*, October 23, 2005, sec. A, 12.

Fitzmyer, Joseph A. *The Acts of the Apostles*. New York: Doubleday, 1964.

———. *Romans: A New Translation with Introduction and Commentary*. New York: Doubleday, 1993.

Fletcher, Joseph F. *Situation Ethics: The New Morality*. Philadelphia: Westminster, 1966.

Foucault, Michel. *The History of Sexuality*. Vol. 1: *An Introduction*. New York: Random House, 1978.

———. *The History of Sexuality*. Vol. 2: *The Use of Pleasure*. New York: Random House, 1985.

———. *The History of Sexuality*. Vol. 3: *The Care of the Self*. New York: Pantheon, 1986.

Fowl, Stephen E., ed. *The Theological Interpretation of Scripture: Classic and Contemporary Readings*. Cambridge, MA: Blackwell, 1997.

———. *Engaging Scripture: A Model for Theological Interpretation*. Oxford: Blackwell, 1998.

Fowl, Stephen E., and L. Gregory Jones. *Reading in Communion: Scripture and Ethics in Christian Life*. Grand Rapids: Wm. B. Eerdmans, 1991.

Fraade, Steven D. "The Nazirite in Ancient Judaism (Selected Texts)." In *Ascetic Behavior in Greco-Roman Antiquity: A Sourcebook*, ed. Vincent Wimbush, 213–23. Minneapolis: Fortress, 1990.

Fraassen, Bas C. van. *The Empirical Stance*. New Haven, CT: Yale University Press, 2002.

Frei, Hans W. *The Eclipse of Biblical Narrative: A Study in Eighteenth and Nineteenth Century Hermeneutics*. New Haven, CT: Yale University Press, 1974.

———. "The 'Literal Reading' of Biblical Narrative in the Christian Tradition: Does It Stretch or Will It Break?" In *The Bible and the Narrative Tradition*, ed. Frank McConnell, 36–77. New York: Oxford University Press, 1986.

Fremantle, W. H., with G. Lewis and W. G. Martley. *The Principal Works of St. Jerome*. Nicene and Post-Nicene Fathers, 2d ser. Vol. 6. Grand Rapids: Wm. B. Eerdmans, 1979.

Fulkerson, Mary McClintock. "Gender—Being It or Doing It? The Church, Homosexuality, and the Politics of Identity." *Union Seminary Quarterly Review* 47 (1993): 29–46.

Fuller, Ronald. Review of Keener, *And Marries Another*. *Journal of Evangelical Theological Society* 38 (1995): 277–78. See Craig Keener.

Funk, Robert, Roy W. Hoover, and the Jesus Seminar. *The Five Gospels: The Search for the Authentic Words of Jesus*. New York: Macmillan, 1993.

Furnish, Victor Paul. "The Bible and Homosexuality." In *Homosexuality: In Search of a Christian Understanding*, ed. Leon Smith, 6–21. Nashville: Discipleship Resources, 1981.

———. "The Bible and Homosexuality: Reading the Texts in Context." In *Homosexuality in the Church*, 18–35. See Jeffrey S. Siker.

———. "Homosexual Practices in Biblical Perspective." In *The Sexuality Debate in North American Churches, 1988–1995: Controversies, Unresolved Issues, Future Prospects*, ed. John J. Carey, 253–73. Lewiston, NY: Edwin Mellen, 1995.

———. *The Moral Teaching of Paul: Selected Essays*. 2d ed. Nashville: Abingdon, 1985.

Gagnon, Robert A. J. *The Bible and Homosexual Practice: Texts and Hermeneutics*. Nashville: Abingdon, 2001.

Galen. *On Semen*. Ed. Phillip de Lacy. Corpus medicorum graecorum 3/1. Berlin: Akademie-Verlag, 1992.

Gardner, Percy. *The Religious Experience of Saint Paul*. New York: G. P. Putnam's Sons, 1913.

Garrett, Susan R. *The Demise of the Devil: Magic and the Demonic in Luke's Writings*. Minneapolis: Fortress, 1989.

Geertz, Clifford. *Local Knowledge: Further Essays in Interpretive Anthropology*. New York: Basic Books, 1983.

Gilhus, Ingvild Saelid. "Male and Female Symbolism in the Gnostic *Apocryphon of John*." *Temenos* 19 (1983): 33–43.

Ginzberg, Louis. *Legends of the Jews*. 7 vols. Philadelphia: Jewish Publication Society of America, 1909–66.

Goldberg, Jonathan, ed. *Reclaiming Sodom*. New York: Routledge, 1994.

Good, D. J. "Reading Strategies for Biblical Passages on Same-Sex Relations." *Theology and Sexuality* 7 (1997): 70–82.

Goodacre, Mark S. *The Case Against Q: Studies in Markan Priority and the Synoptic Problem*. Harrisburg, PA: Trinity Press International, 2002.

Goss, Robert E. *Jesus Acted Up: A Gay and Lesbian Manifesto*. San Francisco: HarperSanFrancisco, 1994.

———. *Queering Christ: Beyond Jesus Acted Up*. Cleveland: Pilgrim, 2002.

Gouge, William. *Of Domesticall Duties: Eight Treatises*. London: John Haviland, 1622.

Goulder, Michael. "Devotion, Divorce and Debauchery." In *Tro og historie: Festschrift til Niels Hyldahl i anledning af 65 års fødselsdagen den 30. december 1995*, ed. Lone Fatum and Mogens Müller, 107–17. Copenhagen: Copenhagen University, Museum Tusculanums, 1996.

Grant, Brian W. *The Social Structure of Christian Families: A Historical Perspective*. St. Louis: Chalice, 2000.

Grant, Robert. "Neither Male nor Female." *Biblical Research* 37 (1992): 5–14.

Grayston, Kenneth. "Adultery and Sodomy: The Biblical Sources of Christian Moral Judgment." *Epworth Review* 15 (1988): 64–70.

Green, Garrett. *Imagining God: Theology and the Religious Imagination*. Grand Rapids: Wm. B. Eerdmans, 1998.

———. *Theology, Hermeneutics, and Imagination: The Crisis of Interpretation at the End of Modernity*. Cambridge: Cambridge University Press, 2000.

Green, Joel B., ed. *Hearing the New Testament: Strategies for Interpretation*. Grand Rapids: Wm. B. Eerdmans, 1995.

Greene-McCreight, Kathryn. "The Logic of the Interpretation of Scripture and the Church's Debate Over Sexual Ethics." In *Homosexuality, Science, and the "Plain Sense" of Scripture*, ed. David L. Balch, 242–60. Grand Rapids: Wm. B. Eerdmans, 2000.

Guenther, Allen R. "The Exception Phrases: Except *porneia*, Including *porneia* or Excluding *porneia*? (Matthew 5:32; 19:9)." *Tyndale Bulletin* 53 (2002): 83–96.

Guerra, Anthony J. *Family Matters: The Role of Christianity in the Formation of the Western Family*. St. Paul: Paragon House, 2002.

Gundry-Volf, Judith M. "Gender and Creation in 1 Corinthians 11:2–16: A Study in Paul's Theological Method." In *Evangelium Schriftauslegung Kirche: Festschrift für Peter Stuhlmacher zum 65. Geburtstag*, ed. Jostein Ådna et al., 151–71. Göttingen: Vandenhoeck & Ruprecht, 1997.

———. "Male and Female in Creation and New Creation: Interpretations of Galatians 3.28C in 1 Corinthians 7." In *To Tell the Mystery: Essays on New Testament Eschatology in Honor of Robert H. Gundry*, ed. Thomas E. Schmidt and Moisés Silva, 95–121. Sheffield: Sheffield Academic Press, 1994.

Guthrie, Donald. *Galatians*. London: Nelson, 1969.

Haller, Wilhelm, ed. *Iovinianus: Die Fragmente seiner Schriften, die Quellen zu seiner Geschichte, sein Leben und seine Lehre*. Leipzig: J. C. Hinrich, 1897.

Halperin, David M. *One Hundred Years of Homosexuality*. New York: Routledge, 1990.

Halperin, David M., et al., eds. *Before Sexuality: The Construction of Erotic Experience in the Ancient Greek World*. Princeton, NJ: Princeton University Press, 1990.

Hannay, Alastair. *Kierkegaard: A Biography*. Cambridge: Cambridge University Press, 2001.

Harink, Douglas. *Paul Among the Postliberals: Pauline Theology Beyond Christendom and Modernity*. Grand Rapids: Baker, 2003.

Harrill, J. Albert. *Slaves in the New Testament: Literary, Social, and Moral Dimensions*. Minneapolis: Fortress, 2006.

Hart, Hendrik. "Reply to Wolters." *Calvin Theological Journal* 28 (1993): 170–74.

———. "Romans Revisited." *The Other Side* 28, no. 4 (July–August 1992): 56–62.

Hauerwas, Stanley. *Vision and Virtue: Essays in Christian Ethical Reflection*. Notre Dame, IN: Fides, 1974.

Hauerwas, Stanley, Nancey Murphy, and Mark Nation, eds. *Theology Without Foundations: Religious Practice and the Future of Theological Truth*. Nashville: Abingdon, 1994.

Hays, Richard B. "Awaiting the Redemption of Our Bodies: The Witness of Scripture Concerning Homosexuality." In *Homosexuality in the Church: Both Sides of the Debate*, ed. Jeffrey S. Siker, 3–17. Louisville, KY: Westminster John Knox, 1994. Originally published in an edited version in *Sojourners* 20, no. 6 (July 1991): 17–21.

———. *Echoes of Scripture in the Letters of Paul*. New Haven, CT: Yale University Press, 1989.

———. *The Moral Vision of the New Testament: Community, Cross, New Creation; A Contemporary Introduction to New Testament Ethics*. San Francisco: HarperSanFrancisco, 1996.

———. *New Testament Ethics: The Story Retold*. Winnipeg, MB: CMBC, 1998.

———. "Relations Natural and Unnatural: A Response to John Boswell's Exegesis of Romans 1." *Journal of Christian Ethics* 14 (1986): 184–215.

Hayter, Mary. *The New Eve in Christ: The Use and Abuse of the Bible in the Debate about Women in the Church*. London: SPCK, 1987.

Hegy, Pierre, and Joseph Martos, eds. *Catholic Divorce: The Deception of Annulments*. New York: Continuum, 2000.

Helminiak, Daniel A. *What the Bible Really Says About Homosexuality*. San Francisco: Alamo Square, 1994.

Henderson, Jeffrey. *The Maculate Muse: Obscene Language in Attic Comedy*. New Haven, CT: Yale University Press, 1975.

Herter, H. "Effeminatus." In *Reallexikon für Antike und Christentum*, vol. 4, 620–50. Stuttgart: Hiersemann, 1959.

Heywood, Leslie, and Jennifer Drake. *Third Wave Agenda: Being Feminist, Doing Feminism*. Minneapolis: University of Minnesota Press, 1997.

Hill, Christopher. *Society and Puritanism in Pre-Revolutionary England*. New York: Schocken Books, 1964.

Hock, C. B., Jr. "The Role of Women in the Church: A Survey of Current Approaches." *Grace Theological Journal* 8, no. 2 (1987): 241–51.

Hofstadler, Douglas R. *The Mind's I: Fantasies and Reflections on Self and Soul.* New York: Basic Books, 1981.

Hooker, M. D. "Adam in Romans I." *New Testament Studies* 6 (1959–60): 297–306.

———. "A Further Note on Romans I." *New Testament Studies* 13 (1966–67): 181–83.

Hopkins, Keith. "The Age of Roman Girls at Marriage." *Population Studies* 18 (1965): 309–27.

Hornsby, Teresa J. "Paul and the Remedies of Idolatry: Reading Romans 1:18–24 with Romans 7." In *Postmodern Interpretations of the Bible: A Reader*, ed. A. K. M. Adam, 219–32. St. Louis: Chalice, 2001.

Horst, P. W. van der. *The Sentences of Pseudo-Phocylides.* Leiden: E. J. Brill, 1978.

Hunter, David G. "Helvidius, Jovinian, and the Virginity of Mary in Late Fourth-Century Rome." *Journal for Early Christian Studies* 1 (1993): 47–71.

———. "Rereading the Jovinianist Controversy: Asceticism and Clerical Authority in Late Ancient Christianity." *Journal of Medieval and Early Modern Studies* 33 (2003): 453–70.

———. "Resistance to the Virginal Ideal in Late-Fourth-Century Rome: The Case of Jovinian." *Theological Studies* 48 (1987): 45–64.

———, ed. *Marriage in the Early Church.* Minneapolis: Fortress, 1992.

Huyssteen, J. Wentzel van. *Essays in Postfoundationalist Theology.* Grand Rapids: Wm. B. Eerdmans, 1997.

Instone-Brewer, David. *Divorce and Remarriage in the Bible: The Social and Literary Context.* Grand Rapids: Wm. B. Eerdmans, 2002.

Irenaeus. *Against the Heresies.* Trans. and annotated by Dominic J. Unger, with further revisions by John J. Dillon. Ancient Christian Writers 55. New York: Paulist, 1992.

Jacobs, Andrew S. "A Family Affair: Marriage, Class, and Ethics in the Apocryphal Acts of the Apostles." *Journal of Early Christian Studies* 7 (1999): 105–38.

Jacoby, Felix. *Die Fragmente der griechischen Historiker.* 3 vols. Leiden: E. J. Brill, 1969.

Jeanrond, Werner G. *Text and Interpretation as Categories of Theological Thinking.* New York: Crossroad, 1988.

Jenkins, Keith. *Re-thinking History: With a New Preface and Conversation with the Author by Alun Munslow.* London: Routledge, 2003.

Jerome, *Commentaire sur S. Matthieu.* Ed. Emile Bonnard. Sources chrétiennes 259. Paris: Éditions du Cerf, 1979.

Jewett, Robert. "The Sexual Liberation of the Apostle Paul." *Journal of the American Academy of Religion Supplement* 47, no. 1 (1979): 55–87.

John Chrysostom. *The Homilies of S. John Chrysostom.* 3d ed. rev. Oxford: James Parker, 1877.

Johnson, Luke Timothy. *The Acts of the Apostles.* Sacra Pagina Series 5. Collegeville, MN: Liturgical, 1992.

———. "Debate and Discernment, Scripture and the Spirit." *Commonweal* (January 1994): 11–13. Reprinted in *Virtues and Practices in the Christian Tradition: Christian Ethics after MacIntyre*, ed. Nancey Murphy, Brad J. Kallenberg, and Mark Thiessen Nation, 215–20. Harrisburg, PA: Trinity Press International, 1997.

———. "Why Scripture Isn't Enough." *Commonweal* 124, no. 11 (June 6, 1997): 23–25.

Johnson, Luke Timothy, and William S. Kurz. *The Future of Catholic Biblical Scholarship: A Constructive Conversation.* Grand Rapids: Wm. B. Eerdmans, 2002.

Johnson, S. Lewis, Jr. "God Gave Them Up." *Bibliotheca sacra* 129 (1972): 124–33.

Jung, Patricia Beattie, and Ralph F. Smith. *Heterosexism: An Ethical Challenge.* Albany, NY: SUNY Press, 1993.

Kähler, Else. "Exegese zweier neutestamentlicher Stellen (Römer 1.18–32; 1 Korinther 6.9–11)." In *Probleme der Homophilie in medizinischer, theologischer, und juristischer Sicht*, ed. Th. Bovet, 12–43. Bern: Paul Haupt, 1965.

———. *Die Frau in den paulinischen Briefen*. Zürich: Gotthalf, 1960.

Kamlah, Ehrhard. *Die Form der katalogischen Paränese im Neuen Testament*. Tübingen: Mohr/Siebeck, 1964.

Katz, Jonathan Ned. "The Age of Sodomitical Sin, 1607–1740." In *Reclaiming Sodom*, 43–58. See Jonathan Goldberg.

———. *Gay/Lesbian Almanac*. New York: Harper & Row, 1983.

Kazantzakis, Nikos. *The Last Temptation of Christ*. Trans. P. A. Bien. New York: Simon & Schuster, 1960.

Keener, Craig S. *And Marries Another: Divorce and Remarriage in the Teaching of the New Testament*. Peabody, MA: Hendrickson, 1991.

Kelly, J. N. D. *Jerome: His Life, Writings, and Controversies*. New York: Harper & Row, 1975.

Kelly, Kevin T. *Divorce and Second Marriage: Facing the Challenge*. 2d ed., expanded. London: Geoffrey Chapman, 1996.

Kelsey, David H. *Uses of Scripture in Recent Theology*. Philadelphia: Fortress, 1975.

Kierkegaard, Søren. *Concluding Unscientific Postscript*. Trans. David F. Swenson and Walter Lowrie. Princeton, NJ: Princeton University Press, 1941.

———. *Philosophical Fragments or A Fragment of Philosophy*. Trans. David Swenson, trans. revised Howard V. Hong. Princeton, NJ: Princeton University Press, 1936, 1962.

———. *Stages on Life's Way: Studies by Various Persons*. Ed. and trans. with introduction and notes by Howard V. Hong and Edna H. Hong. Princeton, NJ: Princeton University Press, 1988.

Kimball-Jones, H. *Toward a Christian Understanding of the Homosexual*. London: SCM Press, 1966.

Kuefler, Mathew. *The Manly Eunuch: Masculinity, Gender Ambiguity, and Christian Ideology in Late Antiquity*. Chicago: University of Chicago Press, 2001.

Kysar, Myrna, and Robert Kysar. *The Asundered: Biblical Teachings on Divorce and Remarriage*. Atlanta: John Knox, 1978.

L'Huillier, Peter. "The Indissolubility of Marriage in Orthodox Law and Practice." In *Catholic Divorce: The Deception of Annulments*, ed. Pierre Hegy and Joseph Martos, 108–26. New York: Continuum, 2000.

Lacey, W. K. *Family in Classical Greece*. Ithaca, NY: Cornell University Press, 1968.

Landow, George P. *Hypertext 2.0*. Baltimore: Johns Hopkins University Press, 1997.

———, ed. *Hyper/text/theory*. Baltimore: Johns Hopkins University Press, 1994.

Laqueur, Thomas. *Making Sex: Body and Gender from the Greeks to Freud*. Cambridge, MA: Harvard University Press, 1990.

Latour, Bruno. *We Have Never Been Modern*. Cambridge, MA: Harvard University Press, 1993.

Laughery, Gregory J. *Living Hermeneutics in Motion: An Analysis and Evaluation of Paul Ricoeur's Contribution to Biblical Hermeneutics*. Lanham, MD: University Press of America, 2002.

Lawler, Michael G. *Marriage and the Catholic Church: Disputed Questions*. Collegeville, MN: Liturgical, 2002.

Lawrence, D. H. *The Man Who Died*. London: Martin Secker, 1931.

Layton, Bentley. *The Gnostic Scriptures*. Garden City, NY: Doubleday, 1987.

Leites, Edmund. *The Puritan Conscience and Modern Sexuality*. New Haven, CT: Yale University Press, 1986.

Lindbeck, George. *The Nature of Doctrine: Religion and Theology in a Postliberal Age*. Philadelphia: Westminster, 1984.

———. "The Story-shaped Church: Critical Exegesis and Theological Interpretation." In *Scriptural Authority and Narrative Interpretation*, ed. Garrett Green, 161–78. Philadelphia: Fortress, 1987.

———. "Toward a Postliberal Theology." In *The Return to Scripture in Judaism and Christianity: Essays in Postcritical Scriptural Interpretation*, ed. Peter Ochs, 83–103. New York: Paulist, 1993.

Loader, William. *Sexuality and the Jesus Tradition*. Grand Rapids: Wm. B. Eerdmans, 2005.

Lowe, Stephen D. "Rethinking the Female Status/Function Question: The Jew/Gentile Relationship as Paradigm." *Journal of the Evangelical Theological Society* 34 (1991): 59–75.

Luther, Martin. *Commentary on the Epistle to the Romans.* Trans. J. Theodore Mueller. Grand Rapids: Zondervan, 1954.

MacDonald, Dennis Ronald. "Corinthian Veils and Gnostic Androgynes." In *Images of the Feminine in Gnosticism*, ed. Karen L. King, 276–92. Philadelphia: Fortress, 1988.

MacIntyre, Alasdair C. "How Moral Agents Became Ghosts or Why the History of Ethics Diverged from that of the Philosophy of Mind." *Synthese* 53 (1982): 295–312.

Mackin, Theodore. *Divorce and Remarriage*. New York and Ramsey, NJ: Paulist, 1984.

Maglin, Nan Bauer, and Donna Perry. *"Bad Girls"/"Good Girls": Women, Sex, and Power in the Nineties*. New Brunswick, NJ: Rutgers University Press, 1996.

Malherbe, Abraham J., ed. *The Cynic Epistles: A Study Edition*. Missoula, MT: Scholars Press, 1977.

Manson, T. W. *The Sayings of Jesus*. Grand Rapids: Wm. B. Eerdmans, 1957.

March, W. Eugene. Review of Instone-Brewer, *Divorce and Remarriage. Journal of Family Ministry* 17 (2003): 74–75. See David Instone-Brewer.

Martin, Dale B. "Contradictions of Masculinity: Ascetic Inseminators and Menstruating Men in Greco-Roman Culture." In *Generation and Degeneration: Literature and Tropes of Reproduction*, ed. Valeria Finucci and Kevin Brownlee, 81–108. Durham, NC: Duke University Press, 2001.

———. *The Corinthian Body*. New Haven, CT: Yale University Press, 1995.

———. "The Promise of Teleology, the Constraints of Epistemology, and Universal Vision in Paul." In *St. Paul Among the Philosophers: Subjectivity, Universality, and the Event*, ed. John Caputo. Forthcoming.

———. Review of Hays, *Moral Vision. Journal of Biblical Literature* 117 (1998): 358–60. See Richard B. Hays.

Martin, Dale B., and Patricia Cox Miller, eds. *The Cultural Turn in Late Ancient Studies: Gender, Asceticism, and Historiography*. Durham, NC: Duke University Press, 2005.

McCane, Byron R. "'Let the Dead Bury Their Own Dead': Secondary Burial and Matt. 8:21–22." *Harvard Theological Review* 83 (1990): 31–43.

McIntyre, Michael. "Gay Texts of Terror?" *Christian Scholar's Review* 26 (1997): 413–34.

McNally, Terrence. *Corpus Christi: A Play*. New York: Grove, 1988.

McNeill, John J. *The Church and the Homosexual*. Kansas City: Sheed Andrews & McNeel, 1976.

Meeks, Wayne A. *Christ Is the Question*. Louisville, KY: Westminster John Knox, 2006.

———. "The 'Haustafeln' and American Slavery: A Hermeneutical Challenge." In *Theology and Ethics in Paul and His Interpreters: Essays in Honor of Victor Paul Furnish*, Eugene H. Lovering Jr. and Jerry L. Sumney, eds., 232–53. Nashville: Abingdon, 1996.

———. "The Image of the Androgyne: Some Uses of a Symbol in Earliest Christianity." *History of Religion* 13 (1974): 165–208.

———. "A Nazi New Testament Professor Reads His Bible: The Strange Case of Gerhard Kittel." In *The Idea of Biblical Interpretation: Essays in Honor of James L. Kugel*, Hindy Najman and Judith H. Newman, eds., 513–33. Leiden: E. J. Brill, 2004.

Meier, John P. "The Historical Jesus and the Historical Law: Some Problems Within the Problem." *Catholic Biblical Quarterly* 65 (2003): 52–79.

———. *A Marginal Jew: Rethinking the Historical Jesus.* Vol. 1. New York: Doubleday, 1991.

Montefiore, H. W. "Jesus, the Revelation of God." In *Christ for Us Today: Papers Read at the Conference of Modern Churchmen, Somerville College, Oxford, July 1967*, ed. Norman Pittenger, 101–16. London: SBM, 1968.

Moore, Stephen D. *God's Beauty Parlor, and Other Queer Spaces in and around the Bible.* Stanford, CA: Stanford University Press, 2001.

———. *God's Gym: Divine Male Bodies in the Bible.* New York: Routledge, 1996.

Morgan, Edmund S. "The Puritans and Sex." In *The American Family in Social-Historical Perspective*, ed. Michael Gordon, 363–73. 2d ed. New York: St. Martin's, 1978.

———. *The Puritan Family: Essays on Religion and Domestic Relations in Seventeenth-Century New England.* Boston: Boston Public Library, 1944.

Motyer, Stephen. "The Relationship Between Paul's Gospel of 'All One in Christ Jesus' (Galatians 3:28) and the 'Household Codes.'" *Vox Evangelica* 19 (1989): 33–48.

Moxnes, Halvor. "Social Integration and the Problem of Gender in St. Paul's Letters." *Studia theologica* 43 (1989): 99–113.

Muehl, William. "Some Words of Caution." In *Male and Female: Christian Approaches to Sexuality*, ed. Ruth Tiffany Barnhouse and Urban R. Holmes III, 167–74. New York: Seabury, 1976.

Muller, Earl C. Review of Instone-Brewer, *Divorce and Remarriage. Catholic Biblical Quarterly* 65 (2003): 470–72. See David Instone-Brewer.

Murphy-O'Connor, Jerome. "Sex and Logic in I Corinthians 11:2–16." *Catholic Biblical Quarterly* 42 (1980): 482–500.

Nelson, James B. "Homosexuality: An Issue for the Church." *Theological Markings* 5 (1975): 41–52.

Nissinen, Martti. *Homoeroticism in the Biblical World: A Historical Perspective.* Trans. Kirsi Stjerna. Minneapolis: Fortress, 1998.

Nolan, John Gavin. *Jerome and Jovinian.* Washington, DC: Catholic University of America Press, 1956.

Nolland, John. "The Gospel Prohibition of Divorce: Tradition History and Meaning." *Journal for the Study of the New Testament* 58 (1995): 19–35.

Noonan, John T., Jr. "Novel 22." In *The Bond of Marriage: An Ecumenical and Interdisciplinary Study*, ed. William W. Bassett, 41–96. Notre Dame, IN: University of Notre Dame Press, 1968.

Nussbaum, Martha. *The Fragility of Goodness: Luck and Ethics in Greek Tragedy and Philosophy.* Cambridge: Cambridge University Press, 1986.

———. "Therapeutic Arguments and Structures of Desire." *Differences* 2 (1990): 46–66.

———. *The Therapy of Desire: Theory and Practice in Hellenistic Ethics.* Princeton, NJ: Princeton University Press, 1994.

O'Flaherty, Wendy Doniger, and Mircea Eliade. "Androgynes." In *The Encyclopedia of Religion*, 1:337–42. 2d ed. New York: MacMillan/Thomson Gale, 2005.

Ogletree, Thomas W. *The Use of the Bible in Christian Ethics: A Constructive Essay.* Philadelphia: Fortress, 1983.

Økland, Jorunn. *Women in Their Place: Paul and the Corinthian Discourse of Gender and Sanctuary Space.* London: T. & T. Clark, 2004.

Olender, Robert G. "Paul's Source for 1 Corinthians 6:10–7:11." *Faith and Mission* 18, no. 3 (Summer 2001): 60–73.

Oppenheimer, Helen. *Marriage.* London: Mowbray, 1990.

Oribasius. *Oeuvres.* Ed. and trans. C. Daremberg and U. C. Bussemaker. Paris: Impr. Nationale, 1858.

———. *Oribasii collectionum medicarum reliquiae*. 4 vols. Ed. Ioannes Raeder. Amsterdam: Adolf M. Hakkert, 1964.

Orr, William F., and James Arthur Walker. *I Corinthians*. Garden City, NY: Doubleday, 1976.

Osborne, Grant R. "Hermeneutics and Women in the Church." *Journal of the Evangelical Theological Society* 20 (1977): 337–52.

Oulton, John Ernest Leonard, and Henry Chadwick, eds. *Alexandrian Christianity: Selected Translations of Clement and Origen, with Introduction and Notes*. Library of Christian Classics, vol. 2. Philadelphia: Westminster, 1954.

Pagels, Elaine. "Paul and Women: A Response to Recent Discussion." *Journal of the American Academy of Religion* 42 (1974): 538–49.

Parker, D. C. *The Living Text of the Gospels*. Cambridge: Cambridge University Press, 1997.

Parvey, Constance F. "The Theology and Leadership of Women in the New Testament." In *Religion and Sexism: Images of Woman in the Jewish and Christian Traditions*, ed. Rosemary Radford Ruether, 117–49. New York: Simon & Schuster, 1974.

Pascual, Josep Moncho. "La asimetría principio rector de la sociedad antiqua." *Cuidad de Dios* 210 (1997): 473–93.

Patte, Daniel. *Ethics of Biblical Interpretation: A Reevaluation*. Louisville, KY: Westminster John Knox, 1995.

Perkins, Judith. *The Suffering Self: Pain and Representation in the Early Christian Era*. London and New York: Routledge, 1995.

Perkins, William. *Works*. Cambridge: Cantrell Legge, 1618.

Petersen, William L. "Can ARSENOKOITAI Be Translated by 'Homosexuals'?" *Vigiliae christianae* 40 (1986): 187–91.

Peterson, Iver. "Bishop Installed Amid Dust-up Over Stand on Governor's Divorce." *New York Times*, May 1, 2004, sec. B, 1.

Phipps, William E. *The Sexuality of Jesus: Theological and Literary Perspectives*. New York: Harper & Row, 1973.

———. *Was Jesus Married?: The Distortion of Sexuality in the Christian Tradition*. Lanham, MD: University Press of America, 1986.

Pippin, Tina. *Death and Desire: The Rhetoric of Gender in the Apocalypse of John*. Louisville, KY: Westminster/John Knox, 1992.

Porter, Stanley E. "Wittgenstein's Classes of Utterances and Pauline Ethical Texts." *Journal of the Evangelical Theological Society* 32 (1989): 85–97.

Preus, James Samuel. *From Shadow to Promise: Old Testament Interpretation from Augustine to the Young Luther*. Cambridge, MA: Harvard University Press, 1969.

Ramsay, W. M. *A Historical Commentary on St. Paul's Epistle to the Galatians*. London: Hodder & Stoughton, 1899.

Ramsey Colloquium. "The Homosexual Movement: A Response by the Ramsey Colloquium." *First Things* 41 (March 1994): 15–20.

Ramsey, Paul. *Basic Christian Ethics*. New York: Scribner, 1950.

Reardon, R. P. *Collected Ancient Greek Novels*. Berkeley: University of California Press, 1989.

Rehm, Bernard, ed. *Die Pseudoklementinen II Rekognitionen in Rufins Übersetzung*. Rev. ed. from the earlier edition by Georg Strecker. Berlin: Akademie, 1994.

Reynolds, Philip Lyndon. *Marriage in the Western Church: The Christianization of Marriage during the Patristic and Early Medieval Periods*. Leiden: E. J. Brill, 1994.

Roberts, Alexander, and James Donaldson, eds. *The Ante-Nicene Fathers: Translations of the Writings of the Fathers Down to A.D. 325*. Grand Rapids: Wm. B. Eerdmans, 1978.

Röhser, Günter. "Mann und Frau in Christus. Eine Verhältnesbestimmung von Gal 3, 28 und 1 Kor 11, 2–16." *Studien zum Neuen Testament und seiner Umwelt* 22 (1997): 57–78.

Rorty, Richard. *Contingency, Irony, and Solidarity*. Cambridge: Cambridge University Press, 1989.

———. *Philosophy and the Mirror of Nature*. Princeton, NJ: Princeton University Press, 1979.

Rosen, Jonathan. *The Talmud and the Internet: A Journey Between Worlds*. New York: Farrar, Straus & Giroux, 2000.

Rudy, Kathy. *Sex and the Church: Gender, Homosexuality, and the Transformation of Christian Ethics*. Boston: Beacon, 1997.

Sadler, M. F. *The Epistle to the Romans, with Notes Critical and Practical*. London: George Bell, 1888.

Said, Edward W. *Orientalism*. New York: Pantheon, 1978.

Saller, Richard. *Patriarchy, Property and Death in the Roman Family*. Cambridge: Cambridge University Press, 1994.

Sanders, E. P., and Margaret Davies. *Studying the Synoptic Gospels*. Philadelphia: Trinity Press International, 1989.

Satlow, Michael L. *Jewish Marriage in Antiquity*. Princeton, NJ: Princeton University Press, 2001.

Scanzoni, Letha, and Virginia Ramey Mollenkott. *Is the Homosexual My Neighbor?* San Francisco: Harper & Row, 1978.

Scarry, Elaine. *The Body in Pain: The Making and Unmaking of the World*. New York: Oxford University Press, 1985.

Schaff, Philip, ed. *Nicene and Post-Nicene Fathers of the Christian Church*. 14 vols. Grand Rapids: Wm. B. Eerdmans, 1979.

Schneemelcher, Wilhelm, ed. *New Testament Apocrypha*. Rev. ed. and English trans. edited by R. McL. Wilson. 2 vols. Philadelphia: Westminster, 1991.

Schrage, Wolfgang. *Der erste Brief an die Korinther*. Zurich: Benziger, 1991.

Schücking, Levin L. *The Puritan Family: A Social Study from the Literary Sources*. 2d ed. New York: Schocken Books, 1969.

Scroggs, Robin. *The New Testament and Homosexuality: Contextual Background for Contemporary Debate*. Philadelphia: Fortress, 1983.

———. "Paul and the Eschatological Woman." In Scroggs, *The Text and the Times*. Minneapolis: Fortress, 1993. Previously published in *Journal of the American Academy of Religion* 40 (1972): 283–303.

———. *The Text and the Times: New Testament Essays for Today*. Minneapolis: Fortress, 1993.

Sedgwick, Eve Kosofsky. *Epistemology of the Closet*. Berkeley: University of California Press, 1990.

Seneca, Lucius Annaeus. *L. Annaei Senecae, Opera quae supersunt*. 3 vols. Ed. F. Haase. Leipzig: Teubner, 1887–97.

Sevenster, Jan Nicolaas. *Paul and Seneca*. Leiden: E. J. Brill, 1961.

Shaw, Brent. "The Age of Roman Girls at Marriage: Some Reconsiderations." *Journal of Roman Studies* 77 (1987): 30–46.

Shedd, William G. T. *A Critical and Doctrinal Commentary on the Epistle of St. Paul to the Romans*. Grand Rapids: Zondervan, 1967 (originally published 1879).

Shield, Mary E. Review of Instone-Brewer, *Divorce and Remarriage*. *Review of Biblical Literature* (2003). http://www.bookreviews.org. See David Instone-Brewer.

Siker, Jeffrey S. "Homosexual Christians, the Bible, and Gentile Inclusion: Confessions of a Repenting Heterosexist." In *Homosexuality in the Church: Both Sides of the Debate*, ed. Jeffrey S. Siker, 178–94. Louisville, KY: Westminster John Knox, 1994.

———, ed. *Homosexuality in the Church: Both Sides of the Debate*. Louisville, KY: Westminster John Knox, 1994.

———. *Scripture and Ethics: Twentieth-century Portraits*. Oxford: Oxford University Press, 1997.

Smalley, Beryl. *The Study of the Bible in the Middle Ages*. Oxford: Clarendon, 1941.
Smith, Abraham. "The New Testament and Homosexuality." *Quarterly Review* 11:4 (1991): 18–32.
Smith, Barbara Herrnstein. *Belief and Resistance: Dynamics of Contemporary Intellectual Controversy*. Cambridge, MA: Harvard University Press, 1997.
Smith, Jonathan Z. *Drudgery Divine: On the Comparison of Early Christianities and the Religions of Late Antiquity*. Chicago: Chicago University Press, 1990.
Smith, Morton. *Clement of Alexandria and a Secret Gospel of Mark*. Cambridge, MA: Harvard University Press, 1973.
———. *The Secret Gospel: The Discovery and Interpretation of the Secret Gospel According to Mark*. New York: Harper & Row, 1973.
Soranus. *Gynecology*. Trans. Owsei Temkin. Baltimore: Johns Hopkins University Press, 1956.
———. *Sorani Gynaeciorum libri IV. De signis fracturarum, de fasciis, vita Hippocratis secundum Soranum*. Ed. Johannes Ilberg. Corpus medicorum graecorum 4. Leipzig: Teubner, 1927.
Spijker, A. M. J. M. Herman van de. *Die gleichgeschlechteliche Zuneigung: Homotropie: Homosexualität, Homoerotik, Homophilie—und die katholische Moraltheologie*. Freiburg: Walter, 1968.
Staley, Jeffrey L. *Reading with a Passion: Rhetoric, Autobiography, and the American West in the Gospel of John*. New York: Continuum, 1995.
Stanton, Elizabeth Cady. *The Woman's Bible*. Boston: Northeastern University Press, 1993 (1895).
Stegemann, Wolfgang. "Paul and the Sexual Mentality of His World." *Biblical Theology Bulletin* 23 (1993): 161–66.
Steinberg, Leo. *The Sexuality of Christ in Renaissance Art and in Modern Illusion*. New York: Pantheon Books, 1983.
Stendahl, Krister. "The Apostle Paul and the Introspective Conscience of the West." *Harvard Theological Review* 56 (1963): 199–215.
———. *The Bible and the Role of Women: A Case Study in Hermeneutics*. Philadelphia: Fortress, 1966.
———. "Biblical Theology, Contemporary." *Interpreter's Dictionary of the Bible*, 1:418–32. Nashville: Abingdon, 1962.
Stone, Ken. *Practicing Safer Texts: Food, Sex, and Bible in Queer Perspective*. London: T. & T. Clark, 2005.
Stone, Lawrence. *The Family, Sex and Marriage In England 1500–1800*. London: Weidenfeld & Nicolson, 1977.
Stowers, Stanley K. *A Rereading of Romans: Justice, Jews, and Gentiles*. New Haven, CT: Yale University Press, 1994.
Stuart, Moses. *A Commentary on the Epistle to the Romans*. Andover: Flagg & Gould, 1832.
Swancutt, Diana. "Sexing the Pauline Body of Christ: Scriptural 'Sex' in the Context of the American Christian Culture War." In *Toward a Theology of Eros: Transfiguring Passion at the Limits of Discipline*, ed. Virginia Burrus and Catherine Keller. New York: Fordham University Press, 2006.
Swartley, Willard. *Slavery, Sabbath, War, and Women: Case Studies in Biblical Interpretation*. Scottdale, PA: Herald Press, 1983.
Tanner, Kathryn E. "Theology and the Plain Sense." In *Scriptural Authority and Narrative Interpretation*, 59–78. See Garrett Green, ed.
Tanner, Kathryn. *Theories of Culture: A New Agenda for Theology*. Minneapolis: Fortress, 1997.
Taubes, Jacob. *The Political Theology of Paul*. Ed. Aleida Assmann et al. Stanford, CA: Stanford University Press, 2004.

Taylor, Charles. *Sources of the Self: The Making of the Modern Identity*. Cambridge, MA: Harvard University Press, 1989.

Taylor, Nicholas. "Paul for Today: Race, Class, and Gender in the Light of Cognitive Dissonance Theory." *Listening* 32 (1997): 22–38.

Taylor, Thomas. *Works*. London: Printed by T. R. & E. M. for J. Bartlet the elder and J. Bartlet the younger, 1653.

Theophilus of Antioch. *Ad Autolycum*. Ed. Robert M. Grant. Oxford: Clarendon, 1970.

———. *Ad Autolycum, libri tres*. Ed. J. C. T. Otto. Corpus Apologetarum Christianorum Saeculi Secundi 8. Wiesbaden: Martin Sändig, 1969; reprint of 1861.

———. *Trois Livres a Autolycus*. Ed. Gustave Bardy. Sources chrétiennes 20. Paris: du Cerf, 1948.

Thiel, John E. *Nonfoundationalism*. Minneapolis: Fortress, 1994.

Thielicke, Helmut. *The Ethics of Sex*. New York: Harper & Row, 1964.

Thiselton, Anthony C. "Can Hermeneutics Ease the Deadlock? Some Biblical Exegesis and Hermeneutical Models." In *The Way Forward? Christian Voices on Homosexuality and the Church*, ed. Timothy Bradshaw, 145–96. London: Hodder & Stoughton, 1997.

Thomas Aquinas. *Summa theologiae*. Ed. and trans. Thomas Gilby. Cambridge: Blackfriars, 1964.

Timmerman, Joan H. "The Sexuality of Jesus and the Human Vocation." In *Sexuality and the Sacred: Sources for Theological Reflection*, ed. James B. Nelson and Sandra P. Longfellow, 91–104. Louisville, KY: Westminster John Knox, 1994.

Tompkins, Jane P., ed. *Reader-response Criticism: From Formalism to Post-structuralism*. Baltimore: Johns Hopkins University Press, 1980.

Tuttle, Robert W. "All You Need Is Love: Paul Ramsey's *Basic Christian Ethics* and the Dilemma of Protestant Antilegalism." *Journal of Law and Religion* 18 (2002–2003): 427–57.

Ukleja, P. Michael. "The Bible and Homosexuality, Part 2: Homosexuality in the New Testament." *Bibliotheca sacra* 140 (1983): 350–58.

Ulrich, Eugene. "Our Sharper Focus on the Bible and Theology Thanks to the Dead Sea Scrolls." *Catholic Biblical Quarterly* 66 (2004): 1–24.

Vanhoozer, Kevin J. "The Reader in New Testament Interpretation." In *Hearing the New Testament: Strategies for Interpretation*, ed. Joel B. Green, 301–28. Grand Rapids: Wm. B. Eerdmans, 1995.

———. "The Spirit of Understanding: Special Revelation and General Hermeneutics." In *Disciplining Hermeneutics: Interpretation in Christian Perspective*, ed. Roger Lundin, 131–65. Grand Rapids: Wm. B. Eerdmans; Leicester, England: Apollos, 1997.

Vasoli, Robert H. *What God Has Joined Together: The Annulment Crisis in American Catholicism*. New York: Oxford University Press, 1998.

Vawter, Bruce. "Divorce and the New Testament." *Catholic Biblical Quarterly* 39 (1977): 528–42.

Vetterling-Braggin, Mary, ed. *"Femininity," "Masculinity," and "Androgyny": A Modern Philosophical Discussion*. Totowa, NJ: Rowman & Littlefield, 1982.

Vogt, Kari. "'Becoming Male': A Gnostic and Early Christian Metaphor." In *The Image of God: Gender Models in Judaeo-Christian Tradition*, ed. Kari Elisabeth Børresen, 170–186. Minneapolis: Fortress, 1995.

Vögtle, Anton. *Die Tugend- und Lasterkataloge im Neuen Testament*. Münster: Aschendorffschen Buckdrockerei, 1936.

Volf, Miroslav. *Exclusion and Embrace: A Theological Exploration of Identity, Otherness, and Reconciliation*. Nashville: Abingdon, 1996.

Vorberg, Gaston. *Glossarium Eroticum*. Rome: L'Erma, 1965.

Wakin, Daniel J. "The Nation: Abortion to Annulment; Communion Becomes a Test of Faith and Politics." *New York Times*, March 9, 2004, sec. 4, 3.

Ward, Roy Bowan. "Why Unnatural: The Tradition Behind Romans 1:26–27." *Harvard Theological Review* 90 (1997): 263–84.

Warner, Michael. *The Trouble With Normal: Sex, Politics, and the Ethics of Queer Life*. New York: Free Press, 1999.

Watson, Francis. *Agape, Eros, Gender: Towards a Pauline Sexual Ethic*. Cambridge: Cambridge University Press, 2000.

———, ed. *The Open Text: New Directions for Biblical Studies?* London: SCM, 1993.

———. *Paul, Judaism and the Gentiles: A Sociological Approach*. Cambridge: Cambridge University Press, 1986.

———. "Spaces Sacred and Profane: Stephen Moore, Sex and the Bible." *Journal for the Study of the New Testament* 25 (2002): 109–17.

———. *Text and Truth: Redefining Biblical Theology*. Grand Rapids: Wm. B. Eerdmans, 1997.

———. *Text, Church and World: Biblical Interpretation in Theological Perspective*. Grand Rapids: Wm. B. Eerdmans, 1994.

Wengst, Klaus. "Paulus und die Homosexualität: Überlegungen zu Röm, 1, 26f." *Zeitschrift für evangelische Ethik* 31 (1987): 72–81.

Wenham, D. "Whatever Went Wrong in Corinth?" *Expository Times* 108 (1997): 137–141.

Wenham, Gordon J., and William E. Heth. *Jesus and Divorce*. Updated edition. Carlisle, Australia: Paternoster, 2002.

Westphal, Merold. "Post-Kantian Reflections on the Importance of Hermeneutics." In *Disciplining Hermeneutics: Interpretation in Christian Perspective*, ed. Roger Lundin, 57–66. Grand Rapids: Wm. B. Eerdmans, 1997.

Whiting, J. W. M. *Becoming a Kwoma*. New Haven, CT: Yale University Press, 1941.

Wiedemann, Hans-Georg. "Homosexualität und Bibel." In *Die Menschlichkeit der Sexualität: Berichte, Analysen, Kommentare ausgelöst durch die Frage: Wie homosexuell dürfen Pfarrer sein?* ed. Helmut Kentler, 89–106. Munich: Chr. Kaiser, 1983.

Wiles, Maurice. "In What Sense Is Christianity a 'Historical' Religion?" *Theology* 81 (1978): 4–14.

———. *Maurice Wiles*. Explorations in Theology 4. London: SCM, 1979.

Williams, Robert. *Just As I Am: A Practical Guide to Being Out, Proud, and Christian*. New York: Crown, 1992.

Wilson, Nancy. *Our Tribe: Queer Folks, God, Jesus, and the Bible*. San Francisco: HarperSanFrancisco, 1995.

Winkler, John J. *The Constraints of Desire*. New York: Routledge, 1990.

Witherington, Ben III. *The Acts of the Apostles: A Socio-Rhetorical Commentary*. Grand Rapids: Wm. B. Eerdmans, 1998.

———. "Rite and Rights for Women—Galatians 3.28." *New Testament Studies* 27 (1981): 593–604.

Witmer, John A. Review of Keener, *And Marries Another*. *Bibliotheca sacra* 151 (April–June 1994): 250. See Craig Keener.

Wolters, Albert. "Hart's Exegetical Proposal on Romans 1." *Calvin Theological Journal* 28 (1993): 166–70.

Wong, Eric K. C. "The Deradicalization of Jesus' Ethical Sayings in 1 Corinthians." *New Testament Studies* 48 (2002): 181–94.

Wood, Charles M. *The Formation of Christian Understanding: An Essay in Theological Hermeneutics*. Philadelphia: Westminster, 1981.

Woodward, Kenneth L. "A Political Sacrament." *New York Times*, May 28, 2004, sec. A, 21.

Wright, David F. "Homosexuals or Prostitutes? The Meaning of ARSENOKOITAI (1 Cor. 6:9, 1 Tim. 1:10)." *Vigiliae christianae* 38 (1984): 125–53.
Wright, N. T. *The Last Word: Beyond the Bible Wars to a New Understanding of the Authority of Scripture*. San Francisco: HarperSanFrancisco, 2005.
Yarbrough, Robert W. "The Hermeneutics of 1 Timothy 2:9–15." In *Women in the Church: An Analysis and Application of 1 Timothy 2:9–15*, ed. Andreas J. Köstenberger and Thomas R. Schreiner, 155–96. Grand Rapids: Baker Books, 1995.
Young, Frances. "Allegory and the Ethics of Reading." In *Open Text: New Directions for Biblical Studies?* ed. Francis Watson, 103–20. London: SCM, 1993.

Scripture Index

Author and Subject Index